Gift
of
Rachel
and
Jerry
Mills

A PROPHET READS SCRIPTURE

ALLUSION IN ISAIAH 40–66

Nostalgia Jewishness is a lullaby for old men
gumming soaked white bread.

J. GLADSTEIN, *modernist Yiddish poet*

CONTRAVERSIONS

JEWS AND OTHER DIFFERENCES

DANIEL BOYARIN AND

CHANA KRONFELD, EDITORS

The task of "The Science of Judaism"
is to give Judaism a decent burial.

MORITZ STEINSCHNEIDER,

founder of nineteenth-century

philological Jewish Studies

A PROPHET READS SCRIPTURE

ALLUSION IN ISAIAH 40–66

BENJAMIN D. SOMMER

Stanford University Press • *Stanford, California*

#39085365

Stanford University Press

Stanford, California

© 1998 by the Board of Trustees of the

Leland Stanford Junior University

Printed in the United States of America

CIP data appear at the end of the book

For my mother and to the memory of my father

לזכר אבי
אברהם בן הינדל ובנימין
ולאמי
חנה לאה בת גולדה רבקה ושאול נתן הכהן

הַבִּיטוּ אֶל־אַבְרָהָם אֲבִיכֶם...
כִּי־אֶחָד קְרָאתִיו וַאֲבָרְכֵהוּ וְאַרְבֵּהוּ

וַתִּתְפַּלֵּל חַנָּה וַתֹּאמַר עָלַץ לִבִּי בַּה'...
כִּי־פָקַד ה' אֶת־חַנָּה וַתַּהַר וַתֵּלֶד שְׁלֹשָׁה־בָנִים

PREFACE

ALL TRANSLATIONS in this book are my own, unless otherwise noted. Chapter and verse references to the Hebrew Bible are to the Masoretic text.

References to commentaries on biblical books and to the Hebrew University Bible Project (edited by Moshe Goshen-Gottstein) are to the section concerning the verse under discussion unless otherwise noted. For example, in a discussion of Isa 40.1, the comment "See Skinner" means "See the section on Isa 40.1 in Skinner's commentary." In a few cases where a commentator's treatment of a verse is extremely long, I add a page number.

Mindful of the Jewish prohibition on pronouncing the four-letter personal name of God, I do not write out that name in full but instead include only its consonants, thus: "YHWH." In Hebrew quotations, I substitute the symbol 'ה for that name, lest the book's pages (and those of the many drafts that preceded it) be rendered sacred according to Jewish law and thus unfit for disposal except in a cemetery. For the same reason, I spell the Hebrew word for "God" א־להים.

I transliterate some items for the benefit of readers who know no Hebrew but may want to appreciate Deutero-Isaiah's often ingenious puns. Because these transliterations are intended for non-specialists, I avoid arcane symbols dear to members of my guild; thus I write not *šeyābînû hammaśkîlîm lᵉbaddām* but *sheyabinu hammaskilim lᵉbaddam*. I do include symbols for phonemes not found in English, such as *ḥ* (pronounced like the "ch" in

"Bach"), ' (a voiced guttural fricative), and ' (a glottal stop); these are necessary in cases of paronomasia to show the close resemblance between Deutero-Isaiah's wording and that of his source. The letters *ei* in transliterations are pronounced as in the English word "weigh."

For the convenience of readers of Hebrew, I include vowels in the first occurrence of most biblical quotations; for the convenience of the publisher, I dispense with vowels in subsequent instances unless they are crucial to the argument.

∾

The first seeds of the harvest that follows were planted during my high school years in a class on Deutero-Isaiah at the Prozdor School of the Jewish Theological Seminary in New York. I was fascinated to learn from the class's teacher, Rabbi Bruce Dickstein, that the exilic prophet had paraphrased several verses from Psalms and Jeremiah; I did not yet know where the excitement of studying these texts would one day lead me. My gratitude to the faculty of that school, and especially to its principal, Rabbi Herbert Kavon, is deep and abiding. More seeds were sown during my years in graduate school, during which I studied Isaiah with Professor Shalom Paul at the Hebrew University, Professor Steven Geller at Brandeis University, and Professor Rolf Rendtorff at the University of Chicago.

I first wrote on this topic in a graduate seminar at Brandeis taught by Professor Michael Fishbane, and I expanded ideas from that paper in my University of Chicago doctoral dissertation. This book presents a substantial revision of the dissertation, which was directed by Professor Fishbane and read by Professors John Collins and Marc Brettler. Professor Collins's helpful observations and friendly manner guided me in directions I would otherwise have missed and enriched my thinking. Professor Brettler read the dissertation with great acuity, and his advice improved both dissertation and book. As an undergraduate, a graduate student, and now a colleague, I have benefited from his challenging rigor and his warmth, from his outstanding pedagogy and his friendship. It is a privilege for me to term myself his student. In many ways and for many years, Professor Fishbane fostered my growth as a scholar. He promoted original thinking, respected differences of opinion, and helped me avoid numerous pitfalls as I moved from paper to dissertation and from dissertation to book. His impact on this book—through his generous and penetrating comments, his own writings, and the example he set as a careful yet bold reader—is vast. My gratitude to him goes beyond words, but I hope that this book's contribution to the study of inner-biblical exegesis, a field he pioneered, pays part of a limitless debt.

Professor Shalom Paul inspired my analyses on Deutero-Isaianic allusion through his own writing, his class on Deutero-Isaiah, and the encouragement and counsel I was fortunate to receive from him as I wrote this book. In its earlier incarnations, this work benefited from my discussions with Stephen Hall, Daniel Klerman, Esther Menn, Michael Satlow, William Schniedewind, Colleen Stamos, and Anthony Tomasino. The book itself has been enhanced by advice from several colleagues: Professors Jacob Lassner, Richard Kieckhefer, Daniel Garrison, and Manfred Vogel. I am especially grateful for the comments of Professors Robert Alter and Chana Kronfeld. I would like to express my thanks to Professors Kronfeld and Daniel Boyarin for accepting the book in the Contraversions Series and for their encouragement, and to Helen Tartar and the editors of Stanford University Press for their many valuable observations.

In the preparation of the manuscript I was capably assisted by Mr. Daniel Shulman, Ms. Aline Linden, Ms. Elisa Marcus, Ms. Karina Hogan, and Ms. Shari Lowin. My thanks go to the Office of the Dean at the College of Arts and Sciences of Northwestern University for awarding me an AT&T Junior Faculty Fellowship, which allowed me to prepare the book for press. I am obliged to Rabbi Steven Forstein for suggesting the book's title; to a lover of Jewish books, Mr. Stanley Batkin, for permitting me to use art from his collection on the cover and for his assistance in finding a fitting image; and to the artist, Mr. Shraga Weil of Kibbutz Ha-'Ogen in Israel, for his consent as well.

As I finish what I hope is a contribution to Hebrew scholarship, I recall with appreciation mentors of my youth who encouraged me to pursue Jewish learning and introduced me to critical and literary approaches to the Bible: Rabbis André Ungar and Matthew Kanig, and my teachers Larry Malitzky and Joel Laitmann.

When I first wrote a paper on Deutero-Isaiah's allusions, I had not yet met Jennifer Dugdale. As I wrote the dissertation on which this book is based she gave me firm support and tender affection; the day after the opening words of Deutero-Isaiah's prophecy were chanted in the liturgy for שבת נחמו of 1995 we were married; and as I wrote the book itself, she gave her advice and love. תְּנוּ־לָהּ מִפְּרִי יָדֶיהָ וִיהַלְלוּהָ בַשְׁעָרִים מַעֲשֶׂיהָ.

For a longer time and with greater effect than any others, my parents nurtured my love of Jewish learning and hoped that I might contribute to it. My only sadness as I complete this work is that my father did not live to see it. I am heartened to know he was confident that this day would arrive and to know of the joy it will bring to my mother. It is dedicated to them.

B.D.S.

August 1997

מנחם אב, תשנ"ז

CONTENTS

A PROPHET READS SCRIPTURE

ALLUSION IN ISAIAH 40–66

הַנְּבִיאִים הַגְּדוֹלִים הִשְׁלִיכוּ אֶת מַחֲצִית נְבוּאוֹתֵיהֶם

. . .

אֲנִי מְלַקֵּט אוֹתָן וְעוֹשֶׂה לִי מֵהֶן נְבוּאוֹת עֲנִיּוֹת.

The great prophets threw out half their prophecies

. . .

I gather them up and make myself poor prophecies from them.

YEHUDA AMICHAI, *"I Am a Poor Prophet"* (1989)

INTRODUCTION

THE ISRAELI POET Yehuda Amichai discloses in these lines a sense of belatedness, even of inferiority. Following a long tradition of Hebrew writing, he is only able to gather up what was discarded, to glean in a field already planted and harvested many times over. The problem this modern Hebrew writer confronts is a common one in twentieth-century literature, but it affects the Hebrew writer with particular intensity: his predecessors wrote not only books but The Book; not only words but The Word. The tradition he wishes to augment does not merely include a canon, a flexible cluster of great works serving as source and context for any new writing. It incorporates *the* canon, a collection of prophecy, narrative, and law sanctified and closed some twenty centuries earlier. More than most writers, Amichai has reason to feel incapable of producing anything truly new; he can only reuse and revise what he inherits. Even as an inheritor, as a revisor, Amichai cannot but see himself as a latecomer, for the most prominent genres in the Hebrew literary tradition have long centered around the reworking or interpretation of the Source. Some of these genres are overtly exegetical: these include the *midrash* of the rabbis, the *pesher* of the Dead Sea community. Others are more bold and revisionary: think, for example, of attempts to create new scripture based on the old, such as the Temple Scroll, produced by the Dead Sea community, or the New Testament. Allusive or anthological genres exist as well: for example, both liturgical and secular poetry written by Jews in the Middle Ages. If Amichai seeks consolation as he attempts to reread what was reread many times before, he can at least recall that he is in good company: Hillel and Jesus and Qumran's Teacher of Righteousness, Akiva and Paul and the kabbalists all stood where he stands, gathered in the field where he gathers.

But it is not only the post-biblical authors who experienced this relationship to texts from the Bible. For, as biblical scholars have increasingly realized in recent years, the biblical authors themselves also comment on, explain, revise, argue with, and allude to texts written by their predecessors.[1] The implications of this phenomenon, which we may call inner-biblical allusion and exegesis, are important both for students of the Hebrew Bible and for students of the religious and literary traditions that grew from it. The presence of biblical exegesis within the Hebrew Bible itself shows that the religion of the ancient Israelites was already a text-based religion, a set of beliefs and practices dependent not only on oral traditions but also on authoritative documents. As prophets, priests, scribes, and psalmists modified tradition in ancient Israel, they had to take these documents into account, whether by revising the earlier texts, explaining them in new ways, applying their principles to new situations, or relying on their authority.

It follows that the religion which *generated* the Hebrew Bible in a crucial respect resembles the religions *generated by* the Hebrew Bible. Israelite thinkers, like those of Judaism and Christianity, looked back to existing texts and constructed new works in relation to those earlier ones. This exegetical and revisionary activity among biblical authors illuminates the parallel activity that was to become central in classical Judaism and Christianity—an activity, indeed, that produced classical Judaism and Christianity. The study of how biblical authors used or reacted to their predecessors, then, can be very suggestive. It allows the historian of religion to note correlations between the way the Hebrew Bible came into being and the way the literature of those who inherited the Hebrew Bible came into being. It suggests that biblical authors bequeathed to their successors not only a text, but ways of relating to and re-creating that text. The study of inner-biblical allusion and exegesis demonstrates that certain concerns are not exclusively post-biblical ones; these include questions of authority, of the relationship between new ideas and an existing canon, of new poetry's status next to older prophecy. Just as Hillel and Amichai grappled with these issues, so too did the biblical authors themselves.

I examine in this work the use of earlier biblical material in one limited, but highly allusive, corpus: Isaiah 40–66. These chapters were written during and after the Babylonian exile in the sixth century B.C.E. We may call the prophet (or perhaps prophets) responsible for these chapters "Second Isaiah" or "Deutero-Isaiah."[2] This prophet lived in Mesopotamia a generation after the Babylonian empire destroyed the Judean state and sent much of its population into exile. Deutero-Isaiah anticipated the victory of the Persian empire over the Babylonian, and he[3] promised his fellow Judean exiles that the Persians would allow them to return to their homeland and rebuild their temple there. Parts of these chapters also treat the situation of the returnees in the Land of Israel itself.

A close examination of these chapters shows Deutero-Isaiah to be one of the most allusive ancient Israelite authors. As he composed speeches of comfort and encouragement, he reformulated single lines and whole sections from the work of his predecessors. By studying these reformulations, we can enrich our understanding of individual passages in this writer's work. Further, we can gather evidence to answer a crucial question: Why does this prophet allude? Why does he rely on his predecessors?[4] The answers to this question illuminate a significant moment in the development of inner-biblical allusion and exegesis, and hence they clarify the activities that later gave rise to Judaism and Christianity. The examination of Deutero-Isaiah's use of earlier material allows us to sharpen the tools with which biblical scholars approach the phenomenon of inner-biblical allusion and exegesis in general. Answers to the question "Why does Deutero-Isaiah allude?" also help us understand the transformations of prophecy in late Israelite religion. The orally delivered oracles that had predominated earlier were eclipsed in the post-exilic era by written works patterned after the older oracles. Through investigating Deutero-Isaiah's use of earlier oracles, we deepen our understanding of this development.

In Chapters 2 through 5 of this book I examine allusions in Isaiah 40–66 in order to uncover their recurrent thematic and stylistic traits. I turn first to Deutero-Isaiah's use of Jeremiah, because the work of Jeremiah is the source for the largest number of allusions in Isaiah 40–66; subsequent chapters treat allusions to Isaiah ben Amoṣ (that is, Isaiah the son of Amoṣ, whom many biblical scholars label "First Isaiah"), the Book of Psalms, and other texts. I do not discuss every allusion in detail; instead, representative examples of certain techniques are used to typify Deutero-Isaiah's use of earlier material. Nearly every case of Deutero-Isaianic allusion I have found, however, is mentioned in the text or endnotes. There is one exception to this comprehensive approach. Identifying allusions to the Book of Psalms is particularly complicated, and therefore my discussion of these examples is more tentative and less comprehensive.

Two methodological matters demand attention before the analysis of the texts themselves commences. First, it is worthwhile to examine how literary critics think about relationships among specific texts. Which approaches in literary theory are relevant to biblical texts, and how might these approaches be applied to them? Discussing this question in Chapter 1, I refine the methods devised by biblical scholars for studying inner-biblical exegesis and allusion generally. Second, a central question underlies this whole project: How can one identify an allusion? How does one know that a similarity between a text in Isaiah 40–66 and another text results from borrowing— from Deutero-Isaiah's use of a specific passage in the other text? This issue forms a major subject of the second chapter. In the final chapter, I examine the theological and historical questions raised by Deutero-Isaiah's allusivity, questions that help us understand not only that prophet and his era but the peculiar recursiveness that marks the Hebrew literary tradition as a whole, whether in the writing of a contemporary poet like Yehuda Amichai or the work of the exilic prophet who insisted that the people Judah yet lives.

My approach to prophetic texts differs from that of many contemporary scholars. Where some of my colleagues detect composite writings and evidence of scribal hands spread over diverse periods, I usually find unified poems; where others sense a need to read several short pericopes atomistically, I encounter longer, highly integrated units.[5] This tendency is evident in my conclusion that Isaiah 40–66 forms a single corpus, probably by one author. It also manifests itself in my approach to individual passages in Deutero-Isaiah and his sources. Some scholars tend to break up a chapter to find a base document (typically consisting of, say, verses 1–2, 5b, and 7aβ– 9bα) that has been supplemented with several distinct additions, each of which can be dated with surprising precision. I regard compositional analyses of this type as unconvincing, not only because I doubt our ability to distinguish among diverse hands in prophetic texts but because many of the passages in question present themselves as readable units of considerable length to begin with. All this is not to deny that occasional glosses and interpolations occur in prophetic literature. I dispute, rather, the practice (especially prevalent in criticism of Isaiah 1–33 and 56–66) of finding a patchwork of textual fragments in passages that make better sense as they stand. The disjunctions and contradictions that allegedly establish the composite nature of prophetic texts often result from hyper-sensitive reading rather than genuine critical acumen. Similarly, I do not deny that some prophetic books are built from originally separate blocks of material; my work on Deutero-Isaiah's use of Jeremiah, on the contrary, lends credence to a classic source-critical approach to the Book of Jeremiah, as I explain at the beginning of the second chapter. Many attempts to find diverse authorship in prophetic texts, however, lack the sort of solid evidence that has been presented by critics of the Pentateuch. Neither the consistent differences of language, style, and outlook nor the lack of internal cohesion which are so manifestly present in the Pentateuch appear in most of the prophetic texts I examine.[6]

A full methodological discussion of this issue would require me to examine the nature of this sort of criticism and its origins. (I suspect these lie in the unfortunate propensity of form critics since Gunkel to assume that units of prophetic discourse must be extremely short, and in the unfathomable supposition of some scholars that a multiplicity of genres points to a multiplicity of authors.) Such an examination would fill a prolegomenon of great length and little interest. It seems better merely to include this *caveat lector* at the outset and to respond to critics by discussing some allegedly composite passages; this I do in endnotes directed toward the specialist.

More important than these case-by-case disquisitions is an implicit cumulative argument that emerges from my work as a whole. If I find one or two cases in which an allusion occurs in a section regarded by others as a hodgepodge of fragments, one might view my findings as coincidental; that is, one might contend that the verses in question do not—indeed cannot—contain extended reference to an earlier text. But if I find scores of such borrowings, and if they display consistent patterns in their reuse of older material, then the notion that all these cases result from happenstance becomes untenable; the repeated occurrence of a single type of borrowing validates my presumption that the passages in which they occur are unified compositions. By the end of this book, I hope it will be clear that the latter situation obtains.

1 LITERARY THEORY AND THE STUDY OF INNER-BIBLICAL ALLUSION AND EXEGESIS

As BIBLICAL authors evoke, interpret, paraphrase, and otherwise employ compositions by their predecessors, they forge textual links of a sort that has been subject to intense consideration among literary theorists in the past quarter century. Before we turn to biblical examples themselves, it will be useful to survey the varied approaches to questions of influence, allusion, and intertextuality current in literary theory and to decide which approaches are relevant to the project at hand. Doing so will make possible a reformulation of conclusions others have reached regarding inner-biblical exegesis. Such a reformulation is relevant not only to my work on Isaiah 40–66 but to the study of the subject generally.[1]

Influence and Intertextuality

Within the plethora of approaches to relationships among texts that have developed in the past twenty-five years, it is possible to distinguish between two broad categories suggested by the literary critics Jay Clayton and Eric Rothstein. One approach is oriented toward "influence" and "allusion," the other toward "intertextuality."[2] Literary critics have long focused on the former approach, asking how one composition evokes its antecedents, how one author is affected by another, and what sources a text utilizes. That approach is diachronic, because it distinguishes between the earlier text (the source or the influence) and the later one (the alluding text or the influenced). It focuses attention on the author as well as on the text itself.

"Intertextuality" (as Clayton and Rothstein use the word) encompasses manifold connections between a text being studied and other texts, or between a text being studied and commonplace phrases or figures from the linguistic or cultural systems in which the text exists. As Ziva Ben-Porat explains, these connections do not arise exclusively from an intentional and signaled use of an earlier text, such as citation (which might be studied under the rubrics of influence or allusion). The connections may result from the way that expressions in a given text reflect linguistic, esthetic, cultural, or ideological contexts of the text at hand; other texts may share those contexts, and hence links among many texts may be noticed, whether the authors of the texts knew each other or not.[3]

The intertextual approach relies heavily on structural linguistics and its postmodern heirs in seeing all signs, including those in a literary text, as meaningful only insofar as they stand in relation and opposition to other signs. As a result, any utterance signifies only in the context of other utterances, or as part of a sign system, such as a language. To understand any utterance is to put it in relationship with other utterances; and thus, any reader of a literary text necessarily connects it with other utterances. These utterances include other literary texts as well as popular expressions and underlying ideologies. For the intertextual approach, texts are part of a larger set of signifying systems, and only in such systems can they can come into being or be understood. This approach can be found in the work of many critics in the last quarter century, especially Roland Barthes, Julia Kristeva, Jacques Derrida, Michael Riffaterre, and Mikhail Bakhtin.

Intertextuality focuses not on the author of a text but either on the text itself (as part of a larger system) or on the reader.[4] It is the reader who interprets signs in the text by associating them with related signs in the reader's own mind. Of course, one reader's matrix of associations will differ from another's, so that the set of signs relevant for the intertextual approach can be quite broad. Sayings, clichés, prevalent notions or ways of thinking, other works of literature (whether earlier or later than the work being read) may contribute equally to the reader's construction of meaning of a given text. Intertextuality, then, concerns itself with the relations among many texts; it is a synchronic, reader-oriented, semiotic method.

These two types of approach differ markedly from each other. Several analysts of intertextuality stress that intertextuality is not merely the study of sources. Jonathan Culler summarizes the distinction: "Intertextuality thus becomes less a name for a work's relation to particular prior texts than a designation of its participation in the discursive space of a culture. . . . The study of intertextuality is thus not the investigation of sources and influences as traditionally conceived; it casts its net wider to include anonymous discursive practices, codes whose origins are lost, that make possible the signifying practices of later texts."[5] Indeed, the commonplace that reappears in a given work or the ideologies or esthetic preferences that inevitably manifest themselves in a text tend to interest the student of intertextuality more than sources from earlier literary works. Further, such a critic would stress that all texts may be read intertextually, because all texts relate to wide-ranging sign systems and can be compared to many other utterances.[6] For the student of influence or allusion, on the other hand, some texts yield little of interest.

This distinction between intertextuality, on the one hand, and allusion and influence, on the other, is basic to contemporary theoretical discussions of the relations between texts,[7] though many readers continue to confuse them.[8] In brief, intertextuality is concerned with the reader or with the text as a thing independent of its author, while influence and allusion are concerned with the author as well as the text and reader.[9] Intertextuality is synchronic in its approach, influence or allusion diachronic or even historicist.[10] Intertextuality is interested in a very wide range of correspondences among texts, influence and allusion with a more narrow set. Intertextuality examines the relations among many texts, while influence and allusion look for specific connections between a limited number of texts.

Which approach serves as a useful model for the study of the relations between Isaiah 40–66 and other parts of the Bible? Some might suggest intertextuality for a number of reasons.[11] Not only is that approach somewhat more fashionable in the humanities at the moment,[12] but certain aspects of the theory appear to lend themselves to the peculiar problems of biblical texts. Students of citation or allusion need to ask whether a resemblance between texts results from one author borrowing from another (in which case it is relevant to their study) or from two authors using common phrases or tropes (in which case it is not). But the intertextual critic does not feel compelled to address this question. On the contrary, the commonplace particularly interests such a critic. Moreover, identifying citations or allusions with confidence poses a particularly acute problem for the investigation of inner-biblical allusion and exegesis because so little ancient Israelite literature is preserved on which to form our judgments.[13] Thus the intertextual approach may appear to be more attractive to the biblical scholar. Further, for the student of allusion in the Bible, the question of which text is earlier and which later often arises: even if one is relatively confident that allusion or influence occurred, one might debate who is the alluder, who the source. But an intertextual critic would not need to ask whether the author of, say, Isaiah 49 borrowed from Isaiah 11, or vice versa. From the vantage point of intertextuality, "a resemblance or parallel is seen as inhering in the mind of the reader in the first place," so that the intertextual critic "does not need to worry about whether the author really read, remembered, and imitated a specific precursor."[14] Finally, given that the status of the author or authors in Isaiah 40–66 is open to question, there may be advantages to an approach which ignores the author in favor of the reader or a larger system of signification.

In this study, however, I will utilize the model of allusion and influence rather than that of intertextuality. While the musings of post-structuralist and other critics on the nature of sign systems are intrinsically interesting, they do not in every study provide the most useful models for the issues at hand. Some authors call attention to their own allusivity; they seem to insist on their relation to earlier texts. In such a case (and, I shall argue, Deutero-Isaiah is such a case), the intertextual model would lead a critic to overlook an important aspect of the text at hand.[15] Further, Isaiah 40–66 (or at least 40–55) are very concretely rooted in a readily identifiable historical situation. These chapters respond to the challenge that the loss of homeland and Temple posed for sixth-century Judean exiles, and they evince the promise that the fall of Babylon offers them. In analyzing such a deeply historical text, diachronic (and even explicitly historicist) approaches will prove both usable and enriching.

If I were writing a purely literary analysis, I might have been able to confine myself to issues of intertextuality, though even in that case certain questions of literary interest would have been neglected. However, I hope that this study will shed light both on the way Deutero-Isaiah uses language to create meaning and on the history of Israelite religion. Consequently, the intertextual approach will not suffice, since I need to address myself to a number of areas outside the scope of such study. Some of those issues may place the critic in a precarious situation: they force decisions about the dating of texts and the sufficient conditions for terming a parallel a borrowing. However, the proper response to such difficulties is not a flight to the synchronic (which at times masks an abdication of critical rigor), but careful construction of an argument. At times such arguments may seem speculative, but this need not vitiate the project as a whole. Dating biblical texts is difficult, but I believe that some methods of biblical criticism, carefully applied, yield justifiable results; the dating of each problematic text needs to be considered individually. Developing criteria to decide what parallels can be termed allusions, citation, or the result of influence is the project of the study of inner-biblical allusion and exegesis—a project I think possible, and to which I hope to contribute. To develop such criteria, it will be necessary to investigate in greater detail methods used in the study of influence and allusion and to examine closely the process of identifying and utilizing influences and sources. It is to this set of questions that I now turn.

Allusion and Influence

The concepts of influence and allusion can be set against an intertextual approach to the study of texts in that the former are more concerned with an author and allow for an element (often a strong one) of diachronic study. However, influence and allusion are not identical. Both concepts, along with some related notions, need to be described on their own.

Allusion

A standard definition of allusion in literary studies is provided by Earl Miner: "tacit reference to another literary work, to another art, to history, to contemporary figures, or the like."[16] Allusion requires "an echo of sufficiently familiar yet distinctive and meaningful elements" and "an audience sharing the tradition with the poet," according to Miner, since, without these, the borrowed material in the later work (i.e., the material in the later work, elements of which derive from the source) will not be recognized as such.[17] Carmela Perri offers another definition of allusion which describes the technique in semiotic terms. In a literary allusion, some signifier in the text refers not only to a signified in the imagined world of the text, but also to a source text. "An allusion refers at least doubly: the sign of the allusion-marker refers within its text's world as well as allusively, to some referent outside this text."[18] Take a brief example: In Wordsworth's "I Saw the Figure of a Lovely Maid,"[19] the words describing "the Lovely Maid" refer doubly. In the imagined world of the text, they refer to the central character of the poem, whom the speaker loved and whose death he mourns. At the same time, those words also refer to another text in which a poet describes a vision of a recently deceased woman whom he loved: Milton's Sonnet XXIII, "Methought I Saw My Late Espoused Saint."[20]

Ben-Porat provides the most detailed and helpful analysis of the act of interpreting an allusion.[21] She describes four stages through which the reader moves as the reader "actualizes" an allusion—that is, as the reader recognizes the allusion and uses elements from the source text to help construct a reading of the alluding text. In describing Ben-Porat's approach, I refer to two examples of allusion: the poem by Wordsworth mentioned above, which borrows from Milton, and a short story by Aharon Meged, "Indecent Act," which refers to Goethe's *Faust*.

First, the reader recognizes what Ben-Porat calls a *marker*, an identifiable element or pattern in one text belonging to another independent text.[22] The marker is one aspect of a *sign* in the referring text. The sign may be a poetic line or a sentence or a phrase, or it may consist of a motif, a rhythmic pattern, an idea, or even the form of a work or its title.[23] In Wordsworth's poem "I Saw the Figure of a Lovely Maid," several types of markers point back to the sonnet "Methought I Saw My Late Espoused Saint." These include words ("I saw"), images (the brightness of the apparition; a woman who appeared corporeal fading away), setting (a vision in sleep interrupted by waking), and theme (recalling a departed loved one). Markers may be simple (consisting of a single element) or complex; short or long; concentrated in a part of the alluding text or dispersed through several lines.[24] In Meged's story, the markers are spread over a long paragraph, and they include several lines from Goethe's poem which are quoted verbatim and discussed at length by one of the characters in the short story. Just as the alluding text contains a marker, the evoked text contains what Ben-Porat calls "the *marked*," the same elements as they appear in the evoked text. The referents of the marker and the marked in the imaginary worlds of the two texts need not be identical or even similar, though they may be.[25] For example, the markers in Wordsworth's poem refer within the world of that poem to a character independent of the woman in Milton's poem (similar though they are). On the other hand, the character in Meged's story uses the word "Gretchen" to refer to the same character who appears in Goethe's drama.

The second stage in the recognition of the allusion is the identification of the evoked text. This is not identical with the first stage, because it is possible that a reader will recognize a marker as referring to another text without recalling what the evoked text is. Most readers have experienced a sense that a phrase in a text they are reading is borrowed without knowing where it is borrowed from. In Meged's story, the second stage is reached easily, since one character in the story tells another that he has been reading a new translation of Goethe's *Faust* and that he disagrees with how some lines were rendered into Hebrew. In Wordsworth's poem, only a reader who has read and recalls Milton's poem can reach stage two.

The third stage is the modification of the interpretation of the sign in the alluding text. The reader brings certain elements of the evoked text or the marked to bear on the alluding text, and these alter the reader's construal of meaning of the sign in the alluding text.[26] For example, in "Indecent Act" a minor character happens to discuss some lines in a new translation of *Faust* into Hebrew. Among the lines he mentions in "Meine Ruh' ist hin / Mein Herz ist schwer" ("My calm is gone / My heart is heavy," lines 3374–75 of the drama). These lines, the reader realizes, describe very well the feelings of the main character in Meged's story, a teacher who has been accused of having sex with a high school pupil of his. Thus the allusion evokes an emotional state from the source which contributes to the portrayal of a parallel emotional state in the alluding text.

Allusions do not always require readers to reach Ben-Porat's fourth stage. In this stage the reader activates the evoked text as a whole to form connections between it and the alluding text which are not based on the markers and marked items themselves. Once the two texts have been linked by the marker's evocation of the marked, the reader may recall other signs within each text which affect the interpretation of the alluding text, even though these signs are not linked as marked and marker. Additional thematic patterns in the texts which initially had not seemed related now come into play, further enriching one's understanding not only of the sign containing the marker but the alluding text as a whole.[27] Certain properties of the source text outside of the marked sign may prove relevant for the alluding text. For example, the reader of Meged's story "Indecent Act" may recall the stanzas from which the line in *Faust* was quoted:

Meine Ruh' ist hin,	My calm is gone
Mein Herz ist schwer,	My heart is heavy,
Ich finde sie nimmer	I shall find rest never
Und nimmermehr.	And nevermore.
. . .	. . .
Die ganze Welt	The whole world
Ist mir vergällt.	Is ruined for me.
. . .	. . .
Mein armer Sinn	My poor mind
Ist mir zerstückt.	is undone.

(Lines 3374–77, 3380–81, 3384–85)[28]

Goethe's lines foreshadow the rest of Meged's story. The character, stripped of the dignity he had always enjoyed as a venerable scholar, and constantly anxious that others view him as a child molester, never again will find rest. Further, the reader may recall the context of the lines: they are spoken by Gretchen, the girl whom Professor Faust seduced. The similarity between the situations in *Faust* and "Indecent Act" is suggestive. It reminds the reader that respected and wise older men in fact do what Meged's character is accused of, and thus the allusion may lead the reader to suspect that the accusation is true. Further, it may strike the reader as significant that Gretchen speaks these lines out of longing for Faust: "Wo ich ihn nicht hab'/Ist mir das Grab" ("Wherever he isn't/Is the grave for me," lines 3378–79). She longs for "Sein Händedruck, / Und, ach, sein Kuß!" ("His hand's touch, / and o! his kiss!" lines 3400–3401). The connection hints that Meged's character, like Gretchen, may be less innocent than he would have people believe. How these questions play themselves out in a reading of Meged's story and how they are affected by further links to Goethe's poem is not my concern here; the example, I hope, shows that the marked not only affects the reading of the marker but establishes a nexus between two texts, which may allow many elements of the evoked text to alter one's understanding of the alluding text as a whole.

Influence

Having described allusion, we are in a position to distinguish between allusion and several closely related phenomena. As used in literary criticism, the term "influence" designates "the affiliative relations between past and present literary texts and/or their authors. . . . Influence-study generally entailed the practice of tracing a text's generic and thematic lineage. . . . [Studies of influence focused] on the ways literary works necessarily comprise revision or updating of their textual antecedents."[29] Influence has comprised a major concern of literary critics (though interest waned somewhat due to the New Criticism). Scholars of English, for example, have written copious studies on topics such as the role of Latin poetry in Milton, or Milton's importance for the romantics. The study of influence often accompanies the study of literary tradition: as writers continue adopting themes, topics, genres, and styles from their precursors, patterns of theme and topic develop which constitute a tradition investigated by literary historians.[30] Influence studies at times note the positive use a poet made of his or her predecessors. On the other hand, Walter Jackson Bate and Harold Bloom stress the burden which poets felt due to their relation with those whom they followed. These two critics examine the attempts by poets to assert their originality or their alleged freedom from their precursors.[31]

The elements which fall under the rubric "influence" need not confine themselves to particular words or even images or tropes. Thus Harold Bloom insists repeatedly that he is not interested in echoes of earlier poets' wording or imagery in the work of later poets: "Poetic influence, in the sense I give to it, has almost nothing to do with verbal resemblances between one poet and another. Hardy, on the surface, scarcely resembles Shelley, his prime precursor."[32] The discovery of resemblances in diction or imagery which constitute the marker and the marked, however, stands near the core of the study of allusion. Further, the study of allusion focuses on an aspect of the relationship between texts which is not the concern of influence study: the *use* to which the earlier text is put in the new one—that is, the way elements of the evoked text affect the reading of the alluding text.[33] Influence, on the other hand, is more likely to contribute to a theory of the genesis of literary texts, to the study of a given period or author (whether biographical, psychological, or historical), or (most of all) to the investigation of traditions or canons. The wider implications of influence study reflect a central difference between influence and allusion: influence is a much broader phenomenon. Whereas allusion posits a relationship between two specific texts (in most cases, between particular sets of lines in those texts), influence refers to relations between authors, whole works, and even traditions. Thus one may speak not only of the influence of one work on another (say, of Spenser's *Faerie Queene* on Milton's *Paradise Lost*) but of a tradition on a work (the aggadic tale on Agnon's story "'Aggadat Hassofer") and of a tradition on a tradition (Greek tragedy on French neo-classicism).

Of course, allusion and influence remain closely linked: both posit diachronic relationships between specific texts or groups of texts. Further, the two may very often appear together (Bloom's example of Hardy and Shelley notwithstanding). Spenser influenced Milton in many ways, and verbal echoes of Spenser appear frequently in Milton. Nonetheless, the concerns implicated in the study of each phenomenon remain distinct: noting allusions belongs to the project of interpretation and is more focused on a specific text, while studying influence connects to wider, less text-specific issues.[34]

In this study, I primarily treat allusion in Deutero-Isaiah's poetry. My interest in influence is more limited: it encompasses the influence of specific works (such as that of the prophet Isaiah) on Isaiah 40–66, but not that of traditions (such as ancient Near Eastern royal ideologies). Nevertheless, on the basis of patterns in Deutero-Isaiah's project of allusion, I shall attempt to arrive at conclusions about his place in prophetic tradition, and this attempt will involve questions similar to those examined by students of influence.[35]

Echo

Ben-Porat identifies at least three and often four stages in the recognition of an allusion: noticing the marker, identifying the source, bringing the marked sign to bear on the interpretation of the sign which includes the marker, and also noting additional aspects of the source text which affect the reading of the alluding text generally. Ben-Porat stresses that a text which allows the reader to note the marker and to identify the source is not an allusion. Only with the fuller interpretation of the alluding text which occurs in the third stage is it possible to assert the presence of an allusion.[36] In other words, allusion consists not only in the echoing of an earlier text but in the utilization of the marked material for some rhetorical or strategic end.[37]

We may ask, then, what do we have in a case where elements of an earlier text reappear in a later one, but the meaning of the marked sign in the source has little effect on a reading of the sign with the marker in the alluding text? I will term this phenomenon "echo," which differs from allusion in that only the first two stages of Ben-Porat's scheme are at play.[38] Some examples will make this clearer. Ben-Porat gives one example of an allusion which she claims moves through the first three stages: a cheese advertisement using the phrase, "This is the smell that launched a thousand barbecues."[39] According to Ben-Porat, the reader of the advertisement recognizes the echo of another phrase ("This is the face that launched a thousand ships"—stage one), identifies the source as Marlowe's play *Dr. Faustus* (stage two), and brings the context of the quote to bear on the advertisement, yielding the interpretation, "Buy this popular cheese because it is a special product for special (intelligent) people" (stage three). It seems unlikely to me, however, that most people who hear or read the advertisement go beyond stage one, viz., recognizing the advertisement as echoing a common phrase. Few would know the source of the quote. Almost none would utilize it to produce a revised interpretation of the advertisement. Thus, this advertisement provides an example of echo. The echo alters nothing in the interpretation of the sign itself, though the presence of a familiar phrase makes the text more interesting.

Cases of echo may go beyond the first stage. An example: in an article on literary approaches to studying biblical narrative, Yair Zakovitch acknowledges the importance both of evidence of multiple compositional layers in a text and of a unifying framework; but he stresses that the structural unity of the final literary form (which he terms המרכבה) has conceptual priority. He summarizes this idea pithily: "סוף מעשה המרכבה במחשבה תחלה" (roughly, "the final literary form has conceptual priority").[40] Any literate reader of Hebrew will recognize two familiar phrases here, and hence reaches Ben-Porat's first stage. מעשה מרכבה (here, "literary structure," but also "deed of the chariot") is the term for an early Jewish mystical movement. סוף מעשה במחשבה תחלה ("final form . . . conceptual priority," but also "last in creation, first in intention") is a line from Solomon Alkabez's famous song for the Sabbath liturgy, לכה דודי, where it refers to the Sabbath itself—the last day in the order of God's creation, the first in His intention. Upon recognizing the source of the line, the reader has reached stage two.[41] However, it does not seem possible in this case to arrive at stages three or four. The original context of the phrase has no bearing on Zakovitch's essay; rabbinic or Lurianic ideas about the Sabbath do not affect our reading of this discussion concerning the relative places accorded to diachronic and synchronic approaches to biblical narrative. Zakovitch's borrowing from liturgical poetry is playful; it is clever; and thus it is a particularly fine example of echo. But it is not an allusion in the sense described above, since it does not relate to the interpretation of the sign (here, the sentence in his essay) in which the marker (the borrowed vocabulary) appears. Nonetheless, his echo is worth noting, because it does tell us something about the author, and because noticing it is part of the process of reading the piece. This leads us to the question of the *purpose* of a mere echo; but I shall defer this issue until I have discussed the purpose of allusions.

The distinction between cases of allusion and echo is rarely clear-cut. I have interpreted Zakovitch's borrowing of a phrase from לכה דודי as an echo, not an allusion, because I cannot discover any respect in which knowing the poem affects my interpretation of the line in the essay. Yet some reader might attempt to do so, and thus that reader would view this as a case of genuine allusion. Ben-Porat views the cheese advertisement as allusive, while I sense overreading in her claims and prefer to classify this as echo. Both techniques may be present in a text, and it is necessary to realize that an examination of one may often lead to the other.[42]

Exegesis

By "exegesis," I mean an attempt to analyze, explain, or give meaning to (or uncover meaning in) a text.[43] Exegesis in this narrow sense is a category distinct from allusion. The marker in an allusive sign refers doubly: to a signified in the textual world of the alluding text and to a signified outside that textual world, viz., to another text. Thus the words and images used by Wordsworth in his poem "I Saw the Figure of a Lovely Maid" refer to a vision experienced by the narrator of the poem, but they also refer to another poem, Milton's "Methought I Saw My Late Espoused Saint." An exegetical comment refers to another text but not to anything in the imagined world of the exegetical text itself. An exegetical text clarifies or transforms an earlier text; an allusive text utilizes an earlier text.[44] An exegetical text[45] is formally dependent on and oriented toward the older text, without which it cannot exist; an alluding one has a formal independence, even if its production of meaning depends to a great degree on older texts.[46] An allusion may help us to recognize elements in the evoked text which we had not noticed before, and hence it may aid in interpreting the evoked text, but this is a secondary feature not present in all allusions.[47] Exegesis, however, necessarily and primarily involves an attempt at helping the reader recognize elements in the older text and offering suggestions regarding its interpretation. As in the cases of influence and echo, the line dividing exegesis from allusion is permeable, and individual cases may straddle the distinction or challenge it. Nonetheless, it will be useful for the sake of conceptual clarity to keep this distinction in mind.

Reasons for Allusion

Why do authors allude? Literary theorists describe many factors that lead authors to recall the language of their predecessors. A lack of confidence may prompt an author to borrow from a work already acknowledged as great. As Johnson explains, the poet, "unsatisfied by his system's own capacity to create permanence, seeks further security. It founds its sign-system and semic substance on a literary substrate already considered permanent. . . . The older text is the 'iron' the poet chooses to run through the 'reinforced concrete' of his poetic world."[48] This may be the case even if an audience is unlikely to recognize older vocabulary in the new text. An author, feeling unable or unworthy to create something entirely new, may nevertheless be willing to fashion a literary artifact from older material.[49]

Allusion may serve as a way of acknowledging, even asserting influence (and here we should again note that influence is not necessarily a burden for all poets).[50] By acknowledging a predecessor, an author may seek to gain entry into a canon; through allusion the poet avows, "This work is worth reading, just as its predecessors were." In such a case, allusion represents an attempt to bolster the authority of the work. Conversely, allusion and its acknowledgment of influence may bolster the authority of a predecessor's work or of the tradition within which the new work claims a place. By alluding, a new work keeps the older works alive and maintains their relevance. Thus allusions (and any acknowledgment of influence) serve a culturally conservative function.[51] At the same time, a new work can also attempt to introduce less well-known works into a canon or to create a new canon, and hence allusion can perform a culturally innovative role.[52]

Allusion not only allows an author to assert closeness to an older text; it also can distance the new work from the old, since it is precisely when one juxtaposes two works (as one is forced to do by allusion) that one notices their differences. In such a case, allusion may, paradoxically, allow the new text to achieve a distinct identity in opposition to the older work.[53]

An allusion may help establish a link between author and audience by appealing to shared knowledge.[54] Allusion may simply allow the author to display his or her erudition.[55] By the same token, allusion gives the readers an opportunity to demonstrate their knowledge (if only to themselves).

Here we arrive at another aspect of allusion: the pleasure that alluding, and recognizing allusion, gives to authors and readers alike. Perri points out that "the etymological origin of 'allusion' is the Latin *alludere*, to joke, jest, mock, play with," and many descriptions of joking apply quite well to literary allusion.[56] Allusions, like jokes, place familiar material in new, often surprising contexts. In joking, the incongruity of the context produces humor. In alluding, the new context is enriched by landmarks from the old, so that the reader experiences a pleasurable recognition of something already known. Perri quotes Freud's comments on techniques of joking such as similarity of sound and modification of familiar phrases, which apply equally well to allusion: "We can single out as their common characteristic the fact that in each of them something familiar is rediscovered, where we might instead have expected something new. The rediscovery of what is familiar is pleasurable."[57]

Similarly, Johnson notes that "phonic and rhythmic forms acquire an independent existence in the poet's memory as a source of satisfaction."[58] While many literary critics focus on more hermeneutically oriented aspects of allusion, this element of play, of sensual enjoyment, in allusion should not be overlooked. I think it often is one of the most important reasons for allusion; at times it may be the only one. We ought not forget that luxuriating in "the pleasure of the text"[59] is perhaps the most crucial aspect of reading literature, and the element of play in allusions encourages just this. The element of play helps explain why allusion usually is covert: it is more challenging, and more fun, for the reader to have to produce the identification.

Most of these reasons for allusion play the same role in cases of echo. Insofar as an echo allows a reader to identify a source, it connects the new work with the old no less than an allusion. Thus it may assert the new work's place in a tradition or bolster the tradition itself through reuse. The element of play may be the exclusive reason for an echo, where no significant effect on the interpretation of the sign at hand can be found. In our examples of echo above, the element of play was strong. The advertisement's use of the line "the cheese that launched a thousand barbecues" does not suggest that Marlowe's play can be brought to bear productively on the interpretation of the advertisement, but it does engender a pleased, even amused, sense of recognition. Zakovitch's echo of a familiar phrase in Jewish intellectual life and of a line from Jewish liturgy does not affect his specific point about how to read biblical narrative. But it does strike the reader as familiar and thus satisfying. It may achieve two further purposes typical of allusion or echo: it displays the author's knowledge and wit; and it may signal Zakovitch's claim to be participating in a tradition of study which is not merely academic or modern. Thus, even in a case which does not allow Ben-Porat's third and fourth stages, a borrowing may tell a good deal about an author and his or her relationship to predecessors.

Inner-Biblical Allusion and Exegesis

The preceding discussion allows us now to focus on allusion, echo, influence, and exegesis as they appear in the Hebrew Bible. In cases where two biblical texts are related as source and borrower, we may classify the nature of the relationship along two axes: one is concerned with form or rhetoric, and the other with meaning, interpretation, or strategy.[60]

Forms of the Use of Older Material

How does a later biblical text connect to a source from an earlier biblical text at a formal level? Three categories emerge: explicit citation, implicit reference, and inclusion. The reasons for this dependence and its implications for interpretation of the later text constitute another issue to be discussed below.

EXPLICIT CITATION.   In an explicit citation, the later text uses some formula to make manifest that it is referring to, depending on, disagreeing with, or explaining an older text. The name of the older text is often given. For example, several post-exilic books explain a religious practice as being performed כַּכָּתוּב בְּתוֹרַת מֹשֶׁה ("as it is written in the Teaching of Moses"— 1 Kgs 2.3, Ezra 3.2, 2 Chr 23.18); similar formulae appear elsewhere. (Even in such cases, however, it is not always completely clear to us what book is referred to. In post-exilic books, תוֹרַת מֹשֶׁה ["the Teaching of Moses"] often appears to mean something very much like our Pentateuch, incorporating priestly, holiness, Deuteronomic, and other material in a single work,[61] but in some pre-exilic writings the term seems to refer specifically to Deuteronomy [see 2 Kgs 14.6 for a particularly clear example]. In Neh 10.35, something called a wood sacrifice is described as being כַּכָּתוּב בַּתּוֹרָה ["written in the Torah"], though no such practice is described in the Pentateuch.)[62] In other cases, the text includes a citation formula but not the name of the text referred to. In the description of sacrifices for holidays in Numbers 29, the text repeatedly notes that, in addition to the special sacrifices, the daily sacrifices should also be offered כְּמִשְׁפָּטָם ("according to their regulation"). The source of each מִשְׁפט (regulation) is not given, though they are known to us from Leviticus or Numbers (e.g., the regulations for the *tamid*-sacrifice in Num 28.3–8).[63] Reference may also be made to a popular saying known to us only from the reference itself (e.g., Jer 31.28 or Ezek 18.2)[64] or to books unknown to us (for example, "The Book of the Wars of YHWH," referred to in Num 21.14). There are many reasons that an older text may be cited; these will be discussed below. Our concern here is only to note the existence of the category of explicit citation at a formal level.

IMPLICIT REFERENCE.   In a larger number of cases, however, the reference to the older text is implicit. Markers (usually borrowed vocabulary) point the reader to the older text, though only if the reader is familiar with them. In such cases, the specific connection to the older text is harder to prove, though we have seen that even when a citation is made explicit the identity of the older text may be debated. In this formal category, the new text reuses vocabulary or imagery from the source. Probably the largest number of cases of what scholars have generally called "inner-biblical exegesis" belongs in this category. For example, Mal 1.6–2.9 and Psalms 4 and

67 contain many vocabulary items found in the ancient priestly benedictions known to us from Num 6.23–27.[65] The abundance of markers pointing back to the older text makes clear that Malachi and the psalmists borrowed from that text, even though none of these authors cites the older text by name.

INCLUSION.   It is also possible for a new work to borrow whole sections word for word from an older text, so that the new text does not merely allude to scattered material but incorporates whole sections of an older work. Chronicles serves as the most obvious example of this phenomenon as it repeats, more or less verbatim, large parts of Samuel and Kings.[66] In cases of inclusion, the new work may make small but highly significant changes in the reused material, but this does not change the *formal* status of the borrowing, which differs from the cases described above. Similar to inclusion is interpolation: by adding material to a text (or by removing material from it), a scribe can drastically change the meaning of the original. For example, Zakovitch argues that the addition of Gen 25.22–23 to a text that did not originally include them helps portray Jacob as divinely ordained to receive the birthright rather than as a swindler.[67] One can describe the formation of Chronicles in these terms. By adding and removing material from the older text in Samuel-Kings, the Chronicler created a new work. In this sort of case, the boundary between the study of inner-biblical allusion and exegesis and the study of tradition history and source criticism becomes blurred.

Purposes for the Use of Older Material

The previous section described the relationships between sources and later texts from a formal point of view. Of course, the texts are also related in terms of content. How does a later biblical text confront the meaning of an earlier text on which it relies? What does the later text say or imply about the message of the earlier? To what use does it put the earlier text? These questions will allow us to explore the types of relationships between biblical texts and their sources at a thematic level. Several categories emerge from this analysis: exegesis, influence, allusion, and echo. Within both influence and allusion, two subcategories appear: revision and polemic. As we examine these, we will want to relate each to the formal categories noted above in order to see which formal categories are most likely to coincide with which thematic, strategic, or interpretive categories. In some cases it will be useful to apply Ben-Porat's analysis of the stages involved in actualizing an allusion, because her concerns shed light on the nature of these categories. Ben-Porat's analysis will be instructive even outside the category of allusion, especially because it allows us to note the difference between allusion and the other categories. Finally, I shall discuss whether the new text takes the place of the older text or coexists with it.

EXEGESIS. I intend the term "exegesis" in the narrow sense outlined above: an exegetical text purports to explain the meaning of a specific older text. (My definition differs from the much broader use of the term in the phrase "inner-biblical exegesis" in the work of Sarna, Fishbane, and Zakovitch. For them this phrase refers to any case in which one biblical passage borrows from or is based on another. Most examples of what they call inner-biblical exegesis are not, strictly speaking, exegetical; they are allusions. It is for this reason that I prefer to call the phenomenon "inner-biblical allusion and exegesis.")[68] Exegesis abounds in post-biblical literature: Qumran pesher, midrash, medieval Bible commentary all focus on allowing readers to understand biblical texts. Exegetical passages may be embedded in larger, non-exegetical texts, as are midrashic passages in the Talmud or explanations of biblical texts in philosophical works.[69] Cases such as this appear frequently in the New Testament, sometimes in the mouths of characters in a narrative and sometimes in the author's own voice: Jesus explains the meaning of a passage in the Hebrew Bible (e.g., in Mark 12.26–27); Paul spends a great deal of time doing the same (e.g., Rom 5.12–17, 11.25–32).

Many examples of this category appear in the Hebrew Bible. In Dan 9.2, Daniel states that he examined the prophecy of Jeremiah according to which the exile was to last seventy years in order to understand what "seventy years" meant. In Ezra, Nehemiah, and Chronicles, attempts are often made to interpret the Torah text which contains apparently contradictory stipulations (attributed by modern scholars to P and D). Most cases of what Fishbane calls "scribal exegesis" in the Bible fall into this category. In such cases, a later hand inserts a clarifying comment into a vague text.[70] For example, in Exod 32.1, the original text must have read, הָאִישׁ אֲשֶׁר הֶעֱלָנוּ מֵאֶרֶץ מִצְרַיִם ("the man who brought us out of Egypt"); a later hand has added the clarifying remark זֶה מֹשֶׁה ("this is Moses") before the word הָאִישׁ ("the man").[71]

Most examples from this thematic/strategic category fall into the formal category of citation. Because the exegetical passages deal with specific older texts, references to them are often explicit. Scribal additions depart from this tendency. Because they are not independent texts, the question of how they relate formally to their predecessors is moot. Those cases where the new text does not name what older text is being explained constitute a second exception; see, for example, Dan 9.26–27, where Daniel applies the prophecy of Israel's return in Isa 10.26–27 to his own day.[72] Daniel does not mention Isaiah by name, so that one can notice his interpretation of Isaiah only through recognizing the markers which point back to the older text. Nevertheless, this is a case of exegesis in the narrow sense: Daniel is attempting to show, albeit implicitly, what the text in Isaiah really refers to (political events of a much later time). In this case of exegesis, the formal relationship between the texts is one of implicit reference rather than citation. (The thematic category of exegesis displays a similar flexibility of form in the New Testament. When Paul interprets Genesis 3 in Rom 5.12–17, he neither quotes the text he discusses nor identifies it explicitly. On the other hand, Rom 11.25–32 is a case of explicit citation: Paul indicates that he is commenting on Isa 59.20–21 and 27.9 by quoting them verbatim.)

The reader in cases of exegesis which are also examples of citation easily and inevitably moves through the first of Ben-Porat's stages, the recognition that an earlier text is coming into play, since the text in question presents itself as a reading of the older text. In cases where the older text is explicitly named, the second stage, identification of the source, also presents no problem. In cases where the exegesis is not explicit, the first two stages may in fact be overlooked by a reader who does not recall (or never knew) the marked vocabulary in the source. Stages three and four of Ben-Porat's scheme are not relevant in cases of exegesis. In those stages, the reader's original perception of the meaning of the alluding text is altered as the reader brings the source to bear on the alluding text. But in a case of exegesis, the new text's surface meaning is simply to make a comment on the older text; once that surface meaning is understood, the older text already has come into play, so that stages three and four are unnecessary. Nonetheless, one might argue that the reader goes through a process resembling, if distinct from, stages three and four. The reader may compare the interpretation of the older text given in the exegetical text to his or her own understanding of the older text. The exegesis may turn out to be merely an explication or clarification of the older text or a tendentious reading of it which works in an unexpected way (for example, Daniel's understanding of "seventy years" in Jeremiah as "four hundred and ninety years"). Analyzing the nature of the exegesis itself then alters or adds to one's understanding of the exegetical text as a whole or the work in which the exegetical passage appears.

An exegetical text does not take the place of the older text. On the contrary, it is relevant primarily because the older text is available and needs explication. If the older text were not read, the new text would be pointless. In fact, by clarifying or updating the meaning of the text under consideration, the new text may help preserve it.

INFLUENCE.   A text may be related to a predecessor in that the viewpoint or ideology of the later text as a whole depends on or reflects the earlier one, regardless of specific connections between individual lines or words in each. For example, the influence of Deuteronomy or an early version of it on the books of Joshua, Judges, Samuel, and Kings is well known; these historical books draw from Deuteronomy a pattern of concerns and ideas. In such a case, the relation between the works falls into the literary category of influence. (As in cases of influence in other literature, the influenced work may also contain passages which allude back to specific passages in the predecessor; for example, 2 Kgs 14.6 alludes explicitly to Deut 24.16, while Josh 9.6–14 alludes implicitly to Deut 21.22–23.) In cases of influence, the new text need not displace the older text (for example, Samuel and Kings do not attempt to displace Deuteronomy; rather, they show the working of its principles in history), but in some examples of influence discussed below, the new text may in fact do so.

Influence may also include the repetition of an older text's verbal content. Such cases may be examples of inclusion from a formal point of view (e.g., the influence of Samuel and Kings on Chronicles). Alternatively, they may involve a less word-for-word reliance on the source as the new text restates the older material largely in its own words. For example, Jubilees and the Temple Scroll repeat with various changes the stories and laws found in the Pentateuch.[73] Influence in these cases usually incorporates one of two thematic relationships, revision or polemic.[74] Each deserves detailed discussion.

REVISION.   At times a biblical text will restate some aspects of an earlier text while altering elements of the older text's message or adding to the earlier message.[75] This often happens in legal codes, in which earlier laws are rewritten. Thus the Covenant Code's law regarding the release of Hebrew slaves after six years of service in Exod 21.2–6 is repeated in Deut 15.12–18, but with a number of changes: the scope of the law is widened so that it covers female as well as male slaves; the slave receives payment on being set free; the location of the ceremony in which a slave may announce his wish not to go free differs. The older law is not entirely rejected, but some of its details are. This category is very frequent in prophecy. Thus Isa 15.1–16.12 contain a lengthy oracle of doom against Moab, which seems not to have been fulfilled. Isa 16.13–14 correct the older prediction, specifying that the events in fact will come to pass in the next three years. The addition neither rejects the older prophecy nor attempts to explain that it always should have been understood to refer to such and such a time. Rather, it acknowledges that the original oracle had not come to pass but asserts that it soon will— that is, it retains but revises the older text.[76]

Revisions of older texts may take a number of the forms described in the previous section. In rare cases, such as Isa 16.13–14, the older text may be specified or cited explicitly (there the new text refers overtly to the older one with the words זֶה הַדָּבָר אֲשֶׁר דִּבֶּר ה' אֶל־מוֹאָב מֵאָז, "this is the word that YHWH had spoken earlier concerning Moab"). More frequently, the texts will be related implicitly through markers such as common vocabulary or, in legal revision such as that found in Deut 15.12–18, common topics. Cases of this thematic category can take the form of inclusion as well. Chronicles is to a large degree a revision of Samuel and Kings, and they are related through extensive quotation into which additions and changes have been introduced. It is even possible that a later text will restate and revise ideas from an older text without citing, alluding to, or quoting a specific passage in the older text. For example, Jubilees retells the stories of Genesis largely in its own words; it tends not to borrow lengthy passages from Genesis verbatim (this case might also be seen as an extended case of implicit reference). Thus all the formal relationships described above occur in the category of revision.

If the revision includes explicit citation of the earlier text, then the first two stages of Ben-Porat's scheme take place inevitably. In other cases, they again depend on the reader's knowledge. As in cases of exegesis, the third and fourth stages need not be an issue. Recognizing the dependence on the earlier text will not change the reading of the later text, but it will lead to a greater appreciation of the position of the later text vis-à-vis its predecessors.

In cases of revision, the new text largely replaces the older one. Deuteronomy 15 is not a mere gloss on Exodus 21; once the new law is available, the old law can (in fact should) be ignored. From the Chronicler's viewpoint, by reading Samuel and Kings one would only gain information which at times is incorrect, while a proper perspective on Judean history can be garnered from his new work.[77] Even if the old text is preserved, the new text attempts to relegate the old one to a noneffective status. It is worth noting, however, that replacement is not identical to rejection. The core ideas of the older text are preserved in the new one along with various improvements. Precisely because that core remains, however, the older text no longer serves any practical role (at least in the view of the author of the new text).

This category is distinct from exegesis because the new text does not claim to explain the older one, but presents an innovative variation of the older text's ideas.[78] However, the effect of the category often becomes exegetical, especially if the source which has been revised is preserved or becomes canonical. For a community that accepts both texts, contradictions between the source and the revisions must be resolved. At times, the resolution involves understanding the earlier one as implying what the later makes explicit; in such a case, readers impose the meaning of the second text on the first. Nonetheless, the exegetical effect of the new text results not from the original relation between the texts but from the decision of later readers to preserve both texts and to read one in light of the other.[79]

Revision may generate exegesis, but revisionary writing relates to older texts quite differently from the manner in which real exegesis does. In exegesis, the older text is already authoritative, and the new text is secondary, not only temporally but ontologically—even if the new text suggests a radical interpretation of the older one. In revision, the new text assumes a more independent and assertive posture. To label Deuteronomy exegetical in the strict sense would imply a misunderstanding of the nature of Israelite religion in that period. The Covenant Code was not canonical for Deuteronomy in the way that the Torah was canonical for the rabbis. Because the Covenant Code in Deuteronomy's day was not unalterably a part of a collection of authoritative writings, biblical authors could revise it or reject it. For the rabbis, however, the written Torah was both closed and authoritative, so that they could not produce a replacement for it or compose additional books which would be part of it. They could only perform exegesis on it. (It is precisely for this reason that their interpretations were at times, of necessity, so extravagant.)[80] Further, the categories of exegesis and revision within the

Hebrew Bible have very different heirs in post-biblical literature. Exegesis leads to pesher, to midrash, to rabbinic Judaism; the tradition of revision continues in Apocrypha, Pseudepigrapha, Qumran texts such as the Temple Scroll, the New Testament, and medieval Hebrew poetry (even though these texts also contain exegetical elements).[81]

POLEMIC. At times a biblical text argues against another biblical text.[82] We have already seen that Ezek 18.2 repudiates a popular saying. (The New Testament also contains examples of this category in relation to the Hebrew Bible; see, e.g., Mark 10.2–12.) An extended series of polemics among several texts involves the divine attribute formula. The version found in Exod 34.6–7 includes assertions that later biblical writers pointedly disavowed. According to that formulation (which appears in condensed form in Exod 32.1–6, 34; Num 14.1–20; 2 Kgs 20.12–19; and Ps 99.8), God punishes children for the sins of their parents, apparently as a sign of mercy to the parents: when a sinner repents, his punishment is deferred to his offspring.[83] Later writers, having abandoned this notion, omitted the wording that describes trans-generational punishment in their versions of the attribute formula: see, e.g., Jonah 4.2, Joel 2.12. Elsewhere they even replaced it with assertions that more pointedly contradict the older formula, asserting that God punishes the sinner directly and does not delay punishment; see, e.g., Deut 7.9–10.[84] In Ps 103.8–9 the formula is repeated without the doctrine of transgenerational deferment of punishment; here again an author stresses that God's anger does not last forever: לֹא לְעוֹלָם יִטּוֹר ("He does not remain angry forever").[85] The rejection of the formula found in the older text is heightened by Psalm 103's punning use of the root נט״ר (which sometimes means "to guard" but is used here in its sense "to be angry") where Exod 34.7 had used the similar-sounding and related word נצ״ר (which always means "to guard").

In rare cases in the Hebrew Bible, a polemic occurs in an explicit citation; Ezek 18.2 exemplifies this. More often in the Hebrew Bible, the older text is not specified, so that the polemic falls into the formal category of implicit citation. Thus, for example, the repetition of certain vocabulary in a particular order serves as a marker in Deuteronomy 7, Joel 2, Jonah 4, and Psalm 103, showing that the new texts are connected to a particular older text (known to us from Exodus 34).

Polemical texts attempt to take the place of the texts against which they argue. This is the case even when the older text survives or is preserved by a citation in the polemical text. At the same time, polemic depends on the older text even while rejecting it. When the reader recognizes the marked vocabulary and identifies the source, he or she takes particular note of the disagreement with the source. The juxtaposition of the texts calls the new idea into sharper focus than would have been possible if the new text had merely asserted an idea without stressing the departure from the older text.

Like revision, polemic is distinct from, yet can result in, exegesis. Thus Lev 25.39–44 appear to abrogate the slave laws found in Exod 21.2–6 and Deut 15.12–18. Leviticus insists that an Israelite can never remain a slave for more than fifty years (because the slave goes free at the Jubilee, which occurs every fifty years), while the other texts allow a Hebrew to remain a slave forever (לְעֹלָם). But rabbinic readers accept all these texts as canonical and therefore disallow contradictions among them. As a result, they understand the word לעולם ("forever") in Exod 21.7 as meaning "until the Jubilee" (*Mek. Nezikin* Parashah 2). In so doing, the rabbis allow Leviticus 25 to regulate the reading of Exodus 21 and Deuteronomy 15, so that the polemic in Leviticus has effectively become an exegesis. Nonetheless, this is a secondary development, and it is important to realize that the passage was not originally exegetical in import but polemical.[86]

Even though the distinctions among polemic, revision, and radical exegesis should be maintained, one must admit that the lines dividing these categories in specific cases are not always clear. When a later author refers to an earlier text and changes some ideas in it, readers may debate whether the later author means to argue against the earlier text, to rewrite it with appropriate changes, or to claim that the earlier text really meant to say what he is saying more clearly now.[87] The boundaries between the categories at hand are difficult to draw; one scholar may classify a text as exegetical, while another sees it as a case of revision or polemic. Nonetheless the categories remain heuristically significant.

ALLUSION. Biblical writers may use an older text to bolster their own text or to help make some claim. For example, according to Jer 2.3, those who consume Israel will incur guilt because "Israel is a holy thing to YHWH." In making this assertion, Jeremiah relies on a legal passage in Lev 22.14–16, which teaches that holy donations are not to be consumed because doing so incurs guilt before God.[88]

Allusion forms one of the most common categories of what Sarna, Fish-bane, and Zakovitch call inner-biblical exegesis and the most common category of aggadic exegesis. However, this category is distinct from the category of exegesis as defined above. A writer alludes to an older text for some purpose in his own text, not to suggest a particular understanding of the old one. Wordsworth imports pathos from Milton's description of his late wife; by alluding to Goethe's *Faust*, Meged introduces into his story the motif of tension between learning or prestige on the one hand and desire on the other. Similarly, in the example discussed in the previous paragraph, Jeremiah neither interprets nor revises the priestly passage. He does not claim that the older passage is a geopolitical warning to Israel's enemies rather than a law concerning the sacrificial cult. Nor does he suggest that the text ought to be such a warning and needs to be rewritten. The prophet's statement does not bear on the status of the older text at all. Rather, Jeremiah borrows the older vocabulary to make his own message readily understood by analogy, or more vivid. James Kugel characterizes the role of allusion within the Bible particularly well: examples of this category serve as "an evocation, an argument by analogy, and . . . an appropriation of divine law and its authority in order to make" a new point not necessarily related to the topic of the older text.[89]

Allusion can overlap with polemic. If an author uses vocabulary bor-rowed from an older text to highlight the extent to which his ideas contrast with that text, the correspondence of marker and marked allows us to call that instance of polemic an allusion. For example, as Deutero-Isaiah argues against Genesis 1, he includes examples of vocabulary from the earlier text, pointing back to the passages in the source which he finds problematic.[90]

Formally, examples of this category may of course be implicit references; alternatively, they may be introduced by citation formulae and refer ex-plicitly to the older text, though in fact this is uncommon.

Applications or appropriations of older material in no way attempt to replace that material. Replacement is a possibility only in cases such as revision, where the new text addresses the same issue as the old, but in an innovative way. There is no need for replacement in cases of allusion; indeed, the new text depends on the old for its impact.

ECHO. We saw above that allusions are distinct from mere echo. The meaning of an alluding text is affected by the content of the source text, while echoes do not suggest any altered understanding of the passage in which they appear. Formally, however, echoes resemble allusions in that both borrow vocabulary, images, or other elements from the older text, and many of the purposes or reasons for allusion apply equally well to echo.

This distinction remains important for the Hebrew Bible. At times a later text may borrow from a specific older text without explaining, expanding, rejecting, or utilizing the content of the older text. Thus Psalms 4 and 67 make liberal use of vocabulary from the Priestly Benediction known to us from Num 6.23–27. But, as Fishbane points out, these psalms are not "aggadic transformations" of the ancient benediction; they "merely re-use its liturgical prototype."[91] This does not mean that the appearance of the vocabulary is a coincidence, or that this is not a genuine case of dependence on an earlier source. The reader can recognize the markers (the many words borrowed from the source) and identify the source, but doing so does not lead the reader to change his or her interpretation of the psalms. The presence of the familiar vocabulary does, however, affect the reader, who experiences the pleasure of recognition and realizes that the psalm is part of a particular liturgical tradition. Further, the reuse of the vocabulary may represent a claim to authority by the psalms or an attempt by them to reinforce the authority of the ancient benediction. The reuse also may shed light on connections between different genres in Israelite worship (blessing, prayer) and between the people who composed or utilized them. Thus, the non-interpretive borrowing of older vocabulary remains significant to the student of inner-biblical allusion and exegesis.

2   DEUTERO-ISAIAH'S USE OF JEREMIAH

Genuine Dependence or Coincidental Similarity?

All students of allusion must distinguish between two types of textual similarity: cases in which one writer relies on another and cases in which two writers use similar language coincidentally.[1] Several texts may use the same vocabulary not because a later author depends on an earlier one but because they utilize a common tradition, or because they are discussing a topic that naturally suggests certain vocabulary. This problem becomes acute in a highly traditional literature such as the Bible. Stock prophetic, legal, or poetic vocabulary[2] or the common use of some familiar trope or type-scene may lead two texts to look similar whether or not one author knew the other. Deutero-Isaiah drew upon many established Israelite traditions: stories concerning the Exodus and the patriarchs; conventional prophetic genres such as the oracle against a foreign nation and the mock trial (*rib*); customary liturgical forms encompassing praise and lamentation.[3] As a result, Deutero-Isaiah's language in, say, a mock trial may resemble that of a mock trial in another book, but the resemblance does not necessarily point to a case of inner-biblical exegesis or allusion.[4] A central methodological principle follows from this: we cannot view an older text as a source for a passage in Deutero-Isaiah if both utilize stock vocabulary,[5] exemplify a literary form such as a lament,[6] or treat a subject that calls for certain words.[7]

The traditions that Deutero-Isaiah utilized were not exclusively Israelite. Scholars have long noticed similarities between parts of Isaiah 40–66 and Akkadian prayers, oracles, and royal inscriptions; Deutero-Isaiah depends on Mesopotamian royal and prophetic ideologies, especially in his depictions of servant figures and of Cyrus, the Persian king who vanquished Babylonia.[8] These ideologies influenced other Israelite prophets as well, and this increases the extent to which Deutero-Isaiah will share vocabulary with other prophets. In other words, not only does Deutero-Isaiah rely on his Israelite predecessors, but they all draw on common ancient Near Eastern traditions. Deutero-Isaiah applies the following vocabulary and ideas to Israel, to servant figures, or to Cyrus; corresponding Akkadian terms appear in the portrayal of the king in Mesopotamian royal traditions:[9]

1. The words "call one's name" (קרא/הזכיר שם = Akkadian *šuma zakāru* or *šuma nâbu*), often followed by "justly" (בצדק = *kēniš*);

2. Various words used to describe God's special favor or love, such as אהב and רצה (corresponding to Akkadian *narāmu* and *migru*);

3. The idea of divine election, expressed in Hebrew with the root בחר (in Akkadian with the words *itûtu* and *naplusu*);

4. The king/nation as servant, or עבד (*[w]ardu*) of the gods;

5. The idea that the figure depicted was created by the god, expressed in Hebrew with the roots בנה and יצר (in Akkadian with *banû*), and perhaps also designated in the womb (בבטן, Akkadian *ina libbi ummi* or *ina šasurri agarinni*) for a certain role (usually involving many nations in both the biblical and cuneiform sources);

6. The words "grasp / hold one's hand / right hand" (תמך/החזיק ביד/בימין = *tiriṣ qāti, qāta tamāḫu/ṣabātu*).

7. The idea that the figure in question is to set captives free (especially bringing them light) and/or to restore a Temple;

8. The words "do not fear, for I am with you to save you" (אל תירא/אל תפחד כי אתך/עמך אני/אנכי להצילך, occurring in Akkadian with the phrase *lā tapallaḫ* and the additional components in a variety of forms).[10]

When these items appear in Deutero-Isaiah and an earlier text, the passage in Deutero-Isaiah cannot be considered an allusion to the earlier text unless some other factor indicates that Deutero-Isaiah utilized that text. We cannot regard these words and motifs as markers of allusion unless more definite markers are present. For example, Deutero-Isaiah has YHWH proclaim to Israel,

> O Israel, My servant (וְאַתָּה יִשְׂרָאֵל עַבְדִּי), Jacob (יַעֲקֹב), whom I chose, seed of Abraham who loved Me: . . . Do not fear, (אַל־תִּירָא) for I am with you (כִּי עִמְּךָ־אָנִי); do not be frightened, for I am your God. I support you, I help you, I uphold you. (Isa 41.8, 10)

These lines (as well as 43.1–7 and 44.1–3) bear a remarkable similarity to a remark made by Jeremiah:

> O Jacob, My servant (וְאַתָּה . . . עַבְדִּי יַעֲקֹב), do not fear (אַל־תִּירָא)—a statement of YHWH—and do not become afraid. . . . For I am with you (כִּי־אִתְּךָ אֲנִי)—a statement of YHWH—to save you. (Jer 30.10–11; see also Jer 1.8)

Yet one cannot conclude that Isa 41.8–10 allude specifically to Jeremiah. All the terms connecting these passages belong to the royal traditions that we know in greater detail from other ancient Near Eastern texts, both biblical and non-biblical. Deutero-Isaiah may have been taking stock language from a widespread tradition just as Jeremiah did, rather than borrowing it directly from Jeremiah 30 or Jeremiah 1. That both authors depended on stock language associated with royal ideologies becomes even more evident in light of terms such as הֶחֱזַקְתִּיךָ ("I held onto you"), בְּחַרְתִּיךָ ("I chose you"), קְרָאתִיךָ ("I called you"), and אֹהֲבִי ("who loves me") in Isa 41.8–10 and בְּטֶרֶם אֶצָּרְךָ בַבֶּטֶן יְדַעְתִּיךָ . . . נָבִיא לַגּוֹיִם נְתַתִּיךָ: ("before I created you in the womb, I singled you out . . . I made you a prophet to the nations") in Jer 1.5, since these terms correspond to those found in Akkadian royal texts (see numbers two, three, five, and six above).

Even when the use of common traditions by two texts is not likely, it can be difficult to confirm that parallel vocabulary results from borrowing rather than coincidence. This difficulty is acute in Deutero-Isaiah, since almost all his allusions are cases of implicit rather than explicit citation. In the absence of explicit citation formulae (such as כַּכָּתוּב, "as it is written"), the sheer number or proportion of words appearing in both texts must point toward borrowing. Such a criterion can be dangerously indeterminate.

However, if an author frequently reformulates marked vocabulary in certain ways, one can verify that a passage from that author's work contains a borrowing when the ostensible markers there conform to a pattern frequently noted in other markers in the author's work.[11] Further, an author may repeatedly allude to certain texts, and the author's preference for those texts increases the probability that additional parallels with them result from borrowing. The argument that an author alludes, then, is a cumulative one: assertions that allusions occur in certain passages become stronger as patterns emerge from those allusions. The critic must weigh evidence including the number of markers and their distinctiveness, the presence of stylistic or thematic patterns that typify the author's allusions, and the likelihood that the author would allude to the alleged source. The weighing of such evidence (and hence the identification of allusions) is an art, not a science.[12]

Identifying Deutero-Isaiah's Allusions

In the remainder of this chapter, I shall argue that in certain passages Deutero-Isaiah draws words, images, and ideas from Jeremiah. At the beginning, such an argument must be tentative. The analysis of more and more examples will allow me to note typical thematic transformations and stylistic adaptations that help isolate genuine allusions in Deutero-Isaiah, as opposed to texts where Deutero-Isaiah and Jeremiah resemble each other for some other reason. Cases of allusion will begin to emerge as strong examples only after other cases are collected.

Other scholars, including John Skinner, Umberto Cassuto, Shalom Paul, and William Holladay, have noted correspondences between Jeremiah and Deutero-Isaiah which they attribute to the dependence of the latter upon the former,[13] and Wolfgang Lau has studied the use of sources including Jeremiah in Isaiah 56–66 (though not in 40–55).[14] These earlier studies are very useful for the investigation of inner-biblical allusion and exegesis in Isaiah 40–66. Several caveats regarding the work of these scholars must nonetheless be noted. They do not, by and large, discuss the problem of distinguishing borrowings from coincidental similarities of vocabulary.[15] Further, they note correspondences between individual verses but tend to overlook correspondences between whole sections, which are very frequent. Finally, these scholars generally do not examine the use to which borrowed material is put—that is, they produce long lists of parallels or of Deutero-Isaiah's sources, but they do not study his strategic transformation of earlier texts.

One group of parallels between the Book of Jeremiah and Deutero-Isaiah will not be examined. Many similarities can be noted between Isaiah 40–66 and Jeremiah 50–51. I do not discuss these because it is altogether likely that Jeremiah 50–51 or large sections thereof were written at the same time as (or even later than) Deutero-Isaiah.[16] Thus we cannot be sure that Deutero-Isaiah would have had access to these chapters. The similarities between them may result from their common message and historical setting. Further, many parallels between Deutero-Isaiah and Jeremiah 50–51 involve vocabulary that appears in several other texts as well, especially Isaiah 14. This circumstance suggests that the parallels in question reflect word clusters popular among exilic and post-exilic writers concerned with the fate of Babylon. While a core of Jeremiah 50–51 may well go back to the work of Jeremiah, and while Deutero-Isaiah may have in fact at times alluded to these passages, it will be safest to avoid reference to them.[17]

Of course, a number of critics maintain that other sections of the Book of Jeremiah are post-exilic as well, but nothing approaching unanimity exists regarding those chapters.[18] Therefore, in collecting examples of Deutero-Isaianic borrowing from Jeremiah, it is sensible to consider parallels from the rest of Jeremiah. An examination of Deutero-Isaiah's dependence on Jeremian traditions produces a startlingly neat picture: Deutero-Isaiah's sources in Jeremiah are limited to specific blocks of material, a finding that dovetails remarkably well with Sigmund Mowinckel's theories regarding the composition of the Book of Jeremiah.[19] More specifically, Deutero-Isaiah utilizes poetic utterances of Jeremiah and a limited corpus of prose material by the pre-exilic prophet, but Deutero-Isaiah never relies on the Deuteronomistic prose speeches attributed to Jeremiah, the biographical narratives describing him, or the oracles against the nations found in his book.[20]

Reversal

Words and images earlier prophets used in rebuking the people or predicting their doom often reappear in passages where Deutero-Isaiah comforts the exiled Judeans or announces their restoration. Thus Deutero-Isaiah consoles the people with language resembling that with which Isaiah or Jeremiah castigated them.[21]

Jeremiah has God complain that his fickle people have forgotten Him more easily than a woman forgets her jewelry:

> Would a young woman forget her jewels, a bride her ornaments
> (הֲתִשְׁכַּח בְּתוּלָה עֶדְיָהּ כַּלָּה קִשֻּׁרֶיהָ)? But my people has forgotten me
> days without number. (Jer 2.32)

Deutero-Isaiah uses similar vocabulary to convey a very different message: that God has not forgotten Zion or her children, the people Israel:

> Zion says, "YHWH has abandoned me, and my Lord has forgotten
> me." Would a woman forget her suckling one, or a young female the
> son of her womb (הֲתִשְׁכַּח אִשָּׁה עוּלָהּ [אוֹ]ם רַחֵם [22]בֶּן־בִּטְנָהּ)? Even if
> these forget, I will not forget you. Look! I have inscribed you on [My]
> palms; your walls are in My sight at all times. Your children are coming
> quickly . . . you will wear all of them like jewelry (כָעֲדִי), you will
> adorn yourself with them as a bride (וּתְקַשְּׁרִים כַּכַּלָּה). (Isa 49.14–18)

Vocabulary found in a single question in Jeremiah occurs also in Deutero-Isaiah, but there it is spread over two verses. First God asks, התשכח אשה עולה ("Would a woman forget her suckling one?"), which recalls the beginning of the question God asked in Jeremiah; several verses later the words כעדי ("jewelry") and ותקשרים ככלה ("you will adorn yourself with them as a bride") appear. The material resembling the older text appears in two halves in Deutero-Isaiah. We shall see parallels of this sort again.

God's statement to Israel in the later text calls to mind His complaint in the earlier. When one reads the passages alongside each other, one senses that YHWH denies abandoning His people, even though they forgot Him in Jeremiah's day—indeed, YHWH would no sooner forget them than a woman would forget her child. Both texts include the metaphor of a woman, but in Deutero-Isaiah the figure is found in a more tender image: in place of a woman who covets her jewels, we read of mother and child. Reference to jewelry does appear later in this passage, but there God does not use the motif to criticize Zion. Instead, He promises that she will have children with whom to adorn herself. Vocabulary and images which had appeared in the Jeremiah passage turn up in Deutero-Isaiah's work as well, and the later prophet repeatedly uses these words and images to encourage where the earlier one had chastised. The consistency of this pattern suggests that the presence of the same elements in both texts is no coincidence. Deutero-Isaiah alludes to Jeremiah's wording, reusing the earlier metaphor of a woman in a new way. He reverses the message of the passage from Jeremiah without denying its accuracy, as he asserts that God, like a mother, reprimands but does not renounce Her child. The people did forsake YHWH. But even though this might lead one to expect that YHWH would ignore Israel, in fact YHWH has not done so.[23] In this passage, as in others we will examine, Deutero-Isaiah provides reasons for God's loyalty which are unrelated to Israel's behavior or worthiness—and which are therefore more believable to a guilt-ridden exilic audience.[24]

In the case just examined, a single line from the source is reversed in a short passage in Deutero-Isaiah.[25] In other cases this type of correspondence involves longer passages. Take, for example, the lament found in Jer 10.17–25:[26]

> [God says:] "Pack your bags to leave the land, O you sitting (יֹשֶׁבֶת) under siege! For thus says YHWH: I am about to cast out the inhabitants of the land (יוֹשְׁבֵי הָאָרֶץ). . . ." [The people lament:] "Woe is me because of my injury! My wound is terrible (נַחְלָה)! . . . My tent (אָהֳלִי) has been destroyed; all my tent-strings (מֵיתָרַי) have been cut; my children (בָּנַי) have gone away from me and are no more. Nobody is left to stretch out my tent or to raise up its flaps (אֵין־נֹטֶה עוֹד אָהֳלִי וּמֵקִים יְרִיעוֹתָי)." For the shepherds are fools . . . all their flock is scattered. Listen! A voice, a report is coming: "Great noise from the north—to make the cities of Judah a desolation (שְׁמָמָה)." . . . O YHWH, chastise me—indeed, [this] is just; but not in anger, lest You make me naught. Pour out your anger on the nations (הַגּוֹיִם) who do not know you . . . for they have devoured Jacob . . . and brought an end to him; they have desolated (הֵשַׁמּוּ) his dwelling places. (Jer 10.17–25)

The vocabulary found in this passage occurs also in the following song in Deutero-Isaiah:

Sing, barren one who has not given birth; break forth in joy and shout, you who have not gone into labor (חָלָה)! For the children from the time of desolation (בְּנֵי שׁוֹמֵמָה) outnumber those of the married years, says YHWH. Widen the space of your tent (מְקוֹם אָהֳלֵךְ), stretch out the flaps (וִירִיעוֹת . . . יַטּוּ) of your dwelling! Don't be stingy—lengthen the strings (מֵיתָרַיִךְ) and strengthen the pegs! For you will spread out to the south and the north and dispossess nations (גּוֹיִם); [your children] will settle the desolate cities (נְשַׁמּוֹת יוֹשִׁיבוּ). . . . And your redeemer will be called the Holy One of Israel, the God of all the earth (הָאָרֶץ). (Isa 54.1–3, 5)

Most of the parallels I note in parentheses consist of a word which appears in both texts. One, however, is based on a similarity of sound. The word מקום (m᾽qom, "space") in Isa 54.2 resembles a word in the Jeremiah passage which has a different meaning but consists of the same three consonants in the same order: מקים (meiqim, "raise up"). The connection between these words is strengthened by their appearance in both texts next to the words אהל ("tent"), יריעות ("flaps"), and נט״ה ("stretch"). The expression in Deutero-Isaiah differs in another way from its counterpart in Jeremiah: the words ומקים יריעותי ("the one who raises up [meiqim] the flaps") in Jeremiah constituted a single phrase. But in Deutero-Isaiah מקום ("space," m᾽qom) is separated from יריעות ("flaps") by an intervening noun, אהלך ("your tent"). Thus, as we saw in the previous example, elements which appeared in succession in Jeremiah occur in Deutero-Isaiah as well, but the sequence is broken in the later text. In this case only one word separates the elements that were together in Jeremiah, while in the previous example the phrase "Would a young woman forget her jewels, a bride her ornaments" was split into two parts by several intervening verses. Nonetheless, the division here is quite palpable because elements of what had been one phrase now belong to separate clauses: "Widen the *space* [m᾽qom] of your tent, the *flaps* of your dwelling stretch out!"

The passage from Deutero-Isaiah seems to reverse the negative images in Jeremiah point by point. The people lamented the loss of their children in the older text, but Deutero-Isaiah tells Zion that she will have children again, and more than before. In Jeremiah the people mourned, "My tent is destroyed, all my tent-strings are broken." Because the children were killed, rebuilding was not feasible: "nobody is left to stretch out my tent, no one to set up the flaps" (10.20). Deutero-Isaiah, on the other hand, assures Zion that not only will she have a tent, she will need to enlarge it to accommodate her abundant offspring. Thus the prophet directs her to do precisely what the people were unable to do in Jeremiah. Both texts tell us that the people will spread out, but for different reasons. In Jer 10.21 the invading nations scattered Israel, but in Isa 54.3 the Israelites, in their great number, reclaim land in all directions from the foreigners.[27] The invaders had made the cities of Judah into desolation (שממה), but now the Israelites repopulate them.

A pattern emerges here which occurred in our first example as well: words, images, and metaphors that signified negatively for the people Israel in Jeremiah herald restoration for the people in Deutero-Isaiah. The consistency of the pattern again suggests that Deutero-Isaiah has deliberately borrowed and reversed elements from the older text. That the relationship between the two texts also displays a stylistic feature found in the first example—the split-up of a single phrase from Jeremiah into two phrases in Deutero-Isaiah—strengthens this impression.[28] The words I have indicated in parentheses above, then, are not merely coincidental parallels, but a set of marked items and markers that comprise a case of literary allusion.[29]

While Deutero-Isaiah's use of Jeremiah indicates his closeness to his predecessor, in some passages he appears to agree with prophets whom Jeremiah criticized. For example, Jeremiah castigated false prophets, saying,

> Great and small, they all pursue unjust gains (בּוֹצֵעַ בָּצַע), while prophet and priest practice deception. They would heal (וַיְרַפְּאוּ) the wound of my people easily, saying, "Things will be fine! Things will be fine!" but things will not be fine (שָׁלוֹם שָׁלוֹם וְאֵין שָׁלוֹם). (Jer 6.13–14)

Deutero-Isaiah, however, expresses an optimistic outlook remarkably similar to that of the false prophets whom Jeremiah opposed:

> For the sin of his [the people's] unjust gains (בִּצְעוֹ) I was angry, and I smote him . . . I have seen his ways and I have healed him (וְאֶרְפָּאֵהוּ). . . . Things will be fine, things will be fine (שָׁלוֹם שָׁלוֹם) for those near and far (God says), and I heal him (וּרְפָאתִיו). But the wicked are like a sea stirred up, for they will not be able to have tranquility. . . . Things will not be fine (אֵין שָׁלוֹם) for the wicked. (Isa 57.17–21).[30]

The two passages share several vocabulary items that do not appear together elsewhere in the Hebrew Bible; moreover, these items appear in the same order in both texts: בצע ("unjust gains"), then the root רפ"א ("heal"), followed by the words שָׁלוֹם שָׁלוֹם ("things will be fine, things will be fine") and אֵין שָׁלוֹם ("things will not be fine"). Again we find that words occurring in succession in Jeremiah appear in two halves in Deutero-Isaiah. Jeremiah's " 'Things will be fine! Things will be fine!' but things will not be fine" is cut in two, the first part applying to the people generally ("Things will be fine, things will be fine for those near and far") and the second to the wicked ("Things will not be fine for the wicked"). The presence of this pattern, which we have seen in the previous two examples, and of other vocabulary items that appear in the same order in both passages, suggests that Deutero-Isaiah is not merely issuing a proclamation that happens to agree with the prophets whom Jeremiah opposed. Rather, he deliberately alludes to the passage from Jeremiah.[31] In so doing, Deutero-Isaiah reverses Jeremiah's message of woe and replaces it with a proclamation of restoration, just as he did in the examples discussed above.[32]

This case of reversal creates an odd situation: Deutero-Isaiah appears to endorse the false prophets. Like them, he predicts that things will go well for the nation. Yet he does not attempt to distance himself from Jeremiah or to maintain his own continuity with the false prophets. The prophets to whom Jeremiah objected had a valid message—but not one valid for their own time. For that era, Jeremiah was the true prophet. Furthermore, in a modified fashion, Jeremiah's words still apply in Deutero-Isaiah's own day, since even then "things will not be fine for the wicked." One might have thought that this sort of allusion signifies Deutero-Isaiah's rejection of his predecessor. On the contrary, he uses the rhetoric of reversal to underscore how apt Jeremiah's warnings were. In prophecy, timing is all, and Jeremiah understood what the other prophets did not: that the time for a message of encouragement had not yet arrived. Further, his negative words, properly recast, would remain appropriate for the future as well. Deutero-Isaiah, then, reinforces Jeremiah's position as a prophet, because in repeating Jeremiah's words in the form proper for his own day he brings them new validity. Deutero-Isaiah does not align himself with the false prophets of the pre-exilic period; instead, he gives focus to Jeremiah's rebuke while stressing a prophecy more relevant for the exiles.

One of the finest examples of reversal involves Jeremiah's letter to the exiles, in which Jeremiah advised the Judeans sent to Babylonia that they must be prepared to live there for some time.[33]

> Thus says YHWH of Hosts, the God of Israel to all the exiles (הַגּוֹלָה) that I have exiled from Jerusalem (הִגְלֵיתִי מִירוּשָׁלַם) to Babylonia. Build houses (בְּנוּ בָתִּים) and settle (וְשֵׁבוּ), and plant (וְנִטְעוּ) gardens, and eat their fruit (וְאִכְלוּ אֶת־פִּרְיָן). Take wives and beget (וְהוֹלִידוּ) sons and daughters, and take wives for your sons and give men your daughters that they may give birth (וְתֵלַדְנָה)[34] to sons and daughters, and you will increase and not be few. (Jer 29.4–6)

Similar vocabulary appears in an exuberant passage in Deutero-Isaiah:

> Rejoice and exult (וְגִילוּ) forever and ever! . . . For, look! I shall create for Jerusalem exultation (גִּילָה), and for its people, joy. I have exulted in Jerusalem (וְגַלְתִּי בִירוּשָׁלַם) and have rejoiced with my people. No more will there be heard in it the sound of crying or the sound of sobbing. . . . They will build houses (וּבָנוּ בָתִּים) and settle (וְיָשָׁבוּ) in them; they will plant (וְנָטְעוּ) vineyards and eat their fruit (וְאָכְלוּ פִּרְיָם). They will not build for another to dwell in it; they will not plant for another to eat it. . . . They will not give birth (יֵלְדוּ) in dismay, for they are seed blessed by YHWH, and their offspring are with them. (Isa 65.18–23)

The motif of building houses and planting gardens appears elsewhere in the Hebrew Bible as well (Deut 28.30, Ezek 28.26, Amos 9.14, Mic 6.15). But Isaiah 65 shares vocabulary with Jeremiah 29 which does not occur in these other passages (e.g., "Jerusalem" and "give birth"). More importantly, Jeremiah's phrases and ideas reappear in Isaiah 65 in the same order: Jerusalem, build houses, settle, plant, eat their fruit, give birth. As a result one begins to suspect that Deutero-Isaiah did not merely utilize a stock motif found throughout the Hebrew Bible, but that he borrowed these items from Jeremiah 29 specifically.

This suspicion receives additional corroboration from the appearance of two additional lexical connections, which also occur in order. At the outset of the passage, Deutero-Isaiah hints at several words in Jeremiah without quoting them; instead, he inserts similar-sounding words. Rather than

Jeremiah's גולה (*golah*, "exile"), he says גילה (*gilah*, "exultation"), and rather than הגליתי מירושלם (*higleiti mirushalayim*, "I have exiled from Jerusalem"), he says גלתי בירושלם (*galti birushalayim*, "I have exulted in Jerusalem"). The similarity in the second set results not only from the repetition of the letters ג״ל and the reference to Jerusalem, but from the repetition of a grammatical form: each text has a first-person singular perfect verb based on the letters ג״ל, and thus each text includes the sounds *g* and *l* followed by the phoneme *ti*.

This wonderful play on a word from the source works on both stylistic and thematic levels. Where Jeremiah spoke of exile, Deutero-Isaiah interjects exultation. The hermeneutic of reversal, the move from tropes of woe to tropes of joy, appears in many of Deutero-Isaiah's allusions to Isaiah and Jeremiah. But nowhere is that hermeneutic so clear, so succinct, and so delightful as in this transformation of גולה (*golah*) to גילה (*gilah*).

Other borrowed terms are used in a new, positive way as well. Jeremiah's letter dashed the exiles' hopes of a speedy return. He bade them to invest effort and time in building houses, planting vineyards, having not only children but grandchildren—activities that point to a long-term residence in Babylonia. These normally auspicious endeavors were therefore harbingers of bad news for the exiles. But Deutero-Isaiah uses them in a promising manner: to predict remarkable longevity. A person who builds a house or plants a vineyard enjoys it for a limited time, while those in the next generations reap most of the benefits of the person's efforts. But in Isaiah 65, we are told that people will live so long that they themselves will derive ongoing benefit from their effort.

In some cases of reversal, Deutero-Isaiah supplies responses to prayers and laments found in the earlier prophet's work. Deutero-Isaiah declares:

> Sing to YHWH a new song, [give] Him praise from the ends of the earth (הָאָרֶץ). . . . Let the wilderness and its cities take up [the song], its villages, where the inhabitants of Kedar (קֵדָר) live. Let the rock-dwellers sing, let them cry out (יִצְוָחוּ) from the top of the mountains . . . YHWH goes forth like a hero (כַּגִּבּוֹר); like a man of war (כְּאִישׁ מִלְחָמוֹת) He rouses up fury. He yells, He even roars; He triumphs over His enemies. "I have held back for a long time; I was quiet, I restrained Myself. [But now,] I will howl, I will pant, I will gasp (וְאֶשָּׁאַף) like a woman giving birth. I will destroy mountains and hills

and dry up all their vegetation (עֶשְׂבָּם). I will turn rivers into islands and dry up pools. I will lead blind people on a path they do not know and guide them on roadways they do not know. I will make what is dark before them light, what is crooked straight. These are the things I have done; I have not deserted them." (Isa 42.10–16)

The passage calls to mind one in which Jeremiah describes the punishment to which the people are subject and their prayer that it end:

> Judah mourns, her gates grow feeble. They are draped in darkness all the way to the ground (קָדְרוּ לָאָרֶץ), and the cry (וְצִוְחַת) of Jerusalem rises up. Their nobles sent youths for water, they went to the cisterns; [but] they found no water, they came back with their buckets empty. . . . For there has been no rain in the land (בָאָרֶץ)[35]. . . Wild asses stand on the bare hilltops, they gasp (שָׁאֲפוּ) for breath like a jackal, their eyes waste away,[36] for there is no vegetation (עֵשֶׂב). "If our sins have testified against us, act for Your name's sake, YHWH! . . . Hope of Israel. . . . Why are You like a stranger in the land (בָאָרֶץ) . . . like a helpless man (כְּאִישׁ נִדְהָם),[37] like a hero (כְּגִבּוֹר)[38] who cannot save? You are in our midst, YHWH! We are called by Your name! Don't abandon us!" (Jer 14.2–9)

That these two passages share many vocabulary items which do not appear together elsewhere suggests that Deutero-Isaiah borrows these elements from Jeremiah. This suspicion is reinforced by a playful correspondence between two semantically distinct but similar-sounding words: קָדְרוּ (qadᵉru) in Jeremiah is a verb meaning "to become dark," but קֵדָר (qeidar) in Deutero-Isaiah is a proper noun. Correspondences such as these have emerged in the examples discussed above as a stylistic characteristic of Deutero-Isaiah. He frequently uses the same root as his source but with a different meaning (as in this example), a phenomenon I shall refer to as word play; and he often hints at a word in his source by using a similar-sounding but unrelated word (for example, גילה [gilah, "exultation"] instead of גולה [golah, "exile"]), which I shall refer to as sound play. Word play and sound play are examples of the sort of stylistic pattern whose presence can make it easier to determine that two passages are related as source and borrower, and they help to confirm here that Deutero-Isaiah depended specifically on Jeremiah 14.

The case of word play in this passage is interesting for another reason. Although Deutero-Isaiah uses the consonants קד"ר to mean something other than what they meant in Jeremiah, he does not abandon Jeremiah's motif of darkness, because that motif appears later in the passage as the word מחשך ("dark"). Thus the word קדרו ("draped in darkness") in the source begets two words in the allusion: the first imitates the sound, the second the idea, of the marked item. One thing did Jeremiah speak; two did Deutero-Isaiah hear.

Several other motifs in the passage in Deutero-Isaiah point back to Jeremiah, although the words used to describe them are new. Thus the theme of the blind people who are led in the wilderness may go back to the wild animals whose eyes fade. God's statement that he has not deserted them is based on the people's cry, "Don't abandon us!" Deutero-Isaiah borrows Jeremiah's drought imagery but transforms it from a token of divine punishment to a figure of God's power: the God who is strong enough to dry up pools, rivers, and cisterns is strong enough to redeem. But where Israel is concerned, the absence of water in Jeremiah is reversed, so that Israel will receive water where there usually is none: in the desert as they return to the Land of Israel. (The word מקוה in Jeremiah, translated above as "Hope," can also mean "pool," a pun certainly intended by Jeremiah. Deutero-Isaiah recognizes the pun, and he picks up the secondary meaning by using the word אגם, which also means "pool.")

The passage in Deutero-Isaiah not only reverses the negative tropes of the passage in Jeremiah; at times, God in the later text responds to the questions which Jeremiah asked YHWH on behalf of the people. The earlier prophet asked God why He ignored the people's plight; in Deutero-Isaiah God announces that He had wanted to help them, but He restrained himself (probably for the reasons cited already in Jeremiah: their sins testified against them). Now He is ending His restraint and will rescue them. YHWH is not "a helpless man" but "a man of wars," not "a hero incapable of saving" but "a hero who triumphs." The people begged, "Don't abandon us"; in Deutero-Isaiah YHWH assures them that He has forgotten neither them nor His own mighty deeds: "I have not deserted them." (The comparison of YHWH to a woman giving birth underscores the unbreakable bond between God and

Israel, even as it expresses the travail that the divinity endures for the nation's sake.)[39] It may be that the form of the passage in Deutero-Isaiah, a psalm of praise, is itself chosen as a response to the lament in Jeremiah 14. This tendency to respond to negative statements of earlier prophets occurs in other cases of reversal as well.[40]

Reprediction

As Fishbane has noted, prophets often repeat predictions first uttered by their predecessors which have yet to be fulfilled, and Isaiah 40–66 abound with examples of this category.[41] Deutero-Isaiah paraphrases prophecies of restoration from Jeremiah. Less frequently, Deutero-Isaiah repeats Jeremiah's warnings or prophecies of doom, creating repredictions of a negative nature. He often reformulates the prophecies he repeats in interesting ways: for example, Deutero-Isaiah omits Jeremiah's references to the restoration of the northern kingdom or rewrites them to refer to the exiles from Judah. By repeating earlier prophecies, Deutero-Isaiah attempts to bolster the authority of his predecessors: he asserts that, contrary to appearances, Jeremiah really was correct when he predicted that punishment would be followed by renewal. At the same time, by revising some of Jeremiah's predictions, he implies that in their original form they were somehow deficient. Thus the category of reprediction discloses the complicated relationship between source and borrowing: in order to renew the older texts' messages, the new author is forced at least in part to overturn them.

Positive Reprediction

POSITIVE REPREDICTION BASED ON JEREMIAH 30–33.   Jeremiah 30–31 and 33 provide the richest mine for Deutero-Isaiah as he restates positive prophecies from Jeremiah.[42] For example, in Isa 43.5–9 the exilic prophet alludes to the prediction of Jer 31.1–8, asserting with his predecessor that the exiles will not languish in Babylon forever. As he repredicts, Deutero-Isaiah introduces small changes. The referents of the markers are not always identical to those of the marked items from the evoked text. In Jeremiah God "gathers" the people Israel (Jer 31.8, 10), while in Deutero-Isaiah the nations "gather together" to witness God's grace toward Israel (Isa 43.9). "Blind" in

Jeremiah is used literally, referring to individuals among the returnees who cannot see, while the same word in Deutero-Isaiah refers metaphorically to the whole nation, who failed in the past to understand so much (43.8).[43] As Deutero-Isaiah repeats the earlier prediction, he lays greater emphasis on the many nations who will witness the salvation of Israel. Jeremiah mentions this theme in 31.10 ("Hear the word of the Lord, O nations"), and 31.7 may give a hint of it; but Deutero-Isaiah devotes all of 43.9–10 to the theme, and he adds that YHWH challenges the peoples regarding the efficacy of their prophets.[44]

Deutero-Isaiah restates other prophecies of return from these chapters as well,[45] but I shall focus on a series of somewhat ambivalent allusions to a passage from Jeremiah 31 in which Jeremiah predicted much more than the return to Zion. Jeremiah said,

> Behold, days are coming (a statement of YHWH) when I will make with the house of Israel and the house of Judah a new covenant (בְּרִית חֲדָשָׁה), not like the covenant I made with their fathers on the day that I took their hand to lead them out of the land (הֶחֱזִיקִי בְיָדָם לְהוֹצִיאָם מֵאֶרֶץ) of Egypt—a covenant they broke, when I became their lord (a statement of YHWH). Rather, this is the covenant which I shall make with the house of Israel after those days (a statement of YHWH): I shall plant My teaching (תּוֹרָתִי) within them, and I shall write it on their hearts. I shall become their God and they shall become My people. A man shall no longer teach (יְלַמְּדוּ) his fellow or his brother, "Know YHWH," for all of them, from the small to the great, will know Me (a statement of YHWH), for I shall forgive their sins, and I will no longer recall their transgressions. Thus says YHWH, who makes the sun for light (לְאוֹר) by day and the moon[46] and stars for light (לְאוֹר) at night, who stirs up (רֹגַע) the sea and makes its waves roar: If these laws would be undone (יָמֻשׁוּ), (a statement of YHWH), then would the seed of Israel cease being a nation for all time. (Jer 31.31–36)[47]

Several passages in Deutero-Isaiah recall the language and theme of this prediction. These passages include the first of the so-called "servant songs":

> Thus says the God YHWH, who created heaven and stretched it out, who spread out (רֹקַע) the earth (הָאָרֶץ) and its offspring. . . . I,

YHWH, called you forth in righteousness, and I took your hand
(וָאַחְזֵק בְּיָדֶךָ); I created[48] you and made you a covenant (בְּרִית) of a
nation,[49] a light (לְאוֹר) of the peoples, by opening[50] the eyes of the
blind and leading (לְהוֹצִיא) the prisoner out of the jail. . . . The former
things have come true, and now I announce the new things (וַחֲדָשׁוֹת).
(Isa 42.5–9)

The dependence of the passage from Deutero-Isaiah on Jeremiah at first
seems unlikely. Two of the markers, the words החזיק ביד ("take one's hand")
and the theme of setting captives free (to which הוציא, "lead," refers in
Deutero-Isaiah) appear in Mesopotamian royal texts on which both of these
passages may depend.[51] Nevertheless, words unrelated to the royal traditions
also appear in both texts. These include Jeremiah's phrase ברית חדשה ("a
new covenant"), which is split in two in Deutero-Isaiah: ברית ("covenant")
appears in 42.6, חדשות ("new") in 42.8. Not only the additional vocabulary
but also the split-up pattern reveal the presence of an allusion. Sound play,
another stylistic feature of Deutero-Isaianic allusion, occurs as well. Jeremiah's רגע (*roga'*, "stirs up") becomes רקע (*roqa'*, "spread out"): the marker
in Deutero-Isaiah hints back at a different but similar-sounding word in the
source. Further, the objects of these two verbs, הים ("the sea") and הארץ
("the land, the earth"), respectively, constitute a stock word pair in poetic
parallelism,[52] and this distant or implied parallel strengthens the connection
between the two texts. Finally, we know that Deutero-Isaiah utilized this
section of Jeremiah frequently, so that the possibility of a borrowing is not at
all remote.

Jeremiah's prediction was radical in a number of ways. He claimed that
God renounced His eternal covenant with Israel, as the destruction of the
temple and dethronement of the Davidic monarchy indicated. A new covenant would be made at the time of the restoration to replace the old one.
Unlike the old covenant, which the people had to learn, the new covenant
would be internalized by the people so that they would never break it.
Therefore, it would truly be eternal.[53] Deutero-Isaiah repeats Jeremiah's
prophecy but shies away from its more surprising aspects. Like Jeremiah, he
predicts that the people will have a covenant with YHWH.[54] But the tense
and aspects of the verbs in the Isaiah passage are ambiguous: they can
describe the creation of a covenant either in the past or in the future.[55] As a
result, the passage leaves open the question of whether Deutero-Isaiah is

referring to an already existing covenant (which seems more likely) or a new one. In any event, he avoids describing the covenant as "new." Thus we see here a reprediction that ignores some of the most radical aspects of the source but restates its main ideas. Further, Deutero-Isaiah stresses the closeness of God and Israel here by portraying Israel as YHWH's servant and applying to the nation the motifs of royal texts, suggesting that the people as a whole enjoy a kingly state. This motif is absent in the passage from Jeremiah.[56]

In 54.10, Deutero-Isaiah again stresses that YHWH's covenant with Israel is steadfast:

> For mountains may move (יָמוּשׁוּ), and hills may quake, but my loyalty to you will not be undone (יָמוּשׁ), and my covenant (וּבְרִית) of well-being will not waver, says YHWH, who has mercy towards you. . . . And all your children will be disciples (לִמּוּדֵי) of YHWH, and the well-being of your children will be abundant. (Isa 54.10, 13)

The idea and the language recall Jer 31.33–35. Again the steadfast nature of the covenant is stressed; again a prophet guarantees that the people will know YHWH, that there will be no question as to whether they have learned his *torah*. But, as in 42.5f., Deutero-Isaiah does not go quite as far as Jeremiah. He refers to an unshakable covenant, but not to a new one. His description of the covenant as permanent is not as radical as Jeremiah's, in which God changes human nature in order to ensure that the covenant will always be in their hearts.[57] In Jeremiah the people's inevitable knowledge of God will remove the need for learning (an idea expressed in Jer 31.34 with the root למ״ד), but Deutero-Isaiah simply predicts that the people will learn God's teaching successfully, so that they are called "disciples" (למודים, from the same root). Deutero-Isaiah uses the figure of the mountains differently as well. Jeremiah compares the permanence of the covenant to natural laws. But for Deutero-Isaiah, a comparison to natural laws is not enough; he remembers that YHWH in Hebrew psalmody is the one who, notoriously, can move mountains.[58] To him, Jeremiah's assurance may seem a double-edged sword. Therefore, Deutero-Isaiah declares that even if the mountains move, the covenant will remain.

Another occurrence of Jeremiah's idea of an inevitable covenant is found in 59.21:

As for me, this is My covenant (בְּרִיתִי) with them, says YHWH: My spirit which is with them and My words which I put in their mouth will not move out (יָמוּשׁוּ) of their mouths, or their descendants' mouths, or their descendants' descendants' mouths, from this time forth and forever. (Isa 59.21)

As in 42.6 and 54.10, the idea here is not quite as drastic as what we find in Jeremiah. Deutero-Isaiah stresses the steadfastness, not the newness, of the covenant.[59] Jeremiah had insisted that YHWH's torah would be a permanent part of the people's heart; Deutero-Isaiah predicts that His spirit would never leave them.[60]

In all these passages based on Jer 31.31ff., Deutero-Isaiah at once repeats and revises the older prediction, reinforcing the older text while restraining it. Here Deutero-Isaiah does not merely allude but alters or interprets. He suggests that we should not take Jeremiah's words too literally, for they imply that YHWH's covenant could be broken (even if only to be renewed). On the contrary, Deutero-Isaiah insists, the covenant is eternal and unshakable. The older prophecy is to be read in light of the newer one, or perhaps in this case we should not attend to the older one at all. Thus Deutero-Isaiah takes a more independent stance in these cases of reprediction. Nonetheless, he does not reject his predecessor. By paraphrasing Jeremiah, Deutero-Isaiah emphasizes his connection with the earlier prophet and stresses that his predictions are valid. The disagreements between the two prophets remain subtle, as though Deutero-Isaiah desires to correct the older text without impugning its status.

POSITIVE REPREDICTION BASED ON JEREMIAH 1–29.   Prophecies of consolation appear in sections of Jeremiah other than chapters 30–31 and 33, and they, too, provide a source for Deutero-Isaiah.[61] For example, Jeremiah wrote a letter to Judean deportees in Babylonia, telling them that the exile would be lengthy, but not indefinite; at the end of a long time ("seventy years"), the people would be permitted to return to the Land of Israel:[62]

For thus says YHWH: When Babylon's seventy years are up, I shall remember you, and I shall fulfill My good word (דְּבָרִי) concerning you: I shall return (לְהָשִׁיב) you to this place. For I am planning for your well-being (statement of YHWH), not for your misery (כִּי[63]

אָנֹכִי חֹשֵׁב עֲלֵיכֶם . . . מַחְשְׁבוֹת שָׁלוֹם וְלֹא לְרָעָה . . .), so that you will
have a future with hope. And you will call to me . . . and pray to me
(וּקְרָאתֶם ⁶⁴אֹתִי . . . וְהִתְפַּלַלְתֶּם אֵלָי), and I will listen to you. You will
search for Me and find Me when you seek Me (וּמְצָאתֶם כִּי תִדְרְשֻׁנִי)
with all your hearts. I will be present (⁶⁵וְנִמְצֵאתִי) for you (a statement
of YHWH), and I will return your captives (⁶⁶וְשַׁבְתִּי אֶת־שְׁבוּתְכֶם)
and gather you from all the nations and all the places to which I
banished you. (Jer 29.10–14)

Deutero-Isaiah has a similar message for the exiles of his own day:

Seek YHWH when He is present (דִּרְשׁוּ ה' בְּהִמָּצְאוֹ); call out to
Him (קְרָאֻהוּ) when He is near! An evil person (רָשָׁע) should forsake
his way, a man of iniquity his plans (מַחְשְׁבֹתָיו), and should return
to YHWH (וְיָשֹׁב אֶל ה'), that He will have mercy on him, and to
God, for He forgives abundantly. "For My plans are not your plans
(כִּי לֹא מַחְשְׁבוֹתַי מַחְשְׁבוֹתֵיכֶם), and your ways are not My ways" (a
statement of YHWH). "As the sky is higher than the earth, so are My
ways higher than yours, and so are My plans higher than yours
(וּמַחְשְׁבֹתַי מִמַּחְשְׁבֹתֵיכֶם). And as rain and snow fall from the sky and
do not return (לֹא יָשׁוּב) there . . . so is My word (דְּבָרִי) . . . : it does
not return to Me (לֹא־יָשׁוּב אֵלַי) unfulfilled. . . . For you will go forth
in joy, and in peace (וּבְשָׁלוֹם) you will be brought in." (Isa 55.6–12)

Much of the vocabulary shared by these two passages relates to the issue of
prayer and response, and the presence of that vocabulary in two texts concerned with that issue is not surprising. Nevertheless, the passages share
other items that are not connected with prayer and do not appear as a cluster
elsewhere in the Hebrew Bible (e.g., מחשבות ["plans"], שלום ["peace/well-
being"], and a word meaning "evil" [רשע in Deutero-Isaiah, רעה in
Jeremiah]). These additional parallels increase the likelihood that Deutero-
Isaiah borrowed from Jeremiah's letter. Further, we know that Deutero-
Isaiah was familiar with chapter 29 of Jeremiah, since (as we saw above) that
chapter serves as a source for the strong case of allusion occurring in Isa
65.18–23. In light of all this, the relationship of Jer 29.10–14 and Isa 55.6–12
can confidently be described as an allusion.

Deutero-Isaiah asserts that the time Jeremiah predicted is imminent—

that is, God is now ready to be sought. The prophet adds two elements in his reformulation of the older promise. He invites the people to appeal to YHWH (vv. 6–7), thus transforming Jeremiah's promise into an exhortation; and he stresses the difference between God's actions and a human's (vv. 9–10). Although God's plans may resemble those of a human, Deutero-Isaiah emphasizes that they are completely different from merely human thoughts (vv. 8–9), and that they are as inevitable and reliable as the downward movement of rain. Such a simile is especially apt in a case of reprediction. Through allusions of this kind, Deutero-Isaiah insists that older prophecies of encouragement issued in YHWH's name are, in spite of appearances, accurate. Thus Deutero-Isaiah has a single goal in his reference to words of God proclaimed earlier through Jeremiah and in his comparison of God's words to rain: the exilic prophet aims to bolster the nation's trust both in his literary sources and in the Source of his prophecies.

Deutero-Isaiah uses the older text's vocabulary to repeat its message, but he does not always use the vocabulary in the same way Jeremiah had done. In 29.10, the term שׁוּב ("return") referred to God's bringing the people back; in 55.11 the same word asserts that YHWH's promises are always fulfilled. Through the new use of this word, Deutero-Isaiah asserts that the promise is based not only on YHWH's mercy (which the audience might have doubted) but on His constancy.

Historical Recontextualization

In the previous example, we saw that Isa 55.6–12 add new elements to the prophecy found in Jer 29.10–4, but the new text's message does not differ: Jeremiah anticipated a restoration in the distant future, and Deutero-Isaiah, living about a half century later, announces that the predicted restoration is at hand. Elsewhere, however, Deutero-Isaiah's restatement involves a historical recontextualization of earlier prophecy and hence a revision of it. In these cases Deutero-Isaiah repeats a prediction Jeremiah uttered in regard to one set of events or to a particular group; the new version relates to a similar but separate set of events or to some other group. Take the following example. Early in his career, Jeremiah directed his attention to the northern kinsmen of the Judeans, variously known as the Ephraimites or as Israel (in the narrow sense of the latter term). Jeremiah lived less than a century after the northern kingdom's collapse at the hands of the Assyrians, and he may have hoped for their return to the orbit of Judean influence in his youth, during the reign of Josiah. God directed Jeremiah as follows:

> Go proclaim these words to the north: Return, apostate Israel! I will not continue to look on you aversely, for I am faithful (a statement of YHWH); I will not be angry forever (לֹא אֶטּוֹר לְעוֹלָם). But acknowledge your sin! For . . . you have gone on motley paths (דְּרָכַיִךְ) among strangers. . . . Return, backsliding (שׁוֹבָבִים) children (a statement of YHWH)! . . . For they have perverted their ways (דַּרְכָּם); they have forgotten YHWH their God. Return, backsliding (שׁוֹבָבִים) children! I will heal your apostasy (אֶרְפָּה מְשׁוּבֹתֵיכֶם)! (Jer 3.12–14, 21–22)[67]

Deutero-Isaiah uses similar vocabulary to convey a similar message to a different audience, the Judean exiles who will return (or have already done so, if chapter 57 is post-exilic).

> I do not contend forever (לֹא לְעוֹלָם אָרִיב), and I do not rage unceasingly. . . . Because of the sin of his [i.e., the people's] unjust gains I was angry, and I smote him . . . , but he went backsliding (שׁוֹבָב) in his own heart's way (בְּדֶרֶךְ). I have seen his ways (דְּרָכָיו) and I have healed him (וְאֶרְפָּאֵהוּ). . . . Things will be fine! Things will be fine!—for those near and far (God says), and I have healed him (וּרְפָאתִיו). (Isa 57.16–19)

A verse resembling 57.16 and Jer 3.5 appears in Ps 103.9 as well, and this might render my assertion that Deutero-Isaiah borrowed from Jer 3.5f. dubious. However, the additional vocabulary shared between 57.18–19 and Jeremiah 3 makes it more likely that this passage in Deutero-Isaiah depends directly on Jeremiah. Further, Deutero-Isaiah uses Jeremiah 3 elsewhere (see below), and the word שׁובב ("backsliding") appears nowhere in the Hebrew Bible outside Jeremiah 3 and Isaiah 57. In light of all this the parallel is almost certainly an allusion.

Deutero-Isaiah repeats the message that God's anger is limited in duration, but he speaks to the southern exiles of his own day. Here again, Deutero-Isaiah not only borrows from but alters an older oracle. But the revision does not amount to rejection. On the contrary, Deutero-Isaiah updates the older prophecy in order to give it ongoing validity. His audience might have thought that Jeremiah was simply wrong, since a return of northern exiles was unlikely. However, by reusing elements from Jeremiah 3 in his own prediction, Deutero-Isaiah allows the original oracle to live on, albeit in a new form. He does not assert that an older text was incorrect. (Other prophets did; for example, Isa 16.13–14 and Ezek 29.17f. make clear that the older oracles that they follow did not come true.)[68] Instead, he seems to camouflage any deficiencies found in his source. Thus this text constitutes a case of revision or perhaps interpretation, but not polemic; Deutero-Isaiah's attitude toward his source remains respectful, even when he alters it. Further, in recasting the Jeremiah passage, Deutero-Isaiah may have followed the lead of Jeremiah himself. Jeremiah 3 as it stands consists of messages to the north, supplemented by extensive messages to the south later uttered by Jeremiah; it is likely that Jeremiah himself put these elements together toward the end of his career, so that the original words to the north were redirected to southerners.[69]

Negative Reprediction

In most cases of reprediction, Deutero-Isaiah appropriates Jeremiah's prophecies of restoration. In a small number of cases, however, Deutero-Isaiah repeats judgment oracles of his predecessor.

One such case occurs in the lengthy denunciation found in 56.9–57.6.[70] There Deutero-Isaiah criticizes the people for idolatrous worship and berates false prophets in particular for misleading the people:[71]

> All beasts of the field, come to feast (כֹּל חַיְתוֹ שָׂדָי אֵתָיו לֶאֱכֹל), all beasts in the forest (כָּל־חַיְתוֹ בַּיָּעַר)! His seers are blind . . . they are shepherds (רֹעִים) who know not how to understand. They all go in their own way, each one to his unjust gain, every last one (אִישׁ לְבִצְעוֹ[72] מִקָּצֵהוּ)! . . . The righteous one perishes, but none pay attention (וְאֵין אִישׁ שָׂם עַל־לֵב); steadfast men are rounded up (נֶאֱסָפִים) without anyone looking on—indeed, because of evil such a righteous one is rounded up (נֶאֱסָף). May peace come (יָבוֹא שָׁלוֹם)! May they rest on their beds. . . . But you—come here, children of a woman who practices sorcery! . . . Your portion is with the smooth stones in the wadi (בְּחַלְּקֵי־נַחַל חֶלְקֵךְ). (Isa 56.9–57.6)

The denunciation contains many terms also found in Jer 12.7–13, in which YHWH calls on the nations to punish his people for their sins, but also laments his people's demise.

> My inheritance became to me like a lion in the forest (כְּאַרְיֵה בַיַּעַר)— it raised its voice at me; therefore I have rejected her. . . . Gather (אָסְפוּ) for the feast, bring in all beasts of the field (כָּל־חַיַּת הַשָּׂדֶה הֵתָיוּ לְאָכְלָה)! Many shepherds (רֹעִים) have ruined my vineyard; they have trampled my inheritance (חֶלְקָתִי); they have made my pleasant inheritance (חֶלְקַת) a waste and a desert. . . . The whole land is destroyed, for none pay attention (כִּי [73] אֵין אִישׁ שָׂם עַל־לֵב) . . . YHWH's sword consumes from one end of the land to the next (מִקְצֵה־אֶרֶץ וְעַד־קְצֵה הָאָרֶץ); there is no peace (אֵין שָׁלוֹם). (Jer 12.8–12)

In both passages the root חל״ק appears twice within a single verse, but Deutero-Isaiah uses it once with the same meaning as it had in Jeremiah ("portion, inheritance") and once in a different sense ("smooth things"). The large amount of shared vocabulary along with the sound play indicate that Deutero-Isaiah borrowed from Jeremiah.[74]

Deutero-Isaiah's admonition restates that of Jeremiah; he warns the people that the sort of punishment which Jeremiah described may return. Thus, Deutero-Isaiah follows Jeremiah in calling for animals to come and consume Israel (Jer 12.9; Isa 56.9). But there are significant differences between the prophecies as well. Jeremiah portrayed a widespread destruction of the whole people; Deutero-Isaiah limits his address to the sinners themselves, while bemoaning the temporary fate of the righteous, who will eventually be vindicated (57.14f.). This idea of selective punishment may represent a reworking of Isaiah's idea of the remnant that will survive the coming disaster.[75] (This notion also appears in Deutero-Isaiah's reworking of Jer 6.13–14 in Isa 57.17–21, where the later prophet makes Jeremiah's words more specific as he asserts that "things will not be fine *for the wicked*.") Deutero-Isaiah utilizes most of the vocabulary he borrows in new ways. In Jer 12.10, the רֹעִים are the foreigners who destroy Israel; in Isa 56.11, they are the prophets (or leaders) who mislead Israel and who will bear the brunt of punishment. Jeremiah complained that the people don't pay attention (שָׂם עַל לֵב) to God's warnings (12.11); Deutero-Isaiah complains that people don't pay attention (שָׂם עַל לֵב) to the plight of the righteous (57.1). In Jeremiah God speaks bitterly of His possession (12.10); in Deutero-Isaiah the same words refer to the inheritance of idolatry which the people themselves choose (57.6). Deutero-Isaiah does not pick up on Jeremiah's idea of the people as God's inheritance, perhaps because the focus of divine choice now shifts to the righteous rather than the people as a whole. Finally, although the passage in Deutero-Isaiah is primarily negative, it includes positive elements that are put into sharper focus when we compare it with the vocabulary on which it is based. In 12.12, Jeremiah states, אֵין שָׁלוֹם ("there is no peace"); when this vocabulary reappears in Deutero-Isaiah, we read, יָבוֹא שָׁלוֹם ("may peace come!" 57.2)—although the verse laments the demise of the righteous, it also predicts a better day.[76]

Deutero-Isaiah recalls another passage in Jeremiah later in chapter 57. Deutero-Isaiah has YHWH complain,

> In your many wanderings (דַּרְכֵּךְ), you did not tire; you did not say (לֹא אָמַרְתְּ), "It's no use (נוֹאָשׁ) [to continue on this evil path]!" You found (מָצָאת) the life of your hand.[77] (Isa 57.10)

The verse reuses vocabulary from the following statement:

> Look at your way (דַּרְכֵּךְ) in the valley, acknowledge what you've done! [You are like] an easy young camel galloping aimlessly on her paths (דְּרָכֶיהָ). . . . In the passion of her desire she snorts the wind. . . . None will tire out looking for her; they will find (יְמְצָאוּנְהָ) her in her heat. Save your foot from becoming bare and your throat from being parched! But you said (וַתֹּאמְרִי), "It's no use (נוֹאָשׁ)! No, (לוֹא),[78] I do love strangers, and I will go after them." (Jer 2.23–25)

In addition to the highlighted markers and marked items in the verses quoted, the idea found in Jer 2.28 ("Where are the gods you made yourself? Let them come to rescue you") is repeated in 57.12–13.[79] In both passages God berates the people for idol worship, described in both as their "way" (דרך). The crucial word נוֹאָשׁ is employed differently, however. In Jeremiah, its sense is, "It's no use! I can't stop! I'm addicted to this way of living." In Deutero-Isaiah, God criticizes the people for not saying, "This idol worship is useless!" Thus, as in the previous example, Deutero-Isaiah repeats Jeremiah's criticism by borrowing Jeremiah's vocabulary, but he uses the vocabulary in a new way. Identical elements create different sentences but express the same theme.

Fulfillment of Earlier Prophecies

YHWH proclaims throughout Deutero-Isaiah that He is unique and trust-worthy and that the audience should realize this because He announced long ago what would take place later (see, e.g., 41.22, 43.12, 44.6–7, 48.3).[80] But Deutero-Isaiah does not only speak of earlier prophecies in general terms. By reusing the wording found in specific older texts, he asserts that the predictions found in them have been fulfilled.[81]

One need go no further than the first utterance of Deutero-Isaiah to find an allusion to a prophecy of Jeremiah which has come to pass. The later prophet hears God calling on His messengers to proclaim to Jerusalem,

> Her term of service is complete! Her punishment (עֲוֺנָהּ) has been accepted! She has received a twofold penalty from YHWH for all her sins (חַטֹּאתֶיהָ)! (Isa 40.2)

Deutero-Isaiah refers again to a twofold punishment later in his book:

> Because they were put to shame doubly (מִשְׁנֶה) and inherited[82] con-tempt as their portion,[83] therefore they will inherit doubly (מִשְׁנֶה) in their land (בְּאַרְצָם). (Isa 61.7)

It seems surprising that the people have received a "twofold penalty" for their sins,[84] but Jeremiah had warned precisely of that:

> I shall first repay double for their transgression and their sin (מִשְׁנֶה עֲוֺנָם וְחַטָּאתָם) and their profanation of my land (אַרְצִי). (Jer 16.18)

Three markers in Isa 40.2 point us back to the text in Jeremiah: the concept of double punishment and two vocabulary items, חטאת ("sin") and עון ("transgression/punishment"). The link between these terms in the two passages is bolstered by three facts. In both Isa 40.2 and Jer 16.18 they appear with possessive suffixes. Further, they occurred next to each other in Jeremiah, but (in an example of a recurrent pattern noted above) they have been split apart in Deutero-Isaiah. Finally, Deutero-Isaiah uses the word עון not to mean "transgression" but in its secondary sense, "punishment." This alteration constitutes a case of word play, which we have seen in other cases of Deutero-Isaianic allusion. The lines' dependence on Jeremiah is likely in light of these stylistic features. Deutero-Isaiah's second reference to the idea of double punishment is also couched in terms Jeremiah used when predicting that such a punishment would occur: משנה ("double") and ארץ ("land"). This further parallel confirms that Jeremiah served as the source for these passages. In both these passages, Deutero-Isaiah asserts that the prophecy of doom uttered by Jeremiah has been realized; God's justified wrath has run its course.[85] In the second reference to Jer 16.18, Deutero-Isaiah also declares that restoration would soon follow; thus the allusion also contains a strong element of reversal similar to those examined above.

The same relationship of prophecy and fulfillment appears in the following case. In Jeremiah, God announced that He would punish the people by treating them like metal which is being smelted:

> Thus says YHWH of Hosts: Behold, I am about to smelt them and refine them (הִנְנִי צוֹרְפָם וּבְחַנְתִּים), for what can I do (כִּי־אֵיךְ אֶעֱשֶׂה) because of my people?[86] (Jer 9.6)

Deutero-Isaiah uses the same vocabulary as he describes the chastisement the people have experienced in exile:

> Behold, I have smelted you (הִנֵּה צְרַפְתִּיךָ), but not for silver,[87] I have tested you ([88]בְּחַרְתִּיךָ) in the furnace of affliction. For My sake, for My sake I acted (אֶעֱשֶׂה), for how could (כִּי אֵיךְ) [My name][89] be defiled? And I shall not give my glory to another. (Isa 48.10–11)

One might doubt that these passages are related as source and allusion, because the image of the people being assayed appears elsewhere (see Isa 1.25, Jer 6.27–29, Zech 13.9, Mal 3.2–3). Isa 48.10–11, however, shares additional vocabulary with Jer 9.6 not found in the other texts where the smelting theme appears: כי איך ("for how") and אעשה ("act, do"). Further, the phrase הנני צורפם ובחנתים ("behold I shall smelt them and refine them") from Jeremiah appears in Deutero-Isaiah, but there the words are divided into two parts: first we read הנה צרפתיך ("behold I have smelted you"), and several words later we read בחרתיך ("I have refined/tested you").[90] The presence of the split-up pattern we have noticed in other cases of Deutero-Isaianic allusion increases the likelihood that this passage refers back to Jeremiah. A rhetorical question comes at the end of both verses, creating additional similarity between the passages. As a result, Deutero-Isaiah's dependence on the passage in Jeremiah becomes clear.

Thematically, the allusion works at several levels. Deutero-Isaiah not only asserts that Jeremiah's prediction has come to pass, but alters the reason God gives for the punishment. Jeremiah stressed the people's deceptiveness and sinfulness, which gave God no alternative but to punish them (see 9.7–8). Deutero-Isaiah, however, shifts the focus from the people to God and His honor. He uses Jeremiah's vocabulary to express a new reason for the assaying: "*For My sake, for My sake* I do *this*, for how can *My name be dishonored*?" Lest the people worry that they have lost any claim to a part in that honor, the prophet continues, "But I will not give My glory to another." The shift in focus from the people's sinfulness to God's honor has great import for Deutero-Isaiah's audience. The exiles may have agreed with Jeremiah that they were terribly flawed; therefore they may have viewed themselves as unworthy of salvation. But Deutero-Isaiah tells them that YHWH has another, more compelling reason to act on their behalf: they are His nation, and God's own pride will be harmed if they remain subservient to their conquerors.

Further, here, as in other cases in which he notes that the grim prophecies of the past have come to fruition, Deutero-Isaiah demonstrates the efficacy of the Judean prophetic tradition and the God who stands behind it. By recalling negative prophecies, Deutero-Isaiah brings encouragement to the nation: for he intimates that the God who was powerful enough to punish Israel will also be powerful enough to save them. Marduk did not defeat YHWH; on the contrary, the victory of the Babylonians was brought about by YHWH Himself, as YHWH's prophets had foretold. But now another prophet of YHWH is predicting restoration, and the new prophecies will be fulfilled no less than the old ones. Paradoxically, by reminding the people of their plight and their sinfulness, Deutero-Isaiah consoles the nation, for he shows that YHWH upholds His covenant—for worse, and therefore also for better.

The negative repredictions have another important function. As he recalls Jeremiah's negative predictions approvingly, Deutero-Isaiah stresses his own distance from the false prophets whom he seems at times to resemble. Like the false prophets, Deutero-Isaiah encourages the nation (sometimes using the same words as the prophets Jeremiah opposed)—but he does not minimize Israel's guilt. Jeremiah, not the false prophets, had been correct when he excoriated the nation's proclivity toward sin and warned that disaster would come. By noting the accuracy of these predictions, Deutero-Isaiah makes clear that he follows in the tradition of Jeremiah rather than the prophets who predicted weal and ignored woe.

Deutero-Isaiah alludes to fulfilled prophecies of Jeremiah in several other passages.[91] Further, the reversals noted above also imply a confirmation of Jeremiah's dire prophecies.

Typological Linkages

Like other biblical authors, Deutero-Isaiah posits correspondences between diverse people, events, and places, thus asserting that one may be understood in light of the other or that one provides a pattern that the other follows. These links may be called "typological."[92] When the description of the person, event, or place that serves as a paradigm stems from a particular older text, the assertion of such a correspondence constitutes an allusion.[93]

In one such allusion, Deutero-Isaiah utilizes a text from Jeremiah as the source of both a typological link and a reversal. Jeremiah predicted the arrival of Nebuchadnezzar to take control of the Land of Israel as follows:

> I made the earth, the human (אָנֹכִי עָשִׂיתִי אֶת־הָאָרֶץ אֶת־הָאָדָם),[94] and the beast which are upon the face of the earth with my great strength and my outstretched arm (וּבִזְרֹעִי הַנְּטוּיָה), and I give it to whoever is right (לַאֲשֶׁר יָשַׁר) in my eyes. And now I have given all these lands into the hands of Nebuchadnezzar, the king of Babylon, my servant. (Jer 27.5–6)

Deutero-Isaiah describes Cyrus using almost identical phrasing when he has God say,

> I made the earth, and the human upon it I created (אָנֹכִי עָשִׂיתִי אֶרֶץ וְאָדָם עָלֶיהָ בָרָאתִי); my own hands stretched out (אֲנִי יָדַי נָטוּ) the

skies, and I commanded all its hosts. I raised him [Cyrus] up in victory, and all his roads I made straight (אֲיַשֵּׁר). He will build my city and let my exiles go. (Isa 45.12–13)

That Deutero-Isaiah relies on Jeremiah becomes clear not only from the shared vocabulary items but from the order of those items: the markers appear in the same order as the marked. One of the markers, יָדִי ("my hand"), is a synonym rather than an exact repetition of the marked word, זְרוֹעִי ("my arm"), but the relationship is clear because both precede the word נטו/נטויה ("outstretched"). Both passages include a word based on the consonants יש"ר, but in Deutero-Isaiah they mean "to make straight," while in Jeremiah they mean "right" or "pleasing." This correspondence between two words which are built from one set of consonants but have distinct meanings constitutes a case of word play, which is (as we have seen) a typical feature of Deutero-Isaianic allusion. The initial sentences of the two passages are nearly identical. However, in Jeremiah the words אֶרֶץ ("earth") and אָדָם ("human") appear next to each other in a single clause, and both are objects of the verb עָשִׂיתִי ("I made"). In Deutero-Isaiah, "earth" and "human" still appear next to each other and following "I made," but they are no longer part of a single clause; "earth" ends one clause and "human" becomes the beginning of another. In other words, what had been subject-verb-object$_1$-object$_2$ becomes subject-verb-object$_1$; object$_2$—*new subject—new verb*.[95]

Shalom Paul notes that in each of these texts "the creator of the universe is the controller of history, and both Nebuchadnezzar and Cyrus are accorded leading roles in the execution of the divine plan."[96] Cyrus, like Nebuchadnezzar, is appointed by the creator to carry out a mission relating to the Land of Israel and its people. Jeremiah taught that Nebuchadnezzar was God's tool; Deutero-Isaiah asserts that one can understand Cyrus in the same way, and thus he posits a typological link between them. However, they have opposite tasks: Nebuchadnezzar destroys and deports, Cyrus restores and rebuilds.[97]

The Character Jeremiah as Type

The life of the prophet Jeremiah frequently serves in Deutero-Isaiah as a paradigm for the experience of both the nation Israel and the servant figures whom Deutero-Isaiah describes. Vocabulary from Jeremiah's dedication scene is repeatedly applied to the people and to the servant of the "servant songs" (in chapters 42, 49, 50, and 53), and descriptions of Jeremiah's suffering serve as models for Deutero-Isaiah's depiction of the nation. Because much of the vocabulary of the dedication scene in Jeremiah comes from royal traditions, one may view the parallels between that scene and passages in Deutero-Isaiah as resulting from their common use of traditional ancient Near Eastern motifs. On the other hand, the link between the prophet Jeremiah and the people Israel in Deutero-Isaiah is clear in light of the passages describing Israel in terms borrowed from reports of Jeremiah's affliction. This makes it more likely that Deutero-Isaiah relied on the dedication scene as a model elsewhere. Because of the particularly strong connections between the "servant songs" and the Book of Jeremiah, it will be best to examine them separately, after discussing other texts that view Jeremiah's life as a paradigm for the role of the people Israel.

Jeremiah and the Nation

God stresses His relationship with Israel in 51.12f., urging the people not to fear mere mortals. He ends His statement with the words,

> I put My words in your mouth (דְּבָרַי בְּפִיךָ), and I cover you in the shade of My hand (יָדִי), that I may plant ([98]לִנְטֹעַ) the heavens and establish the earth and say to Zion, "You are My people." (Isa 51.16)

Several of these phrases also appear in Jeremiah's call:

> YHWH stretched out His hand (יָדוֹ) and touched my mouth and said, "I hereby place my words in your mouth (דְּבָרַי בְּפִיךָ); see, I appoint you today over nations and kingdoms: to pluck up and pull down, and to decimate and destroy; to build and plant (וְלִנְטוֹעַ)." (Jer. 1.9–10)

Deutero-Isaiah uses the motif of God's word being put into the people's mouth in two ways. The phrasing hints that God's teaching is in the people's heart (cf. Isa 51.7),[99] a notion perhaps based on Jer 31.32. At the same time, the phrase "I put my words in your mouth" retains the prophetic meaning it has in Jeremiah: Israel becomes a prophet nation here. It has a task relating to the nations parallel to that of Jeremiah. Through being redeemed, they serve as a witness to the nations of YHWH's might and loyalty. The connection this passage posits between God's redeeming His people and His "planting the heavens" at first seems perplexing, as does the text's linkage between both these ideas and the nation's prophetic role. The medieval rabbinic commentator Radak reminds us that for this author redemption is a cosmological event accompanied by the creation of a new heaven and earth (Isa 66.22, and cf. 51.6). Thus God's protection of the nation and His renewed covenant with them are part of the same series of actions as the planting of heaven and the founding of earth, all of which Isa 51.16 describes. That complex of deeds, which is focused around the people Israel, will broadcast the vitality of YHWH to the nations. Insofar as Israel's role (albeit passive) is central to all this, the nation is the tool through which YHWH's message becomes known to the world, and hence Israel is a prophet nation.[100]

Not only Jeremiah's prophetic task established a pattern which the nation would follow; his tribulations also foreshadowed the calamity which would befall the people. This can be seen in the verses from Deutero-Isaiah preceding the verse analyzed above:

> I, I am the one who comforts you. . . . But you forgot YHWH your creator. . . . You constantly feared the anger of the oppressor when he planned to destroy (לְהַשְׁחִית), but where is the anger of the oppressor? The tree ([101]הָעֵץ) quickly opens up; it does not die (וְלֹא־יָמוּת) from being cut down ([102]לְשַׁחֵת); its fruit ([103]לַחְמוֹ) is not lacking. (Isa 51.12–14)

The comparison of the people to a tree seems odd, until one realizes that it is based on a passage in which Jeremiah likens himself to a tree which is about to be cut down:

> I did not know that they devised plans against me: "Let us cut down the tree with its fruit (נַשְׁחִיתָה עֵץ בְּלַחְמוֹ), and let us remove him from the land of the living so that his name will no more be remembered." . . . The men of Anathot . . . seek my[104] life and say, "Stop prophesying in the name of YHWH, so that you will not die (וְלֹא תָמוּת) by our hands." (Jer 11.19–21)[105]

The plotters in Jeremiah are fellow Judeans who attempt to bring his prophetic career to a close, whether by intimidating him or by killing him. Deutero-Isaiah uses the same phrasing as he describes the fears of the prophetic nation. An oppressor (here, Babylon) threatened Israel and nearly cut it down; but, like Jeremiah, the nation survived and continued to flourish and give fruit.[106]

Jeremiah and Servant Figures

Jeremiah serves as a pattern for Israel, especially when the nation is depicted as a servant figure in what many biblical scholars refer to as the "servant songs" (42.1–4 [or 1–7], 49.1–6, 50.4–9, and 52.13–53.12).[107] Many elements in these songs are modeled on descriptions of Jeremiah's suffering.[108] In Isa 50.4–9, the servant announces that he has been chosen as YHWH's prophet, that he has suffered in executing his duties, and that he has accepted his suffering willingly. The motifs and vocabulary of the description borrow from several passages in Jeremiah,[109] especially Jer 20.7–12. In both texts, the prophet is shamed and then vindicated. When the servant expresses his confidence in his ultimate vindication by YHWH, he uses many of the same words which Jeremiah used to implore God's help: the earlier prophet said, "Righteous (צַדִּיק) Tester. . . . Let me see Your retribution on them! I have revealed my case (רִיבִי) to you!" (Jer 20.12); the servant predicts, "The One who vindicates me (מַצְדִּיקִי) is near—who could fight (יָרִיב) with me?" (Isa 50.8). Deutero-Isaiah's reference back to the root צד״ק constitutes a case of word play, because the root appears with its meaning of "righteousness" in Jeremiah and with that of "vindication" in Deutero-Isaiah.

The motifs which the servant songs borrow from descriptions of Jeremiah's affliction are used in surprising ways. Jeremiah deeply resents the ridicule which YHWH brought upon him by making him a prophet (20.7–9), but the servant announces proudly, "The lord YHWH gave me a prophetic message,[110] and I did not rebel" (50.5). Where Jeremiah would have liked to avoid the abuse heaped on him, the servant says, "I gave my back to the smiters" (50.6). Deutero-Isaiah transfers some of the vocabulary and imagery describing Jeremiah's tormenters to the servant. The same words describe the disgrace the tormenters will face in Jeremiah and the disgrace (and ultimate vindication) of the prophet in Deutero-Isaiah. Jeremiah says,

Those who pursue me will fail and not succeed; they will be ashamed (בֹּשׁוּ) for they will not understand; eternal humiliation (כְּלִמַּת) [will be theirs]. (Jer 20.11)

The servant declares,

I did not hide my face from humiliation (מִכְּלִמּוֹת) and spitting. The lord YHWH will help me; therefore I will not be humiliated (נִכְלָמְתִּי) . . . or put to shame (אֵבוֹשׁ). (50.6–7)

The reverse occurs with fire images: in Jeremiah, the prophet experiences God as a painful fire within (20.9), while in Deutero-Isaiah the tormenters start a fire and get burned by it (50.11).

Another description of the servant's suffering is also based on Jeremiah's laments. In 53.7–8, we read,

He was tormented and afflicted, but he did not open his mouth, like a sheep brought to the slaughter (לַטֶּבַח יוּבָל). . . . He was cut off from the land of the living (מֵאֶרֶץ חַיִּים). (Isa 53.7–8)

The image relies on Jeremiah's description of himself:

I was like a docile lamb brought to the slaughter (יוּבַל לִטְבוֹחַ), but I did not know that they devised plans against me, [saying] . . . let us cut him out of the land of the living (מֵאֶרֶץ חַיִּים)! (Jer 11.19)

The passages share a fair amount of additional vocabulary:

וַ'ה [53.6, 10 // 11.18, 20]
רא"ה [52.14, 15, 53.2, 11 // 11.18, 20]
חָשְׁבוּ מַחֲשָׁבוֹת [11.19] // חֲשַׁבְנֻהוּ {2x} [53.3, 4]
שׁח"ת [52.14 // 11.19]
צֶדֶק [53.11] // יַצְדִּיק צַדִּיק [11.20]
גֻּלֵּיתִי [53.1] // נִגְלָתָה [11.20]
תָּמוּת, יָמֵתוּ [11.21, 22 {2x}] // מֹתָיו [53.9], לַמָּוֶת [53.12]
בְּיָדוֹ [53.10] // בְּיָדֵנוּ [11.20]

"And YHWH" (Jer 11.18, 20 // Isa 53.6, 10)

the root "to see" (11.18, 20 // 52.14, 15; 53.2, 11)

"they thought thoughts" (11.19) // "we thought him to to be" (53.3, 4 [2x])

the root "to destroy" (11.19 // 52.14)

the root "justice/victory" (11.20 // 53.11)

"I revealed" (11.20) // "was revealed" (53.1)

"you will die" (11.21), "they will die" (11.22 [2x]) // "when he dies" (53.9), "to death" (53.12)

"by our hands" (11.20) // "by his hand" (53.10)

Deutero-Isaiah does not transform most of the markers strategically. They underscore his dependence on Jeremiah, but recognizing their source does not alter one's reading of the passage in Deutero-Isaiah. Nonetheless, the link between them continues the trend we saw in the previous passage. Again, the servant's career is modeled on that of Jeremiah. Again, the servant accepts his fate more readily than Jeremiah: whereas Jer 11.19–20 (like 20.7–12) contain the prophet's complaint, the servant "does not open his mouth" (53.7) as he is led to his torment. Here as in Jeremiah 11 and 20, the one chosen by YHWH is ultimately, and surprisingly, vindicated.[111]

Echo

Deutero-Isaiah at times reuses several items of vocabulary from Jeremiah which do not significantly change our reading of the passage. In such an instance we have an echo rather than a full-fledged allusion. Deutero-Isaiah may have used the source in these cases to assert his connection to Jeremiah and his tradition, to experience the pleasure of borrowing older vocabulary, or to give the audience the pleasure of encountering familiar signposts in a new location. Isolated phrasing which may have come from Jeremiah but plays no strategic role occurs throughout Deutero-Isaiah (see, e.g., Isa 51.19, 59.7, and 60.18 // Jer 48.3; Isa 55.11 // Jer 30.24; Isa 57.6 // Jer 9.8; Isa 57.20 // Jer 49.23; Isa 63.6 // Jer 31.8; Isa 63.25 // Jer 31.34; Isa 65.3 // Jer 6.7; Isa 65.13 // Jer 15.13; Isa 66.15 // Jer 4.13). Because these parallels involve only a few phrases, it is difficult in any one of them to be certain that the vocabulary is borrowed, and even when Deutero-Isaiah knew the phrase from Jeremiah, the borrowing may have been unconscious; he may have been unaware that vocabulary from a text he knew came to the fore as he composed.

At times, however, the markers are more numerous, even in cases of echo. In one passage God rebukes the people, saying, "They are skilled at doing evil (לְהָרֵעַ), but they don't know how to do good (וּלְהֵיטִיב לֹא יָדָעוּ)" (Jer 4.22). These items appear in reverse order as Deutero-Isaiah has YHWH address foreign gods. They are, He contends, incapable of any actions that would indicate their effectiveness or existence: "Tell us what will happen in the future, that we may know (וְנֵדְעָה) that you are gods! Do something, do anything (אַף־תֵּיטִיבוּ וְתָרֵעוּ), that we may see and fear!" (Isa 41.23). Both passages immediately go on to use the root רא"ה ("to see," Jer 4.23 // Isa 41.24) followed by the negative particle אֵין (4.24 // 41.26), and then again the root רא"ה ("to see") followed by the phrase וְאֵין הָאָדָם/אִישׁ ("but there was nobody // no person," 4.25 // 41.28). Furthermore, both include the word תֹהוּ ("emptiness"), though in Jeremiah it comes after the first use of רא"ה ("to see," 4.23) and in Deutero-Isaiah at the end of the whole passage (41.29). Deutero-Isaiah recasts some of the vocabulary so that it means something other than what it meant in Jeremiah: in the older text הרע and היטיב are separate verbs meaning "to do evil" and "to do good" (the people are wise when it comes to the former, but don't know how to do the latter), but Deutero-Isaiah employs the terms as a hendiadys (the gods can't do anything). Thus, Deutero-Isaiah's borrowing of these verbs constitutes a case of word play. For all the playfulness and ingenuity which Deutero-Isaiah displays in his use of the prophecy of doom, we see here neither confirmation nor reversal, neither reprediction nor response. Deutero-Isaiah does not utilize the source to affect the meaning in his own text; he simply repeats vocabulary from the source while discussing a different subject altogether. Thus recognizing the markers does not contribute to our construal of the meaning of the later text, even though it may add to our enjoyment of it.[112]

Stylistic Features of Deutero-Isaianic Allusion

At the outset of this chapter, I noted that a stylistic pattern recurrently displayed by borrowed vocabulary can help a reader identify genuine cases of allusion. Such a pattern highlights the vocabulary and emphasizes the dependence on the older text. In the examples of Deutero-Isaiah allusion

discussed above, several such features emerged. Each deserves further attention. I shall discuss one more passage in which Deutero-Isaiah depends on
Jeremiah, because this brief case includes all the stylistic features under
consideration: the split-up pattern, sound play, word play, and identical
word order. In one of the earliest passages in the Book of Jeremiah,[113] the
prophet directed his attention to his northern countrymen who had been
exiled a generation before. Jeremiah has God say to Rachel, who is crying for
her Ephraimite children,

> Hold back your voice from crying (מִנְעִי קוֹלֵךְ מִבֶּכִי), and your eyes
> from tears. For there is a reward for your service (שָׂכָר לִפְעֻלָּתֵךְ), says
> YHWH, and they will return from the enemy's land. (Jer 31.16)

Deutero-Isaiah uses similar vocabulary at the beginning of his book:

> Go up on a high mountain, you who bring good tidings to Zion! Raise
> your voice in strength (הָרִימִי בַכֹּחַ קוֹלֵךְ), you who bring good tidings
> to Jerusalem! Go up, do not fear! Say to the cities of Judah, Behold
> your God! Behold, the Lord YHWH is coming as a strong one, and His
> arm brings dominion for Him. His reward (שְׂכָרוֹ) is with Him and
> His recompense (וּפְעֻלָּתוֹ) before Him. (Isa 40.9–10)

Although these passages share only a few items of vocabulary, Isa 40.9–10
emerges as a particularly strong example of borrowing because of the typical
features of Deutero-Isaianic allusion with which it abounds.

The Split-up Pattern

Deutero-Isaiah often splits up a phrase from his source into two parts
which are separated by several words or even verses.[114] Several cases of this
phenomenon have been discussed above; the case just noted displays it as
well. The phrase שכר לפעלתך ("a reward for your service") from Jer 31.16 is
divided into two phrases in Isa 40.9–10: שכרו אתו ופעלתו לפניו ("His
reward is with Him, and His *recompense for service* is before Him"). The
presence of this pattern confirms other factors, discussed in the following
sections, which indicate that this is a case of one author borrowing from
another, rather than a case of stock prophetic language. In this case, as in a

few others (e.g., the allusion to Jer 10.20 in Isa 54.2), the components of the original phrase are separated by a single word. In a larger number of cases, Deutero-Isaiah inserts much more material between the two components.

We shall find the same pattern in Deutero-Isaiah's allusions to Isaiah ben Amoṣ, Psalms, and other material. This technique constitutes an important element in his project of allusion. He may have hoped that his audience would recognize the pattern so that they would experience greater enjoyment of the text. Hearing the first half of an older phrase might have created a sense of anticipation for a reader or listener who was aware of the technique and deeply familiar with Deutero-Isaiah's sources. This sense of anticipation would be fulfilled when the second half appeared. In addition, Deutero-Isaiah may have wanted his readers to notice the technique in order to help them identify cases of reliance on older material. Though it is impossible to know with certainty whether Deutero-Isaiah contemplated these effects, the technique does in fact aid the scholar of inner-biblical allusion—and increases one's enjoyment of Deutero-Isaiah's artistry.[115]

Sound Play

Deutero-Isaiah delights in alluding to words from his source not only by repeating them but by hinting at them through the use of similar-sounding words. In these cases, the markers and the marked are not identical vocabulary, but the link between them remains palpable. In addition to the examples discussed earlier in this chapter, this phenomenon appears in Isa 40.9–10's allusion to Jer 31.16. In Isa 40.9, Deutero-Isaiah alluded to the phrase from Jer 31.16, מנעי קולך מבכי (minʿi qoleik mibbeki, "hold back your voice from crying"), with the words, הרימי בכח קולך (harimi bakkoᵃḥ qoleik, "raise your voice in strength"). Only the word "voice" is taken verbatim from the source, but the marker sounds even more similar to the marked because both begin with a feminine singular imperative and hence end with the phoneme /ī/: הרימי/מנעי (harimi/minʿi). Further, בכח (bakkoᵃḥ, "in strength") recalls בכי (beki, "crying") because the words share the letters bêt and kāph and because they appear next to the word קולך (qoleik, "your voice") in both texts. Thus similar-sounding words and identical grammatical constructions work together to create an impression of similarity between the marker and the marked.[116]

As is the case with the split-up pattern, sound play occurs in Deutero-

Isaiah's allusions to Isaiah and Psalms as well as his allusions to Jeremiah. Further, sound play characterizes Deutero-Isaiah's writing even outside his allusions to earlier material. He loves to place similar-sounding words near each other: e.g., ונמקו . . . ונמסו (wᵊ-namassu . . . wᵊ-namaqqu, 34.3–4); כנחל שטף . . . כנחל שלום (kᵊnaḥal shalom . . . kᵊnaḥal shoṭeip, 54.8); פאר תחת אפר (pᵊʾeir taḥat ʾeiper, 61.3); מטע . . . מעטה (maᶜᵃṭei . . . maṭṭaᶜ, 61.3); למני . . . ומניתי (la-mni . . . u-maniti, 65.11–12); יִרְעוּ . . . יָרֵעוּ (yirᶜu . . . yareiᶜu, 65.25). Elsewhere, he repeats certain sounds over and over: e.g., sibilants and the letter ḥēṭ in 40.6b–8.[117] Thus the feature of Deutero-Isaiah's poetics of allusion which I note here reflects a characteristic of his style generally.

Word Play

Deutero-Isaiah often employs a word borrowed from his source in a sense different from that found in the source. We have seen this phenomenon in several allusions discussed earlier. Further, Isa 40.10 displays this trait. There Deutero-Isaiah borrows the word פעלה from Jer 31.16. In Jeremiah the word meant "service, punishment," but Deutero-Isaiah uses it in the sense of "reward, payment for service." This feature occurs in Deutero-Isaiah's allusions to other texts as well.[118]

Word play based on homonymy represents a complex variation of the sound plays we saw above. Just as Deutero-Isaiah's use of sound play was not limited to cases of allusion, so too word play characterizes Deutero-Isaiah's poetic style in general. Torrey points out that Deutero-Isaiah loves to utilize both meanings of a homonym in a single verse or passage:[119] e.g., תכן ("measured"; "set in order"), 40.12, 13; גור ("foe"; "sojourner"), 54.15; צדקה ("victory"; "justice"), 56.1; נצח ("victory"; "eternity"), 63.3, 6.

Word Order

In several cases of allusion discussed above, Deutero-Isaiah repeats vocabulary in the order of its appearance in the source. This is also the case in Isa 40.9–10 as they borrow from Jer 31.16: הרימי בכח קולך ("raise your voice in strength") appears first in Deutero-Isaiah, just as מנעי קולך מבכי ("hold back your voice from crying") appears first in Jeremiah. These are followed in both by the word שכר ("reward") and then by the word פעולה ("service/recompense"). This feature is not as common as the split-up pattern, sound play, or word play, but it does appear in several additional cases.

The Role of Stylistic Features in Identifying Cases of Allusion

The stylistic traits discussed above aid in identifying cases of inner-biblical allusion in Deutero-Isaiah. The presence of a pattern in an author's allusions allows a reader to confirm that a similarity between the author and an older text results from deliberate use of the older text rather than from coincidence. As such patterns emerge, it becomes clear that examples displaying the patterns indeed depend on a source. Sound play, word play, and especially the split-up pattern are common enough and distinctive enough to serve as a sort of stylistic signature of Deutero-Isaiah, a flag that points to the presence of an allusion or echo.[120] (These features, which are so common in Isaiah 35 and 40–66, are at best rare in cases of inner-biblical allusion and exegesis culled from other books or even from other parts of the Book of Isaiah, such as chapters 24–27, which often refer to earlier biblical material.)[121] Furthermore, the presence of these techniques makes it less likely that a similarity between Deutero-Isaiah and an older text results from their common use of a literary topos. It is true that two authors may use the same words because both are relying on stock vocabulary or discussing a particular topic, but a cluster or topic does not require a particular order for those words. Thus identical order almost certainly results from borrowing. Indeed, the later author's decision to mimic the order of the marked items may constitute an attempt to signal the borrowing in a particularly clear fashion. Sound play also suggests the presence of an allusion to a particular text rather than the use of a poetic or prophetic word cluster. Stereotyped vocabulary involves just that—words or vocabulary items, not sounds. When Deutero-Isaiah uses words that resemble ones from an earlier text, he is not utilizing a word cluster. Rather, he is playfully hinting at material from a particular earlier text. Similarly, word clusters involve specific uses of the words of which they are comprised. When Deutero-Isaiah plays with a homonym, he draws not on standard vocabulary but on a particular text.

Deutero-Isaiah's markers do not always display these features. But these patterns help one to ascertain the presence of borrowing even for cases that do not contain them. They can do so for two reasons. First, thematic categories emerge from the cases marked by these stylistic criteria. Other apparent allusions seem even more likely to be genuine when they fit into these thematic categories. Second, Deutero-Isaiah's preferences for certain passages becomes clear from the stronger cases of allusion that display these patterns. For example, we have seen several cases of allusion to Jeremiah 30–31, Jeremiah 2, and Jeremiah 16; further, Deutero-Isaiah alludes twice to each of the following passages: Jer 10.17–25, 11.18–21, and 14.2–12. When a text in Deutero-Isaiah shares vocabulary with one of Deutero-Isaiah's favorite sources, one can argue more confidently that the Deutero-Isaianic text in question depends on that source.

My method here, then, resembles what Fishbane calls a "hypothetico-deductive method," by which an examination of several passages yields information on the areas where use of earlier material may be expected; the result becomes hypothesis, which is validated by the degree to which they generate other examples.[122] Stronger examples of Deutero-Isaiah's reliance on older material suggest hypotheses regarding the stylistic and thematic types of revision and the texts most likely to be sources; those hypotheses are validated or disproved by further examination of the material which reveals or fails to reveal additional examples which fit the hypothesis. The hypothesis regarding these stylistic features, then, helps generate new examples by telling us what to look for, but it may be rejected if it does not prove useful in identifying further cases. I have found that attending to these features indeed aids in detecting inner-biblical allusions in Deutero-Isaiah. The usefulness of these features will become even more evident in the following chapters.

3 THE APPROPRIATION OF PROPHETIC TRADITION

DEUTERO-ISAIAH'S ALLUSIONS to Jeremiah fall into several categories: confirmation that Jeremiah's dire prophecies achieved fulfillment; reversal of tropes of condemnation to ones of comfort; reprediction of unfulfilled prophecies (in some of these, a historical figure from Deutero-Isaiah's day replaces one from his source's time); and typological linkage. Deutero-Isaiah utilized material from other prophets in precisely the same ways. He did not differentiate among his many precursors, and the revisionary methods he employs on one prophet are identical to those used for another. From this we learn that he did not position himself as an epigone of one particular figure, nor does his writing contribute exclusively to any one school's collection of prophetic utterances. Rather, he utilizes allusion to situate himself in a broad stream of prophetic tradition. This finding, we shall see, carries weighty implications for our assessment of the relation between the two major parts of the Isaiah scroll.

Not surprisingly, many allusions stem from the largest collection of prophetic texts outside the Book of Jeremiah, to wit, Isaiah 1–39. The complex nature of this source requires detailed attention before we turn to an examination of individual passages. Just as Deutero-Isaiah cannot have utilized the Book of Jeremiah as we know it, so too Isaiah 1–39 surely did not exist in their present form during the exile. Scholars debate whether the bulk of "First Isaiah" can be ascribed to Isaiah ben Amoṣ himself (a minority position)[1] or whether those chapters include a great deal of material from the seventh and sixth centuries and even later (a more commonly held view).[2] For our purposes this question is in part moot. The student of Deutero-Isaiah's allusions need not be concerned whether a passage stems from the eighth-century prophet or from a later pre-exilic (or even early exilic) tradent; in either case, by the time Deutero-Isaiah composed his poetry the material already belonged to the scroll or traditions ascribed to Isaiah.

The issue of passages dated to the late exilic or post-exilic era requires attention, however. Several points of contact exist between Deutero-Isaiah and Isaiah 13.1–14.23. The latter are widely—and I think rightly—viewed as exilic or even post-exilic. Therefore I will not consider parallels between these passages to be cases of Deutero-Isaianic allusion. There are no sustained verbal links with chapters 24–27, which almost all scholars agree date from later than Deutero-Isaiah's day. However, Deutero-Isaiah does borrow from other material viewed by some as post-exilic (for example, chapters 2, 9, and 11). It will be necessary to examine the dating of each of these passages individually. Discussion of this issue appears in the notes wherever appropriate.

Many other scholars have investigated parallels between Isaiah 40–66 and other prophetic books.[3] Most of them have done so in order to gather evidence concerning the growth and redaction of the Book of Isaiah, and they do not pause to consider the exegetical significance of the linkages. Perhaps for that reason they tend to overlook the full extent and depth of many parallels. On the other hand, some points of contact noted by these scholars consist of just one or two words and are not extensive enough to be considered genuine cases of allusion. More recently, scholars (especially those associated with the "Unity of Isaiah" school) have explained the parallels as resulting from the book's redactional history. They attribute sections of Isaiah 1–39 that resemble 40–66 to Deutero-Isaianic editing of, and interpolation in, the sayings attributed to Isaiah ben Amoṣ.[4] My study will lead to a different explanation. Because these parallels follow the patterns found in Deutero-Isaianic allusions to Jeremiah and (as we shall see in this chapter) other prophets, it will become clear that these parallels must be attributed to the same cause—Deutero-Isaiah's borrowing from an older collection, rather than his adding to it.[5]

Reversal

Just as Deutero-Isaiah composed prophecies that both borrowed from and reversed the message of Jeremiah's prophecies of doom, so too he turns negative oracles by other prophets on their heads.[6]

A strong case occurs at the outset of Deutero-Isaiah's prophecies. Isaiah[7] had reproached the inhabitants of Samaria, the capital of the northern kingdom, with these words:

> Woe, haughty crown of Ephraim's drunkards! His magnificent honor (צְבִי) is a flower that fades (וְצִיץ נֹבֵל). Those above the fertile valley (גֵּיא) are smashed with wine.[8] Behold, a strong and powerful one belongs to the Lord (הִנֵּה חָזָק וְאַמִּץ לַא־דֹנָי). Like a stream of hail . . . he will throw [the drunkard of Ephraim] down to earth with [his] hand (בְּיָד). The magnificent honor of the city above the fertile valley (גֵּיא) will be a flower that fades (צִיצַת נֹבֵל). . . . On that day, YHWH of hosts will become a magnificent crown and an honorable diadem for those of His people (עַמּוֹ) who remain. (Isa 28.1–5)

Some of these phrases reappear in Deutero-Isaiah's opening words:

> Comfort, comfort My people (עַמִּי), your God is saying. Speak tenderly to Jerusalem and proclaim to her that her term of service (צְבָאָה) is complete, that her punishment has been fulfilled, that she has received from YHWH's hand (מִיַּד) double for all her sins. A voice calls: Set up the way for YHWH! . . . Every valley (גֵּיא) will be exalted and every mountain and hill will be lowered. . . . A voice proclaims: . . . All flesh is grass, and all its loyalty like the flower in the field (כְּצִיץ הַשָּׂדֶה). The grass withers, the flower fades (נָבֵל צִיץ) when the wind from YHWH blows on it. . . . The grass withers, the flower fades (נָבֵל צִיץ), but the word of our God stands forever. . . . Behold! the Lord YHWH is coming as a strong one (הִנֵּה אֲ־דֹנָי ה' בְּחָזָק יָבוֹא).[9] (Isa 40.1– 10)

The two passages share vocabulary and themes such as the constancy and inconstancy of God and the people, some of which other scholars have noted.[10] These themes and the words עם ("people") and יד ("hand") are quite common, so that they cannot serve as markers indicating that Deutero-

Isaiah draws specifically on Isaiah 28. Similarly, the word נבל ("fade") appears together with botanical terms in figures of human frailty several times in the Hebrew Bible, though that word and ציץ ("flower") appear together only in these two passages. The connection between the passages goes deeper than these frequent terms, however, since both passages also utilize an additional phrase that is unique to them: the words הנה ("behold"), חזק ("strong"), and א־דני ("lord") together. In Isaiah, "behold" occurred immediately before "strong," but in Deutero-Isaiah they are separated by another word: "Behold, a strong . . ." becomes, "*Behold!* the Lord YHWH is coming as *a strong* one." If the repetition of vocabulary suggests the presence of allusion, the split-up of a phrase from the evoked text confirms it, for we saw in the previous chapter that this verbal pattern typifies Deutero-Isaiah's references to older texts. Another characteristic stylistic feature of Deutero-Isaianic allusion, sound play, occurs here as well. The word צבאה (*ṣᵉbaʾah*, "term of service") in Isa 40.2 hints back at the similar sounding word צבי (*ṣᵉbi*, "magnificence") in Isa 28.1 and 28.5.[11]

Figures that in 28.2 served to rebuke and to predict doom reappear in 40.10 as harbingers of hope. In Isaiah, the powerful one whom the Lord sends will punish Israel, but in Deutero-Isaiah the Lord Himself comes as the powerful one to redeem the people. The reversal also involves a change of reference. The passage from Isaiah predicts the punishment of Ephraim brought by the Assyrians. Deutero-Isaiah, however, is no longer concerned with the Assyrians or with the northern kingdom. As he borrows, he shifts the referent of Isaiah's vocabulary to the issue of his own day: the return of Judean exiles from Babylonia. Thus he implicitly contrasts the victory of the Assyrians over Israel with the downfall of the Babylonians, the latter-day counterparts of the Assyrians. This passage, then, provides an example of historical recontextualization, which we have seen also in Deutero-Isaiah's reuse of Jeremiah.[12]

Isaiah is not the only eighth-century prophet whom Deutero-Isaiah reversed. Micah complained of prophets who led the people astray by selling optimistic oracles:

> Thus says YHWH regarding the prophets who mislead My people . . . and proclaim (וְקָרְאוּ), "Things will be fine." . . . You will have night, with a lack of vision; it will be so dark (וְחָשְׁכָה) that you cannot prophesy. The sun will set on the prophets, their day will become

dark ... for there will be no answer (מַעֲנֶה) from God. But I am power-
fully full of the spirit of YHWH and of justice (וּמִשְׁפָּט) ... so that I tell
Jacob its sin and Israel its infraction (לְהַגִּיד לְיַעֲקֹב פִּשְׁעוֹ וּלְיִשְׂרָאֵל
חַטָּאתוֹ). Hear this ... you who build (בֹּנֶה) Zion by means of blood. ...
Her leaders give judgment (יִשְׁפֹּטוּ) for bribes ... and her prophets
prophesy for silver. They claim support from YHWH, saying, "Is not
YHWH in our midst (בְּקִרְבֵּנוּ)? No evil will befall us!" Therefore,
because of you, Zion will be plowed under as a field. (Mic 3.5–12)

Deutero-Isaiah uses similar vocabulary in a passage where he rebukes the
people but also promises better days:

Proclaim (קְרָא) it with your throat, do not hold back (תַּחְשֹׂךְ)! ... Tell
My people its sin, the House of Jacob its infractions (וְהַגֵּד לְעַמִּי
פִּשְׁעָם וּלְבֵית יַעֲקֹב חַטֹּאתָם). They make oracular inquiries of Me constantly ... , as if they were a people who ... had not abandoned the
ordinance (וּמִשְׁפַּט) of its God. They ask Me about righteous judgments (מִשְׁפְּטֵי־צֶדֶק); they desire to be close (קִרְבַת) to God. ... But
you fast in strife and contentiousness. ... Do I ask for such a fast? ... Is
this not the fast I desire: [a day] to loosen evil bonds, ... to free the
downtrodden. ... Is it not a day to distribute your food among the
hungry. ... Then your light would burst open like the morning
sun. ... Then you would call (תִקְרָא) and YHWH would answer
(יַעֲנֶה). ... And your light would shine in the darkness (בַּחֹשֶׁךְ) ... and
your ancient ruins would be rebuilt (וּבָנוּ). (Isa 58.1–11)

At first one may wonder whether these two passages are related as source and
allusion. Almost all the vocabulary they share appears often in the Bible.
However, the appearance in both of הגיד ("tell") followed by פשע and חטא
("infraction" and "sin") suggests that the similarity may be more than a
coincidence; the two sentences are nearly identical. These passages share not
only the vocabulary indicated in parentheses but also certain themes: the
hypocrisy that characterized the people's attempts at making contact with
God, and the motif of light and darkness. The word תחשך (taḥsok, "hold
back") in Deutero-Isaiah hints back to the word וחשכה (wᵉhashᵉka, "dark-
en") in Micah, which constitutes a case of sound play. All this suggests that
the later passage in fact depends on the earlier.

This impression is strengthened by the thematic relationship between the passages. Both prophets complain that the people rely not on religious deeds but on their presumed closeness to God. In both passages that closeness is expressed with the root קר"ב, though in Micah the people assert its presence ("YHWH is in our midst"), while in Deutero-Isaiah the people seek it ("desire to be close to God"). Deutero-Isaiah also includes a reversal of the negative message in Micah. Micah warns that the people are entering a long night, without divination; he announces that Jerusalem will be destroyed. But Deutero-Isaiah encourages the people, telling them that right behavior will halt the situation Micah described. As he does so, he transposes a negative image in Micah, according to which the people build Jerusalem unjustly. Deutero-Isaiah uses similar vocabulary to describe the people successfully rebuilding the ancient ruins. Thus the later prophet both repeats the older prophet's complaint and reverses his prophecy of doom.[13]

The relationship between Deutero-Isaiah and his source is complex, because the later prophet at once aligns himself with Micah and resembles the prophets whom Micah berates. Like the objects of Micah's rebuke, Deutero-Isaiah comforts the nation and announces that evil will not befall Zion. But like Micah, he also acknowledges the nation's sins. The motive behind allusion becomes palpable here: as a prophet who reassures—that is, the sort of prophet whom Micah reviles—Deutero-Isaiah wants to stress his connection with his predecessors; he needs not only to reverse the older message but to repeat it within newly appropriate confines. Lest the audience mistake him for the sort of prophet whom Micah condemns, Deutero-Isaiah first follows Micah's bidding by proclaiming the people's sins. Having thus abrogated not Micah's message but the situation that called it forth, Deutero-Isaiah can proceed to announce the cessation of the punishment Micah foresaw: light will replace the darkness, prophets will again receive answers, and what was destroyed will be rebuilt.[14]

Reprediction

Deutero-Isaiah's restatements of prophecies that have yet to be fulfilled are among the most frequent of his allusions. We have already seen that repredictions based on Jeremiah are extremely common.

Two prophecies in Deutero-Isaiah strongly resemble a famous vision that appears in the writings of both Isaiah and Micah. The vision portrays the peaceful world of the future and Jerusalem's place in it:

> In future days, the mountain of the House of YHWH will be ensconced as the greatest of mountains and raised (וְנִשָּׂא) above the hills. All nations will flow towards it (וְנָהֲרוּ אֵלָיו כָּל־הַגּוֹיִם), and many people will come (וְהָלְכוּ עַמִּים) and will say, Come! Let us go up (וְנַעֲלֶה) to the mountain of YHWH, to the House (בֵּית) of the God of Jacob, so that He will teach us some of His ways . . . for out of Zion comes teaching (כִּי מִצִּיּוֹן תֵּצֵא תוֹרָה), and the word of YHWH from Jerusalem. And He will judge (וְשָׁפַט) among the nations, . . . and they will beat their swords (חַרְבוֹתָם) into plowshares and their weapons into pruning forks; nation will not lift up sword (חֶרֶב) against nation, and they will learn war no more. (Isa 2.2–4; Mic 4.1–4 is almost identical and contains all the marked items)[15]

A similar prophecy appears with similar language in Deutero-Isaiah:

> For YHWH has comforted Zion (צִיּוֹן), comforted all her ruins (כָּל־חָרְבֹתֶיהָ); He has made Zion's wasteland as Eden, her desert as a garden of YHWH. . . . Listen to Me, My nation (עַמִּי), and My folk, give ear! For teaching goes forth from Me (כִּי תוֹרָה מֵאִתִּי תֵצֵא), and I will give My judgment (וּמִשְׁפָּטִי) as a light of the nations (עַמִּים), . . . and My arms will judge nations (עַמִּים יִשְׁפֹּטוּ). Islands will look eagerly to Me, and in My arms they will have hope. (Isa 51.3–5)

The parallels are not limited to the vocabulary noted in parentheses. The idea of peoples gathering appears in both passages, and both predict that nations are taught and judged by YHWH at His mountain. In both passages agricultural images (plowshares and pruning hooks in the source, gardens in the allusion) take the place of figures of destruction expressed with the root חר"ב: swords (חַרְבוֹתָם, ḥarbotam) in the source and ruins (חָרְבֹתֶיהָ, ḥorboteha) in the allusion; the correspondence constitutes a fine case of sound play. The consistent use of several themes in both passages suggests that these parallels are no coincidence. The presence of a typical feature of Deutero-Isaianic allusion shows that the parallel results from borrowing.[16]

Deutero-Isaiah repeats the older prediction, affirming that an era of peace and equity is imminent. But he alters it slightly. His message initially concentrates not on the nations but on what is relevant to the Judeans themselves; his perspective is more national than universal. Further, while Deutero-Isaiah shares the older text's focus on Zion, he clarifies that the source of YHWH's teaching is not merely geographic ("for from Me [rather than Zion] does teaching go forth"). This change may be more than coincidental. Deutero-Isaiah's exilic audience has reason to doubt the power of Zion's God over Babylon or its conqueror. Deutero-Isaiah reminds them that YHWH's might is not constrained by location. Moreover, they may suspect a person claiming to be a prophet of Zion's God, when that person does not speak on or even near the holy mountain.[17] Deutero-Isaiah avers that YHWH's words come from YHWH Himself and can be revealed anywhere in the world He created—even in an enemy's land. This allusion, then, permits a glimpse at Deutero-Isaiah's anxiety regarding his own status. How can he sing the Lord's song, proclaim YHWH's message, in a strange land? His response is to assert his authority by recalling YHWH's universal domain. Indeed, he lays claim to a prophetic status that allows him not only to repeat his predecessors but to supplement them. As Deutero-Isaiah calls the earlier vision to mind, he corrects a misimpression that may arise from it: teaching does not come from Zion alone. Thus this allusion works at three levels to bolster Deutero-Isaiah's position. First, it reminds his audience that YHWH can speak through an exilic prophet. Second, it shows the audience that a later speaker can add to (and even appear to contradict) earlier ones. At the same time, Deutero-Isaiah uses the borrowing to place himself in the same tradition as his source, and hence he draws on its authority even as he revises it.

Another allusion to the same passage occurs later in the book:

Rise, shine, for your light has come, and YHWH's glory has risen above you. For look! Darkness covers the earth, and mist cloaks peoples, but YHWH will shine on you, and His glory will appear over you. Nations will come (וְהָלְכוּ גוֹיִם) to your light, and kings to the splendor of your beacon. Lift up (שְׂאִי) your eyes and see: they have gathered together, they are coming to you—your children from afar. . . . Then you will see and glimmer (וְנָהַרְתְּ), you will be amazed and your heart will grow wide, for the abundance of the sea and the wealth of the nations (גּוֹיִם) will come to you. Riches borne by camels will cover you . . . they will bring (יִשָּׂאוּ) gold and frankincense, and they will proclaim praise to YHWH. All the flocks of Kedar will gather for you; the rams[18] of Nebaioth will serve you. They will go up (יַעֲלוּ) will-ingly[19] on my altar, and I will glorify My glorious House (וּבֵית). (Isa 60.1–7)

Markers in addition to the vocabulary in parentheses occur. Zion, the sub-ject of the passage in Isaiah 2 and Micah 4, is addressed in Isaiah 60, al-though the word "Zion" does not appear explicitly. The allusion includes an extraordinary word play based on the root נה"ר. In the older text the root meant "flow to," but in Isaiah 60, it has its other meaning: "shine, glimmer." The sense of motion the root indicated in the source is nonetheless picked up by another phrase in the allusion: "wealth . . . will *come to* you" (60.5). The verb נהרו (*naharu*, "flow") in the source also suggests ocean imagery, both because what flows recalls water and because the verb hints at the word יָם ("sea"), the standard poetic parallel of the almost identical-sounding noun נהר (*nahar*, "river").[20] This image reappears more strongly in the allusion with the words "wealth of the sea" (60.5). Thus a single marked word in Isaiah 2 yields three markers in Isaiah 60. One marker (ונהרת, "glimmer") recalls the marked item's sound, one ("come to") recalls its meaning, and one ("sea") recalls its imagery (and brings to mind its stan-dard poetic parallel). One thing did the older prophets speak; three did Deutero-Isaiah hear. Though the order of the markers and the marked items is not identical, most of the terms which appear at the outset of the source (נש"א, נהר, הלך) appear at the outset of the borrowing, while those which appear at the end of the source (על"ה, בית) appear at the end of the borrowing.

The passages share a view of the future: Jerusalem will be exalted; nations will go there in great number to acknowledge YHWH. But the focus of the new passage shifts, as Gerhard von Rad notes:

In the former passage all the interest was concentrated on the heathen nations and on the significance which the transfigured Jerusalem had for them. Now, on the contrary, attention is focused almost exclusively on the holy city, which itself shares in the divinely ordered reign of peace. . . . The oracle gives a foretaste of the events as seen from the point of view of the city itself. Zion will be "radiant", its heart will "thrill" (v. 5), and, as in an altogether analogous situation in Isa 49.18ff., Zion will ask with astonishment "who are these that fly like a cloud?" (v. 8)[21]

Further, Deutero-Isaiah offers a different picture of what the nations will do when they arrive at Zion. In the earlier oracle, the nations came for instruction and, apparently, for the peaceful arbitration of international disputes. In the later one, the peoples come to contribute to the sacrificial cult and to add to the city's wealth.[22] Each passage envisions a wonderful future in a distinct way: the earlier text looks forward to universal peace, while Deutero-Isaiah hopes for the prosperity of Zion and the return of the exiles. Thus we find here the same shift from a universal to a national point of view which we saw in the reuse of the older vision in Isa 51.3–5.

In the cases just examined, Deutero-Isaiah asserts that an older prophecy is accurate and will soon be fulfilled, though he stresses new concerns within the context of the already existing predictions. The examples, then, belong more to the literary category of revision than to allusion. In other cases, Deutero-Isaiah genuinely alludes to an older prophecy: he utilizes its language to produce a new prediction. Take the following example. In the seventh century the prophet Nahum predicted the downfall of Nineveh and the Assyrian empire, news that would be greeted happily in Jerusalem:

> Behold on the mountains the legs of a herald who announces well-being (הִנֵּה עַל־הֶהָרִים רַגְלֵי מְבַשֵּׂר מַשְׁמִיעַ שָׁלוֹם)! Celebrate your holidays, O Judah! Bring your vow-offerings! For base men will not continue to move through you (כִּי לֹא יוֹסִיף עוֹד לַעֲבָר־בָּךְ בְּלִיַּעַל); they have ceased. . . . For YHWH has returned (שָׁב ה׳) the pride of Jacob as the pride of Israel. (Nah 2.1–3)

These phrases appear again in Deutero-Isaiah:

> Wake up, Zion, wake up! Clothe yourself with might! Clothe yourself, Jerusalem, O holy city, with your glorious garments! For the uncircumcised and the impure will not continue to walk through you (כִּי לֹא יוֹסִיף יָבֹא־בָךְ עוֹד עָרֵל וְטָמֵא). . . . For thus says my lord YHWH: My people went down to Egypt to live there at the beginning,

and Assyria mistreated them for nothing. But now—what am *I* doing here (a statement of YHWH)?[23] . . . My name is constantly reviled! Therefore My people will know My name . . . [they will know] that I am the one who says, "Behold, here I am." How splendid on the mountains are the legs of a herald who announces well-being (:הִנְנִי מַה־נָּאווּ עַל־הֶהָרִים רַגְלֵי מְבַשֵּׂר מַשְׁמִיעַ שָׁלוֹם), a herald (מְבַשֵּׂר) of good news, who announces (מַשְׁמִיעַ) victory, who says to Zion, "Your God has taken the throne!" The voice of your watchmen rises up, together they sing as each eye sees YHWH's return (בְּשׁוּב ה') to Zion. (Isa 52.1–8)

The passage in Deutero-Isaiah contains two sentences that repeat almost exactly the phrasing of the verse in Nahum. Nonetheless, several small stylistic changes are of interest. In Nahum, the word הִנֵּה is the beginning of a statement: "*Behold* on the mountains the legs of the herald." In Deutero-Isaiah, the word הִנְנִי precedes the statement describing the herald on the mountain (as in Nahum), but it does not introduce that statement. Rather, it is the last word of the previous utterance: "I am He that says, *Behold, here I am*." Further, these words also contain a case of the split-up pattern. In Nahum, "behold" is followed immediately by the words "on the mountains," while in Deutero-Isaiah the words "how splendid" intervene. Other stylistic changes occur as well. As in several other allusions, Deutero-Isaiah amplifies a brief phrase or figure from the source: Nahum speaks of "a herald who announces well-being." Deutero-Isaiah not only restates those words but adds reference to "a herald of good news, who announces victory, who says to Zion, 'Your God has taken the throne!' "[24]

The earlier prediction is not repeated here; rather, it serves as the paradigm for an entirely new one. Both Deutero-Isaiah and Nahum predict the downfall of a great Mesopotamian city that had oppressed Judah, and both anticipate a day in the near future when this good news will reach Jerusalem. Then the city will be inhabited only by those who ought to be there. But Nahum spoke of the Assyrians, and his book describes the destruction of Nineveh, while Deutero-Isaiah is concerned with Babylon. Thus this re-prediction also involves historical recontextualization.

Deutero-Isaiah alters as he repredicts. The new element in Deutero-Isaiah's use of the phrases from Nahum is noted by Menahem Haran:

In spite of the verbal parallel between the two passages, they are divided by a different outlook that is immediately recognizable: Nahum speaks in ethical terms ("base men" [בליעל]) and promises Judah and Jerusalem freedom from invasion and military incursions and from the acts of cruelty and destruction that accompany them. Our prophet promises the city's freedom through ritual purity, since it will be "the holy city." . . . He understands this holiness in a specific way. . . . The entire city changes into an extended temple area. For this reason, the promise appears here that its ritual purity will be protected; the uncircumcised and the impure (ערל וטמא) will not be allowed to enter it. . . . [Other biblical writers view Jerusalem as holy, but Deutero-Isaiah is the only prophet who uses the term עיר הקדש {the holy city} to describe it {also in 48.2, and cf. 64.9}, and] only our prophet casts this holiness in ritual-cultic terms. He does this by granting the holy status of the temple mount to the entire area of the city, as if the entire city formed one giant temple-complex.[25]

Other examples of representation could be cited,[26] but two types deserve attention on their own. First, many represdictions display a particular thematic revision, the nationalization of royal motifs. A smaller number are based on prophecies of doom rather than optimistic oracles.

Represdiction of Royal Prophecies

Deutero-Isaiah alludes several times to the passage in Isaiah 11 that foresees the reign of a just Davidide king.[27] He repeats the earlier prediction of a glorious future from Isaiah 11 but ignores its references to the king by shifting its predictions regarding the Davidic line to the people as a whole. The source reads:

A branch will go forth (וְיָצָא) from the trunk of Jesse . . . and YHWH's spirit (רוּחַ) will rest on him—a spirit (רוּחַ) of wisdom and understanding, a spirit (רוּחַ) of counsel and might, a spirit (רוּחַ) of knowledge and awe before YHWH. . . . He will not judge (יִשְׁפּוֹט) [merely] by the sight of his eyes (עֵינָיו), nor will he decide cases [merely] by what his ears hear (וְלֹא־לְמִשְׁמַע). He will judge the poor righteously, and he will decide the case of the humble of the land (אָרֶץ) in justice. . . . Righteousness will be the clothing he wears, and truthfulness (וְהָאֱמוּנָה) his garment. . . . And on that day, the enduring root of Jesse will be a standard for nations (עַמִּים); peoples (גּוֹיִם) will seek him out, and his rest shall be glorious (כָּבוֹד). (Isa 11.1–10)

The longest reference to chapter 11 occurs in the first of the "servant songs," Isa 42.1–9:

Behold My servant, whom I support; My chosen one . . . I have given My spirit (רוּחִי) to him, so that he might send forth (יוֹצִיא) justice (מִשְׁפָּט) to the nations (לַגּוֹיִם). He does not cry out . . . he does not make his voice heard (וְלֹא־יַשְׁמִיעַ). . . . . He would not break even a crushed reed, nor would he extinguish a dim flame; he puts forth (יוֹצִיא) justice in truth (לֶאֱמֶת). . . . . The distant coastlands look towards his teaching. Thus says the God YHWH, who created the heavens . . . and spread forth the earth (הָאָרֶץ) and its inhabitants, who gives breath to the people (לָעָם) on it and spirit (וְרוּחַ) to those who walk it: I, YHWH, called you in justice (בְצֶדֶק), and I took your hand. I created you and made you a covenant-people, a light of nations (גּוֹיִם) by opening the eyes (עֵינַיִם) of the blind and taking (לְהוֹצִיא) the prisoner out of the jail.[28] I am YHWH; that is My name, and I shall not give My glory (וּכְבוֹדִי) to another. (Isa 42.1–8)[29]

Both passages describe an ideal figure who will judge justly. In each, the position of the lowly is of special concern: the king hears their cases fairly in chapter 11, while they are set free in 42. In both texts, the situation described has implications for the entire world. The outcome of the justice described in 11.1–5 includes knowledge of YHWH among the peoples, who now look toward the king in Jerusalem, as described in 11.6–10. Deutero-Isaiah articulates the connection between these themes more explicitly. The ideal figure he describes will be a source of teaching for the nations, who will look toward the figure.[30] Thus the allusion is a case of reprediction: both prophets look forward to an era of justice, of freedom for Israel, and of knowledge of YHWH among the nations, who recognize the greatness of an ideal figure.

Yet Deutero-Isaiah repeats only part of Isaiah's prophecy. He does not foresee the renewal of the Davidic line: the ideal figure he describes is not a king, and the passage includes no assertions regarding the monarchy.

Rather, the description of the king in Isaiah 11 provides a pattern that the servant's career follows. Thus the allusion also exemplifies the category of typology. The lack of reference to the renewal of the Davidic line throughout Deutero-Isaiah has often been noted,[31] but it becomes particularly pointed here, as the Davidic elements from Isaiah 11 are consistently removed in the allusion. This absence is startling given the continued existence of the Davidic family in Deutero-Isaiah's day and the hope for the dynasty's re-enthronement expressed in other exilic and early post-exilic texts, such as Jer 33.14–16; Ezekiel 37; Zech 3.8, 4.6–10, 6.12; Hag 1.12–14, 2.21–23.[32]

Isaiah's promises regarding the monarch are not simply dropped. When Deutero-Isaiah speaks of the servant in terms he borrows from Isaiah's description of the ideal Davidic king, he implies that the promises Isaiah vouchsafed to the Davidic line now apply to the people as a whole. The transfer from the king to the nation is clear in the first half of the passage because the servant (as in almost all the servant passages) is the nation Israel itself.[33] Even if one doubts the identification of the servant with the people, the nationalization of Davidic motifs is made explicit later in the passage. In Isa 11.2 the Davidide was infused with "spirit"; in 42.5 the whole people are so infused. In 11.10, the nations seek the Davidide; in 42.6 the whole people are the light of nations;[34] the coastlands look toward the light and the teaching it brings (42.4).[35]

Other elements of the reprediction are new as well. Deutero-Isaiah shares Isaiah's concern for the return of exiles, but in 11.11–16 Isaiah describes northerners who fled from or were deported by the Assyrians, while Deutero-Isaiah is concerned with Judean exiles in Babylonia. Thus the passage also displays the historical recontextualization we have noted in several other allusions. Several vocabulary items are used in new ways. In Isaiah 11 ארץ refers to the "land" that the king rules, i.e., the Land of Israel. In Deutero-Isaiah the word has its other, more global meaning: nations throughout the world will recognize the One who stretched out the "earth." If משפט in chapter 42 means "way of behaving, religion" or "salvation,"[36] then even the royal function of judging is no longer present. In such a case, the different use of משפט is itself transformative.

Another allusion to Isaiah 11 occurs in 60.17–61.1.[37] Several markers appear: נצר ("sprout," 11.1 // 60.21); רוח ("spirit," 11.2 // 61.1); the root צד"ק, expressing just rule (11.3–5 // 60.17); ארץ ("land," 11.4 // 60.21). One might object that the parallel involves fairly common vocabulary items (though

"sprout" is an important exception, appearing only four times in the Hebrew Bible). Further, the linkage may initially appear weak because at least
two of the parallel terms reflect an ancient Semitic motif associated with
royalty: both Hebrew and Phoenician texts describes kings with a word for
"shoot" or "branch" alongside the word צדק, meaning "just" or "legitimate."[38] It might follow that Isa 60.17–61.1 transform a royal motif rather
than Isaiah 11 specifically. However, the texts are linked by additional themes
that do not often appear with the terms in question. Both texts mention
peace within the city (11.6–9 // 60.18). The idea of nations coming to Zion,
which appears in 11.11f., occurs earlier in the passage containing the allusion
as well (60.5–10).[39] Given the presence of shared vocabulary along with
shared themes, and in light of Deutero-Isaiah's earlier use of these verses
from Isaiah, it seems likely that Isa 60.17–61.1 indeed rely on Isaiah 11. Like
chapter 11, this passage looks forward to an ideal era of justice and its
inevitable consequence, peace. But Deutero-Isaiah does not mention the
king who will bring in that time of respite by ruling equitably. Vocabulary
which in Isaiah described the king's role is applied to the people as a whole in
the allusion. The "sprout" in 11.1 refers to the new or future Davidic king, but
in 60.21 the nation Israel is the "sprout" planted by YHWH. The king
governs in justice (בצדק) and wears justice (צדק) as a garment in 11.4–5, but
in 60.21 we are told, "Your whole people are the just ones (ועמך כלם
צדיקים)." Here again, as Deutero-Isaiah restates Isaiah's prophecy from
chapter 11, he omits any prediction of a new king and transfers royal prerogatives to the nation.[40]

These multiple borrowings from Isaiah 11, like the multiple borrowings
from Isaiah 2/Micah 4, resist easy classification. It is not clear whether the
relationship between these passages should be termed revisionary or exegetical. Does Deutero-Isaiah use these allusions to challenge his predecessor,
claiming that Isaiah was wrong when he looked forward to a glorious and
just monarchy? Or does he rather cue the reader to reinterpret Isaiah's
prophecy? In the latter case, Deutero-Isaiah counsels the reader to understand chapter 11's references to a Davidic monarch allegorically: we should
recognize that when Isaiah mentions the king, he means to speak of the
nation Israel as a whole. I suggest tentatively that Deutero-Isaiah does not
intend a thorough exegesis of the earlier passage, if only because he picks up
borrowed elements in various ways. For example, both chapter 42 and chapter 60 borrow the word ארץ from the source, but in chapter 60 the word

retains the sense it had in the source ("land"), while chapter 42 gives it a new meaning ("world, earth"). If Deutero-Isaiah were reading the earlier chapter in a novel sense, it is more likely that both his references to it would have retained that sense. His variable use of the marker suggests that he was engaged in revision, not exegesis: he comes to correct a misimpression that the older text can create (the Isaian notion of a future Davidic king), not to correct the reader's misreading of the older text (a reading according to which the king in Isaiah 11 really is a king rather than a cipher standing for the nation).

Negative Reprediction

The cases of reprediction examined thus far involve the restatement of optimistic prophecies. As was the case with the repredictions based on Jeremiah, however, a very small number repeat prophecies of doom. The most extensive negative reprediction is found in Isa 56.10–57.6, in which, as we have seen, Deutero-Isaiah restates the prophecy of destruction from Jer 12.7–13. As he does so, he concentrates on a reason for the judgment not found in the Jeremiah passage: the people's love of false prophecy. Deutero-Isaiah borrows this theme from Isa 30.9–14, which condemn the Israelites for their refusal to listen to genuine prophets. The allusion to Isa 30.9–14 becomes clear from vocabulary which the passages share:[41]

רֹאִים [30.10] // רֹעִים [56.11]
חֹזִים [30.10] // הֹזִים [56.10]
נְכֹחוֹת [30.10] // נְכֹחוֹ [57.2]
חֲלָקוֹת [30.10] // בְּחַלְּקֵי־נַחַל חֶלְקֵךְ [57.6]
דֶּרֶךְ [30.11] // לְדַרְכָּם [56.11]

seers (*roʾim*, 30.10) // shepherds (*roʿim*, 56.11)
prophets (*ḥozim*, 30.10) // sleepers (*hozim*, 56.10)
straight (30.10 // 57.2)
smooth things (30.10) // smooth stones of the wadi are your
     inheritance (57.6)
path (30.11 // 56.11)

The first two items are cases of sound play. The third involves word play: חלקות means "smooth words, lies," while the two occurrences of the root in 57.6 mean "smooth stones of a river" and "inheritance."

In the source, Isaiah complains that the Israelites tell prophets to lie to them; in the allusion, Deutero-Isaiah accuses the prophets of lying to the Israelites. In Isaiah 30, the people say to the seers, "Do not see!" In Isaiah 57, we are told that the prophets are blind. In both, the people are warned that the result of false prophecy will be disaster.

Isaiah 57 repeats another negative prediction from Isaiah in a more complex fashion. The passage bases its imagery and its critique of idolatry on 2.6–21, which read:

> Indeed, You have rejected your people, the House of Jacob, because they have been filled with divination[42] and sorcerers (וְעֹנְנִים) like the Philistines. . . . Their land is filled with no-gods; they bow down to the work (מַעֲשֵׂה) of their own hands, to what their fingers have made. A person makes himself lowly, and a man humbles (וַיִּשְׁפַּל) himself—do not forgive (תִּשָּׂא) them! Go into a rock and hide yourself in the dust away from the dread of YHWH. . . . Haughty human eyes will be lowered (עֵינֵי גַבְהוּת אָדָם שָׁפֵל), and the loftiness of men will be made humble (וְשַׁח רוּם אֲנָשִׁים), but YHWH will alone remain exalted on that day. For YHWH of hosts has a day in store for all who are proud and haughty (כָּל־גֵּאֶה וָרָם), for all who are lifted up—they will be brought low (כָּל־נִשָּׂא וְשָׁפֵל): for all the cedars of Lebanon which are high and mighty (הָרָמִים וְהַנִּשָּׂאִים) . . . and for all the high mountains (הֶהָרִים הָרָמִים) and all the lofty towers (הַנִּשָּׂאוֹת). . . . On that day, people will throw away their no-gods of silver and gold, which they made so they could bow down to them. . . . They will go into the crags of rocks and the clefts of boulders (וּבִסְעִפֵי הַסְּלָעִים) away from the dread of YHWH. (Isa 2.6–21)

Deutero-Isaiah criticizes using similar language:

> And you—come here, children of a sorceress (בְּנֵי עֹנְנָה), seed of an adulterer and one who acted like a prostitute! . . . who got excited by gods under every leafy tree, who slaughtered children in the wadis, under the clefts of boulders (סְעִפֵי הַסְּלָעִים). . . . On a tall and lofty mountain (עַל הַר־גָּבֹהַּ וְנִשָּׂא) you put your bed—yes, there you went up to make a sacrifice! . . . You sent your messengers far away; you went as low (וַתַּשְׁפִּילִי) as Sheol. . . . What you have made (מַעֲשָׂיִךְ) will

not help you. When you cry out so that your abominations[43] might save you, the wind will lift (יִשָּׂא) them up, a gust will take them off. But the one who trusts in Me will inherit the land and acquire My holy mountain.[44] . . . For thus says the One who dwells eternally high up above (רָם וְנִשָּׂא), whose name is "Holy:" I dwell up above in holiness, but also with those who are contrite and lowly in spirit (וּשְׁפַל־רוּחַ), to revive the breath of the lowly (רוּחַ שְׁפָלִים). (Isa 57.3–15)

In addition to the vocabulary indicated in parentheses, the passages share several themes, though they express them with slightly different vocabulary. Each contrasts the people's trust in idols with their lack of fear of YHWH, and each announces that the people will soon have reason to fear YHWH (2.10, 21; 57.11). In Isaiah, the once-haughty people will lower themselves to hide in caves and dust (2.10, 21); in Deutero-Isaiah they go as far down as Sheol (57.9). Idols vanish in both texts: in Isaiah they are swept up (2.18) and their owners fling them away (2.20), while in Deutero-Isaiah the wind carries them off (57.13).[45]

Some critics would object to the suggestion that this passage is an example of Deutero-Isaianic borrowing because they feel that 56.9–57.13 are a collection of pre-exilic oracles interpolated into the exilic or post-exilic collection.[46] Child sacrifice, idolatry, and the like are notoriously pre-exilic tendencies of Israel. The passage resembles judgment oracles of Hosea and Ezekiel, who berate the people's Canaanite practices. If Isaiah 57 is indeed pre-exilic, then it cannot contain a case of Deutero-Isaianic borrowing because it predates Deutero-Isaiah. However, not all critics agree with this dating. Some maintain that the situation it describes does reflect the practices of the generations after the return.[47] A more persuasive alternative is provided by Kaufmann. He attributes the chapter to Deutero-Isaiah, arguing that the prophet described sins of the pre-exilic era here.[48] In that case, 57.3–4 need to be understood literally: you are the children of the ones who practiced sorcery, the seed of people who whored after other gods. The composition, then, is not a criticism by Deutero-Isaiah of his contemporaries, but rather an explanation, based on earlier prophets (especially Isaiah 2), for the disaster that has already occurred. It functions not as prediction but as historical interpretation based on older texts, and perhaps also as an implicit warning against renewed Canaanite practices in the Land of Israel to which the people were now returning. An additional argument for Deutero-Isaiah's authorship of the passage is that it contains several exemplary cases of his style of allusion, each of which I discussed earlier. Its allusion to Jer 12.8–12 includes cases of sound play. The allusions to Isa 30.10–11 and Jer 2.23–25 involve word play.

The probability that chapter 57 borrows from chapter 2 increases when we realize not only that these chapters share vocabulary and themes but that in chapter 57 the shared elements follow carefully worked-out patterns. Isaiah described punishments that would befall the nation in certain places; Deutero-Isaiah describes sins that had occurred in those same locations. God's anger causes the haughty to flee to crags (2.21); Deutero-Isaiah accuses the people of having slaughtered children there (57.5). God will wreak vengeance on high mountains (2.12–14); Deutero-Isaiah identifies high mountains as the site of some sort of religious or sexual misconduct (57.7). The people flee underground from YHWH's anger (2.11f.); Deutero-Isaiah maintains that the people were willing to go to extraordinary lengths to send their gifts to the underworld (57.9).[49] According to Deutero-Isaiah, YHWH decided that the people should receive their punishment in the precise locations where they had come to deserve it. Deutero-Isaiah supplies crimes that fit Isaiah's punishments in other ways as well. In Isaiah, God strikes the people with an overwhelming fear that causes them to hide (2.9–10); Deutero-Isaiah quotes God as complaining that the people did not fear Him (57.11). Deutero-Isaiah intensifies themes from Isaiah 2 or makes them more vivid (just as he often amplified motifs borrowed from Jeremiah, e.g., when borrowing from Jer 31.7–9 in Isa 35.4–10). Thus the motif of the lowly who are raised up and the high who are brought down pervades both, but Deutero-Isaiah takes the idea a step further. Not only will haughty men be brought low (as punishment) (2.9, 11, 12f.), but God, the High and Lofty One, will join the humble and lowly (57.15).[50] In Isa 2.18, idols disappear, though Isaiah does not specify precisely how (the verse probably means that idolatry will cease, not that the idols will literally fly away); in 57.13, the wind carries them off.

Deutero-Isaiah adds a small note of comfort even as he recalls his predecessor's reproach: he announces that the anger will not last forever (57.16).[51] This comment answers the prophet's question in 6.11, "Until when [will this punishment go on], my Lord?" Chapter 57 also contains Deutero-Isaiah's response to the theological problem of Isa 6.9–10, viz., God's apparently spiteful decision to blind the people so that they cannot repent. Deutero-

Isaiah explains in 57.16–18 that the people refused to repent even though God attempted to reprove them. Therefore, there is nothing wrong with God's plan to prevent them from repenting in 6.9—they had their chance but spurned it. Further, Deutero-Isaiah adds that God, realizing their nature, will bring them comfort anyway; He will not merely wait for their repentance.[52] That chapter 57 responds to these verses from chapter 6 is clear given the additional terms that the chapters share.[53]

Chapter 57 represents an extended allusion to Isaiah 2, reusing its portrayal of the nation's sin and its theme of a reversal of high and low.[54] If Kaufmann is correct that chapter 57 refers to the sins of the exiles' fathers rather than those of the returning exiles themselves, this passage is less a reprediction than an explanation of a historical fact: Israelites were punished in certain ways because they deserved it. In such a case, this rereading of older prophecy is oriented to a better understanding not only of the future but of the past. The stress on the sins of the pre-exilic generations works in a positive manner: by showing the nation's punishment to be deserved, Deutero-Isaiah assures his audience that the covenant remains valid, and that YHWH keeps His promises. His audience understood that this dynamic would now work for the better, since it had already worked for the worse.

As was the case in Deutero-Isaiah's allusions to Jeremiah, only a few other cases of reprediction of negative oracles occur.[55]

Historical Recontextualization

In several of Deutero-Isaiah's allusions to earlier prophets, the later prophet recontextualizes elements that referred to Assyria in his source so that they now refer to Babylonia. We have seen that this phenomenon is especially common in cases of reprediction. Thus Isa 52.1–8 apply to Babylon Nahum's prophecy regarding Assyria from Nah 2.1; Isa 11.11–16 referred to the victims of Assyrian expansion, but the captives mentioned in the allusion in 42.1–9 are Judeans in Babylonia. Recontextualization also occurred in cases of reversal described above. The disaster which Isaiah prophesied in 28.2 was to be wrought by the Assyrians, but the restoration Deutero-Isaiah predicts in 40.10 in fact reverses Babylonian actions. In these cases, Deutero-Isaiah does not merely refer to an older text but updates it.[56] Historical recontextualization occurs in several other cases of reprediction (and in one case of confirmation) based on the prophecies of Isaiah and Zephaniah.[57] Allusions to Isaiah are especially rich with recontextualization, which is fitting; given the great time span between Isaiah and Deutero-Isaiah, we should expect that the later prophet will need to adapt the markers so that they fit the changed world of his own day. In allusions to Jeremiah (who lived only a generation or two before Deutero-Isaiah), this trope becomes necessary less often.

Typological Linkage

In several passages examined above, Deutero-Isaiah patterns his predictions about the nation or the servant of YHWH on Isaiah's prophecies regarding Davidic monarchs. These cases of reprediction involve typology: they assert a link between an individual and some other figure, whether another individual or a nation. (Using a similar strategy of personal typology, Deutero-Isaiah applies motifs from the life of Jeremiah to the nation as a whole.) In several other allusions a figure from Isaiah's prophecy provides the pattern for the servant.

A complex case of personal typology occurs in 52.13–53.12, the single passage in which the servant's identity as the nation Israel is in doubt.[58] We have already seen that the passage depends on Jeremiah 11, since the servant here is patterned after the prophet there. In addition, this passage resonates with vocabulary borrowed from Isaiah 6.[59] Markers link the servant primarily to Isaiah himself, at times to the nation, and once to YHWH. The earlier text reads:

> In the year of King Uzziah's death, I saw the Lord sitting on a high and lofty (רָם וְנִשָּׂא) throne . . . I said, "Woe is me, for I am undone! For I am a man of unclean lips, and I dwell among a people of unclean lips, and my eyes have seen the king, YHWH of hosts." One of the seraphs flew towards me with a coal in his hand . . . and he touched (וַיַּגַּע) my mouth (פִּי) with it and said, "Now (הִנֵּה) that this has touched (נָגַע) your lips, your guilt is gone" (וְסָר עֲוֹנֶךָ). . . . And I heard (וָאֶשְׁמַע) the voice of My Lord saying, "Whom (מִי) shall I send, and who (וּמִי) will go for us?" And I said, "Here I am, send me!" and he said, "Go say to this people, 'Listen well, but do not understand (שִׁמְעוּ שָׁמוֹעַ וְאַל־תָּבִינוּ)! See well, but do not know (וּרְאוּ רָאוֹ וְאַל־תֵּדָעוּ)!' Make this

people's mind dense and their ears blocked up, and cover their eyes, lest they see with their eyes and hear with their ears and understand with their minds and repent, so that they would be healed (וְרָפָא לֹו)." And I said, "How long, My Lord?" He said, "Until cities are destroyed and have no inhabitants, houses are empty (מֵאֵין אָדָם), and the land becomes an utter waste (וְהָאֲדָמָה . . . שְׁמָמָה)." (Isa 6.1–11)

Remarkably similar vocabulary appears in Isaiah 52–53:

Behold (הִנֵּה), my servant will prosper; he will be high and lofty (יָרוּם וְנִשָּׂא) and very exalted. Just as many were horrified by him[60]—for[61] his appearance was more disfigured than any man's, his form, more than any person's (שָׁמְמוּ . . . אָדָם)—so too . . . kings will gape in surprise at him. For they will see (רָאוּ) what nobody told them; they will understand what they had never heard (וַאֲשֶׁר לֹא־שָׁמְעוּ הִתְבּוֹנָנוּ). "Who (מִי) would believe what we have heard (לִשְׁמֻעָתֵנוּ)? The arm of YHWH has manifested itself through whom (מִי)? . . . Seeing him—it was not a sight (וְנִרְאֵהוּ וְלֹא־מַרְאֶה) to be enjoyed: . . . a man of sorrows, who knew (וִידוּעַ) disease. . . . We had thought him afflicted (נָגוּעַ), abused by God and tortured. It is he who was defiled by our sins, made contrite by our transgressions—the discipline (מְעוֹנֹתֵינוּ מוּסַר) for our well-being rests on him, and through his wound we have been healed (נִרְפָּא־לָנוּ)! . . . He would not open his mouth (פִּיו); like a lamb brought to the slaughter, like a ewe before those who shear her, he remained silent; he would not open his mouth (פִּיו)." . . . He was banished from the land of the living for the sin of my people, for their wound. . . . He did no violence, there was never falsehood in his mouth (בְּפִיו). . . . Therefore I shall give him a portion along with the many; along with strong ones he will take spoils, for he exposed himself to death[62] and allowed himself to be counted among sinners; he carried the sin of the many and interceded for the sinners. (Isa 52.13–53.12)

The markers exhibit many Deutero-Isaianic features. Sound play occurs as the word וסר (wᵉsar, "went away") from the source becomes מוסר (musar, "discipline") in the allusion. The connection between these two words is conspicuous because both appear next to the word עון ("guilt/transgression"). The words הַאֲדָמָה (*ha’ᵃdama*, "land") and אָדָם (*’adam*, "human") constitute an additional case of sound play. Word play also occurs: שְׁמָמָה in 6.11 means "destruction," but שָׁמְמוּ in 53.14 means "they were surprised."[63]

The words borrowed from Isaiah 6 repeatedly display a pattern of inversion: what happens to the servant recalls what happened to Isaiah yet turns the Isaian prototype on its head. The servant is the one chosen by YHWH to represent the people and to suffer on their behalf; Isaiah is chosen by God to represent Him and to prevent the people from repenting so that they will suffer. The servant does not object to his fate, does not open his mouth (53.7); Isaiah opens his mouth to lament his fate (6.5). The servant brings healing (רפ״א) to the people (53.5); Isaiah forestalls healing (רפ״א) among the people (6.9–10). Isaiah's guilt (עון) is purged (סר) when he is struck (נג״ע) on the mouth (6.7); the corporate guilt (עון) of the people is purged when the discipline (מוסר) of the people is placed on the servant, who receives an injury (נגע) (53.4–5). The passage in chapters 52–53 contains good news for the people (whose sin is purged) and bad news for the servant (who suffers); the passage in chapter 6 contains bad news for the people (who will suffer) and good news for Isaiah (whose sin is purged).[64] Insofar as the Deutero-Isaian passage contains good news for the people and ends with a report of the servant's vindication, the passage also represents a case of reversal: the national guilt described in Isaiah 6 has been lifted.[65]

Additional typological linkages occur between the passages. Not only Isaiah but also the people serve as a type for the servant (though to a lesser extent), in that the servant receives the punishment designated for the people in chapter 6. The servant also recalls YHWH in the earlier passage, since a phrase that described God in 6.1 ("high and lofty") is applied to the servant in 52.13. Finally, like Israel in 6.9, the nations and their kings in 52.15 lack understanding—but the latter gain it by observing the servant.

This servant passage may also allude to other passages from Isaiah. Isa 11.1–10 share vocabulary items with Isa 52.13f.: שֹׁרֶשׁ ("root," 11.1 // 53.2), דעת ("knowledge," 11.2 // 53.11), and יונק ("infant" in Isa 11.8, but "sapling" in Isa 53.2 via word play). The connection may seem meager; but the link between the servant and the Davidide described in 11 is known from 42.1–9, which bolsters the probability that this passage also depends on Isaiah 11. In both Isaiah 52–53 and Isaiah 11 the nations have a role as spectators (11.10, 53.15); in both the central figure brings justice tempered with mercy (11, passim; 53.11–12). Isa 53.4–5 contain vocabulary found in Isa 1.5–6 as well: the words "beaten" (a hophal form of the root נכ"ה), "sickness" (חלי), and "wound" (חבורה).[66] Because all these words belong to a single semantic field, however, their appearance in two texts may be merely coincidental. On the other hand, the word חשבנהו (ḥashabnuhu, "we thought him") in 53.4 may recall חבשו (ḥubbashu, "bandaged") in 1.6 by sound play. If these texts do in fact represent an allusion, they associate the servant and the nation Israel. The link between the nation and the servant is reinforced by the common use of the phrase "high and lofty" in 52.13 and 2.12–14.[67]

The servant song in 52–53 constitutes a complex reworking of several passages from Isaiah and Jeremiah: it borrows copiously from chapter 6 of the former and chapter 11 of the latter while also evoking chapters 1, 2, and 11 of the former. Almost every phrase hints back to at least one earlier prophetic passage (and one section of the song echoes the Psalter as well).[68] In this chapter, Deutero-Isaiah's allusive art reaches a high point. Multiple cases of sound play and word play appear in concert with highly ramified thematic transformations. The passage describes a figure whose career follows patterns set by two prophets, the nation Israel, and God in the older texts. The difficulty that the passage has presented to generations of commentators, traditional and modern, results in part from the allusive artistry with which it was composed. The many pieces of the mosaic that is chapter 53, coming now from Isaiah and now from Jeremiah, pointing at times to a prophetic paradigm for the servant and at times to a national prototype or divine exemplar, send interpreters in a slew of directions at once. The study of Deutero-Isaiah's allusions cannot solve the interpretive crux. However, by showing that the text is based on an intermingling of many borrowed elements, such study does allow readers to understand that the passage is so multivalent precisely because it is a mosaic: it is as rich in possible meanings as it is dependent on earlier sources.[69]

Fulfillment of Earlier Prophecies

At times Deutero-Isaiah employs allusion in order to assert that certain prophecies have been fulfilled. Examples which belong to this category exclusively are fairly infrequent, just as they seldom appear in Deutero-Isaiah's allusions to Jeremiah. At the same time, many of the reversals (noted above) also confirm, albeit implicitly, that dire predictions have come to pass.

A number of scholars have suggested that when Deutero-Isaiah speaks of "former things" (רָאשֹׁנוֹת), he means the fulfilled prophecies of Isaiah.[70] Some (though not all) of these passages do refer to older prophecies which have come to pass.[71] However, there is no indication that the term רָאשֹׁנוֹת in those passages (Isa 41.22; 42.9; 43.9, 12, 18; 44.6–7; 48.3) points specifically to the prophecies of Isaiah ben Amos rather than to those of other prophets whom Deutero-Isaiah utilizes. Thus these passages express Deutero-Isaiah's concern for attesting to the fulfillment of older prophecies in general, not those of Isaiah in particular.

In several cases Deutero-Isaiah does confirm specific predictions made by Isaiah.[72] The earlier prophet accused the people of being rebellious and announced judgment in the following passage:

> It is a rebellious people (עַם מְרִי הוּא); they are deceptive children who would not consent to listen to the teaching of YHWH (לֹא־אָבוּ שְׁמוֹעַ תּוֹרַת ה'), who said to the seers (לָרֹאִים), "Do not see (לֹא תִרְאוּ)! . . . Depart from the path (דֶּרֶךְ), turn aside from what is right! . . ." Therefore, this punishment will be to you like a broken wall which falls . . . whose breach comes all of a sudden. . . . Even a shard (חֶרֶשׂ) to snatch up a firebrand from kindled wood or to scoop up water from a cistern will not be found among the ruins [of the wall]. (Isa 30.9–14)

Isaiah describes the people as refusing to listen to what the prophets tell them—worse, they demand that the prophets alter their statements to reflect what the people want to hear. Put differently, they have eyes and ears but they make themselves blind and deaf. As a result, God will bring destruction on them. Deutero-Isaiah agrees that the people are morally deaf and blind, and he describes their plight as matching Isaiah's prediction of an utter, apparently irremediable disaster.

> O deaf ones (הַחֵרְשִׁים), hear (שְׁמָעוּ), and blind ones, look carefully (לְרְאוֹת)! . . . You saw (רָאוֹת) much but did not pay attention; with open ears, you would not hear (יִשְׁמָע). . . . And it is a people (וְהוּא עַם) that has been plundered and spoiled. . . . They have been plundered and there is none to save them. . . . Who among you will give ear to this, will pay attention and hear (וְיִשְׁמַע) concerning the future? Who gave Jacob over to plunder and Israel to those who take spoils? Was it

not the One against whom we sinned, by not consenting (וְלֹא־אָבוּ) to follow His paths (בִּדְרָכָיו), by not listening (שָׁמְעוּ) to His teaching (בְּתוֹרָתוֹ)? He poured down His furious anger on them. . . . Flames engulfed them all around and they did not understand; [the flames] burned them, but they did not pay attention. (Isa 42.18–25)

Some of the shared vocabulary occurs in other passages that treat the theme of obedience: for example, שמע ("hear") and אבה ("consent") are used in Ezek 3.7–8 and 28.12 (cf. also Ezek 12.1–3). Other items, however, do not elsewhere occur together as they do here (note רא"ה ["see"] and the word עם ["people"] next to הוא ["it"]), and this diminishes the possibility that the parallel merely reflects a common use of formulaic vocabulary. Further, while the verb שמע ("hear") and the noun תורה ("teaching") appear often in the Hebrew Bible, it is quite rare that this verb takes this noun as an object; aside from these two passages, this occurs only in two later texts (Zech 7.12 and Neh 13.3) as well as in Prov 28.9.[73] Typical stylistic features of Deutero-Isaianic allusion are present, and this makes clear that the similarity between the passages results from Deutero-Isaiah's borrowing. The clause from Isaiah, "who would not consent to listen to the teaching," is split into two clauses in Deutero-Isaiah: "did *not consent* to follow His paths, did not *listen to His teaching*." The parallel vocabulary also includes a case of sound play, another frequent characteristic of Deutero-Isaiah's allusion to Jeremiah: החרשׁים (haḥeirªshim, "the deaf ones") in Deutero-Isaiah points back to חרשׁ (ḥeres, "shard") in Isaiah. This word in Deutero-Isaiah also recalls the theme of the people who refused to listen, who made themselves deaf, in the source. The marker, then, alludes doubly. Two things did Isaiah speak, one did Deutero-Isaiah hear. In addition to the marked vocabulary, Deutero-Isaiah adopts the fire imagery from the source.

Recognizing the allusion in 42.18–25 helps solve an exegetical crux. The tone of the passage is surprisingly bleak and angry in comparison with most of this section of Deutero-Isaiah, and it appears to indict the exilic audience for sins against YHWH. Such an accusation hardly matches an attempt to comfort them, as the commentators point out. It may be, however, that here as in other passages Deutero-Isaiah is referring to the sins of the past, those described by his predecessors, in order to explain to the people why they are in their current state. They need not despair of YHWH's attention or power to save; the nation's plight is fully understandable and justifiable. At the same time, just as the negative prophecies of the past were fulfilled, so too the people can have confidence that the new, positive ones will come true. Thus this apparently bleak pericope functions in a optimistic way in its exilic context.

The same move from prediction to confirmation is found in the following case. YHWH condemns the people to blindness, which will result in disaster:

> Act stupid and be stupefied, act blind and be blinded! Become drunk, but not from wine (שִׁכְרוּ וְלֹא־יַיִן), stagger, but not from liquor![74] For YHWH has poured out on you a spirit of stupor (תַּרְדֵּמָה). He closed your eyes (the prophets) and covered your ears (the seers).[75] (Isa 29.9–10)

Deutero-Isaiah acknowledges that the people have become drunk with God's wrath:

> Wake up, wake up, arise, Jerusalem, who drank from YHWH's hand His cup of anger, who drank, who guzzled His goblet[76] of reeling (הַתַּרְעֵלָה). . . . Your children fainted, they sank . . . full of the anger of YHWH. . . . Therefore hear this, afflicted one, you who are drunk but not from wine (וּשְׁכֻרַת וְלֹא מִיָּיִן): Thus says your lord YHWH . . . I have taken from your hand the cup of reeling (הַתַּרְעֵלָה), the goblet of my wrath; you will not continue to drink from it. (Isa 51.17–22)

Although the idea of the cup of God's anger appears in several other biblical passages (Ps 60.5, Hab 2.16, Ezek 23.31f., etc.), the nearly identical phrases in these two passages, שׁכרו ולא־יין/ושׁכרת ולא מיין ("become / you-who-are-drunk, but not from wine"), suggest that Deutero-Isaiah relied specifically on Isaiah. One wonders further if his use of the word תרעלה (tar'eila, "reeling") hints back via sound play to Isaiah's תרדמה (tardeima, "stupor").

Deutero-Isaiah's words contain several elements not found in Isaiah's prophecy of doom. While Isaiah said that God made the people drunk so that they would not listen to true prophecies, lest they repent (cf. 6.10), Deutero-Isaiah declares somewhat more ambiguously that they are drunk with the wrath of YHWH. This ambiguity obscures Isaiah's assertion that YHWH directed prophets to mislead the nation so that it would not repent. (We have seen in other passages that Deutero-Isaiah tends to shy away from this surprising aspect of Isaiah's message, especially in allusions to chapter 6.)[77] Further, this example of the category of fulfillment includes elements of another tendency of Deutero-Isaianic borrowing, historical recontextualization. The punishment which Isaiah envisioned was to be implemented by the Assyrians; the first part of chapter 29 predicted the Assyrians' severe, though not fatal, siege of Jerusalem. The punishment Deutero-Isaiah witnessed, on the other hand, was carried out by the Babylonians. The later prophet suggests that what the earlier prophet predicted in regard to one empire in fact came true with another.

This text, then, straddles the lines separating revision, allusion, and exegesis while also introducing historical recontextualization. Deutero-Isaiah may wish merely to recall the older prediction (in which case this is an allusion) or to update it and correct it (in which case the link is a case of revision). Alternatively, by asserting that the earlier oracle has been fulfilled in the Babylonian conquest, he may attempt to suggest we understand it in a novel way (so that the borrowing is a case of exegesis). Deutero-Isaiah's silence regarding how the people became drunk according to Isaiah (God forced them to drink so that they could not repent) may also work interpretively: he shifts the readers' focus away from that theme. On the other hand, the fact remains that these references occur in a new text, and thus their role in changing one's view of the source is at best indirect. For this reason, it is safest to conclude that the borrowing is not a case of full-fledged exegesis. While Deutero-Isaiah revises or omits some of Isaiah's ideas, it is not clear that he intends to change our reading of the older text.[78]

Multiple Categories

A final allusion deserves attention because it exemplifies several types of Deutero-Isaianic revision and reworking. Isa 54.1–13 repeat both themes and vocabulary from Hosea 1–2. The lengthy passage from Hosea has two sections. In each the prophet initially foretells God's rejection of the people and then announces that He will take the nation back after its punishment. The relevant verses read:

> God said to Hosea, "Go marry a woman of fornication (אֵשֶׁת זְנוּנִים)
> and get children of fornication, for the land has acted like a fornicator,

abandoning YHWH." And he went and married Gomer, the daughter of Diblaim. . . . And she conceived . . . and gave birth (וַתֵּלֶד) to a daughter. And [YHWH] said to [Hosea], "Call (קְרָא) her name (שְׁמָהּ), 'Not-pitied (לֹא רֻחָמָה),' for I shall not have compassion for the House of Israel any more. . . ." And [Gomer] weaned Not-pitied (לֹא רֻחָמָה). She conceived and gave birth to a son. And He said, "Call (קְרָא) his name (שְׁמוֹ), 'Not-My-People,' for you are not My people, and I am not yours."

Yet the number of the children of Israel will be like the sand at the sea. . . . Instead of being told, "You are not My people," they will be called, "Children (בְּנֵי) of the living God." . . . Say to your brothers, "[You are] My people!"—and to your sisters, "[You are] pitied (רֻחָמָה)!" . . .

Argue with your mother, argue! For she is not My wife, and I am not her husband. . . . I shall not have compassion (אֲרַחֵם) on her children, for they are children (בְּנֵי) of fornication. . . . I shall destroy (וַהֲשִׁמֹּתִי) her vines and fig trees. . . . I shall punish her for the days she sacrificed to the baʿalim (הַבְּעָלִים) . . . and followed her lovers and forgot Me (a pronouncement of YHWH). . . .

But on that day (a pronouncement of YHWH), you will call (תִּקְרְאִי) Me, "My husband,"[79] and you will no more call (תִקְרְאִי) Me, "My baal (בַּעְלִי)."[80] I shall remove the names of the baʿalim (הַבְּעָלִים) from her mouth, and they will be remembered no more (וְלֹא־יִזָּכְרוּ עוֹד). . . . And I shall make a covenant (בְּרִית) with them on that day. . . . And I shall wed you forever (לְעוֹלָם). And I shall wed you in righteousness (בְּצֶדֶק) and justice and mercy and compassion (וּבְחֶסֶד וּבְרַחֲמִים). And I shall wed you in truth, and you will know YHWH. . . . I shall pity Not-pitied (וְרִחַמְתִּי אֶת־לֹא רֻחָמָה), and I shall say to Not-My-people, "You are My people," and he will say, "[You are] My God." (Hos 1.2, 3, 6; 2.1, 3, 18–22, 25)

Deutero-Isaiah uses the same vocabulary in similar ways:

Rejoice, O barren one, who has not given birth (יָלָדָה)! . . . For the children (בְּנֵי) from the time of desolation (שֹׁמֵמָה) outnumber those of the married years (מִבְּנֵי בְעוּלָה), says YHWH. . . . Do not fear, do not be ashamed . . . for no more you will remember (לֹא תִזְכְּרִי־עוֹד)

the shame of your youth or the reproach of your widowhood. For the one who made you will become your husband (בֹּעֲלַיִךְ); YHWH of hosts is His name (שְׁמוֹ). Your redeemer, the Holy One of Israel, will be called (יִקָּרֵא) the God of all the earth. For YHWH called you (קְרָאָךְ) as an abandoned wife, [as] a wife of one's youth (וְאֵשֶׁת נְעוּרִים).... For a short moment I left you, but with great compassion (וּבְרַחֲמִים) I shall gather you in. . . . With eternal mercy I treat you compassionately (וּבְחֶסֶד עוֹלָם רִחַמְתִּיךְ), says your redeemer, YHWH. . . . My mercy (וְחַסְדִּי) will not move away from you, and my covenant (וּבְרִית) of well-being will not waver, says YHWH, the one who treats you compassionately (מְרַחֲמֵךְ). Poor one, buffeted one, not-comforted (לֹא נֻחָמָה).... all your children (בָּנָיִךְ) will be disciples of YHWH, and the well-being of your children will be abundant. You will be established in victory (בִּצְדָקָה). (Isa 54.1, 4–8, 10–11, 13–14)

The two sets of passages share not only the vocabulary indicated in parentheses but also several motifs: divine rejection of the nation; subsequent reconciliation; bestowing of names on God and Israel. Hosea's portrayal of Israel as a whore when young may lie behind Deutero-Isaiah's statement (54.4), "You will remember no more the shame of your youth or the reproach of your widowhood," especially since the word for reproach used here (חרפה) can refer to sexual shame or dishonor (see 2 Sam 13.13, Isa 47.3, Ezek 16.57, Prov 6.33). The word לֹא רֻחָמָה (lo' ruḥama, "not pitied") from Hosea 1.8 is a marked item to which two markers in Isaiah 54 point: the root רח"ם ("pity, compassion"), which appears in 54.7, 8, and also in the reference to Israel as לֹא נֻחָמָה (lo' nuḥama, "not comforted") in 54.11, a case of sound play. The phrase "wife of one's youth" (אשת נעורים, 'eishet n⁵urim) in Deutero-Isaiah recalls Hosea's "woman of fornication" (אשת זנונים, 'eishet z⁵nunim) not only because they begin with the same word (translated variously as "wife" and "woman") but also because the subsequent words share a single vowel pattern. Although the markers and marked items are spread over large passages, words which appear together in one often appear together in the other. The resemblance between the two passages emerges as a genuine allusion because of a large number of terms not found together elsewhere, sound play, and the shared themes.

The passage in Hosea contains both a warning and a reversal of that warning: YHWH announces that He rejects the people, but He also reveals

His intention to accept them back after they have been chastened. Deutero-Isaiah acknowledges that God had indeed repudiated the nation, but He did so only temporarily, and now He is about to return to them. Thus Isaiah 54 works as a reversal (of Hosea's prophecy of doom), a confirmation (that a disaster indeed occurred), and a reprediction (of Hosea's prophecy of reconciliation between YHWH and Israel).[81] When Deutero-Isaiah asserts that the children of destruction will outnumber the children of marriage (54.1), he negates Hos 2.6 ("I shall not have compassion on her children, for they are children of fornication"); at the same time, he repeats Hosea's promise of abundant offspring from 2.1 ("the number of the children of Israel will be like the sand at the sea"). The harsh description of the children in Hos 2.6 is further reversed in Isa 54.13: instead of dismissing Israel's offspring as "children of fornication," YHWH announces that they will be His disciples—indeed, they will enjoy great well-being. Hosea talked to the northern Israelites, but Deutero-Isaiah directs his message to southern exiles, so that this passage also displays historical recontextualization. Thus this single allusion exemplifies several thematic categories that typify Deutero-Isaiah's reuse of prophetic material.

In Hosea, God insists that He not be called by the Hebrew word בעל (baʿal), which means both "husband" and "master" and also designates a type of Canaanite god. YHWH insisted instead that He is Israel's איש ("man, husband"). Deutero-Isaiah, however, avoids calling God an איש ("man, husband") and uses the root of the word baʿal to refer to His relationship with Israel. The reason for the converse use of terminology is clear. A central complaint of the Book of Hosea is that the nation Israel prays to the various Canaanite gods known by the term baʿal. Hosea may also have faulted the nation for regarding YHWH as one of the many gods called by that name rather than as a distinct and unique God.[82] The eighth-century prophet therefore argued against calling YHWH by the name baʿal even when he described YHWH as Israel's husband; instead he used the term whose primary meaning is "man" to intimate that YHWH is married to the nation. In Deutero-Isaiah's day, however, baal-worship is no longer a problem.[83] As a result, the exilic prophet does not hesitate to use the root בע"ל when he announces that YHWH marries Jerusalem. Deutero-Isaiah's rejection of the term "man" to describe that relationship further results from his shunning of even traces of anthropomorphism (a tendency that becomes prominent in his polemic against the priestly creation account in Genesis 1, discussed below in Chapter 5). In spite of their difference regarding nomenclature, both Hosea and Deutero-Isaiah emphasize that YHWH is Israel's God, as Isa 54.5 and Hos 2.25 make clear.[84]

Echo

Deutero-Isaiah at times borrows clusters of vocabulary from earlier prophets without transforming them in any particular way. These are cases not of full-fledged allusion but of echo. Although noticing the borrowed elements in these cases does not change one's reading of the passages, the echoes underscore Deutero-Isaiah's connection to his precursors, and they provide the audience the pleasure of recognizing familiar material in a new work. Isa 48.11 contains phrases appearing in Ezek 20.9–22, and Isa 60.6 points to Ezek 26.10, but the parallels do not alter one's reading of the later texts.[85] Several parallels with Zephaniah also fall into the category of echo rather than allusion.[86] Isaiah 65–66 contain a good deal of vocabulary shared with Isaiah 1, most of which falls into this category: while composing Isaiah 65–66, our prophet seems to have had Isaiah 1 in mind and to have borrowed vocabulary from it, but he did not utilize most of that vocabulary in a transformative manner; indeed, one cannot be sure that the borrowing was entirely conscious.[87] Similarly, 44.9–14 are full of vocabulary from 6.9–13,[88] but in chapter 6 that vocabulary referred to issues largely unrelated to those of chapter 44. In the source the people and the land are burned as a punishment, while in the echo wood is burned for a fire in a kitchen. This is a playful borrowing rather than one in which recognizing the source affects the reader's understanding of the later text. Isa 45.9–15 share a tremendous amount of vocabulary with Isa 29.14–21, which include cases of sound play and word play.[89] The older vocabulary is not transformed, nor does recalling its earlier setting affect our reading of the new passage.[90]

Isaiah's Influence in the Context of Deutero-Isaianic Allusion

Deutero-Isaiah's heavy dependence on Isaiah ben Amoṣ, when considered alongside the fact that the utterances of both prophets appear on the same scroll, has led to speculation that the connection between these two prophets is particularly significant.[91] Deutero-Isaiah may have seen himself as the successor of Isaiah ben Amoṣ and his prophecies as a continuation of those in the first part of the scroll. It is possible that the exilic prophet himself appended his work to that attributed to his eighth-century predecessor. However, in light of Deutero-Isaiah's allusions to Jeremiah and to other prophets, it becomes clear that Deutero-Isaiah did not attempt to connect himself to First Isaiah in any special or unique way, and thus it does not seem likely that it was Deutero-Isaiah who brought together his own writings with those going back to Isaiah of Jerusalem.

Deutero-Isaiah's allusions to Isaiah fall into the same thematic categories as his allusions to other prophets: he confirms that the dire prophecies of his predecessors have achieved fulfillment; he reverses their tropes of condemnation to ones of comfort; he repredicts their unfulfilled prophecies (this often involves historical recontextualization, in which Deutero-Isaiah's Babylonia takes the place that Assyria held in Isaiah, Nahum, Zephaniah, and Jeremiah); he forges typological links between figures in his text and individuals or nations in the older texts. Moreover, these categories occur with similar frequency in Deutero-Isaiah's allusions to both Jeremiah and Isaiah. Cases of confirmation are relatively rare in both. Reversals are common, as are typological linkages. Repredictions are the most frequent. He restates prophecies of restoration or triumph most often, but in a small number of cases he repeats accusations or predictions of disaster from both Jeremiah and Isaiah. Further, Deutero-Isaiah repeats one prophecy from each source several times and revises that prophecy by leaving out some salient element: he recalls Isaiah 11 in numerous passages but consistently demurs regarding its vision of an enduring Davidic line, and he alludes to Jer 31.31–36 again and again but always passes over its description of a new covenant impervious to infraction. The single difference in the distribution of Deutero-Isaiah's allusions to these two prophets is found in his response to accusations and laments (a subcategory of reversal). This subcategory occurs more frequently when Deutero-Isaiah uses Jeremiah, perhaps because Isaiah's writing contains fewer laments than Jeremiah's. The exilic prophet does not refer to any one of the other prophets with great frequency (which is not surprising given the smaller extent of their writings), and thus we cannot expect that each of the thematic categories will be attested in the allusions to, say, Micah or Zephaniah. It is significant, however, that all the thematic categories (with the possible exception of confirmation, which is less common in any event) appear in the allusions to the other prophets taken as an aggregate, and that again reprediction and reversal are the most common. Not only does Deutero-Isaiah relate to the content of all these older texts in a consistent fashion; he recasts the wording from older prophets with a single set of stylistic techniques: the split-up pattern, word play, sound play, and (less often) the repetition of borrowed vocabulary in the source's order.

The resemblance between Deutero-Isaiah's allusions to Isaiah and his references to Jeremiah and other prophets indicates that no single precursor manifests a unique influence in Deutero-Isaiah's work. Deutero-Isaiah does not function merely as a disciple in an Isaianic school or a devotee in a Jeremian circle; he participates in a wider prophetic tradition, using the same techniques to recast the work of more than one predecessor in his own oracles.[92]

It is of particular importance to note that Deutero-Isaiah depends on Isaiah and Jeremiah in similar ways—but not to the same extent. His affinity to Jeremiah is stronger. This becomes evident in two ways. First, he displays a greater familiarity with the Jeremiah traditions. There are twenty-seven discrete statements[93] of Jeremiah to which Deutero-Isaiah clearly alludes, and twelve additional statements from Jeremiah to which he may allude.[94] There are only sixteen statements of Isaiah to which Deutero-Isaiah certainly alludes, and another eight to which he may allude.[95] Second, passages that contain allusions to Jeremiah are slightly more frequent than passages containing allusions to Isaiah.[96] Thirty-three passages contain allusions to Jeremiah; of these, six allude to more than one passage in Jeremiah. An additional nineteen passages may contain allusions to Jeremiah. Thirty-two passages contain allusions to Isaiah; of these, eight contain allusions to more than one passage in Isaiah. An additional four cases may contain allusions to Isaiah.

These statistics indicate a stronger connection between Deutero-Isaiah and his more immediate predecessor. What is most impressive, however, is his single method of relating to both Jeremiah and Isaiah and indeed to all his prophetic forebears. This single method demonstrates that Deutero-Isaiah did not have a unique relationship with any one prophet. His work represents a continuation of prophetic tradition generally, not an appendix to any particular collection. In the next chapter, I shall examine Deutero-Isaiah's use of the Books of Psalms and Lamentations in order to see how he appropriated a literary inheritance that included not only prophecy but also songs of praise, lament, and supplication.

4 FROM POETRY TO PROPHECY

TRANSFORMATIONS OF PSALMS AND LAMENTS

DEUTERO-ISAIAH EMPLOYS material from older prophets in order to assert his place among them to create new prophecies out of the old. At the same time, he draws on other types of Israelite and Judean texts, bringing together disparate streams of tradition, articulating their congruence, and demonstrating their vitality. Prominent among these nonprophetic sources are poetic texts: prayers, hymns, and laments known to us from the Books of Psalms and Lamentations. Deutero-Isaiah's allusions in these texts display many of the features found in his references to the prophets, at both thematic and stylistic levels. However, they also reflect other sides of his allusive venture, because the prophet's use of nonoracular material poses a special problem: how can a prediction sanctioned by the divine unfold from a human being's prayer or testimony, from a mortal's exclamation of praise or cry of woe? A survey of Deutero-Isaiah's allusions to psalms and lamentations respectively will exemplify these bold transformations of genre.

Identifying Allusions to Psalms

At the outset of Chapter 2, I discussed the problems involved in distinguishing between cases where a later writer borrows from a specific older text and cases where two writers use similar language coincidentally. Mere happenstance or common reliance on a tradition can create similarities between two texts even when one author did not utilize the other. Furthermore, questions regarding the dating of the putative source can complicate an attempt to assert that one author alludes to another. These difficulties apply with particular intensity in passages where Deutero-Isaiah may have borrowed from a psalm.[1]

The psalmists were among the most traditional of Hebrew writers. They expressed praise, lament, supplication, and wisdom by means of highly formulaic language. Thus clusters of related vocabulary and at times even whole lines appear in more than one psalm. For example, the words "Great is YHWH, and highly praised" appear in Ps 96.4 as well as Ps 145.3; the words "YHWH reigns; indeed, the world stands firm and will not totter" are found in Ps 93.1 and Ps 96.10 (in the former, an additional line separates the first clause from the rest). At times a stock idea will appear in several psalms with minor variations. Ps 29.1 reads, "Ascribe to YHWH, O divine beings, ascribe to YHWH glory and strength!" while Ps 96.7 reads "Ascribe to YHWH, O families of nations, ascribe to YHWH glory and strength!" Ps 113.4 proclaims, "Exalted is YHWH over all peoples," while Ps 99.2 announces, "He is exalted over all nations." Songs of praise, thanksgiving, lament, and supplication which appear outside the Book of Psalms also utilize stock lines. For example, Ps 113.7–8 are identical to 1 Sam 2.8a except for a minor grammatical variation; Ps 68.2 resembles Num 10.35. Some of these parallels may occur because a later writer borrowed a specific line from an older text, but in most of these cases two singers simply used stereotyped lines from a common tradition of hymnody.[2]

Deutero-Isaiah also relies on that tradition. He employs vocabulary clusters associated with the psalms, and many of his poems are based on a genre or structure known to us primarily from the Book of Psalms.[3] Consequently, comparison of Deutero-Isaiah and the Book of Psalms discloses an enormous number of parallels that cannot be classified as borrowings. For example, Deutero-Isaiah opens one passage with the words, "Sing a new song to YHWH, [sing] His praises from the ends of the earth" (Isa 42.10–11), which recalls the opening lines of Psalms 96, 98, and 149. Even though Isaiah 42 shares additional motifs with Psalms 96 and 98,[4] it is difficult to assert that the similarities result from his use of a specific text. Because the passage in which these words appear can be described form-critically as a short psalm of praise,[5] it seems likely that the authors of all these texts utilized formulaic vocabulary associated with that genre. Similarly, the theme of prayer and response, which occurs occasionally in Deutero-Isaiah as well as in many psalms, suggests certain vocabulary. Thus Isa 49.8 ("Thus says YHWH: at a time of favor [בְּעֵת רָצוֹן 'ה], I answer you [עֲנִיתִיךָ]; on the day of triumph [יְשׁוּעָה], I aid you") shares several items with Ps 69.14 ("And as for me, my prayer to you is that . . . you answer me [עֲנֵנִי], O YHWH, at a time of favor [עֵת רָצוֹן 'ה], in your reliable triumph [יִשְׁעֶךָ]"), but these shared items cannot suffice to show that Deutero-Isaiah borrowed from Psalm 69.[6]

These difficulties are compounded by uncertainty regarding the dating of individual psalms, a highly contested issue within biblical studies. Even when the relationship between a psalm and Deutero-Isaiah is strong enough to be considered a borrowing, one often does not know which text is earlier and which later. Some parallels may result from Deutero-Isaiah's influence on a psalm, rather than the other way around.[7]

Several scholars have listed parallels between Isaiah 40–66 and the Book of Psalms. Some, such as Armond Kaminka and Moshe Seidel, attribute these to the prophet's reliance on the psalmist; others, such as Yehezkel Kaufmann and John Skinner, point out similarities without describing all of them as cases of borrowing.[8] In light of the difficulties discussed above, one must approach skeptically any claim that Deutero-Isaiah relied on a particular psalm. In the following discussion, many possible examples of allusion will be passed over in silence because the parallel may result from the use of stock language or because the psalm is probably later than Deutero-Isaiah.[9]

Of course, cases in which Deutero-Isaiah uses stock psalm-language and psalm-forms themselves constitute transformations of older material, and they help us arrive at a fuller understanding of this prophet and his place in the history of Israelite religion.[10] My concern in this study, however, lies with Deutero-Isaiah's use of specific older texts. Therefore, I shall attempt to limit the following examples to cases in which Deutero-Isaiah borrows language from a particular psalm rather than ones in which he calls on stock vocabulary. At the same time, due to the acute nature of the problem of differentiating between these two types of resemblance in the use of psalms, my assertions that certain parallels represent genuine allusions must remain more tentative than the examples found in previous chapters.

Repetition of a Promise

Deutero-Isaiah's allusions to psalms do not fall into the thematic categories that typify his allusions to prophecies. This is not surprising, since psalms do not make predictions whose fulfillment Deutero-Isaiah can confirm or whose content he can reverse, alter, or repeat. Nevertheless, Deutero-Isaiah's allusions to psalms contain thematic elements reminiscent of his allusions to prophecies. For example, a psalm may contain a promise to the worshiper which Deutero-Isaiah repeats or alters (just as he repeats and alters predictions from Isaiah and Jeremiah). This occurs in the following case.

The psalmist urges people to shun evil and declares that the righteous will have well-being:

> [A righteous man] is always (כָּל־הַיּוֹם) kind. . . . Go away from evil and do good (וַעֲשֵׂה) and dwell forever (לְעוֹלָם). . . . For YHWH loves justice and does not abandon His faithful ones; they are protected eternally (לְעוֹלָם). . . . The righteous will inherit the land (צַדִּיקִים יִירְשׁוּ־אָרֶץ) and they will live on it eternally. (Ps 37.26–29)

Deutero-Isaiah uses similar vocabulary when he predicts a glorious future for the righteous of the nation:

> Not only by day (יוֹמָם) will the sun be your light. . . . Your sun will never set, nor your moon go away. For YHWH will be your eternal (עוֹלָם) light. . . . And your people—all of them righteous—will eternally inherit the land (כֻּלָּם צַדִּיקִים לְעוֹלָם יִירְשׁוּ אָרֶץ); they are a shoot that I planted, the work (מַעֲשֵׂה) of My hand in which I take pride. (Isa 60.19–21)

Because all the terms shared by these passages are fairly common in the Bible, one might doubt that Deutero-Isaiah borrowed them from the psalm specifically. On closer inspection, however, the parallel seems more impressive. The words צַדִּיק ("righteous") and יר"שׁ ("inherit") appear together only in these two verses. More importantly, words which had occurred in sequence in the psalm are split up in Deutero-Isaiah: "The righteous will inherit the land" becomes "your people—all of them *righteous—will* eternally *inherit the land*." The tendency to sever a phrase from a source into two parts by the addition of a single word or of a whole clause is one of the most prominent features of Deutero-Isaiah's allusions, as we have seen in previous chapters. Its presence here increases the probability that the similarity between the psalm and Deutero-Isaiah results from borrowing rather than mere coincidence. Finally, other verses from the psalm may also have influenced Deutero-Isaiah. The prophet refers to the nation as "a people who have My teaching in their heart (תּוֹרָתִי בְלִבָּם)" (Isa 51.7). This description calls to mind a phrase from later in this psalm: "The teaching of his God is in his heart (תּוֹרַת אֱ־לֹהָיו בְּלִבּוֹ)" (Ps 37.31). That verse also hints back to Jeremiah's idea of a covenant which the nation inevitably upholds, so that Deutero-Isaiah borrows a line from a psalm in order to summarize and alter an idea from Jeremiah.[11]

Deutero-Isaiah's prophecy restates what the psalm had promised. Thus his use of the psalm recalls Deutero-Isaianic oracles that were shaped by Isaiah's and Jeremiah's prophecies. In this case, however, the allusion has involved a change of genre: a hymn has given rise to a prophecy. Such transformations occur especially in texts concerned with one particular type of promise, the Davidic covenant. This deserves detailed attention.

Nationalization of the Promise to David

Several times Deutero-Isaiah repeats prophecies of Isaiah concerning the Davidic dynasty but broadens their scope so that they refer to the entire nation (11.1–10 // 42.1–8, 60.17–61.1, etc.). Such allusions involve typology (since they pattern the experience of the nation after that of the Davidides), reprediction, and perhaps exegesis. Deutero-Isaiah utilizes royal psalms (psalms that refer to YHWH's promises to David or his descendants) in precisely the same fashion.

Psalm 132 consists of a prayer on behalf of a Davidic king.[12] The psalmist reminds YHWH of the promises He had made to David concerning David's progeny and city:

May Your priests wear victory (כֹּהֲנֶיךָ יִלְבְּשׁוּ־צֶדֶק) and Your faithful ones exult! For the sake of Your servant David, do not turn aside from your anointed one (מְשִׁיחֶךָ)! YHWH swore to David faithfully

(אֱמֶת) . . . , "I shall place on your throne one of your offspring. If your descendants keep My covenant (בְּרִיתִי) and the laws which I teach them, their descendants also will sit on your throne for eternity. For YHWH has chosen Zion, He desires it as His seat. . . . I shall certainly bless (בָּרֵךְ אֲבָרֵךְ) its food supply, and I shall satisfy its poor with sustenance. I shall let its priests wear salvation (וְכֹהֲנֶיהָ אַלְבִּישׁ יֶשַׁע). . . . I shall make success flourish (אַצְמִיחַ) for David; I have set up a lamp for My anointed one (לִמְשִׁיחִי). I shall make his enemies wear humiliation (אַלְבִּישׁ בֹּשֶׁת), and the crown will glimmer on him." (Ps 132.9–18)

Deutero-Isaiah uses many of the same terms as he describes the future well-being and exaltation of the nation as a whole:

The spirit of the Lord YHWH is on me, for He has anointed (מָשַׁח) me to bring good news to the lowly, . . . to give the mourners of Zion a turban rather than dust.[13] . . . The ancient ruins will be built, . . . and the ruined cities renewed. . . . And you will be called, 'the priests (כֹּהֲנֵי) of YHWH'. . . . You will consume the wealth of nations. . . . Because they were put to shame (בָּשְׁתְּכֶם) doubly and inherited[14] contempt as their portion, therefore they will inherit doubly in their land. I shall reward you faithfully (בֶּאֱמֶת) and establish an eternal covenant (וּבְרִית) with them. And their seed will be known among the nations . . . for they are seed whom YHWH has blessed (בֵּרַךְ). I rejoice greatly in YHWH . . . for He has let me wear a garment of salvation (הִלְבִּישַׁנִי בִּגְדֵי־יֶשַׁע); He covers me with victory (צְדָקָה), [making me] like a bridegroom who sports (יְכַהֵן) a turban or a bride decked out in her jewelry. For as the land brings out its vegetation (צִמְחָהּ), and as a garden lets a thing sown flourish (תַצְמִיחַ), so the Lord YHWH will allow victory to flourish (יַצְמִיחַ צְדָקָה) along with praise before all the nations. (Isa 61.1–11)

Not only do these passages share ample vocabulary, but they both refer to certain themes as well. The psalm focuses on YHWH's choice of Zion as well as on the Davidides. Though the word "Zion" does not appear in Isaiah 61, the chapter nonetheless refers to that city: it mentions the rebuilding of ancient ruins and renewed priestly service in them; of course, priests served in Zion.[15] Both texts express a concern for the poor and lowly, though the words used to describe them differ. Finally, both refer to royal headdress: the psalm speaks of a crown (נִזְרוֹ) and the prophecy of a turban (פְּאֵר). The abundance of shared vocabulary and themes begins to suggest that the parallel is no mere happenstance. A typical stylistic feature of Deutero-Isaianic allusion adds to the impression that the prophet borrowed from the psalmist. The psalm includes the clause יִלְבְּשׁוּ־צֶדֶק ("wear victory"). Similar words appear in Deutero-Isaiah, but there they are split apart by intervening words (one of which appeared later in the psalm) so that they are part of two separate clauses: הִלְבִּישַׁנִי בִּגְדֵי־יֶשַׁע מְעִיל צְדָקָה יְעָטָנִי ("He has let me *wear* a garment of salvation; He covers me with *victory*").[16] This line also splits apart a clause which occurred later in the psalm, אַלְבִּישׁ יֶשַׁע ("I shall let [its priests] wear salvation").

If the presence of this stylistic pattern strongly suggests a borrowing, the relationship between the passages on a thematic level confirms it. These verses recall Deutero-Isaiah's allusions to the predictions of Isaiah ben Amos regarding the Davidic dynasty: the promises vouchsafed to David and his descendants in the psalm are transferred to the nation as a whole in Deutero-Isaiah. According to the psalmist, a covenant is made with David and his offspring. But in Deutero-Isaiah the covenant is with the nation. Similarly, the psalm describes the Davidic ruler as wearing a crown, while in Deutero-Isaiah it is the mourners of Zion and the speaker, not the royal family, who receive turbans. Not only do the people acquire royal prerogatives; they are also described as YHWH's "priests." An additional transfer of royal and priestly motifs occurs in the beginning of the passage, where a speaker (who is either the prophet himself[17] or the servant introduced earlier in the book,[18] which most likely depicts the nation Israel) announces that he has been anointed; the king was anointed in the psalm. Further, the speaker in Isaiah 61 is the subject of the verb יכהן ("to wear a turban"), which suggests his priestly status, since the same root provides the noun "priest." The final verses of the chapter make the surrender of royal and priestly motifs to the nation particularly clear. In Ps 132.17 YHWH causes salvation to flourish for David. This wording is repeated in Deutero-Isaiah, but without the reference to David; there YHWH causes victory to flourish for the speaker. In the psalm YHWH clothes the priests with victory, but in Deutero-Isaiah the speaker wears salvation.

The covenant described in the psalm is revised in an important way. The psalm's covenant is couched in conditional language: "If your descendants keep My covenant (בריתי) and the laws which I teach them, their descendants also will sit on your throne for eternity."[19] But Deutero-Isaiah eliminates any reference to conditionality in the agreement between Israel and YHWH. Instead, he stresses that the covenant is an eternal one (ברית עולם). By so doing, the prophet brings the vocabulary borrowed from Psalm 132 into agreement with the Davidic promise as it appears in most other texts, such as Psalm 89 or 2 Samuel 7, where that covenant is unconditional. As elsewhere in his messages to the post-destruction audience, Deutero-Isaiah emphasizes the people's ongoing relationship with YHWH while ignoring the element of contingency and its threat that God will punish the nation or even renounce the covenant. The audience, after all, had already experienced the punishment, so there was no reason to stress it; and the prophet denies that YHWH ever would overturn His promises.

A similar affinity between a psalm concerning the Davidic dynasty and a chapter in Deutero-Isaiah bearing on the nation as a whole occurs in several passages that depend on Psalm 72: Isa 44.28–45.8, 49.7–23, and 60.1–21. These allusions omit any reference to the Davidic dynasty. What happens to the king in the psalm provides the pattern for what happens to the people as a whole in the later texts. In the psalm, the foreign rulers bow down before the king, but in Deutero-Isaiah they pay obeisance either to the city of Jerusalem or to the people as a whole. Thus the allusions underscore once again the absence of a king in Deutero-Isaiah's view of the post-exilic period. The allusions also involve shifts of genre, as Psalm 72's prayer yields Deutero-Isaiah's predictions or prophecies.[20]

In one allusion, Deutero-Isaiah asserts that Davidic prerogatives are vouchsafed to a foreign king as well. In Psalm 2 YHWH declared His special favor for David and his descendants:

Why do the nations (גּוֹיִם) rage and the peoples utter emptiness? The kings of the earth (מַלְכֵי־אֶרֶץ) take their stand . . . against YHWH and against His anointed one (מְשִׁיחוֹ). . . . The one who sits in heaven laughs (בַּשָּׁמַיִם יִשְׂחָק) at them. . . . He speaks to them in anger: "I have anointed My king (מַלְכִּי) on Zion, My holy mountain." Let me tell you of YHWH's edict: He said to me, "You are My son; I have given birth to you. Ask it of Me, and I will give you nations as an inheritance (וְאֶתְּנָה גוֹיִם), the whole earth as your portion (וַאֲחֻזָּתְךָ אַפְסֵי־אָרֶץ). You can shatter them (תְּרֹעֵם) with an iron (בַּרְזֶל) rod; you will demolish them like a potter's (יוֹצֵר) vessel." Now, beware, you kings (מְלָכִים)! Take discipline (הִוָּסְרוּ), rulers of the earth (אָרֶץ)! (Ps 2.1–10)

Deutero-Isaiah uses similar language as he describes Cyrus's position in relation to other kings and to YHWH:

Thus says YHWH . . . who fulfills the word of His servant . . . and says that Jerusalem will be inhabited . . . who calls Cyrus, "My shepherd" (רֹעִי). . . . Thus says YHWH to His anointed one (לִמְשִׁיחוֹ), to Cyrus, whose right hand I have grasped (הֶחֱזַקְתִּי) as I tread down nations (גוֹיִם) before him and ungird kings (מְלָכִים) . . . : I shall go before you and make your path[21] straight (אֲיַשֵּׁר). I shall break bronze doors and hew down iron (בַרְזֶל) bars. I shall give (וְנָתַתִּי) you treasures of darkness . . . so that you will know that I, YHWH, am the one who summons you, the God of Israel, for the sake of My servant, Jacob, and My chosen one, Israel . . . so that they will know from east to west that there is none (אֶפֶס) besides Me. . . . I form (יוֹצֵר) everything from light to darkness, I create everything from well-being to harm (רָע). . . . Let victory flow from heaven (שָׁמַיִם) above; from clouds (וּשְׁחָקִים) let it stream. Let the land (אָרֶץ) be fruitful with salvation as victory flourishes. (Isa 44.24–45.8)

In addition to the vocabulary items noted in parentheses, the passages share themes that each expresses using different language. Ps 2.8 mentions the spoils of war, an idea present in Isa 45.3. In both Ps 2.9 and Isa 45.1–2, a king destroys his adversaries. Ps 2.10 speaks of kings recognizing YHWH; Isa 45.3 speaks of the nations doing same.

Some of the terms these passages share characterize ancient Near Eastern royal texts generally: "my shepherd," "grasp with a hand," and of course "king." Others appear frequently throughout the Hebrew Bible: "evil/harm," "heaven," "nation," "give." The parallel terms as they appear in Deutero-Isaiah, however, display typical features of Deutero-Isaianic allusion: the split-up pattern, sound play, and word play. The psalm describes YHWH's laughter with the clause יוֹשֵׁב בַּשָּׁמַיִם יִשְׂחָק ("the one who sits in the heavens laughs [yishaq]"). The last two words become the subject of both sound play and the split-up pattern, as Deutero-Isaiah calls on the skies to stream with victory: הַרְעִיפוּ שָׁמַיִם מִמַּעַל וּשְׁחָקִים יִזְּלוּ־צֶדֶק ("Let victory flow from *heaven* above; from *clouds* [*u-sh'ḥaqim*] let it stream"). The psalm's יִשְׂחַק ("laughs") is replaced with a similar-sounding but completely unrelated word, וּשְׁחָקִים ("clouds"). The two words which were together in the psalm are separated by the word "above," so that what had been part of a single clause in the psalm is spread over two clauses in Deutero-Isaiah. The word הֶחֱזַקְתִּי (*heh'zaqti*, "I grasped") in the allusion hints back at the source's אֲחֻזָּתֶךָ (*'aḥuzzatka*, "your portion") since they share several sounds: the letters *zayin*, *ḥēt*, and *tāw* along with an unvoiced velar consonant (an emphatic one in Deutero-Isaiah [*qōf*] and a non-emphatic one in the psalm [*kaf*])[22] and an unvoiced glottal consonant at the beginning of the word (a stop ['ālef] in the psalm, and a fricative [*hê*] in Deutero-Isaiah). The word תְּרֹעֵם (*t'ro'eim*, "shatter") in the source produces two words in the allusion by means of sound play: רֹעִי (*ro'i*, "shepherd") and רַע (*ra'*, "evil, harm").[23] In light of the abundant stylistic features that characterize the shared vocabulary, one can confidently assert that Deutero-Isaiah borrowed from Psalm 2 specifically.

While Deutero-Isaiah often reapplies Davidic promises to the nation, here they are bequeathed to the Persian king, Cyrus. The transfer of Davidic blessings to Cyrus matches Deutero-Isaiah's reference to him as מָשִׁיחַ ("messiah, anointed one"; see Isa 45.1), a term normally reserved in the Hebrew Bible for an Israelite king or priest. According to the psalm, the Davidic king was to have acquired dominion to "the ends of the earth" through his divinely aided warfare; according to Deutero-Isaiah, it is Cyrus whom YHWH will aid, so that nations throughout the world will be trampled down and kings will surrender before him. Thus the career of the Davidide in the psalm provides the prototype for Cyrus's experience in the later text. The source and the allusion both display a concern with widespread recognition of YHWH. In the psalm, foreign kings are warned that they should recognize YHWH and His anointed. In Deutero-Isaiah, YHWH announces that He has chosen Cyrus to return the exiles to Zion so that the nations will recognize the work of YHWH. The promises of Psalm 2 are reapplied to Cyrus in order that the people achieve their royal state; Cyrus's victory is for the sake of Israel (v.4f.). Even in this example, the formerly Davidic covenant that is now applied to a foreign king redounds to the favor of Israel as a whole.

Deutero-Isaiah again reassigns the Davidic covenant to the nation in Isa 55.1–5. These verses contain many terms that they share with both 2 Samuel

7 and Psalm 89; the psalm (as Sarna has shown) itself depends on the passage from Samuel.[24] As a result, it is difficult to ascertain whether Deutero-Isaiah alludes to one or both of these texts. His transformation of the themes found in the earlier texts has been described excellently by O. Eissfeldt, whose discussion need not be repeated here.[25] What Eissfeldt found in regard to Isaiah 55 coincides with what we have seen elsewhere. For example, both Psalm 89 and Isaiah 55 use the terms "chosen one" and "servant" to describe a figure who enjoys a close relationship with YHWH, but that figure is the king in the former text and the nation in the latter.[26] As in his use of Psalms 132 and 72, Deutero-Isaiah transforms the prayer in Psalm 89 into a prophecy; as in his use of Psalm 2, he recasts the promise of 2 Samuel 7 as a prediction.

All these passages suggest the question, how does Deutero-Isaiah view the royal family? Other exilic and post-exilic authors remained loyal to the Davidic dynasty and anticipated their return to the throne.[27] That Deutero-Isaiah nowhere refers to a king in the renewed commonwealth intimates that he did not look forward to a restoration of the monarchy.[28] Deutero-Isaiah's allusions to Davidic promises nullify the special status of the royal family, since the whole people now share in what had been the Davidides' unique relationship with YHWH. This question is bound up with another issue: the literary classification of Deutero-Isaiah's appropriation of Davidic material generally. By transferring promises from the royal family to the nation, Deutero-Isaiah engages not merely in allusion but in revision. As he depends on his sources, he implicitly argues against them: yes, YHWH has established an unbreakable covenant, but not (only) with the Davidides. The psalmists, like Isaiah ben Amoṣ, understood only part of the divine message. Deutero-Isaiah's attitude toward his source is not polemical; on the contrary, his use of the psalms start from the presupposition (his and his audience's) that the older texts are sacred. But that sacrality does not prevent him from altering ideas that might mislead.

One might, conversely, argue that Deutero-Isaiah's references constitute not revisions but interpretations of the psalms. The borrowed elements call older texts to the listener's mind, and the older texts now become associated with a new message. As the new text draws items from its sources, it deposits new meaning into them. Such an argument, I think, seems stretched. If the exilic prophet intended his work to act as commentary, it does so in an exceedingly subtle fashion.

The impetus behind this revision is clear. In Deutero-Isaiah's day, one could easily have argued that God's promise to the Davidides, expressed unambiguously in the psalms, had been broken (primarily as a result of human infractions). But Deutero-Isaiah does not do this. As Eissfeldt points out,[29] in Isa 55.4 the prophet notes that David (or one of his descendants, whether Solomon, Hezekiah, or Josiah) indeed became what 2 Sam 7.8 promised: a ruler and a leader of nations. He asserts that the promise to David has already been fulfilled. Thus the defeat of the Davidic rulers at the hands of the Babylonians does not mean that YHWH went back on His word; He had previously implemented it, and now He will extend it further. Deutero-Isaiah avoids nullifying the promises to David as they had appeared in the psalms and the prophecies of Isaiah ben Amoṣ by reinventing them as a promise to the nation as a whole. The older texts had to be updated, lest the tradition they represent become enmeshed in the collapse of the Davidic dynasty.

Response

In the previous section, we saw that Deutero-Isaiah alludes to laments containing prayers on behalf of the Davidic ruler, such as Psalm 89 and Psalm 132. In so doing, he provides a response to those laments, assuring the listeners that YHWH would rouse Himself to act on behalf of His people. Deutero-Isaiah also utilizes other texts in which a psalmist pleaded for help or confessed his sins. The prophet reacts to the personal prayers of the psalms on a national level, as if the individual "I" of the psalms stood for the collective "we" of the exiles.[30]

Deutero-Isaiah employs vocabulary known to us from several laments as he predicts that YHWH will answer prayers favorably. However, due to the widespread nature of stock lament vocabulary, it is often impossible to assert that Deutero-Isaiah depended on a particular text; he may have drawn upon wording traditionally used by those in need, recasting it by incorporating it in a prophecy rather than a prayer.[31]

At times, however, a passage from Deutero-Isaiah and a psalm share additional vocabulary items that are not characteristic of the lament genre, and the shared items display typical features of Deutero-Isaianic allusion. This increases the likelihood that the similarities result from Deutero-Isaiah's use of the specific text from the Book of Psalms. For example, Isaiah

46 contains a great deal of vocabulary which occurs in the personal lament in Psalm 71:

> May you rescue me through your righteousness (בְּצִדְקָתְךָ) and re-deem me (וּתְפַלְּטֵנִי)! Listen to me and save me (וְהוֹשִׁיעֵנִי). . . . My God, redeem me (פַּלְּטֵנִי) from an evil one. . . . I have depended on You since I was in the womb (מִבֶּטֶן); since I was in my mother's belly, You have been my protector. . . . My mouth will be filled with Your praises, with Your glory (תִּפְאַרְתֶּךָ) at all times. . . . Do not cast me off when I become old (זִקְנָה); when my strength fails, do not leave me! For my enemies spoke of me, and those who want to take my life have conspired (נוֹעֲצוּ) together, saying, "God has abandoned him—chase him, grab him, for none will rescue him!" O God, do not be distant from me (אַל־תִּרְחַק מִמֶּנִּי). . . . My mouth will tell of your righteous-ness (צִדְקָתֶךָ) always, of your salvation (תְּשׁוּעָתֶךָ). . . . I shall tell of Your unique righteousness (צִדְקָתֶךָ). . . . Even in old age, when I have gray hair (עַד־זִקְנָה וְשֵׂיבָה), do not abandon me, O God. . . . Your righteousness (וְצִדְקָתְךָ), O God, is without limit. You have performed wonders, O God; who is like You (כָמוֹךָ)? (Ps 71.2–19)

Similar concerns and vocabulary appear in Deutero-Isaiah:

> Listen to Me, O House of Jacob! . . . who were carried since you were in the womb (מִנִּי־בֶטֶן), who were borne from the time you were in the belly! Until you are old (וְעַד־זִקְנָה), I am He; until you are gray (וְעַד־שֵׂיבָה), I shall bear you. I did [it then] and I shall carry [you now]; I shall bear [you] and rescue (וַאֲמַלֵּט) [you]. To whom might you compare Me? . . . To one who is carried on [human] shoulders and borne, and placed down so that it will stand and not move? Let one cry out to it—it will not answer! Even when [the caller is] in distress, it will not save him (יוֹשִׁיעֶנּוּ)! . . . For I am God, and there are no gods beside Me; none is like Me (כָמוֹנִי) . . . who says, "My plan (עֲצָתִי) shall come true. . . ," who calls an eagle from the east, the man brought on by His plan (עֲצָתוֹ) from a far country (מֶרְחָק). . . . Listen to Me . . . you who are distant from victory (הָרְחוֹקִים מִצְּדָקָה): I bring My victory (צִדְקָתִי) near; it is not distant (תִרְחָק). My salvation (וּתְשׁוּעָתִי)

will not tarry. I shall give salvation (תְּשׁוּעָה) to Zion and My glory (תִּפְאַרְתִּי) to Israel. (Isa 46.3–13)

Initially, it may seem unlikely that the latter passage depends on the earlier, because some of the words they share are very common. But a comparison of the use of the terms in each passage yields a repeated pattern. YHWH in Deutero-Isaiah grants the people the boons which the psalmist requested or for which he praised God. The psalmist appealed to God's צדקה (used there in the sense of "righteousness"), while Deutero-Isaiah announces that YHWH will soon bring צדקה (meaning "victory" here) to the nation. The individual in the psalm hoped to acknowledge God's salvation (תשועה), while Deutero-Isaiah announces its imminent arrival. The psalmist praised God's glory (תפארתך); in Deutero-Isaiah God gives His glory (תפארתי) to the people. A similar pattern of response appears in other items as well. The psalmist begged, "O God, do not be distant from me." Deutero-Isaiah has God acknowledge that He has distanced the people from His salvation ("Listen to Me . . . you who are distant from victory"), but He also reassures them, saying, "I bring My victory near; it is not distant." The psalmist pleaded, "Rescue me (פלטני)," and goes on immediately to remind God that God had supported him in the past. In Deutero-Isaiah God recalls that in the past He (She?) had carried the people in the womb, and continues by assuring the people God will uphold them now: "I shall bear [you] and rescue (ואמלט) [you]." Here Deutero-Isaiah employs sound play as he replaces the psalm's פלטני (pallᵉṭeini) with the similar sounding אמלט (ᵃmalleiṭ). The rhetoric of response is most evident in Isa 46.4. The psalmist prayed, "Even in old age, when I have gray hair, do not abandon me, O God." In Deutero-Isaiah YHWH proclaims, "Until you are old, I am He; until you are gray, I shall bear you." These lines furthermore display the split-up pattern as עַד־זִקְנָה וְשֵׂיבָה ("Until old age and gray hair") becomes וְעַד־זִקְנָה אֲנִי הוּא וְעַד־שֵׂיבָה אֲנִי אֶסְבֹּל ("*Until old age*, I am He, *and until gray hair*, I shall bear you").

Other themes are shared by the passages as well. The idea of planning, expressed by the root יע״ץ, appears in both texts, but its significance is reversed. In the psalm, the enemies planned together (נוֹעֲצוּ) to cause the psalmist's downfall. In the later text the root refers to a foreigner but not an enemy. Now the object of YHWH's irrevocable plan ("the man brought on by His plan" [עצתו]) is Cyrus, the foreign king who will bring the people's restoration. The large number of shared terms (some of them, to be sure, common words) which do not appear together elsewhere suggests that the similarities between these two passages are no coincidence. In view of the split-up pattern and the consistent thematic transformation that a comparison of the terms reveals, it becomes clear that Deutero-Isaiah utilized Psalm 71 specifically.[32]

Deutero-Isaiah introduces a number of important changes as he borrows. The psalm is a personal lament, but Deutero-Isaiah appropriates it as if the speaker were the nation Israel. The figure of the womb is used in a startling way. In the psalm, God had been the psalmist's protector since the psalmist's mother was pregnant with him ("since I was in my mother's belly, You have been my protector"). Deutero-Isaiah rearranges the image, however, so that God is the mother: YHWH carried the nation in the womb ("O House of Jacob! . . . who were carried since you were in the womb, who were borne from the time you were in the belly! . . . I shall bear you. I did [it then] and I shall carry [you now]"). As elsewhere in his work, Deutero-Isaiah provides here a reason for God's reliability that goes beyond a covenant or contractual relationship that can be broken by one side. YHWH, as Israel's mother,[33] is bound irrevocably to the nation and will never fully forsake it. Indeed, YHWH is a unique sort of mother: while typically the roles between parent and child reverse, so that the grown child must care for the aged parents, YHWH will never cease to care for Her child; She will continue to carry Israel even into old age.[34]

Repetition and Echo

Deutero-Isaiah repeats the message and vocabulary of some psalms with minor variations. In these cases, his use of the older material comes close to the category of mere echo, since it is not always clear that recognizing the source affects one's reading of the new text. However, some transformations of the older material can be noted, so that the markers do not appear gratuitously.

In Psalm 82 we read the following statement about the אלהים (divine beings) who are being judged:

They don't know, they don't understand (לֹא יָדְעוּ וְלֹא יָבִינוּ). They go round and around in darkness—and all the foundations of the earth totter (יִמּוֹטוּ כָּל־מוֹסְדֵי אָרֶץ)! I had thought, "You are gods, you are all sons of Elyon." But in fact you will die like humans; you will fall like any of the princes. Rise up, O God, and judge the earth (שָׁפְטָה הָאָרֶץ), for You possess all the nations (בְּכָל־הַגּוֹיִם). (Ps 82.5–8)

Similar elements appear in Deutero-Isaiah as the prophet attempts to convince the exiles that YHWH is mightier than the empires that seemingly control their fate:

All the nations (כָּל־הַגּוֹיִם) are like nothing before Him. . . . To whom would you compare God, and what likeness would you set up in comparison to Him? . . . A skilled artificer seeks to establish for himself an idol that will not totter (יִמּוֹט). Don't you know (הֲלוֹא תֵדְעוּ)? Did you not hear? Was it not told to you from the beginning? Don't you understand (הֲלוֹא הֲבִינֹתֶם) the foundations of the earth (מוֹסְדוֹת הָאָרֶץ)? The one who sits above the vault of the earth so that its inhabitants are like grasshoppers, . . . who overturns leaders— He has made the rulers of the earth (שֹׁפְטֵי אֶרֶץ) into nothing. (Isa 40.17–23)

That Deutero-Isaiah depends on the psalm is clear from several factors. The terms they share are not exclusively associated with a single theme, nor do they constitute a stock vocabulary cluster. The split-up pattern is evident: a phrase from one sentence ("tottering are all the foundations of the earth") is divided into two parts: "A skilled artificer seeks . . . an idol that will not *totter*. . . . Don't you understand *the foundations of the earth*?" The first half of the split-up phrase becomes the conclusion of one set of verses (Isa 40.19–20, which describe the idolaters). The second becomes the central point of the next set of verses (Isa 40.21–24, which describe YHWH's role as creator). As in many other Deutero-Isaianic allusions, the words that break up the phrases are also markers: "they don't know, they don't understand," from the psalm become "Don't you know . . . don't you understand" in Deutero-Isaiah.[35]

A number of themes in the pericope in Isaiah 40 restate those of Psalm 82.

The passage in Deutero-Isaiah shares with the psalm a concern for the issue of a divine court. Psalm 82 distinguishes between God and any members of an alleged pantheon. A similar idea makes a subtle appearance in Deutero-Isaiah as well. Isa 40.18 stresses that none can be compared to YHWH. Moshe Weinfeld has shown that this verse is part of Deutero-Isaiah's polemic against several aspects of the priestly creation account in Genesis 1.[36] As Weinfeld demonstrates, this verse opposes the notion that divine or angelic advisers were present at the creation along with YHWH. Thus in this pericope the prophet at once argues against Gen 1.26, which hints at the existence of a heavenly council headed by YHWH, and alludes approvingly to Psalm 82, which attempts to put members of the pantheon in their proper—which is to say, lowly—place. The confluence of sources here is not likely to be a coincidence. Writers often bolster the authority of a new work by demonstrating their dependence on texts that are already respected; an attempt to reinforce one's legitimacy within a tradition constitutes one of the most commonly cited reasons for allusion. As Deutero-Isaiah disputes with one older text (Gen 1.26), he may have felt an acute need to appropriate authority from another one (Psalm 82). By echoing a psalm even as he argues against the priestly writer of Genesis 1, the prophet shows that his polemic against the idea of a pantheon is not altogether new and demonstrates that he remains part of the tradition, in which a debate such as this can and does occur.

Psalm 82 and this pericope in Deutero-Isaiah share one additional theme: a concern with human leadership as it relates to the divine. As Matitiahu Tsevat has argued,[37] the speaker in Psalm 82 comes to the realization that the other divine beings are like mortals, that God can vanquish them as he vanquishes any mortal king. This idea is expressed especially in Ps 82.7–8: "All of you will die like humans; you will fall like any of the princes. Rise up, O God, and judge the earth (שפטה הארץ), for You possess all the nations." Deutero-Isaiah reuses this vocabulary as he stresses that YHWH brings leaders and rulers to naught: "The one who overturns leaders—He has made the rulers of the earth (שפטי ארץ) into nothing." The exilic author further appropriates the end of Ps 82.8, with its reference to "all the nations" whom God controls. The prophet stresses that "all the nations are like nothing before Him." Deutero-Isaiah simply reiterates theological statements of his predecessor, just as he repeats prophecies of Isaiah and Jeremiah elsewhere.[38]

Deutero-Isaiah also echoes themes and language found in Psalm 81, which contains YHWH's grievance over the people's failure to be loyal to Him despite the many boons He gave them:

God placed a statute in Joseph when He went forth against (בְּצֵאתוֹ) the land of Egypt. [YHWH complains:] "I heard (אֶשְׁמָע) a speech I did not recognize. . . . In distress you called, and I saved you. I answered you in a secret place (בְּסֵתֶר) of thunder. . . . Listen (שְׁמַע), O nation, and I will admonish you; O Israel—if you just listen to me (תִּשְׁמַע־לִי)! You will have no strange god; you will not bow down to a foreign god. I, YHWH, am your God, who led you up from the land of Egypt. . . . And yet My people did not listen (וְלֹא־שָׁמַע) to My voice. . . . If only My people would listen to Me (לוּ . . . שֹׁמֵעַ לִי)! If only Israel would walk in My paths (בִּדְרָכַי יְהַלֵּכוּ)! I would soon (כִּמְעַט) make their enemies bow down. . . ." Those who hate YHWH will cringe before Him; their appointed time (עִתָּם) will not end. He fed[39] him [Israel] the best part of the wheat; "I sated you with honey drawn from a rock (וּמִצּוּר)!" (Ps 81.6–17)

The psalm calls to mind a passage from Deutero-Isaiah:

Listen to Me (שְׁמַע אֵלַי), O Jacob, and Israel whom I call. . . . Gather together and listen (וּשְׁמָעוּ)! Who among you foretold this? The one whom YHWH loves is executing His will against Babylon. . . . Draw near and listen (שִׁמְעוּ): I did not speak of this in secret (בַּסֵּתֶר) from of old; from the time (מֵעֵת) it began, I was there. . . . Thus says YHWH your redeemer, the Holy One of Israel: I, YHWH, am your God who teaches you for your benefit, who guides you on the path you will take (מַדְרִיכֲךָ בְּדֶרֶךְ תֵּלֵךְ). If only (לוּא) you had paid attention to My commands, your well-being would have been like a river, your victory like the waves of the sea; your seed would have been like the sand, and the offspring of your loins like its granules (כִּמְעֹתָיו[40]). . . . Get out (צְאוּ) of Babylon! . . . With a joyous voice announce this, make it known (הַשְׁמִיעוּ)! Let it go forth (הוֹצִיאוּהָ) to the ends of the earth; say: YHWH has redeemed His servant Jacob! They will not be thirsty in the dry places where He leads them (הוֹלִיכָם); He makes water flow from a rock (מָצּוּר) for them. (Isa 48.12–21)[41]

Much of the shared vocabulary concerns the issue of obedience, while other items are connected to the theme of the Exodus and desert wanderings, and thus these terms on their own cannot demonstrate the presence of a borrowing. The presence of sound play, however, increases the likelihood that Deutero-Isaiah relied on the psalm: the psalm's כמעט (kim'aṭ, "soon, immediately") yields the word כמעתיו (kim⁺otaw, "like granules, grains of sand") in Deutero-Isaiah.

Deutero-Isaiah borrows elements from the source which referred to the Exodus from Egypt and God's guidance of the people through the Sinai desert. He uses these elements to refer to the nation's imminent departure from Babylon and their journey through the Syrian desert. Thus, in his echoing of Psalm 81, as in his use of the Exodus theme elsewhere, Deutero-Isaiah forges a typological link between the two events, suggesting that the people can understand the return to the land of Israel in light of the great historical event of the past.[42] By recalling YHWH's sustenance in the desert, Deutero-Isaiah allays the fears of his listeners, whom he urges to journey through the desert to the land of Israel. Deutero-Isaiah repeats YHWH's complaint regarding the people's lack of obedience, but he refers exclusively to past infractions and their results, while the psalmist spoke of both past and future sins.[43] As he alters his source's language, Deutero-Isaiah shifts the focus from a general threat to an explanation of a specific calamity: he justifies the exile to his listeners, lest they conclude that it demonstrates a lack of either desire or ability on YHWH's part to save them. Some of the markers are used in entirely new ways: the psalmist uses the words הלך and דרך together as an idiom meaning "to obey" (בדרך הלך); the subject of the verb there is the nation who fails to follow YHWH's commands. In Deutero-Isaiah these words are used in a literal sense: the nation will walk (תלך) on a path (דרך) guided by YHWH.

The borrowing also includes elements of exegesis. The prophet stresses, against one possible understanding of the psalm, that YHWH did not speak His prophecies in secret, but that He predicted the downfall of Babylon publicly, so that His people have no reason to doubt His power to foretell or to save. Another exegetical reworking may occur in the sound play involving the words כמעט (kim'aṭ) and כמעתיו (kim⁺otaw). In the psalm, כמעט indicates that God will respond to Israel's covenant obedience quickly, by making her enemies cringe "soon" or "immediately." When Deutero-Isaiah imitates the sound of this word with the word כמעתיו ("like grains of sand"), he may suggest we read the psalm's כמעט to have another meaning more similar to כמעתיו: "as a small thing." This would yield the following translation of Ps 81.15: "If only Israel would walk in My paths, I would make their enemies bow down like some small thing." The exilic prophet may have preferred this reading of the psalm because it describes real events more accurately: Babylon, Israel's enemy, will indeed cringe before Cyrus "like a small thing" (rather than a great empire); but this hoped-for event did not happen "immediately" upon Israel's repentance in the exile. The sound play Deutero-Isaiah employs in this borrowing helps clarify what to him is the correct message of the psalm and of history: though the mills of God grind exceedingly small, yet they grind slowly.[44]

Deutero-Isaiah and the Book of Lamentations

Scholars including Yehezkel Kaufmann and Norman Gottwald have argued that Deutero-Isaiah was influenced by the Book of Lamentations.[45] We have seen that Deutero-Isaiah reverses laments found in the Books of Jeremiah and Psalms, and thus it is no surprise to discover that he approaches material from the Book of Lamentations in the same way. Nonetheless, an assertion that Deutero-Isaiah knew a specific passage from the Book of Lamentations can pose several problems. Deutero-Isaiah responds to despondent comments of the exiles (Isa 40.27, 49.14, 50.1), and (as Westermann points out) he patterns some proclamations after the form of a lament.[46] Because the lament genre in ancient Israel typically included certain vocabulary, it is difficult to assert that verbal affinities between the Book of Lamentations and Deutero-Isaiah result from borrowing.[47] Some parallels, however, involve terminology not associated with lament traditions, so that we may consider them to demonstrate Deutero-Isaiah's use of Lamentations. In addition, certain parallels display typical features of Deutero-Isaianic allusion, and this further strengthens the claim that Deutero-Isaiah utilized not only vocabulary clusters that happen to be found in the Book of Lamentations, but texts from that book as well.[48]

For example, a passage toward the end of Deutero-Isaiah's corpus resembles the following comment in Lam 2.17–19:

[YHWH] has made the enemy (אוֹיֵב) rejoice over you. . . . O wall (חוֹמַת) of Zion, let your tears flow like a river day and night (יוֹמָם וָלַיְלָה)! Do not give yourself any break (לָךְ אַל־תִּתְּנִי פוּגַת), let not your eyes rest (אַל־תִּדֹּם בַּת־עֵינֵךְ)! Get up, sing during the night (בַלַּיְל), at the beginning of the watches (אַשְׁמֻרוֹת), pour out your heart like water in the presence of my Lord. (Lam 2.17–19)

Similar vocabulary appears in Deutero-Isaiah:

I shall set watchmen (שֹׁמְרִים) on your walls (חוֹמֹתַיִךְ), O Jerusalem, all day and night (כָּל־הַיּוֹם וְכָל־הַלַּיְלָה); those who mention YHWH will never be silent—you should have no rest (אַל־דֳּמִי לָכֶם). And do not give Him rest (וְאַל־תִּתְּנוּ דֳמִי לוֹ) until He establishes and makes Jerusalem a glorious place in the land. YHWH has sworn . . . "I shall never give your grain as food to your enemies (לְאֹיְבַיִךְ)." (Isa 62.6–7)

The shared vocabulary is not associated with the lament tradition. It follows that the similarity between these passages points to a case of genuine allusion.

Deutero-Isaiah reverses the lament: in Lamentations the wall of Jerusalem is told to weep day and night, to give itself no rest as it mourns the loss of YHWH's protection and the enemy's victory. In Deutero-Isaiah, Jerusalem is told that it will have well-guarded walls, for God will never again give the enemy license to destroy. In Lamentations the lack of rest was negative: Zion mourns ceaselessly. But in Deutero-Isaiah the absence of rest is positive, a figure of vigilance: the watchmen will not rest because they guarantee the city's safety day and night. Further, YHWH Himself will not rest until the city is fully rebuilt.[49] The allusion involves one other minor change: Deutero-Isaiah replaces the rare word פוגת from Lamentations (which means "benumbing, cessation") with the more familiar דמי (which also means "rest, cessation").

The same text in Lamentations resembles another passage elsewhere in Deutero-Isaiah. In order to note the similarities, it is necessary to examine several additional verses in the source:

What shall I compare to you, O daughter Jerusalem (יְרוּשָׁלַםִ), what shall I liken to you that I might comfort you (וַאֲנַחֲמֵךְ), O maiden

Zion? Your injury (שִׁבְרֵךְ) is as enormous as the sea! Who will heal you (מִי יִרְפָּא־לָךְ)? . . . All your enemies gape at you . . . saying, "We have swallowed them up! Oh! this is the day we have waited for—it has come (מָצָאנוּ), we have seen it!" . . . Get up (קוּמִי), sing during the night, at the beginning of the watches, pour out your heart like water in the presence of my Lord . . . for the life of your infants, who fainted (הָעֲטוּפִים) in hunger (בְּרָעָב) at the top of all the streets (בְּרֹאשׁ כָּל־חוּצוֹת). (Lam 2.13–19)

The same vocabulary appears in Deutero-Isaiah:

Arise, arise, get up (קוּמִי), O Jerusalem (יְרוּשָׁלַם), who drank from YHWH's hand His cup of anger, who drank, who guzzled (מָצִית) His goblet[50] of reeling. There is none to lead her from among all the children she bore[51]. . . . Two things have befallen you—who will console you (מִי יָנוּד לָךְ)? Disaster and injury (וְהַשֶּׁבֶר), hunger (וְהָרָעָב) and war—who will comfort you (מִי אֲנַחֲמֵךְ)? Your children fainted (עֻלְּפוּ), they sank at the top of all the streets (בְּרֹאשׁ כָּל־חוּצוֹת) . . . full of the anger of YHWH. . . . Therefore hear this, afflicted one, you who are drunk but not from wine: Thus says your lord YHWH . . . I have taken from your hand the cup of reeling, the goblet of my wrath; you will not continue to drink from it. (Isa 51.17–22)

One might wonder initially whether the similarities demonstrate that Deutero-Isaiah borrowed from the specific text in Lamentations. Three of the markers appear also in Nah 3.10–17: "at the top of all the streets," "who will console you," and the root נח״ם (comfort).[52] This suggests that all three authors utilize a standard vocabulary cluster. However, additional items do not appear in Nahum. Further, two cases of sound play occur. Deutero-Isaiah's מצית (maṣit, "you guzzled") recalls a similar-sounding but lexically unrelated word in Lamentations, מצאנו (maṣanu, "we found it"—i.e., "it has come"). Finally, two different words meaning "fainted" are used in these texts (העטופים and עלפו), but each includes the letters ʿayin and pêh. The sound-similarity in the second case becomes even more clear since both of these words appear next to the words "at the top of all the streets." The large amount of shared vocabulary not appearing elsewhere and the typical stylistic features of Deutero-Isaianic allusion make clear that Deutero-Isaiah utilized the passage from Lamentations. This conclusion is strengthened by the realization that Deutero-Isaiah alludes again to these lines in Isa 62.6–7, as we have seen above.

The identification of Deutero-Isaiah's source helps to solve a crux. In Isa 51.19, one would have expected the phrase מִי יְנַחֲמֵךְ ("who will comfort you?") parallel to the question מִי יָנוּד לָךְ ("who will console you?"), rather than the phrase מִי אֲנַחֲמֵךְ, with its first-person verb (literally, "who—I will comfort you").[53] The odd first-person form in Deutero-Isaiah results from exact quotation of the first-person form in Lamentations (אֲנַחֲמֵךְ). Deutero-Isaiah borrowed from his source without harmonizing one of its grammatical forms with its new context. This practice, which results in slight incongruities, occurs often in allusion in the Hebrew Bible and the ancient Near East.[54]

The verses in which the borrowed vocabulary is clustered do not so much reverse the earlier lament as repeat it. The subsequent verses, however, announce that the disaster described in both texts is coming to an end. Thus the passage as a whole reverses the negative message found in its source.

Other passages in Deutero-Isaiah also reverse texts from the Book of Lamentations.[55] It may be significant that no strong cases stem from the fifth chapter of Lamentations, which suggests that Deutero-Isaiah did not know that chapter. Deutero-Isaiah may have had access to the laments found in chapters 1 through 4 as discrete texts, before they were brought together into the Book of Lamentations. Alternatively, the first four chapters may have circulated on a single scroll known to Deutero-Isaiah at the end of the exile before the fifth chapter was added at a later date.

Deutero-Isaiah's Use of Poetic Texts and His Allusive Project

Deutero-Isaiah's allusions to texts from the Book of Lamentations correspond to the reversals frequently appearing in his references to Jeremiah, Isaiah, and other prophets. However, his approach to texts found in the Book of Psalms differs somewhat. The categories of reversal and confirmation, which were prominent in his use of Isaiah and Jeremiah, play no role in his allusions to psalms. This deviation occurs simply because the Psalter contains a different type of material: songs of praise, lament, and supplication rather than predictions and warnings. Nonetheless, his allusions to psalms are often analogous to his use of prophetic material. Whereas he repredicts a prophecy, he repeats the promise of a psalm. His reworking of the Davidic promises remains consistent whether he alludes to Isaiah ben Amoṣ or to a psalm. Similarly, the category of response appears not only in his allusions to psalms but in his borrowings from the prophets as well (albeit rarely). Further, the same stylistic features characterize his use of psalms and prophecy.

Deutero-Isaiah's manifold references to older texts (full-fledged allusions as well as mere echoes) serve to connect him with his Israelite and Judean predecessors, whether prophets or poets. Just as the strong influence of Jeremiah and Isaiah indicates that Deutero-Isaiah participated in a prophetic tradition, so too his dependence on psalms and on laments for the city of Jerusalem shows that this exilic author laid claim to a wide circle of precursors. He alluded to earlier texts as he composed, not merely to update the work of one figure or school, but to reinforce and revitalize a complex, varied Hebrew literary tradition that had experienced a crisis.

5 DEUTERO-ISAIAH'S USE OF PENTATEUCHAL TEXTS

Jeremiah, Isaiah, and Psalms provide the sources for most of the allusions in Isaiah 40–66 and 35. The exilic author also employs the work of other prophets, always in the same ways he employs Jeremiah and Isaiah. Further, he reverses laments found in the Book of Lamentations, just as he turns on their heads laments from Jeremiah and the Book of Psalms. Deutero-Isaiah makes reference to one other type of biblical text: documents known to us from the Pentateuch. Of course, it would not be accurate to say that Deutero-Isaiah borrowed from the Pentateuch itself, since that anthology as we know it probably did not exist in Deutero-Isaiah's day. However, most of the bodies of material that were later brought together to form the Pentateuch already did exist, and Deutero-Isaiah knew them in some form. Thus when I use the term "Pentateuchal text" in this chapter, I mean a text that appears in the Pentateuch we have received, even though Deutero-Isaiah encountered these texts in earlier literary settings.[1] Some of his allusions to Pentateuchal texts involve historical and personal typologies similar to those found in his allusions to prophets and psalms. Deutero-Isaiah's references to priestly texts in the Pentateuch also include examples of polemic, a strategic relationship we have not seen in his use of other material.

My concern in this chapter lies with Deutero-Isaiah's allusions to specific and identifiable Pentateuchal texts, not with his use of motifs or narratives that also happen to occur in the Pentateuch. Distinguishing between these two textual phenomena at the outset is therefore crucial.

Deutero-Isaiah often creates typological linkages between the exiles of his day and characters known to us from the Pentateuch, but in most of these cases it is impossible to ascertain whether he knew these characters from texts that comprise the Pentateuch or from other traditions. For example, in Isa 54.9 the prophet refers to the Noah story, comparing YHWH's promise not to destroy the world (a promise He kept) to His new promise not to destroy the people (a promise which, by implication, He will also keep). Deutero-Isaiah's appropriation of the older story resembles his allusions to prophets and psalms: he asserts an analogy between new and old promises. But the verse does not share enough vocabulary with any verse in Genesis' Noah stories to assert that this typological link is a case of inner-biblical allusion. He could be relying on a widespread tradition about Noah rather than on a particular text. A similar situation emerges in other apparent linkages to the Pentateuch. The prophet connects the Israelites' journey from Egypt to Canaan and the exiles' journey from Babylon to the Land of Israel (e.g., Isa 43.16–21, 51.9–11, 63.11–14). Further, he often uses the term "Jacob" to refer to the exiles because, like their ancestor, the community went from Canaan to Mesopotamia and entered servitude there; moreover, the prophet implies, like Jacob, the exiles would eventually return home.[2] Here again, it is possible that Deutero-Isaiah used widespread Israelite stories or ideas rather than any particular text in which those stories appear. His use of such elements belongs, then, to the study of tradition history rather than to the study of inner-biblical allusion and exegesis.

In some cases, vocabulary items do point to a particular text, but even then the link between them may result from common use of a theme rather than from one text's borrowing from the other. For example, Deutero-Isaiah urges the people to remember the past with the following words:

> Look to Abraham your father and to Sarah who bore you, for he was a solitary person (אֶחָד) when I called him (קְרָאתִיו), but I blessed him (וַאֲבָרְכֵהוּ) and made him many (וְאַרְבֵּהוּ). (Isa 51.2)

The theme of YHWH's blessing Abraham and Sarah so that they had many descendants occurs several times in Genesis. In the story of the binding of Isaac, we read:

The messenger of YHWH called (וַיִּקְרָא) a second time from heaven, saying, "I swear (a statement of YHWH): because you have done this thing and because you have not held back your single (יְחִידְךָ) son from Me, I shall certainly bless you (בָּרֵךְ אֲבָרֶכְךָ) and make your seed many (וְהַרְבָּה אַרְבֶּה) like the stars of heaven." (Gen 22.15–17)

The typological relationship between Abraham and the exiles is straightforward: just as Abraham and Sarah were vouchsafed an unlikely—indeed unbelievable—promise of abundant progeny, so are the exiles; just as the ancestors went in small numbers from Mesopotamia to Canaan, so will the Judean community; just as the ancestors trusted in YHWH and acted accordingly, so must the exiles.[3] Clearly the prophet depends on older Israelite material, but can we be sure that this case draws on Genesis 22 specifically? Similar themes occur in other passages: for example, Gen 12.2–3, where the word for "blessing" occurs repeatedly, and Ezek 33.24, where אֶחָד and רב"ב are also found. As a result one must be wary of asserting that Deutero-Isaiah refers to Genesis 22 rather than to some other text or tradition.

A reference to a biblical story, then, is not necessarily an allusion to a biblical text. Authors (whether biblical or post-biblical) utilize oral and popular traditions as well as documents preserved in writing and known to us. However interesting Deutero-Isaiah's references to widespread traditions are, such references are not literary allusions, and thus they stand outside our area of concern. Nonetheless, in a few cases enough vocabulary or stylistic features occur to suggest that Deutero-Isaiah had a particular Pentateuchal source (though not necessarily our redacted Pentateuch) before him. The bulk of Deutero-Isaiah's references to the Pentateuch stem from the Book of Deuteronomy, while a smaller number are known to us from each of the other books.[4]

Deutero-Isaiah's Use of Deuteronomy

Deutero-Isaiah alludes several times to the poems at the end of the Book of Deuteronomy. For example, Moses had proclaimed in one of the poems,

YHWH's portion is His people; Jacob (יַעֲקֹב) is His allotted inheritance (נַחֲלָתוֹ). . . . YHWH alone led him (יַנְחֶנּוּ); no strange god was with Him. He brought him up onto the high places of the earth (וַיִּרְכִּבֵהוּ עַל־בָּמֳתֵי אָרֶץ), where he eats (⁵וַיֹּאכַל) the abundance of the field. He lets him drink honey from a rock, oil from a flinty stone. (Deut 32.9–13)

Deutero-Isaiah uses remarkably similar vocabulary in the following passage:

YHWH will always lead you (וְנָחֲךָ) and will satisfy your thirsty throat. . . . If you refrain from abusing the Sabbath, from doing your business on My holy day, and instead call the Sabbath a delight . . . then you will take delight in YHWH, and I shall bring you up onto the high places of the earth (וְהִרְכַּבְתִּיךָ עַל־בָּמֳתֵי אָרֶץ); I shall let you eat (וְהַאֲכַלְתִּיךָ) the inheritance (נַחֲלַת) of your father Jacob (יַעֲקֹב); indeed, YHWH's mouth has proclaimed it. (Isa 58.11–14)

A single phrase not found elsewhere appears in both texts ("He/I brings you/him up onto the high places of the earth"); only the aspect and person of the verb change. Additional vocabulary strengthens the link between the two passages. Further supporting the conclusion that Deutero-Isaiah knew and utilized the older text is his use of the phrase כִּי פִּי ה' דִּבֵּר ("For YHWH has spoken"), which sometimes is a formula indicating reliance on an older oracle or text.[6]

Fishbane summarizes the new use to which the old text is put:

[Deuteronomy 32] is a warning and an inspired premonition of future Israelite behavior, but it is non-revelatory, versus the oracle in Isa 58.14, which makes use of it. We thus have YHWH [in Deutero-Isaiah] citing a human *traditum* [from Deuteronomy], though a close examination of the shifts in voice involved . . . shows the individual prophet struggling to suppress his own authority. Furthermore, . . . the selection from the song is descriptive of past benefactions, not prescriptive of future ones—and does not even hint of such. The re-interpretation is thus a *tour de force*. And finally . . . Isa 58.14 refers to the land as the inheritance of the people, not the people as YHWH's inheritance. Such a transformation fully accords with the pervasive post-exilic concern with return to the land, with the added factor that true Sabbath observance is the key to sustained tenure there.[7]

This example, then, does not fit into the categories I described in the chapters on Deutero-Isaiah's reuse of earlier prophecies. We find here not a reprediction but a transformation of a non-oracular text into an oracular one, a shift that recalls Deutero-Isaiah's use of several psalms to create prophecies. Deutero-Isaiah uses history as the basis for prophecy: what occurred in Moses' time, he announces, will occur again, if the nation's behavior warrants it.[8]

Deutero-Isaiah also includes material from a Mosaic poem in the following passage:

> Thus says YHWH: . . . They will bow down to you, they will pray to you, [saying], Only among you does a God dwell, and there is no other God (אֵ־ל וְאֵין), none . . . Israel is saved by YHWH (יִשְׂרָאֵל נוֹשַׁע בַּה׳) with eternal (עוֹלָמִים) salvation. . . . Thus says YHWH, the creator of heaven (הַשָּׁמַיִם)—He is God, who formed the earth (הָאָרֶץ) . . . I am YHWH and there is none (וְאֵין) other. I did not say to the seed (לְזֶרַע) of Jacob, "Seek Me in vain." I, YHWH, speak righteously and declare just things. (Isa 45.14–19)

These vocabulary items had appeared together already in Moses' song:

> O Jeshurun, there is none like God (אֵין כָּאֵ־ל), who rides in heaven (שָׁמַיִם) to rescue you . . . The ancient God is a dwelling place; underneath are the Eternal's arms (זְרֹעֹת עוֹלָם).[9] . . . Israel dwelt secure . . . in a land (אֶרֶץ) of grain and wine whose heavens (שָׁמָיו) exude dew. Happy are you, O Israel (יִשְׂרָאֵל)! Who is like you, a nation saved by YHWH (נוֹשַׁע בַּה׳)? . . . Your enemies will cringe before you. (Deut 33.26–29)

One might doubt that the similarities noted here result from borrowing. Some of the vocabulary the passages share is common, or connected with the theme of YHWH's incomparability. Several factors, however, suggest that Deutero-Isaiah does allude specifically to Deuteronomy. The parallel between these passages includes an instance of sound play, since the root זר״ע forms the word זְרֹעֹת (zᵊroʿot, arms) in Deuteronomy and the word זֶרַע (zeraʿ, seed) in Deutero-Isaiah. The parallel phrases "a people saved by

YHWH" and "Israel saved by YHWH" appear nowhere else. Further, neither this phrase nor the root ע׳׳זר ("arms"/"seed") is associated with the vocabulary cluster concerning YHWH's incomparability. In addition to these words, the two passages share the theme of foreigners who humble themselves before Israel.

Deutero-Isaiah composes a prophecy on the basis of a text that is not, strictly speaking, an oracle. The promise of Deuteronomy 33 does not refer to any particular situation, but the prediction in Isaiah 45 pertains to a specific historical moment. On the other hand, recognizing the source does not alter our reading of the later text, so that we see here a case of echo, not of full-fledged allusion.

Deutero-Isaiah also refers to at least one law known to us from Deuteronomy. The prophet uses a rhetorical question to deny that YHWH has rejected Zion:

> Where is your mother's letter of divorce (סֵפֶר כְּרִיתוּת) by which I sent her away (שִׁלַּחְתִּיהָ)? (Isa 50.1)

The vocabulary appears also in the law of divorce in Deuteronomy:

> If a man takes a wife and marries her, but she does not please him, for he found her guilty of sexual misconduct, and he writes her a letter of divorce (סֵפֶר כְּרִיתֻת) and puts it in her hand and sends her away (וְשִׁלְּחָהּ) from his house, and she leaves his house and goes to another man, and the latter man rejects her and writes her a letter of divorce (סֵפֶר כְּרִיתֻת) and puts it in her hand and sends her away (וְשִׁלְּחָהּ) from his house, or the latter man who married her dies, then her first husband who divorced (שִׁלְּחָהּ) her cannot marry her again. (Deut 24.1–3)

One might doubt that Deutero-Isaiah refers to Deuteronomy specifically. The shared items consist of technical terms relating to the issue of divorce, so that any two authors discussing divorce might independently use that vocabulary. Indeed, the term שׁלח ("send away, divorce") in this technical sense occurs again in Jer 3.1–8, where YHWH asks whether He would accept back the nation that had cuckolded Him. Consequently, one might argue that Isa

50.1 contains a reversal of Jer 3.1–8 rather than an allusion to Deut 24.1–3. However, it is difficult to assert with complete confidence that Deutero-Isaiah alludes to the passage in Jeremiah; he may as easily have been referring to a widespread notion among the exiles that YHWH had permanently rejected Israel. (Further, Deutero-Isaiah and Jeremiah share only a single term, "send away.") On the other hand, both Jeremiah and Deutero-Isaiah presuppose the law from Deuteronomy, not only insofar as they share technical terminology with that law, but in that they both assume that a husband cannot take back a divorced wife. No such law appears elsewhere, so the reference to this specific law known to us from Deuteronomy 24 seems clear.[10] Deutero-Isaiah does not stress the textual source of his reference but simply uses the known legal custom as the basis for his statement. He thus differs from Jeremiah, who introduces his reference to the text from Deuteronomy with a citation formula (לאמר).

This passage also bears comparison with Hosea 1–3, in which YHWH divorces Israel but takes her back later on. Deutero-Isaiah and Hosea agree that God and Israel will be reconciled, while Jeremiah views reconciliation as impossible, at least for the north, and potentially for the south. However, Hosea and Deutero-Isaiah express these similar ideas in different ways. Isa 50.1 denies that a divorce had ever really occurred, while according to Hos 1.9 God utters a divorce formula to Israel (which was then reversed in 2.25).[11] The reason for this difference is clear. Hosea wrote before the Book of Deuteronomy existed, and consequently he was able to say that God and Israel could be remarried after their divorce. Deutero-Isaiah, like Jeremiah, already views some form of Deuteronomy as authoritative, and thus he must deny that there had been a divorce at all. For Hosea, there can be, and is, return after divorce; for Jeremiah, there cannot be, and will not be, return after divorce; for Deutero-Isaiah, there can be no return after divorce, but (his main point) no divorce has really occurred. YHWH never gave Zion a formal bill of divorce, but merely compelled a temporary separation. Consequently, Deutero-Isaiah stresses, there is no impediment to the nation's restoration.[12]

While the allusions to Deuteronomy in the previous examples do not fall into the categories I noted in earlier chapters, other cases do resemble his references to prophets. For example, in the curses toward the end of the book, Moses warned the people not to break the covenant because dire consequences would follow. Among the misfortunes that would result from covenant infraction, he mentions the following:

YHWH will smite you with insanity and blindness and a panicked heart. You will falter in the afternoon as a blind man falters in the pitch black (מְמַשֵּׁשׁ בַּצָּהֳרַיִם כַּאֲשֶׁר יְמַשֵּׁשׁ הָעִוֵּר בָּאֲפֵלָה), and you will not succeed in your journeys (דְּרָכֶיךָ). Indeed, you will be oppressed (עָשׁוּק). (Deut 28.28–29)

Deutero-Isaiah uses similar wording to describe the nation's plight after 587 B.C.E.:

They did not know the way (דֶּרֶךְ) of peace . . . they twisted (עִקְּשׁוּ) their paths. . . . Therefore, justice is far from us; we cannot attain victory. We hope for light but behold darkness; for illumination, but we go about in pitch-black (בָּאֲפֵלוֹת). We flounder like blind men (נְגַשְׁשָׁה כַעִוְרִים) along a wall; like someone without eyes we flounder (נְגַשֵּׁשָׁה). We stumble in the afternoon (בַּצָּהֳרַיִם) as if it were dusk. (Isa 59.8–10)

Ancient Near Eastern covenants and treaties traditionally included curses. Thus one might suspect that Deutero-Isaiah relied on a widespread vocabulary cluster rather than on the covenant curses from Deuteronomy specifically. However, none of the terms these passages share appears in the covenant curses in Leviticus, nor do similar terms appear in the curses in Hittite, Assyrian, or Aramaic treaties that resemble the covenant curses found in the Hebrew Bible.[13] Thus it is likely that Deutero-Isaiah borrowed the terms from the text in Deuteronomy rather than from a cluster of terms associated with covenant curses. Further, several typical features of Deutero-Isaianic allusion occur here. Instead of the word עָשׁוּק (ʿashuq, "oppressed"), Deutero-Isaiah uses a semantically unrelated word built from the same consonants, עקשו (ʿiqqᵊshu, "twisted"). Similarly, Deutero-Isaiah does not repeat the word ממשש (mᵊmasheish, "grope, falter") but substitutes for it another word with a similar meaning built from some of the same consonants: נגששה (nᵊgasheisha, "grope, flounder"). (Interestingly, both of these words appear twice in their respective texts.) The split-up pattern occurs as well. Elements of the clause "falter in the afternoon as a blind man falters in the pitch black" are split into several parts appearing over two verses. In light of these stylistic features, it becomes clear that Deutero-Isaiah alludes to the specific passage in Deuteronomy.

Just as Deutero-Isaiah often notes that the negative prophecies of Jeremiah and Isaiah have come to fruition, so too he notes here that the curses Moses anticipated have been put into effect. Thus this is a case of what I called in earlier chapters "confirmation."[14]

Deutero-Isaiah's Use of Other Pentateuchal Material

Typology

While most of the typological relationships between Deutero-Isaiah and Pentateuchal material may involve use of a tradition, in a few cases, reference to a specific text does seem likely. One such case involves Isa 43.22–28, which criticizes Jacob for failing to serve YHWH with offerings. Klaus Baltzer has pointed out that the text uses several vocabulary items found in the story of Jacob's flight to and sojourn in Mesopotamia.[15] Some of these are common terms connected to the theme of sacrifice (for example, שֶׂה ["sheep," Isa 43.23; Gen 30.32], מִנְחָה ["gift, offering," Isa 43.23; Gen 32.14, 21], זב"ח ["sacrifice," Isa 43.23; Gen 31.54]), and others are relatively common: for example, the roots עב"ד and יג"ע ("work" and "toil"; these appear together in both Isa 43.22–23 and Gen 31.41–42) and the words כִּי, קָרָא, and יַעֲקֹב ("for," "call," and "Jacob," which appear together in Isa 43.22 and Gen 27.36). Baltzer also notes correspondences between words that sound similar but have distinct meanings; this feature, as we have seen, is a common one in Deutero-Isaiah's allusions to older texts, and its presence increases the likelihood that these parallels result from borrowing. The word לְבוֹנָה (lĕbona, "incense") in Isa 43.23 recalls לְבְנֶה (libne, "poplar tree") in Gen 30.37. The words מִקְנֶה קִנְיָנוֹ (miqnei qinyano, "the livestock he owned/bought") in Gen 31.18 yield not only קָנִיתָ (qanita, "you bought") but also קָנֶה (qane, "reed") in Isa 43.24. These further correspondences, which display Deutero-Isaiah's allusive style and involve language that is less common, suggest that Isa 43.22–28 were composed with the Genesis passage in mind.

Baltzer notes that all these vocabulary items in Genesis were used to describe something that Jacob worked to acquire. Deutero-Isaiah, however, complains that Jacob did not labor on YHWH's behalf. The prophet implies a moral lesson: as the nation follows the lead of its ancestor by returning from Mesopotamia to the Land of Israel, it must attend not only to its material needs but also to its obligations to the God who brings about the return. By noting an allusion to the story in Genesis, Baltzer may also solve an exegetical crux in Isa 43.22–28. These verses seem not to fit their exilic context: the Judeans in Babylon had no temple, and thus they were unable to offer sacrifices to YHWH (at least according to Deuteronomistic ideology). In light of this, it would be odd to criticize their failure to do so. The prophet may have the patriarch Jacob in mind rather than the nation as he utters this criticism—that is, he refers to an instance of neglect from the distant past which ought not be repeated.[16]

Other cases of allusion to the Pentateuch are much pithier. According to Leviticus, every fiftieth year Israelites who have lost their land (usually through debt) and have been forced into indentured servitude may leave their servitude and regain their land:[17]

> And you shall sanctify the fiftieth year and proclaim a release (וּקְרָאתֶם
> דְּרוֹר) in the land, to all its inhabitants . . . every man will return to his
> property, every man to his clan. (Lev 25.10)

Deutero-Isaiah maintains that the nation Israel received the benefits prom- ised by priestly law to a person sold into debt-slavery.

> The spirit of the Lord YHWH is on me, for He anointed me to bring
> good news to the lowly, to heal those wounded in heart, to proclaim
> (לִקְרֹא) release (דְּרוֹר) to captives and freedom to those in chains. (Isa
> 61.1)

In 587 B.C.E. the nation, like a debt-slave, lost its land and was sent to live elsewhere. Fifty years later, its period of service ended when the Edict of Cyrus allowed the people to leave Babylonia and regain their ancestral land. As he alludes to the older passage, the prophet employs its motifs meta- phorically: while Leviticus spoke of people who were literally, concretely indigent and bound to their master's land, the prophet uses the words "captives" and "those in chains" to refer to Judeans who were exiled but neither economically disadvantaged nor politically oppressed.[18] He trans- forms a social and economic institution into an eschatological or political trope. This allusion, then, falls into the category of typology: what happened to the individual Israelite in the source provides the model for what happens to the nation Israel in the allusion.[19]

One might argue that Deutero-Isaiah does not refer to the specific law known to us from Leviticus but employs a common legal term concerning the release of slaves or the return to ancestral lands. A similar term, *andurāru* (or *durāru*), occurs in Akkadian, indicating that the terminology Deutero-Isaiah utilizes stems from a widespread ancient Near Eastern legal tradition. The Akkadian term refers to the remission of commercial debts, the manumission of slaves, and the return of real estate to original owners.[20] Unlike the Levitical דרור, the *andurāru* did not take place every fifty years; instead, it was proclaimed at will by a king, especially at the beginning of his reign. In Hebrew also the term דרור can refer to a release proclaimed at will by a king (rather than a release that follows a fifty-year Levitical cycle), as indicated by Jer 34.8, 15, 17; this sense of the term is precisely identical to its Akkadian cognate.[21] The question presents itself, then: does Deutero-Isaiah use the term דרור in its wider sense, known from Jeremiah 34 and from Akkadian, or does he use the narrow sense specific to Leviticus? Significantly, Leviticus 25 and Isaiah 61 share an element not known from any other legal texts, Israelite or otherwise, that speak of a דרור/*andurāru*: that of a fifty-year cycle at the end of which return to ancestral land takes place.[22] In light of this additional correspondence, it becomes clear that Deutero-Isaiah does in fact refer to the priestly law of return known to us from Leviticus, and thus in Isaiah 61 Deutero-Isaiah does not merely use a widespread technical term but engages in inner-biblical allusion.[23]

Polemic

Deutero-Isaiah relates to texts from the Pentateuch in a manner we have not seen in his allusions to prophetic and poetic works: he contests ideas found in some Pentateuchal passages. Allusions of this sort fall into another thematic category, that of polemic.

Moshe Weinfeld has shown that Deutero-Isaiah rejected four central ideas of the priestly creation account in Gen 1.1–2.4a.[24]

First, according to the priestly account, God created the world not *ex nihilo* but from various sorts of pre-existent matter. Before God accomplished His first creative act (described in Gen 1.3), formless matter, including chaos, water, darkness, and the abyss, already existed. This becomes clear in the opening verses of Genesis:[25]

When God began to create (בָּרָא) heaven and earth (אֵת הַשָּׁמַיִם וְאֵת הָאָרֶץ)[26]—the earth (וְהָאָרֶץ) having been utter chaos (תֹהוּ וָבֹהוּ), with darkness (חֹשֶׁךְ) on the surface of the abyss (תְהוֹם) and a wind from God fluttering on the surface of the waters—God said, "Let there be light!" And there was light. (Gen 1.1–3)

But Deutero-Isaiah, alone among the biblical writers, insists that YHWH created everything in the world—not only light but also darkness:

I am YHWH and there is none other. I form light and create darkness (וּבוֹרֵא חֹשֶׁךְ); I make well-being and create misfortune[27]—I, YHWH, make all these things. (Isa 45.6–7)

Deutero-Isaiah denies that the earth ever was as chaotic as Gen 1.2 would have us believe:

For thus says YHWH, creator of heaven (בּוֹרֵא הַשָּׁמַיִם) (He is God), who forms the earth (הָאָרֶץ) and makes it (He constructed it). He did not create it as a chaos (תֹהוּ בְרָאָהּ); He formed it that it might be inhabited: "I am YHWH and there is none other. I did not speak in secret, nor in a place of a dark land (אֶרֶץ חֹשֶׁךְ)." (Isa 45.18–19)

As Weinfeld explains, Deutero-Isaiah argues against Genesis' implication that God had not created darkness; further, lest one suggest that the world He created was chaotic at its outset, the prophet denies that there was chaos at all in the beginning.[28]

Second, the priestly writer, like most biblical authors, imagined God as a physical being who had a form, and he claimed that God created human beings with a similar form:

God said, "Let us make a human being with our form, according to our likeness (בְּצַלְמֵנוּ כִּדְמוּתֵנוּ)." (Gen 1.26; cf. Gen 5.1)

But Deutero-Isaiah repeatedly stresses that YHWH has no form, no likeness:[29]

To whom would you compare (תְּדַמְיוּן) God, and what form (דְּמוּת)
would you attribute to Him? (Isa 40.18; cf. Isa 40.25; 46.5)

Third, the prophet objected to another implication present in Gen 1.26
and other verses in the creation account: the participation, however inconse-
quential, of other heavenly beings in the creation. The first-person plural
verbs depict God as discussing His plans with others, probably the heavenly
court. But Deutero-Isaiah insists,

Thus says YHWH your savior, who formed you in the womb: I,
YHWH, am the maker of all. I stretched forth heaven (שָׁמַיִם) by
Myself; I spread out the land (הָאָרֶץ)—who was with Me?[30] (Isa 44.24;
cf. 40.13–14)

Here again Deutero-Isaiah opposes an idea found in Genesis 1.[31]
Fourth, according to the priestly writers, God rested when He completed
the creation of the world:

He rested on the seventh day from all the work that He had done.
(Gen 2.2)

In six days YHWH made the heaven and earth, and on the seventh
day, He rested and took a deep breath. (Exod 31.17)

But Deutero-Isaiah insists that YHWH, unlike a human being, never rests:[32]

The eternal God, YHWH, the creator of the ends of the earth, neither sleeps nor slumbers; there is no limit to his understanding.
(Isa 40.28)

Any one of these correspondences between Genesis 1 and Deutero-Isaiah
might be dismissed as a coincidence. All four taken together, however, establish that the prophet knew the priestly creation account and found it unac-
ceptably anthropomorphic. For Deutero-Isaiah, YHWH was completely unlike human beings: stronger, incorporeal, solitary, unmistakably older than
the world. In order to stress these characteristics of the divinity, Deutero-
Isaiah weaves into his preaching statements that react subtly to Genesis 1,

thus promoting a new understanding of God. In so doing, he does not merely reread or interpret the older text, but argues against it.[33]

Deutero-Isaiah takes issue with the priestly authors in regard to another question as well: who can officiate at the sanctuary?[34] According to Numbers 18, only members of the tribe of Levi can work in the sanctuary, and descendants of Aaron alone are permitted to carry out the more limited priestly functions there. Israelites from tribes other than Levi are barred from drawing near to the sanctuary:

> YHWH said to Aaron, "You and your sons and your father's house with you shall bear the punishment of the sanctuary; you and your sons with you will bear the punishment of your priesthood (כְּהֻנַּתְכֶם). You shall allow your brethren, the tribe of Levi, your father's clan, to draw near to you; they shall be attached (וְיִלָּווּ) to you and shall serve you (וִישָׁרְתוּךָ) when you and your sons with you are in the presence of the Tent of Witness. They shall serve as guards for you (וְשָׁמְרוּ מִשְׁמַרְתְּךָ), for the tent, and for the sacred vessels, but they shall not draw near to the altar. . . . They will attach themselves (וְנִלְווּ) to you and will guard (וְשָׁמְרוּ אֶת־מִשְׁמֶרֶת) the Tent of Meeting in regard to service at the Tent. A stranger (וְזָר) shall not draw near to you. . . . I have hereby taken your brethren, the Levites, from among the Children of Israel to be a gift to you, to be attendants of YHWH, that they may perform (לַעֲבֹד) the service (עֲבֹדַת) of the Tent of Meeting. But you and your sons with you will retain your priestly status (כְּהֻנַּתְכֶם) in anything relating to the altar. . . . The stranger (וְהַזָּר) who draws near shall be put to death. . . . I hereby give you the guardianship over My gifts in regard to all the holy donations of the Children of Israel; I give them to you as an allocation. . . . At the Holy of Holies you shall eat (תֹּאכֲלֶנּוּ) them. . . . The children of Israel shall no more approach the Tent of Meeting, which would make them incur guilt and die. (Num 18.1– 10, 22)

A three-tiered system is established here: only Aaronides may serve as priests, working at the altar; Levites may not approach the altar, but may work in the Tent of Meeting; other Israelites may not approach the Tent of Meeting.[35] Further, priests (and members of their families) alone may eat the "sacred gifts" of the Israelites (that is, parts of certain sacrifices; see vv. 9–

20); Levites alone may eat the tithes (vv. 21–24), which, however, are not described as sacred. Israelites may not partake in either of these foods.

Deutero-Isaiah, however, imagines a more egalitarian priesthood, in which any Israelite could serve. That all Israelites would be able to participate in the cult becomes clear when the prophet says,

> Strangers (זָרִים) will stand and tend your flocks; foreigners will be your farmers and vinedressers. And you will be called the priests (כֹּהֲנֵי) of YHWH; you will be termed the ones who serve (מְשָׁרְתֵי) our God. You will eat (תֹּאכֵלוּ) the wealth of nations. (Isa 61.5–6)

In this passage, the prophet unambiguously describes the whole nation as priestly. (A similar notion is found in Exod 19.6, which may influence Deutero-Isaiah here. Indeed, Isa 61.6 may represent a literalization of the verse from Exodus.) Thus the Israelites receive the status that was limited to Aaronides in Numbers 18. Similarly, the nations play a role parallel to one the Israelites had in Numbers 18: they bring food to the Israelites/priests. Deutero-Isaiah may imply that, in the future, Israelites will serve as priests for the nations of the world, just as the Levites and Aaronides had earlier served as cultic functionaries for the nation Israel. Deutero-Isaiah uses one marker in a manner differing significantly from the source. For him זר meant a foreigner, a non-Judean, as the parallelism in the verse demonstrates. In the priestly passage, זר is a technical term referring to anyone who was not allowed to approach the altar—i.e., non-Aaronides, including Levites, other Israelites, and foreigners.[36]

One other passage reflects Deutero-Isaiah's less restrictive feelings toward the altar. This widely misunderstood passage deserves attention.

> Thus says YHWH of the eunuchs[37] who observe (יִשְׁמְרוּ) My Sabbaths and choose what I desire, who embrace My covenant: I shall give them a monument[38] in My House better than sons and daughters. I shall give them[39] an eternal name that will not cease.[40] And as for the foreigners[41] who join (הַנִּלְוִים) YHWH to serve (לְשָׁרְתוֹ) Him and to love the name of YHWH as His servants (לַעֲבָדִים), each of whom observes (שֹׁמֵר) the Sabbath without profaning it and embraces My covenant: I shall bring them to My holy mountain, and I shall make them happy in My house of prayer. Their offerings and sacrifices will

be acceptable on My altar, for My house is a house of prayer for all the nations. (Isa 56.4–7)[42]

The passage does not attribute priestly roles to the eunuchs or the foreigners (since they are not said to approach the altar). It merely stresses that their presence and their offerings are welcome on the holy mountain, a notion that is not itself new.[43] Nonetheless, the passage does pointedly apply to the foreigners and eunuchs vocabulary that was expressly limited to Levites in Numbers 18: the terms נלוה ("join") and שרת ("serve"). These words are often, though not always, used as technical terms connected to temple service.[44] By employing them in reference to foreigners and eunuchs, Deutero-Isaiah suggests an analogy between these groups and those who enjoy the priesthood. This analogy was shocking to some ancient readers: the technical term "to serve" (לשרתו) is omitted from the great Isaiah scroll of Qumran (1QIsaᵃ) and paraphrased by the Greek translators of the LXX.[45] As we have seen, foreigners (along with non-Levite Israelites) are excluded from temple service by the priestly writers in Numbers 18; and eunuchs are also disqualified from serving at the sanctuary by the priestly writers in Lev 21.16–23.[46] Thus Isaiah 56 deviates from the priestly writers in tone—and perhaps even opposes their view of the position of foreigners and eunuchs in the cult.

Isaiah 56 also opposes the views expressed by several post-exilic writers regarding the acceptance of foreigners into the community of YHWH-worshipers. Although related to the question of the priestly status of foreigners, the inclusion of foreigners in the covenant is a distinct issue. Priestly literature did not address this question, but post-exilic figures did. The Books of Ezra and Nehemiah tell us that two governors of Judah, Zerubbabel (a contemporary of Deutero-Isaiah) and Ezra (who lived later) used Deut 23.4–5 to reject the entrance of foreigners into the community. In Isaiah 56, Deutero-Isaiah strenuously opposes this viewpoint.[47] Thus in Isa 56.1–8 Deutero-Isaiah polemicizes regarding two issues that are connected but distinct. The first issue involves the status of foreigners in the cult; in this regard his tone differs markedly and deliberately from that of Numbers 18. The second is entrance of foreigners into the community of returned Judean exiles; Deutero-Isaiah's polemic on this latter question is directed at figures like Zerubbabel, but *not* against priestly literature known from the Pentateuch.[48]

Deutero-Isaiah may ascribe a role in the cult to foreigners (thus abrogating Numbers 18) in two other passages, but both are ambiguous. The first of these is Isa 60.7, which may be translated in two ways: "All the flocks of Kedar will gather for you; the rams of Nebaioth will serve you (יְשָׁרְתוּנֶךְ). They will go up willingly on My altar, and I will glorify My glorious House." (In this translation, the rams are the subject of the *qal* verb יַעֲלוּ.) The second possibility is: "All the flocks . . . will serve you (יְשָׁרְתוּנֶךְ). They will offer acceptable offerings on My altar." (In this translation, foreigners are the implied subject of a hiphil verb, יַעֲלוּ, whose object is understood to be the animals.) If the latter translation is correct, then Deutero-Isaiah affirms that foreigners will be accorded priestly privileges that even regular Israelites do not have in priestly law. However, the tone of this passage is not particularly favorable to foreigners. The passage describes foreign kings as serving (שר״ת) the Israelites (not serving YHWH), and it predicts that Israelites will benefit by receiving the foreigners' wealth. Hence it does not seem likely that the latter translation is correct.

The second passage in question appears in the last chapter of the book. Isa 66.21 reads, "Even from them I shall take some to be Levitical priests." The word "them" may refer back to the exiled Judeans brought back from among the nations (66.19), or to the nations themselves. If the latter is the case, Deutero-Isaiah directly opposes the priestly writers' exclusion of foreigners from the cult. While the passage remains ambiguous, the phrasing "*even* from them" suggests that the more surprising of the options is more likely—that the prophet does anticipate priestly service performed by foreigners.[49]

Deutero-Isaiah may involve himself in another old debate reflected in Pentateuchal sources, and by doing so he implicitly argues against one text. According to a passage attributed to E, a messenger from God accompanies the people in their desert journey and leads them into the Land of Israel:

> I am about to send a messenger (מַלְאָךְ) before you to guard you on the way and to bring you to the place I have prepared. . . . For My messenger (מַלְאָכִי) will go before you and bring you into [the land of] the Amorites. (Exod 23.20, 23)

But a passage attributed to J insists that YHWH Himself, or rather His Presence, accompanied the nation on their journey:

[YHWH] said: My Presence (פָּנַי) will go and will treat you graciously. And [Moses] said, If Your Presence (פָּנֶיךָ) does not go, do not bring us out of here. (Exod 33.14–15)[50]

Deutero-Isaiah agrees with the latter passage against the former:

[YHWH] was their savior in all their affliction; not an envoy or a messenger (וּמַלְאַךְ) but His presence (פָּנָיו) saved them.[51] (Isa 63.8–9)

That the passage refers to the exodus becomes clear in the subsequent verses (Isa 63.11–13), which explicitly mention the splitting of the Reed Sea and the desert wandering. It is difficult to ascertain, however, whether the prophet alludes specifically to the verses from the Book of Exodus cited above, or to more widespread traditions. Thus we cannot assert positively that this is a genuine case of inner-biblical allusion or polemic.

Deutero-Isaiah's Use of Pentateuchal Texts in the Context of His Inner-Biblical Allusions

Deutero-Isaiah had a wide knowledge of the sources that comprise the Pentateuch as we know it. He utilizes material from several sections of the Book of Deuteronomy, including poetry, covenant curses, and (in all likelihood) legal texts. His knowledge of Pentateuchal material was not limited to Deuteronomy, however; he borrows from priestly and JE texts as well. The evidence from Deutero-Isaiah's allusions does not allow us to know whether Deutero-Isaiah knew these as separate documents or in a redacted form.[52] Nor do the allusions make clear whether the priestly texts were much older or nearly contemporary with him. However, his willingness to dispute priestly texts evinces a temerity that he never displays in regard to other texts. This anomalous treatment of priestly material might be less surprising if the edition of priestly texts he used was redacted in Deutero-Isaiah's time, so that he did not approach it as venerable and esteemed.

The extent of Deutero-Isaiah's quarrel with priestly texts ought not be overstated. This needs to be stressed, since much recent scholarship, particularly that of Paul Hanson, claims to have discovered a rift in the early post-exilic period between a priestly or hierocratic party (seen in P and

Ezekiel) and a prophetic or visionary party (of which the last part of the Book of Isaiah is a prime example).[53] However, other scholars have argued otherwise: to the extent that the early post-exilic community was polarized, the priestly and the prophetic groups were aligned with, not against, each other. The opponents against whom the last chapters of Isaiah argue are the same groups that Ezekiel and the editors of the Pentateuch attacked—Judeans who prayed to various gods in addition to YHWH. Thus the dichotomy Hanson draws between the visionary authors of Isaiah 56–66 (an allegedly disenfranchised and oppressed group of idealists) and the hierocratic authors of Ezekiel 40–48, Zechariah 9–14, and the P document (priests who enjoy political power and are interested in ritual rather than justice) is a false one. On the contrary, the last part of Isaiah shares with priestly literature a love of the Temple and an abhorrence of improper forms of worship.[54] Thus Deutero-Isaiah's polemics against priestly literature are not evidence of a social and ideological rift in the Persian era; rather, they represent disagreements on specific, albeit important, issues within a single group.

In fact, in one of the passages containing Deutero-Isaiah's polemic against priestly material, he also echoes priestly material approvingly. Isa 56.1–8 not only argue against Numbers 18 but also borrow language relating to the Sabbath from Exod 31.12–16, which is also a priestly text (more specifically, a text that includes PT and HS elements).[55] Among the many items shared by these passages are several that do not appear in other Sabbath texts (such as the Decalogues; Ezekiel 20, 22, and 44; Nehemiah 10 and 13): these include the verb נכרת ("cut off," Exod 31.15 and Isa 56.5) and the root קר״ב (Exod 31.15 and Isa 56.1). This suggests that the prophet borrowed specifically from Exodus 31 rather than from a vocabulary cluster. Typical stylistic features appear as well. The root קר״ב means "midst" in Exod 31.15 (מִקֶּרֶב, *mi-qereb*), but it is transformed through sound play to "near" (כִּי־קְרוֹבָה, *ki-qʾroba*) in Isa 56.1. Further, Exod 31.16, uniquely among passages relating to the Sabbath, describes the seventh day as בְּרִית עוֹלָם ("an eternal covenant").[56] Deutero-Isaiah splits this phrase in two: "For thus says YHWH to the eunuchs who observe My Sabbaths and . . . embrace My covenant (בְּרִיתִי): . . . I shall give you an eternal name (עוֹלָם)" (Isa 56.4–5). In this passage, then, the prophet not only implies a disagreement, in tone if not in content, with the priestly authors; he also echoes one of their central Sabbath laws approvingly, extending its regulations and restrictions to all who embrace the covenant (though not, of course, to all gentiles). Thus a text that allegedly shows the distance between the visionary and hierocratic parties in fact bases itself on a priestly regulation.

We have seen that some of Deutero-Isaiah's allusions to passages known to us from the Pentateuch resemble his allusions to prophetic texts and psalms. He uses these sources as the basis for typological linkages between figures from the past and the nation in his own day. At times, however, he relates to P (and one passage from E) differently. He does not merely refer to this material but disagrees with it; he opposes aspects of priestly ideology, and he attempts to correct them. The thematic category of polemic occurs only in his allusions to Pentateuchal material. Even when he reverses prophecies of doom, Deutero-Isaiah does not argue that the older texts were wrong; he merely announces that the situation they describe was coming to its end. Texts from the Pentateuch were sufficiently well-known to Deutero-Isaiah that they were worth citing, but they were not so authoritative that he refrained from debating with them. This fact will play a role in the following discussion of Deutero-Isaiah's place in the history of Israelite religion.

אֲדֹנָי ה׳ נָתַן לִי לְשׁוֹן לִמּוּדִים

My Lord YHWH has given me a learned tongue.

(ISA 50.4)

6 LEARNED TONGUE, INSPIRED TONGUE

DEUTERO-ISAIAH'S was a peculiar sort of prophetic inspiration. He experienced the presence of the divine voice by ruminating on divine voices from the past. More than his pre-exilic forerunners, Deutero-Isaiah based his prophecies on older texts, recasting their words in order to create new but derivative oracles for his own day. Thus he augured what was to come, for writers in the Second Temple period and later fashioned themselves as interpreters and imitators of prophecy. Deutero-Isaiah's reuse of older texts, then, comes to bear not only on the nature of inner-biblical allusion but on the history of prophecy and the rise of hermeneutically based religion. These issues deserve detailed attention.

The Poetics of Allusion in Isaiah 40–66

Allusions in Isaiah 35 and 40–66 repeatedly display certain stylistic and thematic features. Because Deutero-Isaiah reworks borrowed material in a consistent fashion, a carefully executed and distinct method of allusion emerges from his work. It will be worthwhile to review the patterns evident in his appropriation of older texts and to discuss their implications.

Thematic Patterns

Allusions in Isaiah 40–66 and 35 fall into set thematic categories: confirmation, in which Deutero-Isaiah asserts that dire prophecies of yore have achieved fulfillment; reprediction, in which he restates prophecies that have yet to be fulfilled; reversal, in which vocabulary taken from laments and prophecies of doom is used to construct predictions of restoration; historical recontextualization and typology, which link persons and nations in the past with others in the present; and response, in which the prophet implicitly answers complaints, accusations, or laments in an older text. (Reprediction does not occur in allusions to psalms, but a similar phenomenon, repetition of a promise, does.) In previous chapters I discussed examples of these categories; at this point it is possible to ask what we can learn from the fact that Deutero-Isaiah confirmed, repeated, revised, and reversed older prophecies.

Through the confirmations, Deutero-Isaiah asserts that the prophets who came before him spoke accurately. In so doing, he accomplishes several goals. He bolsters Israelite tradition, avowing that YHWH and his messengers are reliable. The disaster that struck the nation does not indicate that YHWH is weak. On the contrary, it demonstrates that He knew in advance what was to occur and that He is powerful enough to carry out His will. Just as the nation saw YHWH's power working against them, they can be confident that it will work for them when appropriate. By noting that YHWH's earlier pronouncements came to pass, Deutero-Isaiah also bolsters his own authority: he suggests that the predictions of comfort he utters are believable, since they come from the same source as the accurate (albeit grimmer) predictions of Jeremiah, Isaiah, and the others. Allusion to the negative prophecies of pre-exilic figures also reminds listeners of their nation's sinfulness. In an unexpected way, such a reminder can reassure them. According to the covenant, the nation was to be punished for infractions. The fulfillment of the older prophets' threats shows that the covenant mechanism works. It follows that, once the nation has completed its term of service, there is no reason for them to continue suffering, and they will be restored.[1]

In the repredictions Deutero-Isaiah affirms the accuracy of earlier prophecy in a different way. He repeats the messages of comfort found in his predecessors, asserting that their visions of restoration would, eventually, prove as reliable as their warnings of doom. Here, however, the implications of Deutero-Isaiah's allusions, which involve revision and perhaps exegesis, are more complex. Some older promises and predictions seemed to be inaccurate, and their inaccuracy resulted in cognitive dissonance for those who believed in the word of YHWH: promise and reality diverged.[2] Deutero-Isaiah attempts to resolve this dissonance by masking elements of the prophecies that no longer appear likely or meaningful. For example, he apparently did not regard predictions concerning an eternal Davidic kingship as tenable. Those predictions, after all, had been contradicted by the facts of history, since in Deutero-Isaiah's day, no son of David reigned. As a result he found it necessary to pass over in silence the references to a Davidic ruler. (This becomes evident in the allusions to Isa 11.1–9 in Isa 42.1–9 and 60.17–61.1, and more subtly in the reworking of Isa 8.22–9.5 in 60.1–5; in the allusions to Psalms 2 and 72 in Isa 44.24–45.8 and 60.1–21; in the reference to Psalm 132 in Isa 61.1–11; and in the use of Psalm 89 in Isa 55.1–5.) Deutero-Isaiah responds to the difficulty posed by the older texts by excision—which amounts to tacit admission that the older texts had erred. This maneuver presents one early attempt to grapple with a question that would emerge as central in post-biblical traditions: what does one do when a sacred text proves wrong? Deutero-Isaiah's approach was not the only possibility; other reactions to the failure of the Davidic promise were more common. Several exilic and post-exilic authors (in Jer 33.14–16; Ezekiel 37; Zech 3.8, 6.12, 4.6–10; Hag 1.12–15, 2.21–23) affirmed the promise in defiance of historical events, maintaining that it pertained to the future rather than the present. (As a result, an assurance that the dynasty would never end was understood, somewhat paradoxically, to refer to its revival.) Deutero-Isaiah's view, however, was largely forgotten.[3] The expectation of renewed Davidic kingship became widespread in Second Temple Judaisms, while Deutero-Isaiah's eschatology *sans* human redeemer left few traces in later Jewish texts.[4]

Similarly, Isaiah and Jeremiah looked forward to the return of northern Israelites exiled by the Assyrians, but by Deutero-Isaiah's day texts containing these predictions had become anachronistic. Deutero-Isaiah uses language from these passages so that it refers to Judeans exiled by Babylonians, as if to assert that the older prophecies of restoration were accurate but slightly misspoken—when Isaiah and Jeremiah said "Israel" or "Ephraim," they must have meant, or they ought to have meant, "Judah." (This revision occurs in the following allusions: Isa 35.4–10 // Jer 31.8–9; Isa 40.9–10 // Jer 31.15; Isa 45.12–13 // Jer 27.5–6; Isa 40.10 // Isa 28.2; Isa 42.1–9 // Isaiah 11; Isa

46.5–12 // Isa 14.24–25; Isa 51.17–22 // Isa 29.9–10; Isa 60.1–5 // Isa 8.22–9.5; Isa 66.12–24 // Isa 30.27–33. See also his allusion to Nahum 2 in Isa 52.1–8 and to Zeph 2.13–15 in Isa 47.5–11.) Deutero-Isaiah does not brand his predecessors as false prophets, but he does imply that they were at least to some extent wrong. What seems most significant, however, is that he minimizes these differences. He stresses the reliability of his predecessors through the confirmations. Where their accuracy is in question, he upholds their words by repetition, omitting problematic items or substituting contemporary figures for inapplicable characters from the past. Thus Deutero-Isaiah obscures problems in the older texts.

Deutero-Isaiah's method of modifying predictions he restates bears comparison with Deuteronomy's revision of an older law code from Exodus. The problems facing the Deuteronomist and Deutero-Isaiah are similar, but their solutions differ. Bernard Levinson has described the situation in Deuteronomy masterfully:

> Once a law is attributed to God [as is the case in the Covenant Code in Exodus 21–23], how can it be superseded, which is to say, annulled, without the prestige or authority of divine law being thereby impaired? How can a specific component of divine revelation become obsolete? Can one imagine a human editor emerging from the text, the voice of which is otherwise divine or prophetic, to announce the obsolescence of a particular divine commandment? Could one imagine, for that matter, that the divine should suddenly deem inadequate one of his rules? . . . As a result of this tension the biblical authors developed a number of sophisticated literary and exegetical strategies to present new law as not in fact involving the revision or annulment of older laws ascribed to God. The biblical authors develop . . . a "rhetoric of concealment" which serves to camouflage the actual literary history of the laws.[5]

This summary applies no less to Deutero-Isaiah than to Deuteronomy. But Levinson shows that "Deuteronomy is, on the one hand, among the most radically innovative literary units in the Hebrew Bible, and on the other hand, among those which most loudly silence the suggestion of innovation." The Deuteronomists' rhetorical and exegetical strategies effectively deny human authorship and thus conceal their own legal innovations. They employ these strategies precisely because they intend not merely to supplement but to replace their literary predecessor, the Covenant Code found in Exodus 21–23.[6] Thus Deuteronomy is, its protestations notwithstanding, surprisingly free in rejecting earlier material, precisely because it supersedes that material. In the eyes of the Deuteronomists, the text of the Covenant Code need not be preserved. Deutero-Isaiah, however, supplements his predecessors rather than annuls them. He attempts to conceal not his derivative status but errors in the work of the prophets he follows. Deutero-Isaiah is no less innovative, but he is less cavalier in his relation to earlier texts. He positions himself as a "team player" in the prophetic tradition by attempting to cover up problems in the work of his fellow prophets. Deuteronomy, on the other hand, insists on working alone—indeed, it pushes its predecessors off the field.

What accounts for the different relation to literary forebears in these two texts? In part, the disparity is one of genre: a new legal text such as Deuteronomy cannot allow for the continued existence of an alternative, since the law must be defined one way or the other. In addition, the historical circumstances of the two texts may have affected their attitudes. Deuteronomy stems from an earlier time, when the authority of older scriptural writing may have been less compelling. By Deutero-Isaiah's day, the status of older traditions had solidified. Moreover, the exilic prophet wrote after a crisis, when the tradition as a whole was beset by threats from disappointed Israelites and competing ideas. In that era, the need to bolster tradition outweighed other factors.

A third category of allusion also evinces the complexity of Deutero-Isaiah's relationships with his precursors. The reversals suggest that Deutero-Isaiah disagreed with earlier prophets, but this is not in fact the case. In allusions that invert a prophecy of doom, Deutero-Isaiah does not reject the older prophecy. He agrees with Jeremiah and Isaiah, Micah and Hosea, Ezekiel and others, that the people were guilty and deserved their fate, but he stresses that the term of punishment has come to an end. At the same time, by calling to mind prophecies of doom, he reminds the audience that YHWH foretold this justified disaster. Thus reversals include an element of confirmation, and like the confirmations they bolster prophetic tradition rather than challenge it.

In one respect, however, the reversals create a more ambiguous or tense relationship between Deutero-Isaiah and his predecessors. Jeremiah and

Micah criticized prophets who gave the nation empty assurances when they ought to have delivered criticisms or warnings. Deutero-Isaiah proclaims a message very similar to that of the prophets whom Jeremiah and Micah berated: he reassures, but he rarely criticizes or warns, at least in the first part of his book. The link between the false prophets and Deutero-Isaiah is especially clear in Isa 57.17–21, which allude to Jer 6.13–14. In that passage, Deutero-Isaiah himself utters the words once proclaimed by the false prophets ("things will be fine")—words that Jeremiah rejected in favor of a harsh threat. However, Deutero-Isaiah does not disavow Jeremiah's warning. He applies it exclusively to evildoers among the people by supplementing Jeremiah's statement "Things will not be fine" with the words "for the evil ones." Thus Deutero-Isaiah avoids repeating the false prophecies of the pre-exilic period; instead, he gives greater focus to Jeremiah's rebuke while stressing an optimistic prophecy more relevant to his own day. For Deutero-Isaiah, the false prophets had a correct message, but they delivered it at the wrong time. What absolves him from the crime Jeremiah describes is his understanding that the right words have merit only if delivered at the right time.

This tension also comes to the fore in the allusion to Mic 3.6–12 in Isa 58.1–11. Deutero-Isaiah borrows from a passage in which Micah condemned prophets whose message of encouragement closely resembles his own. Perhaps as a result of the friction between his message and Micah's, Deutero-Isaiah feels a need to begin the passage by specifying the people's sins—that is, Deutero-Isaiah does precisely what Micah had excoriated his opponents for failing to do. Only then does Deutero-Isaiah reverse Micah's message of doom. This allusion, then, lays bare (and effectively resolves) an anxiety of affiliation in Deutero-Isaiah's work: he wants to align himself with the tradition of the prophets whom the disaster of 586 B.C.E. authenticated, but his message is one that recalls that of their opponents.[7] In light of this anxiety, the categories of confirmation and negative reprediction take on additional significance. As he repeats some negative predictions approvingly, Deutero-Isaiah makes clear how he differs from the false prophets. By noting that prophecies of doom were correct, he shows that he follows in the tradition of true prophets. He demands we acknowledge that he should not be counted among the prophets who, overlooking the nation's faults, predicted weal. Confirmation and negative reprediction, then, temper the potentially radical impression created by reversal.

Examples from several categories have a further role: they highlight the new aspects of Deutero-Isaiah's message. Allusion not only helps authors express closeness to a tradition but provides an opportunity to distance their message from their predecessors'. Through including elements borrowed from an older text, an author can, paradoxically, demonstrate originality, because it is precisely when one juxtaposes two passages (as allusion forces a reader to do) that one notices differences between them and recognizes what is new in the alluding text. Deutero-Isaiah's use of older material frequently works in this way. In cases of reversal, the same words and images that an earlier prophet used to castigate the people serve in Deutero-Isaiah to comfort them. Deutero-Isaiah's message of consolation has a greater impact against the background of the predictions of catastrophe whose vocabulary he reuses and reverses. Similarly, new elements in a reprediction become especially distinct when the new prediction is read alongside its source. For example, Deutero-Isaiah leaves out any reference to David's descendants when he alludes to passages in which Isaiah or the psalmists promised them eternal rule. Realizing this, one sees with particular clarity that Deutero-Isaiah did not look forward to the renewal of kingship in the post-exilic era. The deliberate exclusion of Davidic promises—which becomes evident only when one examines the text Deutero-Isaiah adapts—makes a stronger impression than their mere absence.

Finally, allusions from all these categories provide Deutero-Isaiah with a means of constructing his own authority. By weaving elements from older works into his new one, Deutero-Isaiah (like most allusive authors) avows that his work is as worthwhile as his predecessors'.[8] Inclusion of borrowed material helps him to claim his place in the prophetic tradition. Allusion furnishes a credential; it becomes a conduit through which Deutero-Isaiah draws on the authority of recognized works. At the same time, his use of older material bolsters that tradition's authority.[9] By alluding, Deutero-Isaiah helps to maintain his sources' relevance. This culturally conservative effect (potentially a function of any allusive literature) played an important role in Deutero-Isaiah's day, when belief in the credibility of Israel's prophets and in the power of the God for whom they spoke was challenged by the apparent defeat of that God, the destruction of His Temple, and the exile of His people. (Further, as passages such as Ezek 12.21–28 show, even before the exile many Judeans were skeptical of prophets.) This bolstering effect is most prominent in cases of confirmation and reprediction.

Allusion in Isaiah 40–66 and 35 serves as a form of rhetoric in the primary sense of the term: a means of persuasion. Deutero-Isaiah attempted to convince a despondent nation that salvation drew near, and his literary art is best understood in the context of this historical circumstance.[10] By reusing familiar phrases from older texts, he drew his audience into his work, and hence made them more likely to attend to it. Listeners or readers who recognize a borrowed phrase experience a sense of enjoyment, a *plaisir du texte*, which begins with the basic act of recognition and increases as the ramifications of the allusion are processed. Deutero-Isaiah's references to older texts entertain his audience and thus motivate them to continue listening, absorbing, contemplating. Several stylistic techniques add to the enjoyment of his allusions. As listeners or readers anticipate the second half of a source's wording in a case of the split-up pattern, or delight in the brilliance of a sound or word play, they are captivated by medium, and hence also by message. These techniques merit further consideration.

Stylistic Patterns and the Identification of Allusions

When Deutero-Isaiah borrows vocabulary from an earlier text, he often subjects it to one of several revisionary techniques.[11] In the technique I have called the split-up pattern, the prophet separates a phrase from his source into two parts and inserts several words or even verses between them. (The technique serves as a fine metaphor for Deutero-Isaiah's use of earlier material generally: by splitting open an older phrase, Deutero-Isaiah creates a space into which he inserts his own words, adding something new to the tradition he passes on.)[12] Many allusions in Isaiah 40–66 and 35 point back to a source not only by repeating the source's words but also by hinting at one or two items with a similar-sounding but distinct word. I call this technique sound play. Another stylistic technique is based on the creative use of homonyms, and I call this word play. In these allusions the prophet employs a borrowed word in a sense different from that found in the older text. These techniques of allusion are especially typical of Deutero-Isaiah;[13] others that are not unique to this prophet appear more sporadically in his work. In some allusions, borrowed words appear in the same order they had in the source. Occasionally Deutero-Isaiah borrows an entire phrase word for word from an older text. The frequency of these stylistic techniques is noteworthy: the split-up pattern occurs in at least thirty-two allusions, sound play in thirty-seven, and word play in sixteen (some of these texts contain more than one case of the technique in question). Stylistic techniques that are less peculiar to Deutero-Isaianic allusion occur less frequently: identical word order occurs twelve times, and word-for-word borrowing ten times. (Incidentally, allusions that display each technique are distributed proportionally among chapters 40–55, 56–66, and 35, a finding whose implications I discuss in the Appendix.)

These stylistic features, along with the thematic patterns, can aid in the identification of allusions. Biblical texts may resemble each other for many reasons other than the reliance of one on the other: these include the common use of formulaic vocabulary, the treatment of a topic that naturally calls for certain words, or simple coincidence. A large number of shared vocabulary items cannot suffice to classify a parallel as a borrowing, although it may suggest the possibility. If many of the shared terms are uncommon ones, the possibility of allusion grows, but coincidence may still be responsible. However, patterns or techniques found throughout passages in which an author uses older texts help the reader confirm an allusion's presence. If a parallel between two texts exhibits a pattern that recurs in allusions in the later text, the possibility of allusion is high. Consequently, when a parallel between Deutero-Isaiah and an earlier text displays the split-up pattern, sound play, word play, or identical word order, it becomes likely that the parallel results from genuine borrowing. The same conclusion holds for parallels that fit into the thematic categories described above, or when the earlier text is one that Deutero-Isaiah has utilized elsewhere.

The Dynamics of Allusion

Allusions in Isaiah 40–66 and 35 frequently replicate dynamics found in biblical poetic parallelism.[14] Most lines of ancient Hebrew or Canaanite verse consist of two (sometimes three) members, which echo each other in a variety of ways. Ps 145.1 provides as apt an example as any: "I exalt You, my God, the King / and I bless Your name forever and ever." The two members (or versets, to use Robert Alter's term) display the same basic semantic content: in both the subject is "I," the verb is one of adoration, the object is the divinity. The versets share phonological features as well.[15] The initial word of each begins with a glottal stop, ends with the phoneme k, and includes the phoneme *r* and a labial consonant in between: אֲרוֹמִמְךָ (*^{ʾa}romimka*, "I exalt you") in the first verset, וַאֲבָרֲכָה (*wa-^{ʾa}bar^aka*, "and I bless") in the second. But (as James Kugel and Robert Alter have pointed out) the second half of a biblical poetic line not only repeats the first; it typically varies it in one of a few ways.[16] The second verset may intensify or specify the first. For example, Ps 118.9 echoes the wording of the previous verse but replaces a single term with a more powerful and particular one: "Better to depend on YHWH than to trust in *people* / Better to depend on YHWH than to trust in *princes*!" (Ps 118.8–9). An even more basic example of intensification occurs when a number is replaced with that number plus one: "We will raise up *seven* shepherds against him / *eight* leaders of men" (Mic 5.4).[17] The second half of a poetic line may identify an ambiguous item from the previous half-line. Take Ps 29.3: "The *qol* (קוֹל) of YHWH is on the water / The glorious God thunders." The subject of the first verset is equivocal, since *qol* can mean either "voice" or "the noise that accompanies lightning." The verb in the second verset ("thunders") makes clear that the latter is intended. A similar relationship appears in one of the earliest pieces of Hebrew poetry: "Let me sing to YHWH for He triumphed in triumph / The horse and its rider He threw into the sea!" (Exod 15.1). The second verset answers a question about the rather general statement in the first: "Just how did He triumph?—By throwing horse and rider into the sea!" At times, a second verset overturns its predecessor while retaining complementary language: "A wicked man borrows but does not repay / A righteous man is generous and giving" (Ps 37.21).

Deutero-Isaiah's allusions unfold from their sources in the same manner that second versets build on first versets: through structures of specification, antithesis, and intensification. In cases of reprediction, an earlier prophecy is made more specific. Jeremiah or Isaiah spoke broadly of better days, and Deutero-Isaiah answers the question, when are those better days coming? Isaiah or Nahum spoke of the fate of the enemy; the exilic prophet explains that this enemy is Babylon. The category of reversal calls to mind the characteristic of a second verset to mimic the semantic content of its predecessor while presenting its antithesis: the markers consist of words and images taken directly from the evoked text, but their message is one of reassurance, not rebuke.

A dynamic of intensification motivates allusions in several thematic categories, recalling a basic structure of biblical parallelism described above: "A, and what's more, A+." Deutero-Isaiah frequently expands on his sources' figures, either by adding to them through a logic of metonymy or by repeating them insistently. This trope reflects the enthusiasm (and perhaps the anxiety) of the exilic prophet. Deutero-Isaiah seems eager that the reader not miss something, whether an interesting idea only touched on in the evoked text or the fact of the allusion itself. A fine example of this tendency appears already in Isaiah 35.[18] Jeremiah had stated:

> Thus says YHWH: Sing (רָנּוּ) to Jacob joyously (שִׂמְחָה), and shout to the chief (בְּרֹאשׁ) of nations. . . . Make it known! Give praise! And say (וְאִמְרוּ): . . . I am about to bring (הִנְנִי מֵבִיא) them from a northern land, and I shall gather them from the ends of the earth; the blind and the lame ([19]עִוֵּר וּפִסֵּחַ) will be among them, together with those who are pregnant and giving birth. A great multitude will return here (יָשׁוּבוּ הֵנָּה). With weeping they will come (יָבֹאוּ) and because of supplications[20] I shall bring them in (אוֹבִילֵם). I shall lead them (אוֹלִיכֵם) to streams of water (נַחֲלֵי מַיִם) on a straight path (בְּדֶרֶךְ); they will not falter on it. (Jer 31.7–9)

Deutero-Isaiah uses the same images when he describes the returnees of his day:

> Say (אִמְרוּ) to the anxious, Be strong! Do not fear. Behold your God will come with requital (הִנֵּה . . . יָבוֹא). . . . Then the eyes of the blind (עִוְרִים) will open and the ears of the deaf will be unsealed. Then the lame (פִּסֵּחַ) will jump like gazelles, and the tongue of the mute will sing (וְתָרֹן). For water (מַיִם) gushes in the desert, and streams (וּנְחָלִים) in the desolate places. The dry land will become a pool, and a parched wilderness—founts of water (מָיִם). . . . And there will be a way and a path (וְדֶרֶךְ), and it will be called the path (וְדֶרֶךְ) of the Holy One. . . . Those who go on this path, even fools (וֶאֱוִילִים), will not err. No lion will be there. . . . The redeemed will go (וְהָלְכוּ). Those ransomed by YHWH will return (יְשֻׁבוּן), and they will come to Zion in song (וּבָאוּ צִיּוֹן בְּרִנָּה), with eternal happiness (וְשִׂמְחַת עוֹלָם) on their heads (עַל־רֹאשָׁם); they will achieve joy and happiness (וְשִׂמְחָה), and sorrow and sighing will flee. (Isa 35.4–10)

The many shared words already suggest that the correspondence between these two passages is more than a coincidence. Moreover, vocabulary in the later passage relates to vocabulary from Jeremiah in ways we have seen in other Deutero-Isaianic allusions. Jeremiah refers to "the blind and lame" in a single phrase: עור ופסח. These words are split apart in Isaiah 35, occurring in two separate clauses: first Deutero-Isaiah says אָז תִּפָּקַחְנָה עֵינֵי עִוְרִים ("then the eyes of *the blind* will open"); then, after mentioning the deaf, he says אָז יְדַלֵּג כָּאַיָּל פִּסֵּחַ ("then *the lame* will jump like gazelles"). A combination of this split-up pattern and Seidel's law[21] affects Jeremiah's "streams of water," so that the individual words "water" and "streams" appear in reverse order separated by several new words. A delightful sound play evokes Jeremiah's word אוֹבִילֵם (*'obileim*, "I shall bring them in"). The later writer does not repeat that word, but he hints at it with the similar-sounding word אֱוִילִים (*'ewilim*, "fools").[22] In light of these typical stylistic patterns, it is clear that Deutero-Isaiah utilized Jer 31.7–9 specifically.[23]

Deutero-Isaiah amplifies many of his predecessor's figures, just as the second verset of a parallel line in biblical poetry often intensifies the first. Some markers are insistently repeated, as if to make sure one can't miss them: דרך ("way") appears three times, מים ("water") twice. Jeremiah mentioned the blind and the lame briefly, but Deutero-Isaiah devotes two verses to describing them along with the deaf and the dumb. A few words announcing that no one will stumble on the straight path God prepares become two verses describing the holiness of the path, assuring listeners that even fools will not err on it, and mentioning several wild animals that are sure not to be seen on the way. Jeremiah's short comment regarding the availability of water on the way back from Assyria gives Deutero-Isaiah an opportunity to describe water in the desert, streams in desolate places, pools in dry land, founts in a parched wilderness. Thus a passing remark in Jeremiah is transformed into a description of a new Exodus in Deutero-Isaiah, since the water motif as it appears in the later text clearly imitates descriptions of the people's journey after leaving Egypt.[24]

The same phenomenon occurs in other allusions. Nahum spoke of "a herald who announces well-being" (Nah 2.1). In his evocation of that passage, Deutero-Isaiah repeats those words exactly and then adds reference to "a herald of good news, who announces victory, who says to Zion, 'Your God has taken the throne!'" (Isa 52.7). A psalmist asked that respect for the king and his descendants last as long as the moon and the sun:

Let them fear you with the sun (שֶׁמֶשׁ) and before the moon (יָרֵחַ) for all generations (דּוֹר דּוֹרִים). . . . May his name remain forever before the sun (שֶׁמֶשׁ). (Ps 72.5, 17)

Yet one cannot deny that the moon does wax and wane, and even the sun sets every day. Deutero-Isaiah therefore announces (in the course of an elaborate reworking of Psalm 72) that the people will not merely enjoy well-being; at least for purposes of metaphor, nature itself will be altered so that the sun will never set on them:

I will make you an eternal majesty, a thing of joy for all generations (דּוֹר וָדוֹר). . . . The sun (הַשֶּׁמֶשׁ) will be your light not only by day, and as for the brightness of the moon (הַיָּרֵחַ)—it will not shine for you only by night.[25] . . . Your sun (שִׁמְשֵׁךְ) will never set, nor your moon (וִירֵחֵךְ) go away. For YHWH will be your eternal light. (Isa 60.15, 19–20)[26]

Deutero-Isaiah recoils from any ambiguity that would allow his audience to entertain doubt regarding YHWH's unending, uninterrupted favor. By exaggerating the figures of speech found in the source, he also clarifies it, thus treating it like the first half of a poetic line. The exilic author also responds to the source: where the psalmist articulated a request ("Let them fear. . . . May his name remain"), the prophet announces that the people as a whole will be granted what the psalmist sought for the king. (The substitution of nation for monarch can itself be seen as an intensification ["not just the king but his whole nation!"] and also a specification ["David's seed really means David's family, which is all Israel"].) Similar structures of intensification appear elsewhere as well: see the allusions to Isa 2.6–21 in Isa 57.3–15; to Jer 31.33–35 in Isa 54.10–13; and to Ps 102.25–27 in Isa 51.6–8.

A related phenomenon involves parallel word pairs. In biblical (and other Canaanite) poetry, a word appearing in one verset is regularly joined by a particular word in the next. For example, שמע ("hear") parallels האזין ("give ear") in Ps 39.13, 49.2, 54.4; Isa 1.2; Deut 32.1; and elsewhere.[27] Some allusions in Deutero-Isaiah make use of this phenomenon. At times, a text evoked by Deutero-Isaiah includes one term but not the item with which that term is typically paralleled in biblical poetry. In such a case, Deutero-Isaiah may introduce the standard parallel in the allusion. Thus he treats his source as an initial verset and constructs his allusion as a distant second verset. For example, Isa 2.2 includes the verb וְנָהֲרוּ ("they streamed"), which is almost identical with the noun נָהָר ("river, current"). The standard poetic parallel of this noun is יָם ("sea"),[28] which does not appear in Isa 2.1–4 but does occur in Deutero-Isaiah's borrowing from that passage in Isa 60.5. A complex variation of this pattern appears in Isa 42.5–9, which evoke Jer 31.31–36. Isa 42.5 describes God as רֹקַע הָאָרֶץ ("who spread out the earth"). This phrase recalls the description of God in Jer 31.35 as רֹגַע הַיָּם ("who stills the sea"), and not only due to the sound play of *roqaʿ* ("spread out") and *rogaʿ* ("stills"). The former verb's object, "earth," is a standard poetic parallel for the latter verb's object, "sea."[29] Deutero-Isaiah supplies a word that corresponds to his source according to the poetics of the Hebrew parallel line, hence tightening the connection between the marked item and its punning marker. Similar cases occur elsewhere (e.g., Isa 52.13, which begins a lengthy allusion to Isaiah 6 by supplying יַשְׂכִּיל ["discern"], a frequent parallel for two verbs in Isa 6.9, יד״ע ["know"] and בי״ן ["understand"]).[30] In these passages, Deutero-Isaiah does not repeat a particular word from the source, but articulates an echo the source implies to the ear well-versed in Hebrew prosody. These subtle references back to the evoked text show Deutero-Isaiah to be poet as much as prophet.

The Centrality of Allusion in Isaiah 40–66

One further aspect of the poetics of allusion in Deutero-Isaiah deserves attention. Many (to an extent, all) literary creations rely on their predecessors, but in some compositions the use of older texts becomes a primary concern. Deutero-Isaiah's prophetic corpus represents such a composition. Allusions occur in every chapter of Isaiah 40–66 and 35; most passages draw upon several sources. Moreover, particularly allusive works tend to identify themselves as such, especially in their opening lines. By beginning with a bevy of allusions, an author signals that older material will play a crucial role in the text at hand.[31] The opening passage of Deutero-Isaiah, Isa 40.1–11, functions in precisely this way.[32] It alludes to Isa 28.1–2, Jer 16.16–18 and 31.15, and Ezek 21.2–12; in addition, it may allude to Isaiah 6, Exod 32.14–15, and Lamentations' frequent refrain, "There is no comforter"

(Lam 1.2, 9, 16, 21). Further, this passage includes the phrase, "For the mouth of YHWH has spoken" (v. 5), which sometimes serves as a citation formula in biblical texts that quote an earlier work.[33] The remainder of the first chapter continues this vigorous pace of allusion. Isa 40.12–31 refer the reader back to Isa 6.9–10, Psalm 82, Genesis 1, and, perhaps, Isa 5.27 and Jer 10.1–16.

These initial references to the prophet's sources not only introduce the reader to the allusive predilection of this work; they also present nearly all the methods of allusion which characterize the next twenty-seven chapters. In the first thirty-one verses of Deutero-Isaiah, we find most of the thematic categories I have discussed: confirmation (of the prediction of double punishment in Jeremiah 16), reprediction with historical recontextualization (of Jeremiah 31's prediction of restoration for the Assyrian exiles), repetition of a psalm's message (based on Psalm 82), several cases of reversal (which abrogate negative predictions from Jeremiah 10, Isaiah 6 and 28, and Ezekiel 21), and polemic (against anthropomorphic attitudes in Genesis 1). Each of the stylistic traits appears as well: the split-up pattern occurs twice, sound play one or possibly two times, word play and identical word order once each.

Thus one could summarize the poetics of allusion in Isaiah 40–66 and 35 as a whole simply by analyzing allusions in the first thirty-one verses of that collection; almost every aspect of the prophet's method appears. This density of reworked material does not continue uniformly through the rest of the work. Some chapters (especially the so-called servant songs) match this density; many others do not, though every chapter in 40–66 and 35 contains at least a few cases that display typical features of Deutero-Isaianic allusion. The presence of so many allusions at the outset of the work proclaims that the reuse of older material is central to Deutero-Isaiah's project. Further, the stylistic techniques that appear throughout these chapters also signal the dependence on predecessors. By making the allusions more identifiable and enjoyable to the reader, the techniques highlight the presence of borrowed material.

The exilic prophet announces: I am a reader, a traditionalist, a recycler. He wants his audience to know that he invests the great labor necessary to inherit a tradition. In so doing, he emphasizes at once his dependence and his originality: he shows that he knows and reveres older texts—and that he differs from them in specific and identifiable ways. Why he needs to do so is discussed at the end of this chapter.

Deutero-Isaiah's Sources

In the body of this work and elsewhere, I discuss the extent of Deutero-Isaiah's sources.[34] I argue, for instance, that he knew an early version of Jeremiah's prophecies which did not yet include all the bodies of material found in the canonical forms of the Book of Jeremiah known from the MT and the LXX. On the other hand, I contend that he utilized a collection of Isaiah's oracles that already contained many texts dated by some critics to the post-exilic period. I also show that Deutero-Isaiah drew from several types of material: prophecy, lamentation, psalms, and (far less frequently) narrative and law. Two larger questions regarding his sources need further elaboration.

First, we may ask, what is the relative place of the different types of material in Deutero-Isaiah's project of allusion, and does he relate to these different types of material in different ways? Second, did Deutero-Isaiah know his sources in oral or written form?

The Relative Place of Different Types of Material

Deutero-Isaiah's sources are not limited to any single stream of Israelite tradition. He utilized Deuteronomistic sources (the Book of Deuteronomy itself as well as prophets connected to that stream of tradition, such as Hosea) and knew priestly traditions (HS and PT from the Pentateuch and probably Ezekiel as well). He alluded to both northern and southern prophets, and to prophets of the eighth, seventh, and sixth centuries. The diverse nature of his sources may result from the mixing of various traditions in the exile, where the collecting and preservation of earlier texts is likely to have been a priority; further, Deutero-Isaiah's allusions may have been designed to promote that mixing. Deutero-Isaiah emerges, then, as a unification text: by alluding to such a wide range of older works, he validates all these streams of tradition, intimating that post-exilic Judaism's library will be a wide-ranging one.[35]

Although Deutero-Isaiah used many sorts of material, he shows strong preferences for some texts. Prophecy was his most frequent and most important source. This is hardly surprising, given Deutero-Isaiah's own claim to prophetic inspiration, a claim that was at once problematic and at least in part dependent on his predecessors. Two prophets provided the bulk of his sources: Jeremiah and Isaiah (in that order). He utilized other prophets more sporadically. He evokes only one or two passages from Micah and Nahum. There are a few more allusions to or echoes of Hosea, Ezekiel, and Zephaniah, but the number of firm cases is small, perhaps not more than two for each prophet. Deutero-Isaiah may have alluded most often to Jeremiah and Isaiah because, as well-known figures, they were more useful sources of authority than the others. Shorter works such as Hosea, Nahum, and Zephaniah may not have been well-known enough to reinforce Deutero-Isaiah's work. Thus, Deutero-Isaiah deliberately focused his allusive project on larger corpora. At the same time, it is important to note that the other prophetic collections were smaller than those of Jeremiah and Isaiah, so that one would expect fewer allusions to them in any event; while only a few references to each of these prophets appears, taken together they comprise a significant source. Ezekiel's place in Deutero-Isaiah's allusive project differs. Though Ezekiel's work is fairly lengthy, he was nearly a contemporary of Deutero-Isaiah, and both were prophets of the exile. Consequently, if Deutero-Isaiah's audience was suspicious of his prophetic authority (or if Deutero-Isaiah himself entertained self-doubt), they might have had a similar view of Ezekiel. Hence allusion to Ezekiel helped Deutero-Isaiah only marginally.[36]

Several types of prophetic material prove productive for Deutero-Isaiah: rebuke, encouragement, lament, and eschatology. On the other hand, Deutero-Isaiah seems less interested in the biography of prophets and the historical information included within prophetic books. Although he does base typologies on descriptions of Jeremiah and Nebuchadnezzar found in Jeremiah's work, he does not borrow vocabulary and themes from narrative passages that describe Isaiah, Jeremiah, or other prophets. Even when he borrows from Hosea 1–2 (chapters in which Hosea makes his own life a metaphor for God's relationship with Israel), he does not exploit the chapters' biographical aspects. The absence of allusion to narratives about Jeremiah almost certainly results from their not having been available to Deutero-Isaiah;[37] but his tendency not to use material of this sort even from other prophets also reflects his lesser interest in prophetic biography.

Deutero-Isaiah alluded to psalms more frequently than do other Hebrew prophets, whether pre-exilic or post-exilic. The reason for his greater dependence on songs of promise and praise has been described well by Hugo Greßmann: Deutero-Isaiah's predictions were mostly positive, and hence they shared more in tone with the psalms than did older prophecies, which were often full of rebuke, warning, and predictions of doom.[38]

Texts known to us from the Pentateuch provide the source for a small fraction of Deutero-Isaiah's allusions. Our prophet knew priestly, Deuteronomic, and other Pentateuchal texts, but he did not underscore his dependence on them. Indeed, he approached that material boldly: his references to the Pentateuch include several cases of polemic. Whereas Deutero-Isaiah was at pains to stress his continuity with prophetic traditions, he felt free to disagree with priestly ones; while he attempted to bolster the former, on occasion he clashed with the latter. Nonetheless, it is important not to misunderstand the nature of Deutero-Isaiah's quarrels with priestly writers. Deutero-Isaiah is not opposed to torah in the sense of law; antinomianism plays no role in his utterances. On the contrary, he affirms the importance of observing the Sabbath (Isa 56.2, 4, 6), a concern he shares especially with the priestly writers;[39] he criticizes Jacob for his failure to sacrifice to YHWH (Isa 43.22–28); he attributes the exile to the nation's disobedience of YHWH's torah (Isa 42.18–25); he tells them they would have enjoyed well-being if only they had observed the commandments (Isa 48.17–19); he denounces cultic improprieties (Isa 57; 66.3–4, 17). But he seems to differ with priestly writers on the composition of the priesthood (see Isa 56.4–7; 61.5–6), and he pointedly contradicts those aspects of priestly theology he finds too anthropomorphic (Isa 40.12–31; 44.24; 45.6–7, 18–19).

Significantly, passages that break with priestly material also incorporate positive references to older texts. In Isa 40.12–31, Deutero-Isaiah subtly rebuts the priestly creation account from Genesis 1, insisting that heavenly beings other than YHWH had no role whatsoever in creation. Yet in these same verses, Deutero-Isaiah weaves in material from Isaiah 6 and perhaps also from Isa 5.27 and Jer 10.1–16, thus making clear that he does not reject all, or even most, of his predecessors. Moreover, he calls the audience's attention to Psalm 82, a pre-exilic text that had already belittled the heavenly host. In chapter 56 he demurs from the Holiness School's rules regarding the priesthood, but in the same passage he recalls approvingly that school's emphasis on the Sabbath, and he stresses the theme of covenant observance. In both these passages Deutero-Isaiah integrates authoritative words into his text precisely as he impugns aspects of priestly teaching. To dispel the impression that he stands against the tradition, Deutero-Isaiah highlights his affiliation with his predecessors, an affiliation that remains firm even though he disagrees with some of them. Allusion, then, serves to minimize what might be seen as presumption in his references to priestly literature.

Other types of material played no role or a much smaller role. The almost total absence of allusions to wisdom literature shows that Deutero-Isaiah was either unfamiliar with or (more likely) uninterested in this stream of Israelite tradition.[40] This is not surprising, since Deutero-Isaiah was most concerned with the unique aspects of Israelite religion: the one God, the land He gave to His people, and the reliable prophets He sent them. Wisdom literature offered less to Deutero-Isaiah. It was as well-known among the Babylonians as among the Judeans they conquered. Thus it did not help the exilic prophet place himself in a particularly Hebrew literary tradition, nor did wisdom literature contribute to a demonstration of the tradition's incomparability.[41] Deutero-Isaiah does not allude to the historical works incorporated in Joshua, Judges, Samuel, and Kings. It is impossible to know whether Deutero-Isaiah did not have access to these works or was simply less interested in them.

Deutero-Isaiah's Sources: Oral or Written?

In the view of many scholars, the prophecies upon which Deutero-Isaiah relied were delivered orally and later committed to writing.[42] Similarly, psalms and laments were composed to be recited, though they were also written down for purposes of preservation. Did Deutero-Isaiah know these sources in their original oral form, or did he utilize written sources?

It initially seems likely that he knew his sources in written form. Deutero-Isaiah repeatedly displays knowledge of a large number of passages from his sources. It follows that his knowledge was based on collections to which he could have made frequent reference, and such a reference work, one assumes, must have been written. But this assumption is not incontrovertible. Large bodies of texts were committed to memory in antiquity, and even the formal study of texts was sometimes based not on written texts but on recitation of memorized passages. This was the case, for example, among the *tanna'im* (literally, "the repeaters") in early rabbinic Judaism.[43] It is not inconceivable that Deutero-Isaiah memorized earlier prophetic collections or that he studied them, and referred to them, in an oral form.

One might object that Deutero-Isaiah's highly stylized and extensive use of lengthy passages must result from the study of a written document.[44]

Stylistic features (especially the split-up pattern and identical word order) and the length of some passages to which he alludes indicate a high level of complexity in his use of sources. That complexity might have required a source he could look at rather than one he merely heard.[45] On the other hand, however, one should recall that Milton's *Paradise Lost*, a peerless *tour de force* of allusive literature, was composed orally by a "poet blind yet bold" (as Andrew Marvell called him in the introduction to the poem's first edition). Having lost his sight years before he composed the poem, Milton was unable to look at the sources he used so richly; he knew some by heart, and others he heard when he directed his daughters to read them to him.[46] There exists empirical evidence, then, that highly complex and recurrent allusions can be made to sources known orally.

Nevertheless, evidence such as Isa 8.16 and Jer 36.4 indicates that prophecies, even if delivered orally, were written down in Israel. Similarly, from the metaphor in Ezek 2.8–3.4 one can surmise that prophecies existed on scrolls. Thus, while one should not discount the possibility that Deutero-Isaiah knew his sources as oral texts, it remains more likely that he consulted them in written form. Of course, these two possibilities are not incompatible. Texts that were written down were almost certainly recited in liturgical or educational settings, and Deutero-Isaiah's knowledge of written texts would have come from both seeing and hearing them.[47]

Deutero-Isaiah's Allusions in the Context of Inner-Biblical Exegesis and Allusion

In the first chapter, I outlined several formal and thematic categories into which cases of inner-biblical allusion and exegesis tend to fall. How does Deutero-Isaiah's work relate to these broad categories?

At a formal level, biblical texts connect to their sources in three ways: through implicit reference, explicit citation, and inclusion. In Deutero-Isaiah, only the first of these appears. The prophet does not announce that he is alluding to or revising an older text, and he never mentions his sources by name. The only possible exceptions involve passages in which he uses the phrase כִּי פִּי ה' דִּבֵּר ("for the mouth of YHWH has spoken"), which may be a formula indicating reliance on an older oracle.[48] Even in those cases (Isa 58.14, which relies on Deut 32.9–14, and Isa 40.5, which relies on Ezek 21.2–

12), the prophet does not refer to his source by name. Similarly, the stylistic features can flag the presence of allusion: they help the audience identify his reliance on sources, and the prophet may well have intended them to act that way. Nonetheless, the work of identifying a reference to an older text is left to the reader or listener.[49]

By requiring the audience to detect the presence of allusion, Deutero-Isaiah increases the pleasure they experience as they interpret his work. This sense of play (an important aspect of literary allusion) encourages the audience to engage themselves actively as they read or listen to the poetry. In addition, a text that refers implicitly rather than explicitly gives the appearance—illusory, to be sure, but nevertheless important—of independence in relation to its precursors. Such a work does not deny that it has predecessors; on the contrary, authors like Deutero-Isaiah use allusion to spotlight their participation in a tradition. But a work whose allusions are implicit appropriates for itself a status roughly equal to that of its predecessors, while a work that cites older authorities by name tends to identify itself as secondary. This formal tendency, therefore, will play a role in our discussion of Deutero-Isaiah's self-understanding and his place in prophetic tradition.

At a thematic or strategic level, biblical texts relate to their sources through influence, allusion, exegesis, and echo; the first two of these at times overlap with the categories of revision and polemic. The bulk of cases in Deutero-Isaiah fall into the category of allusion: the prophet usually borrows words, images, and ideas from his predecessors in order to enrich his own work, not to alter our reading of the predecessors (in which case they would be exegesis), nor to replace the works of the predecessors (in which case they would be revision). Cases of echo occur frequently as well. Polemic is rare: it is limited to a few references to the Pentateuch.

Deutero-Isaiah's references to older texts occasionally involve revision or exegesis. Several times the prophet borrows language from Isaiah ben Amoṣ and the Book of Psalms which promises eternal kingship to the Davidic family. As he does so, he omits any reference to a human king in these passages, and he alters the promise so that it refers to Israel as a whole. Similarly, Deutero-Isaiah refers several times to Jeremiah's notion of a new covenant that will replace the old one and will never be broken by Israel. Although the later prophet repeats this prophecy often, he always shies away from its radical aspects. In both these cases, one senses that Deutero-Isaiah disagrees with one element of his predecessors' thought and suggests a revised version of their doctrines. Indeed, the exilic prophet may attempt to interpret the older texts, albeit in a tendentious manner. He may imply that one should understand "house of David" in Isaiah and the psalms broadly, to include all the members of the nation David ruled rather than David's descendants alone. In such a case, the references in question represent not so much allusion as exegesis. Similarly, Deutero-Isaiah refers to personal laments in the Book of Psalms, but he treats those psalms as if the first-person singular speaker were the nation Israel (see, for example, his extensive reworking of Psalm 72 in Isa 44.28–45.8, 49.7–23, and 60.1–21). In so doing, the prophet may imply that one should understand the individual speaker in these psalms metaphorically as Israel personified—that is, that one read the psalms in question as national laments.

In these cases Deutero-Isaiah's inner-biblical allusion may beget inner-biblical exegesis. But this is exegesis of a very subtle sort. The prophet does not overtly tell his audience how to understand older texts in the way a commentator does. Rather, the audience, having heard a new idea (e.g., the Davidic promise applied to the whole nation), may incorporate it into the older text when they read it subsequently. The interpretation of the older text functions silently, even unconsciously. Because the exilic prophet revises ideas from the older texts, readers may begin to understand the older texts in a new fashion; but it is not clear that this was Deutero-Isaiah's goal. Thus the exilic prophet points the way toward the post-biblical period, in which exegesis played an increasingly important role, but he is by no means a commentator in the sense that the authors of Qumran pesher, rabbinic midrash, or patristic homilies were.[50]

Deutero-Isaiah and the Decline of Prophecy

That Deutero-Isaiah found it necessary or desirable to refer to his predecessors tells us a great deal about his self-understanding and about his place in the history of Israelite prophecy. Before examining these issues, however, it will be necessary to discuss the nature of prophecy in the post-exilic period.

Attitudes Toward Prophecy in the Post-Exilic Era

Israelite prophecy became less common and ultimately ceased a few generations after the exile—or, to speak with greater precision: after the first century of the Second Temple period, Jews tended not to accept the possibility that God still communicated with the Jewish people by speaking directly to certain individuals.[51] Several factors led to this shift in attitude. The termination of kingship contributed to the deterioration of prophecy in two ways. Pre-exilic prophecy was closely related to the institution of kingship. Already David had a prophet on his staff, and even peripheral or unpopular prophets such as Jeremiah often had messages for the king.[52] The absence of a royal audience for prophecy resulted in the institution's decline.[53] A second, even more important factor was the loss of the ideological and imaginative world in which prophecy functioned. Relationships between heaven and earth in ancient Near Eastern thinking were well-defined. The structure of earth imitated that of heaven, in that kingship and temple below reflected parallel institutions above. Closely aligned with those institutions (not only practically but also philosophically) were others that allowed contact between heaven and earth: prophecy, divination, prayer, and sacrifice. If there were no king on the throne, then the world was amiss, and communication between heaven and earth was no longer possible—or at least the old methods of liaison were no longer intact, and new ones had to be sought out.[54] After the dethronement of the Davidic kings, Judean writers were exiles, not merely geographically but metaphysically. Even though some of them lived in their own land, they remained in an exilic situation as long as their own king was not on the throne.[55]

Hence, from 586 (or really 597) B.C.E. onward, the conceptual matrix in which Israelite prophecy existed was broken, and prophecy inevitably began to wane. The destruction of the Temple also contributed to this decline. As the central nexus between heaven and earth, the Temple allowed for the possibility of communication between God and human. (I mean this phenomenologically and not in the sense that prophecy could only occur in the Temple.) If the Temple did not stand, the very notion of prophecy was suspect. Even after it was rebuilt around 518, Judeans knew that the new Temple was not the equal of the one built by David's son, architecturally or metaphysically. Thus the status of prophecy continued to be precarious in the Second Temple period.[56]

Post-exilic prophets at the outset of the Second Temple period displayed a consciousness of their secondary status, of being slightly less close to YHWH than the great prophets of yore. Early in the Persian era, Haggai, Zechariah, and Malachi relayed divine messages to the nation, but their access to YHWH appears limited when compared to that of the classical prophets. Often they are addressed not by God but by an angelic intermediary. At times they fail to understand what they are told or what they see. Compare Jer. 1.11–14, for example, with Zech 2.1–14: the later prophet is more distant both from YHWH (in that he is addressed by an angel) and from YHWH's message (in that he must have it explained to him). Further, Zechariah hints that he received his visions while asleep—that is, his prophecies were revealed through dreams (4.1). Dream-visions were considered a lesser form of prophecy (see Num 12.7), and some writers even associated dream-visions with false prophecy (Jer 23.25–29). Of course, Zechariah does not by any means present himself as a false prophet; like pre-exilic prophets, he claims to have genuine access to the divine council.[57] But his prophetic experiences are in many ways inferior to those of his predecessors.[58] Although this tendency is not ubiquitous among the last prophets (in Hag 1.1, the prophet is addressed directly), it does reveal the beginning of a sense of distance between them and their classical forebears.[59]

As prophecy faded, new ways to ascertain or articulate YHWH's will arose. Scribes collected, edited, and perhaps revised existing records of prophetic discourse, and in so doing they presented the material in a way relevant to their own day.[60] Later in the Second Temple period, people who composed religious documents came increasingly to attribute their work to older, recognized figures, such as the patriarchs or Jeremiah's secretary, Baruch. This turn towards pseudepigraphy discloses a feeling that revelation or divinely sanctioned religious instruction must come from the mouth of a pre-exilic authority.[61] The reading of existing prophetic texts also helped take the place of prophecy during the Second Temple period and thereafter. The beginnings of this process can be found already in the Bible. William Schniedewind shows that Levitical prophecies in the Book of Chronicles relied heavily on the words of classical prophets,[62] and the same has long been noticed in regard to Haggai and Malachi.[63] Reliance on older texts became more intense later in the Second Temple period as claims to prophecy ceased altogether. In Daniel 9 (written around 167 B.C.E.), Daniel meditates on the words of the prophet Jeremiah and prays that he might understand them, whereupon the angel Gabriel appears to explain the older works to him. In Qumran during the second and first centuries B.C.E. and the first century C.E., a whole literature developed in which the meaning of prophetic texts for the present was laid out. While the Habakkuk pesher makes clear that the Teacher of Righteousness whose interpretations are found in these *pesharim* was himself inspired (1QpHab 7.2–4), the Teacher did not compose his own prophecies; he limited himself to commenting on already existing texts.[64] By the time of the rabbis, even this more limited claim to inspiration had faded. The rabbis did not generally suggest that their interpretations were inspired. Indeed, the fact that they engage in debate regarding correct understandings of biblical verses indicates that they saw their readings as fallible, and this fallibility shows that the readings were human in origin.[65] The decline of inspiration and the rise of interpretation form a continuum: as the decline became more acute, interpretation became more important.

Deutero-Isaiah's Self-Understanding

Many scholars suggest that already in Isaiah 40–66 we can observe the decline or even cessation of prophecy. Julius Wellhausen states,

> The writer of Isaiah xl. seq. might . . . be called a prophet, but he does not claim to be one; his anonymity, which is evidently intentional, leaves no doubt as to this. He is, in fact, more of a theologian: he is principally occupied in reflecting on the results of the foregoing development of which prophecy had been the leaven; these are fixed possessions now secured; he is gathering in the harvest.[66]

Other scholars, especially those associated with the "unity of Isaiah" school, suggest that his anonymity is a form of pseudepigraphy: the author of these chapters attributes (or at least connects) his own work to a respected prophet of old by adding it to the scroll of Isaiah ben Amoṣ.[67] This suggestion is dubious, however. There is no evidence that Deutero-Isaiah himself appended his work to that of Isaiah ben Amoṣ. Moreover, the material presented above in Chapters 2 and 3 shows that Deutero-Isaiah's connections to Isaiah are not as strong as his connections to Jeremiah and do not differ in kind from his links with a wide range of prophets. These circumstances render implausible the notion that Deutero-Isaiah regarded himself primarily as supplementing Isaiah.[68] Some scholars would make much of the fact that the author of 40–66 is never termed a prophet (נָבִיא), but this is hardly persuasive: Isaiah ben Amoṣ, Micah, and Amos are never described in their books by this term, but none would doubt that they are among the prophets.[69]

How, then, can one characterize Deutero-Isaiah's discourse? Deutero-Isaiah claims that he conveys YHWH's words, not his own, and hence it is appropriate to term Deutero-Isaiah a prophet.[70] That he attributes his message directly to YHWH is clear from the opening words of Isaiah 40: " 'Comfort, comfort my people,' your God is saying (יֹאמַר אֱ־לֹהֵיכֶם)." Throughout the book, Deutero-Isaiah introduces pronouncements with the words "Thus says YHWH (כֹּה אָמַר ה')"[71] or the formula "an utterance of YHWH (נְאֻם ה')."[72] Deutero-Isaiah appears far less affected by the decline of prophecy than Zechariah, who came after him: like Isaiah or Jeremiah, Deutero-Isaiah hears YHWH's words directly, not through an angelic mediator. Post-exilic prophets experience obscure, dream-like visions in need of interpretation, which is usually provided by an angel, but these do not occur in Isaiah 40–66. In short, Deutero-Isaiah resembles the prophets who preceded him more than those who came after him.

Nevertheless, Deutero-Isaiah has already experienced the disturbances that would eventually lead to the dissolution of prophecy and its replacement by exegetical practices: the Temple's destruction, the monarchy's termination, the nation's exile. As a result, the decline of prophecy begins to affect his work, if only slightly. His status as a prophet may have appeared suspect, both to his audience and to himself. Deutero-Isaiah delivered oracles in the name of Zion's God even though he lived in exile, far from Zion.[73] He worked after the destruction of the Temple, which had been thought to provide a nexus between heaven and earth, thus allowing for communication between YHWH and His people. Unlike Ezekiel (who had lived in pre-destruction Jerusalem before he prophesied in exile, and whose first prophetic revelations took place before the Temple's destruction), Deutero-Isaiah in all likelihood had never seen the Land of Israel when he began his career, and his first encounter with prophetic spirit occurred after the Temple was no more. As a result, he may have grappled with a dilemma regarding his prophetic stature. This crisis of authority and his response to it become most evident in his allusion to Isa 2.1–4/Micah 4.1–4 appearing in Isa 51.3–5.

This predicament expresses itself in the first passage of the collection. Deutero-Isaiah does not report a traditional initiation or call scene of the sort that Moses, Isaiah, Jeremiah, and Ezekiel experienced.[74] But the opening verses of his work do contain hints of an initiation, and some elements of the classical call appear later in his work.[75] Prophetic objection and divine reassurance typify the initiation form; they occupy the bulk of Moses' call (see Exod 3.11–4.17) and are found in the commissioning of Jeremiah and Isaiah as well (see Jer 1.6–8 and Isa 6.5–7). These elements occur in Isa 40.6–8, but in an ambiguous fashion. Deutero-Isaiah's objection may consist merely of his query in 40.6, "What shall I proclaim?"[76] This question is not so much a protest as a laconic request for additional information. God answers in Isa 40.6b–8: you should proclaim that God's word endures, in contrast to the work of frail humans, who wither like grass in a hot wind from YHWH (רוח ה׳). According to this response, the nation can be sure that YHWH will prove more powerful than its Babylonian captors, who are mere flesh. But the text allows another interpretation: the prophet's words may continue through all of verses 6 and 7. In this case, the רוח ה׳ that withers human flesh must be rendered not just as "wind" but as "the spirit of prophecy." Hence Deutero-Isaiah expresses in these verses his fear that the divine spirit will destroy him. (The "flesh" of verse 6, according to this reading, refers not to the Babylonians but to the prophet himself, who worries that the prophetic spirit may injure him or mar his life, as indeed it marred Jeremiah's.) The divine response appears in verse 8: regardless of human anxieties, God's word endures and will be proclaimed.[77] Thus objection and reassurance appear, but their extent and nature cannot be pinned down, and one of the possible readings suggests an objection of exceeding subtlety.

Other elements of the classical prophetic call are present as well, though often in an attenuated fashion. The setting of the call seems to be the divine council (as indicated by God's plural imperatives in Isa 40.1–2, which do not address the prophet alone), a locus that recalls Isaiah 6 and Ezekiel 1–3. However, this setting is not emphasized or specified. Only some of the typical vocabulary of a prophetic initiation appears. The words "do not fear" occur in Isa 40.9 (cf. Jer 1.8, Ezek 2.6, 3.9), but they are addressed to Zion, whereas in the calls of Jeremiah and Ezekiel they are spoken to the prophet.[78] The words for "mouth" and "speech" that occur so often in other initiation scenes (Exod 4.11, Isa 6.5–7, Jer 1.9, Ezek 3.2) are not found here, though the word "voice" is (Isa 40.3, 9; cf. Isa 6.4, Ezek 1.28). Many other elements of the initiation do not appear at all: the vocabulary items "send," "go," and "for I am with you,"[79] the physical contact between a heavenly being and the prophet's mouth, the vision. The presence of some elements in a passage that nonetheless is not a full-fledged commissioning scene intimates that Deutero-Isaiah experienced only a partial admission into the prophetic vocation. The echoing of the scene serves as an apt metaphor for Deutero-Isaiah's status: he is a prophet, but already something less than his predecessors.[80]

The prominence of allusion in Isaiah 40–66 reflects Deutero-Isaiah's in-between status. Like any prophet Deutero-Isaiah proclaims the message of YHWH, but he reports that message using words reminiscent of his predecessors. Further, he borrows with greater frequency than his predecessors. (One might compare the role of inner-biblical allusion and exegesis in Jeremiah. As Holladay demonstrates,[81] many passages of the Book of Jeremiah recall earlier biblical books, but the proportion of allusions in Jeremiah is not as high as in Deutero-Isaiah, and many of the parallels Holladay mentions are less far-reaching than the ones I have discussed; further, I would hesitate to label many of these parallels genuine allusions. The proportion of allusions is even lower in earlier prophetic works, such as Isaiah.) Moreover, Deutero-Isaiah probably hoped that his audience would recognize his dependence. The density of allusion at the outset of the work indicates its import for the corpus as a whole. Further, Deutero-Isaiah may have used the stylistic features discussed above to help signal the presence of borrowed material. All these features demonstrate Deutero-Isaiah's acute need to draw on classical prophets' authority and hence indicate his belated status. On the other hand, unlike the author of the Book of Kings or the authors of much post-biblical literature, Deutero-Isaiah does not mark his references to older texts explicitly. His dependence remains thinly veiled, his allusions implicit. Deutero-Isaiah hopes that the audience will see through the veil, but he does not remove it himself. His position as a late prophet manifests itself in this subtlety: Deutero-Isaiah relies on his predecessors, but he is not so dependent that he must limit himself to explicit citation and explication.

Deutero-Isaiah sees himself, then, at once as prophet and disciple. This self-understanding is beautifully expressed in Isa 50.4, where he proclaims that YHWH has given him a לְשׁוֹן לִמּוּדִים. The phrase allows for two translations, both appropriate metaphors for the language of Deutero-Isaiah. His was a "learned tongue," which called forth the words of his predecessors, invigorating them in profound and clever ways. His was also a "disciple's tongue," for through his allusions to his forebears, he implicitly affirmed his dependence on them. At the same time, he is no mere interpreter, collector, or scholiast. According to 50.4, his learning comes directly from YHWH, not just from study and reflection. His language is both erudite and inspired; he acknowledges that he is a student of his prophetic forebears but claims also to be their peer.

The realization that Deutero-Isaiah terms himself a disciple raises the question: whose disciple does he claim to be? Martin Buber suggested that the use of the term לִמּוּדִים in Isa 50.1 and 50.4 indicates that Deutero-Isaiah saw himself as a student and interpreter of Isaiah ben Amoṣ, since this term appeared already in Isa 8.16.[82] In that earlier passage Isaiah sealed a document for his disciples, who were to act as witnesses that he issued certain prophecies. H. G. M. Williamson has amplified his idea, arguing that Deutero-Isaiah saw himself as the witness anticipated by Isaiah in chapter 8.[83] Deutero-Isaiah's work as a whole, then, forms a supplement to (or, perhaps, culmination of) Isaiah's prophecies. This notion appears also in the work of the "unity of Isaiah" school, which stresses the organic (not merely redactional) connection between the work of Deutero-Isaiah and the material in chapters 1–39; according to this approach, Deutero-Isaiah's work was written to be appended to that of Isaiah.

This viewpoint is seriously flawed for three reasons. In light of this study of Deutero-Isaiah's use of older biblical texts, it is clear that Deutero-Isaiah positions himself as a disciple of pre-exilic prophets generally, not of Isaiah ben Amoṣ specifically. He utilizes prophetic material in a consistent fashion, whether it comes from Isaiah or Jeremiah or Hosea or Micah or others. He approaches texts from the Pentateuch, Psalms, and Lamentation in similar ways as well. Deutero-Isaiah displays no preference for Isaian texts; indeed, he borrows more frequently from Jeremiah.[84] Further, the connection between Isa 8.16 and the witness theme in Deutero-Isaiah is not strong. Most of the passages that Williamson claims rely on Isa 8.16–17 share few vocabulary items with it, and even those are usually quite common.[85] Thus it seems most likely that in Isa 50.4 Deutero-Isaiah describes his relationship to older prophets including, but by no means limited to or concentrating on, Isaiah ben Amoṣ. Finally, the description of Deutero-Isaiah as merely an editor and interpreter who added to the collection ascribed to Isaiah implies (*à la* Wellhausen and Buber) that Deutero-Isaiah was something less than a prophet. This view fails to take into account Deutero-Isaiah's claim (however anxious) to prophetic status, a claim reflected in his repeated attribution of his words to YHWH and his assertion in 50.4 that it was YHWH Himself who provided the learned tongue. Deutero-Isaiah does not borrow to indicate that his utterances were a continuation of Isaiah's work. Rather, he alludes to show that he augments prophetic tradition, broadly conceived. Allusion, then, is a trope of affiliation for Deutero-Isaiah—and also a figure of ambivalence. He employs copious references to predecessors to show that he is indeed a prophet, but his need to do so evinces his apprehensions: he and his audience doubt whether he, or any exile, can truly deliver living words of YHWH.

Canon, Tradition, and Revelation

Deutero-Isaiah's allusivity discloses (and responds to) a crisis of prophetic authority. This crisis generated new forms of expression later in the post-exilic era. Those who wrote religious documents after the outset of the Second Temple period either attributed them to authoritative figures from the past or limited themselves to composing interpretations of older texts. Jews seeking the word of God increasingly consulted not an individual with special access to the divinity but the words of earlier figures which were thought to have meaning for the present. Deutero-Isaiah precedes this development; he is still a prophet, and he identifies his utterances as pronouncements of YHWH. But close examination shows that to an extraordinary degree these pronouncements consist of revisions of earlier ones. Thus Deutero-Isaiah is a pivotal figure in the movement from the predominantly oracle-based religion of ancient Israel to the more hermeneutically based ones of the Second Temple period and later. Deutero-Isaiah represents a new type of writing prophet, a type that includes other exilic and post-exilic figures such as Ezekiel and Zechariah. These prophets based their work in part on an idea that older sources remain significant and must be interpreted. While Deutero-Isaiah did not have a closed canon of sacred writings in the sense that Judaism and Christianity do, his recourse to authoritative texts reflects the beginning of such a notion.[86] Indeed, Deutero-Isaiah's use of those texts may itself have fostered that notion.

We may make this point with greater precision: Deutero-Isaiah had *scripture,* but he did not have *canon.* He regarded some older texts as authoritative and sacred, and through his allusions he attempted to enhance both their prestige and his own. But Deutero-Isaiah had no finite list of sacred works—new prophecies could occur, and hence new scripture could be composed.[87] Deutero-Isaiah supplemented an evolving library by introducing a text that itself developed out of that library. In this respect he differs at once from some biblical authors and from post-biblical writers. On the one hand, unlike the author of Deuteronomy or Chronicles, he did not attempt to replace the works on which he relied. For the Deuteronomist, for the Chronicler, and perhaps also for the author of Qumran's Temple Scroll, an older text could be superseded by a newer one; the older text's authority did not guarantee its permanence.[88] Their attitude toward their predecessors is more liberal and less bound than Deutero-Isaiah's. Yet Deutero-Isaiah is more liberal and less bound than some works that came later. For the rabbis, the canon was closed, and thus its works could only be interpreted; they could not be supplemented by new works of a comparable stature, much less replaced.

The difference between Deuteronomy and Deutero-Isaiah does not result simply from the fact that Deutero-Isaiah is later; after all, the Chronicler and the author of the Temple Scroll resemble the Deuteronomist in this respect, and they postdate Deutero-Isaiah. The difference, rather, is in part a function of the natures of the works in question: new prophecy need not overturn old prophecy, even if they differ on some points, since contradictory prophecies can coexist. But new law must supplant an old one, since contradictory laws cannot coexist. Thus, while the authors of Deuteronomy had to develop what Levinson terms "a rhetoric of concealment which serves to camouflage the actual literary history of the laws,"[89] Deutero-Isaiah develops a rhetoric of allusion which highlights his use of older prophecies and psalms.

While Deuteronomy's rhetoric of concealment hides the extent to which that book is a new (and hence suspect) revelation, for Deutero-Isaiah it is precisely a rhetoric of allusion that permits access to new revelation. Deutero-Isaiah's utterances issue from a new sort of inspiration, one that draws deeply from an existing reservoir of older and accepted divine words. But it is also a final form of inspiration, because for him new revelation involved—indeed demanded—recycling: God's new words could only emerge from intense examination and reordering of words that were not new at all. From this notion it is a small leap to Qumran pesher, in which the interpretation of older revelation results from new inspiration; and it is only a slightly longer leap to the idea that the interpretation of the revealed text takes the place of revelation, that interpretation is a sacred act, or even that scripture itself is the interpretation of revelation. Thus Deutero-Isaiah's allusions contributed to a process that led, ultimately, to traditions that transfigured the religion of the Hebrew Bible. Those traditions would claim that their reformulations, however far-reaching they appeared, stood within the biblical tradition itself. In light of the phenomenon of inner-biblical allusion and exegesis, such a claim seems justified.

I began this book by quoting a latter-day follower and colleague of Deutero-Isaiah's, the poet Yehuda Amichai. Deutero-Isaiah created new prophecies by gathering and reworking the old, and hence Amichai's description of himself works well as a comment about Deutero-Isaiah. Other lines Amichai wrote might be understood to describe the process of renewal and revision that has always formed Hebrew literature; they can even be refigured to pertain to those of us who study that tradition and its transformations:

מִלִּים הָיוּ צְרִיכוֹת לִהְיוֹת רֵיקוֹת
וְצָרוֹת וְקָשׁוֹת, כְּמוֹ פָּרָשַׁת מַיִם
יֵאוּשׁ וְתִקְוָה, שִׂמְחָה וָעֶצֶב, שַׁלְוָה וָזַעַם
צְרִיכִים הָיוּ לִזְרֹם לִשְׁנֵי הַצְּדָדִים
לְמַחֲזוֹר חָדָשׁ.

אֲבָל הַמִּלִּים שֶׁאֲנִי עַצְמִי אוֹמֵר
הֵן עַכְשָׁיו, כְּמוֹ אֲבָנִים שֶׁאֲנִי זוֹרֵק
לְתוֹךְ בְּאֵר בַּשָּׂדֶה לִבְדֹּק
הַאִם הִיא מְלֵאָה אוֹ רֵיקָה,
וּמָה עֲמֻקָּה.

Words ought to be empty
And narrow and hard, like a watershed.

Despair and hope, happiness and pain, tranquility and anger
Ought to stream down the two sides
Into a new cycle.

But the words that I myself say
here, now, are like stones that I throw
into a well in the field to check
whether it is full or empty
and what is its depth.

(Yehuda Amichai, "I Am a Poor Prophet" and "Summer's Rest and Words" [1989])

APPENDIX

APPENDIX: WAS THERE A TRITO-ISAIAH?

DEUTERO-ISAIANIC ALLUSION AND THE UNITY OF 35, 40–66

How Many Second Isaiahs?

Since the late nineteenth century, most biblical scholars have separated Isaiah 40–66 into two parts. These scholars view the last eleven chapters of the book as the work either of a post-exilic writer who lived as much as a century after Deutero-Isaiah or as the work of a group of writers, some of whom lived shortly after the exile and others of whom lived more than a century later. These scholars point to several features of the latter chapters that suggest the presence of a new author. Chapters 40–55 contain little prophetic rebuke and emphasize consolation and exuberant promises of restoration.[1] In chapters 56–66, on the other hand, religious and social criticism appear with greater frequency (e.g., 57.3–13, 58.1–12, 59.1–8, 63.7–64.12). These prophecies differ from the preceding ones not only in tone but in literary style: while chapters 40–55 contain mostly poetry,[2] chapters 56–66 mix prose compositions with poetry. Furthermore, unlike chapters 40 and following, the latter chapters seem to stem from the post-exilic period. Isa 56.8 ("I shall gather in again, in addition to those gathered in") indicates that at least a partial ingathering of exiles has already taken place. A sense of disappointment pervades some of these chapters, and this might be attributed to the failure, after the exile had ended, of Deutero-Isaiah's more spectacular prophecies (e.g., predictions concerning the exalted position of the restored

Jerusalem, the obeisance of foreign kings, the universal recognition of YHWH). References to a temple in these chapters (56.7, 60.7, 62.9, 65.11, 66.6) lead some scholars to assert that they must have been composed after the rebuilding of the Temple in 516 B.C.E., though none of these verses actually describes the Temple as already standing. More persuasive evidence of a post-exilic dating occurs in the interest these chapters display in issues that concerned other authors in that age: the inclusion of foreigners in the Judean community (Isa 56.1–7; cf. Ezra 9.1–4, Neh 9.2); the nature of the priesthood (Isa 61.5–6; cf. Ezekiel 44); the cleavage between different factions (Isa 57.19–21, 65.13; cf. Ezra 4.1–5). These distinctive characteristics are not evenly distributed throughout 56–66, and chapters 60–62 especially resemble 40–55 in tone and style. But these features lead most biblical scholars to posit separate authorship for chapters 56–66.[3]

German- and English-language scholars in the last several decades have given less attention to the older view that a single author composed Isaiah 40–66.[4] Recent studies tend to note only perfunctorily that some scholars defend the unity of 40–66, and most neglect to mention the work of Yehezkel Kaufmann and Menahem Haran, who offer the most important arguments in favor of this position.[5] Further, one of the most commonly cited discussions of the issue, that of Paul Hanson, dismisses the work of those who view 40–66 as a unity by means of a sort of argument *ad hominem*. To a great extent Hanson's rejection of this position is in fact a rejection of the work of Charles Torrey, whom he characterizes as the most important figure in that school of thought. But Hanson never really discusses the evidence marshaled in support of the unity of these chapters. Having rejected Torrey's ill-advised attempt to attribute these chapters to a Jerusalemite living in the late fifth century, Hanson dismisses his work, failing to realize that Torrey's attempt to defend the unity of chapters 40–66 constitutes a distinct argument and requires individual attention.[6] Because the reasoning in favor of the view that these chapters stem from a single author is less well known in the English-speaking world, it will be worthwhile to review some of the main points made by Torrey, Kaufmann, and Haran.

Scholars who argue that Isaiah 40–66 stem from a single author note characteristics that appear throughout these chapters. Torrey and Kaufmann discuss the poetic style of Deutero-Isaiah, and the examples they cite occur not only in 40–55 but in 56–66 as well.[7] The author of these chapters has a unique penchant to repeat imperatives: "Comfort, comfort My people!" (Isa

40.1); "Pass through, pass through the gates!" (Isa 62.10; see also Isa 51.9, 52.11, 57.14; and cf. 48.11, 15; 51.12).[8] He also loves to put similar-sounding words next to each other.[9] Take the following verse in the first part of the book: "Your seed would have been like the sand and the offspring of your loins (מֵעֶיךָ) like its granules (כִּמְעֹתָיו)" (48.19). The same tendency appears later on as well: "He anointed me . . . to give the mourners of Zion a turban rather than dust (פְּאֵר תַּחַת אֵפֶר) . . . a covering (מַעֲטֵה) of praise instead of a broken spirit . . . and they will be called 'the ones planted (מַטָּע) by YHWH'" (Isa 61.2–3). Similarly, this author often emphasizes certain letters and sounds. He repeatedly uses sibilants alongside the letter ḥêṭ in the following verse from the first chapter in the book: "All flesh is grass, and all its loyalty like the flower of the field (כָּל־הַבָּשָׂר חָצִיר וְכָל־חַסְדּוֹ כְּצִיץ הַשָּׂדֶה)" (Isa 40.6). The following verse from later in the book contains an analogous concatenation of words that resemble each other because they contain the letters ḥêṭ, nûn, mêm, and lāmed: "O you who are inflamed by the gods (הַנֵּחָמִים בָּאֵלִים) . . . who slaughter children in the wadis (בַּנְּחָלִים). . . . Your portion is in the smooth stones in the wadi (בְּחַלְּקֵי־נַחַל חֶלְקֵךְ)" (Isa 57.6–7).[10]

The repetition of the word חלק in the last verse introduces another tendency of the writer: he loves to use a word twice in a verse, once with one meaning and once with another.[11] This happens not only in the latter chapters (as in the previous example) but in the first part of the book as well: for example, "He will not break a reed that is bruised (רָצוּץ), nor will he put out a wick that grows dim (כֵהָה). He will not rebuke (יִכְהֶה), nor will he crush (יָרוּץ)" (Isa 42.3–4). Other biblical authors at times engage in sound play or use homonyms creatively, but Isaiah 40–66 display a consistent and ongoing tendency to do so. Because the predilection for punning and affection for alliteration occur throughout these chapters, not in one section alone, Isaiah 40–66 can be treated as a single corpus that is marked by particular poetic techniques.[12]

Other characteristics, of major and minor import, occur in all sections of the book. Haran points out a great many themes that appear in the early and the late sections of the book.[13] These include, for example, the motif of the road that YHWH and the exiles will take (40.3–5, 48.21, 52.11–12, 57.14, 62.10–11), the language and ideas concerning servant figures (e.g., 42.1–4, 49.1–6, 50.4–9, 52.13–53.12, 59.21, 61.1–3),[14] the Zion songs (a set of songs addressed to Zion in chapters 49, 51, 54, 60, and 62, which share a common style, theme, and vocabulary; similar passages concerning Zion but addressed to the exiles occur in 40.9, 41.27, 44.26),[15] and the consistently positive view of the cult.[16] Torrey notes minor but telling similarities between the early and later chapters; for example, Deutero-Isaiah displays a "kindly interest in dumb animals" in 43.20, 63.13, and elsewhere.[17] Mayer Gruber has noted that Isaiah 40–66, almost uniquely among biblical texts, repeatedly attribute feminine and maternal metaphors to YHWH (Gruber cites Isa 42.13–14, 45.10, 49.14–15, and 66.13).[18]

Haran acknowledges that the early and later parts of the corpus display differing areas of focus, but he does not see these as indicating separate authorship. Haran shows that the shift in focus noted by proponents of Isaiah 56–66's separate authorship occurs not at chapter 56 but at chapter 49.[19] After Isa 49.14, Deutero-Isaiah speaks directly and at length to Jerusalem, whereas before that verse he referred to her only in the third person and in passing.[20] Further, while the prophet mentioned Zion in 40–48, he pays greater attention to Zion and Jerusalem in 49–66. Cyrus and the fall of Babylon are mentioned frequently in the early part of the book, but not after chapter 48.[21] It follows that the shift in focus does not result from a change in authorship, since all scholars agree that a single author wrote 40–48 and 49–55. Haran argues that Deutero-Isaiah wrote chapters 40–48 in Babylonia on the eve of the restoration. He must have been among the first Judeans to move to Judah, and he wrote the remaining chapters of the book there during the next two decades.[22] Haran is not alone in suggesting that the author of Isaiah 40–66 moved from the exile to the Land of Israel; late-nineteenth-century scholars had already developed this thesis,[23] and more recently Fritz Maass has defended it.[24]

Why, then, did the idea develop that more than one author must have composed these chapters? Kaufmann and Haran offer trenchant critiques of the consensus positions,[25] and I need not repeat this material, which is already available to scholars. It may be worthwhile, however, to comment on the more recently published work of Hanson, who argues for the division at chapter 56. Hanson's reasoning is threefold.[26] First, he argues that Deutero-Isaiah utilized classical poetic techniques found in the work of pre-exilic prophets, but that the authors of Isaiah 56–66 did not. These techniques involved especially certain regular metric patterns. In the post-exilic era, according to Hanson, these techniques broke down and were replaced by "baroque" or "grotesque" metric patterns and prose forms that can be found in the work of Trito-Isaiah.[27] Second, he maintains that classical prophetic eschatology is still in evidence in Deutero-Isaiah, but that in Isaiah 56–66 it is replaced with post-exilic apocalyptic eschatology. An early version of apocalyptic eschatology is evident in chapters 60–62, while more fully developed versions are found elsewhere in chapters 56–66.[28] Third, Hanson finds different genres in chapters 40–55 and 56–66: while Deutero-Isaiah uses genres appropriate for announcing salvation to Israel and judgment against the nations, Trito-Isaiah's genres concentrate on judgment against specific groups of Judeans.[29]

I doubt that one can arrive at sound conclusions regarding authorship based on this sort of evidence. It is not clear that ancient Hebrew poetry had any regular metric pattern;[30] moreover, if it did, one can question whether modern scholars can find it. Any argument based on the reconstruction of such patterns and on the analysis of their relative presence or absence is doubly suspect. (Or perhaps triply: Even if such a pattern in earlier poetry did exist, and even if it can be found, it is hardly the case that a single author must have limited his work to any one style.) Similarly, the subtle changes in eschatological outlook Hanson finds in 40–66 fail to demonstrate that these chapters stem from more than one author. The developments that lead to such changes could occur in the work of an individual, especially if that individual lived through the major shifts of setting that occurred to the Judean exiles and returnees.[31] Finally, the argument from genre involves a difference not of authorship but of subject and setting. Deutero-Isaiah in the exile stressed salvation for all Israel; he looked forward to a glorious future and to an Israel worthy of it. Deutero-Isaiah in the Land of Israel, confronted with a somewhat disappointing reality, may have altered his message so that only those in Israel who deserved salvation would receive it. Hanson and others may be correct to notice the beginnings of a rift within the Judean community in certain parts of 56–66, but this hardly constitutes evidence of a new author or even of a distinct era.[32]

Was there in fact a Third Isaiah or perhaps several Third Isaiahs? It seems to me that no convincing evidence has yet been marshaled to demonstrate such a thesis. And yet the similarities in language, thought, and style between 40–55 and 56–66 that scholars such as Torrey, Kaufmann, and Haran stress cannot prove beyond doubt that the latter chapters were written by the same author as the former; it remains at least possible that the similarities result from the attempt of a follower or followers to imitate the work of a master.[33] Minimally, however, it seems clear that chapters 40–66 display enough elements of unity that one is justified in treating them as a literary corpus.

This corpus includes at least one, and perhaps two, additional chapters: Isaiah 34–35. Already Heinrich Graetz noticed that the setting, ideas, language, and style of Isaiah 35 closely resemble what is found in Isaiah 40–66,[34] and many scholars have followed him in attributing Isaiah 35 to Deutero-Isaiah. Some scholars include chapter 34 as well.[35] Both these chapters display typical Deutero-Isaianic themes: the motif of the road through the desert that YHWH and the exiles will take is found in 35.4–10; the prophet's love of dumb animals appears in 34.16.[36] Torrey finds in chapters 34–35 many of the typical characteristics of the poet who composed chapters 40–66. Deutero-Isaiah's love of sound play occurs in chapter 34: "Mountains will melt away (וְנָמַסּוּ) in blood, and the host of heaven will rot (וְנָמַקּוּ)" (Isa 34.3–4). Similarly, sibilants are repeated in the following verse from chapter 35: "They will achieve joy and happiness, and sorrow and sighing will flee (שָׂשׂוֹן וְשִׂמְחָה יַשִּׂיגוּ וְנָסוּ יָגוֹן וַאֲנָחָה)" (Isa 35.10). As a result, it will be useful to see whether allusions in those chapters also display tendencies found in chapters 40–66.

Given the elements of unity, and especially in light of the consistent poetic style noted throughout Isaiah 34–35 and 40–66, it makes sense to examine allusions from all these chapters together. Doing so has revealed features that are consistent through those chapters and unique to them.

Isaiah 35 and 56–66 and Patterns of Allusion in Isaiah 40–55

A study of allusions in Isaiah 35 and 40–66 reveals that a single poetics of allusion runs through all these chapters, thus supporting the claim that they should be regarded as a single corpus. No clear cases of allusion occur in chapter 34.

All the thematic categories (confirmation, reversal, reprediction, typology, and response) are found in both chapters 40–55 and 56–66. Chapter 35 includes only cases of reprediction and typology, but the absence of the other categories in so short a unit is not surprising. Polemic against some ideas found in priestly texts occurs in both sections of the book. Similarly, the stylistic patterns appear throughout these chapters. Allusions including the split-up pattern are found in all sections of the book: eighteen times in Isaiah 40–55, thirteen times in Isaiah 56–66, and once in Isaiah 35.[37] Sound play occurs twenty-five times in Isaiah 40–55, ten times in Isaiah 56–66, and twice in Isaiah 35. Allusions that include word play occur eleven times in Isaiah 40–55, three times in Isaiah 56–66, and twice in Isaiah 35. Identical word order and word-for-word borrowing occur less frequently, but they too are broadly distributed. Allusions in which borrowed words appear in the same order they had in the source occur six times in Isaiah 40–55 and six times in Isaiah 56–66. The prophet borrows an entire phrase word for word from a source eight times in Isaiah 40–55 and twice in Isaiah 56–66.

The even distribution of these thematic and stylistic features in Isaiah 35 and 40–66 is highly significant.[38] It suggests that a single author wrote all these chapters, relating to older texts in a consistent fashion throughout. Alternatively, one might suggest that a group of authors utilized a single style of allusion, or that a master who composed some chapters taught a method of borrowing to disciples who composed the rest. The distinction between these alternatives seems largely moot to me; in either case, we are justified to regard Isaiah 35 and 40–66 as a single corpus.[39] In light of this study, and in light of the research of other scholars cited in this appendix, the notion of a division between chapters 55 and 56 of Isaiah should be discarded. (I do not mean to deny that there are differences of thematic emphasis or ideological concern within Isaiah 40–66 and 35, nor would I gainsay the claim that the earlier chapters, which emphasize consolation, were written in the exile, while the later ones were written in the Land of Israel and include a stronger element of disappointment. But the division between earlier, exilic, chapters and later, Palestinian, chapters probably occurs at the end of chapter 48 rather than 55, as scholars such as Haran have noted.)[40] Similarly, the highly complex speculations of scholars such as Odil Steck, Seizo Sekine, and Wolfgang Lau, who find multiple strata of base-text, insertion, and redactional revision in Isaiah 40–66, seem even less likely in view of the thematic and stylistic consistency I have noted here.[41]

Even within chapters 56–66 the allusions are widely distributed. This is an important finding, since some scholars suggest that within chapters 56–66 certain sections are more closely linked to 40–55 than others. Westermann claims that only Isaiah 57.14–20, 60–62, 65.16b–25, and 66.6–26 were penned by the original Trito-Isaiah, who was a disciple of Deutero-Isaiah; the remainder of 56–66 stem from other writers who worked later.[42] The passages attributed by Westermann to Trito-Isaiah (i.e., those resembling Deutero-Isaiah) do indeed contain an abundance of allusions in the style of Deutero-Isaiah. However, the allegedly late material elsewhere in 56–66 also includes allusions resembling those found in Isaiah 40–55. The allusion to Deut 28.29 in Isa 59.8–10 displays reversal and sound play, which are typical features of Deutero-Isaianic allusion. Isa 56.10–57.6 utilize Isa 30.10–11, and this allusion contains several cases of sound play. Isa 66.12–24 is a reprediction including identical word order, two cases of the split-up pattern, two cases of sound play, and one case of word play.[43] In short, the idea that some parts of Isaiah 56–66 lie outside the thematic and stylistic unity of the corpus consisting of 40–66 finds little support from analyzing the poetics of allusion in these chapters.[44] My conclusion is precisely the opposite of Wolfgang Lau's conclusion from his study of "Schriftgelehrte Prophetie" in Isaiah 56–66.[45] This is not to deny that some texts in 56–66 use earlier material more or less than others (as Lau argues); but those differences themselves do not demonstrate that the texts in question must have different authors, since an allusive author is under no obligation to allude at a steady rate in all pericopes. The consistent poetics of allusion, even in texts that allude less often, argue that the chapters do constitute a single document and suggest that hyper-source-criticism of these chapters is not only speculative but *a priori* unwise.

Significantly, the stylistic features that appear so often in Isaiah 35 and 40–66 are rare in cases of inner-biblical allusion and exegesis culled from other books or even from other parts of the Book of Isaiah. For example, several studies of the use of earlier biblical material in Isaiah 24–27 have been published, including especially works by John Day and Marvin Sweeney.[46] The many cases of inner-biblical allusion and exegesis noted by Day and Sweeney do not display an affinity for the split-up pattern, word play, or sound play; however, common ordering of borrowed elements plays an important role in the allusions to Hosea in Isaiah 26–27.[47] Further, most of the allusions to Hosea in these texts contain only one or two shared terms and are based more on thematic parallels;[48] in this respect, they differ greatly from the Deutero-Isaianic allusions, which usually borrow a good deal of vocabulary. Thus it seems clear that the stylistic features (other than common order) are specific to the corpus consisting of Isaiah 35 and 40–66, and are not characteristic of the Book of Isaiah as a whole or of inner-biblical allusion generally. Similarly, the thematic tendencies that Sweeney notes in allusions in chapters 24–27 (especially a move toward universalism)[49] play little or no role in allusions occurring in Isaiah 35 and 40–66. Finally, the alleged allusions to Deutero-Isaiah by Trito-Isaiah[50] do not match the poetics of allusion found in Deutero-Isaianic use of any other texts; indeed, most of the parallels noted as examples of Trito-Isaiah's borrowings from Deutero-Isaiah consist of common vocabulary. These items reflect the vocabulary preferences of a single author or school rather than the complex appropriation of an older passage that marks literary allusion.

REFERENCE MATTER

ABBREVIATIONS

1QIsa^a	The large Isaiah scroll from Qumran cave 1

1QIsa^a The large Isaiah scroll from Qumran cave 1

1QIsa[a]   The large Isaiah scroll from Qumran cave 1
1QIsa[b]   The fragmentary Isaiah scroll from Qumran cave 1
1QpHab   The commentary (*pesher*) on Habakkuk from Qumran cave 1
1QS   The Community Rule (*Serach*) from Qumran cave 1
4QIsa   Fragments of Isaiah from Qumran cave 4
AB   Anchor Bible
ABRL   The Anchor Bible Reference Library
AnBib   Analecta Biblica
ANET   *Ancient Near Eastern Texts Related to the Old Testament* (ed. James Pritchard)
AnOr   Analecta Orientalia
AOAT   Alter Orient und Altes Testament
Apoc Bar   *The Apocalypse of Baruch*
b.   Babylonian Talmud
B. Bat.   *Baba Batra*
San.   *Sanhedrin*
BDB   *The Brown-Driver-Briggs Hebrew and English Lexicon* (ed. Francis Brown, S. R. Driver, and Charles Briggs)
BHS   *Biblia Hebraica Stuttgartensia* (ed. K. Elliger, W. Rudolph, et al.)

Bib	*Biblica*
BJS	Brown Judaic Studies
BM	*Beth Miqra*
BZAW	Beihefte zur *Zeitschrift für die alttestamentliche Wissenschaft*
CAD	*The Assyrian Dictionary of the Oriental Institute of the University of Chicago*
CBQ	*Catholic Biblical Quarterly*
CBSC	Cambridge Bible for Schools and Colleges
Chr	Chronicles
ConBOT	Coniectanea biblica, Old Testament
CRINT	Compendia rerum iudaicarum ad novum testamentum
Dan	Daniel
Deut	Deuteronomy
ErIsr	*Eretz Israel*
Esth	Esther
Exod	Exodus
Ezek	Ezekiel
Gen	Genesis
Gen Rab.	*Genesis Rabbah*
GKB	The Gesenius-Kautzsch-Bergsträsser *Hebräische Grammatik* (ed. G. Bergsträsser)
GKC	The Gesenius-Kautzsch-Cowley *Grammar of the Hebrew Language* (ed. E. Kautzsch)
Hab	Habakkuk
Hag	Haggai
Heb	Hebrew
Hos	Hosea
HS	Holiness School
HUCA	*Hebrew Union College Annual*
IB	*Interpreter's Bible*
Isa	Isaiah
JAOS	*Journal of the American Oriental Society*
JBL	*Journal of Biblical Literature*
Jer	Jeremiah
Josh	Joshua
JQR	*Jewish Quarterly Review*

JSOT	*Journal for the Study of the Old Testament*
JSOTSup	*Journal for the Study of the Old Testament* Supplement Series
JTS	*Journal of Theological Studies*
KAI	*Kanaanäische und aramäische Inschriften* (ed. H. Donner and W. Röllig)
Kgs	Kings
KTU	*Die keilalphabetischen Texte aus Ugarit* (ed. M. Dietrich, O. Lorentz, and J. Sanmartín)
Lam	Lamentations
LBH	Late Biblical Hebrew
Lev	Leviticus
LXX	The Septuagint
Macc	Maccabees
Mal	Malachi
m.	Mishna
Mek.	Mekhilta
Mic	Micah
MT	The Masoretic Text
Nah	Nahum
NCB	New Century Bible
Neh	Nehemiah
NJPS	The New Jewish Publication Society Version (*Tanakh: A New Translation of the Holy Scriptures*)
Num	Numbers
Num Rab.	*Numbers Rabbah*
OTL	Old Testament Library
Pesiq. Rab. Kah.	*Pesiqta deRav Kahana*
PT	Priestly Torah
Prov	Proverbs
Ps	Psalm
RB	*Revue biblique*
Rev	Revelations
Rom	Romans
S. 'Olam Rab.	*Seder 'Olam Rabbah*
Sam	Samuel
SANT	*Studien zum Alten und Neuen Testament*

SBLDS	Society of Biblical Literature Dissertation Series
SBS	*Stuttgarter Bibelstudien*
SBT	Studies in Biblical Theology
ST	*Studia theologica*
STDJ	Studies on the Texts of the Desert of Judah
TBü	*Theologische Bücherei*
Tg	Targum
UT	*Ugaritic Textbook* (ed. Cyrus Gordon)
VT	*Vetus Testamentum*
VTSup	Supplements to *Vetus Testamentum*
WMANT	Wissenschaftliche Monographien zum Alten und Neuen Testament
y.	The Jerusalem Talmud
Taʿan	*Taʿanit*
ZAW	*Zeitschrift für die alttestamentliche Wissenschaft*
Zech	Zechariah
Zeph	Zephaniah

NOTES

INTRODUCTION

1. See Michael Fishbane, *Biblical Interpretation in Ancient Israel* (Oxford: Oxford University Press, 1985); Yair Zakovitch, *An Introduction to Inner-Biblical Interpretation* (Even-Yehuda: Reches Publishing House, 1992) [Heb.]. Earlier studies that sparked interest in this phenomenon include I. L. Seeligmann, "Vorausetzungen der Midraschexegese," *VTSup* 1 (1953), 150–81; Nahum Sarna, "Psalm 89: A Study in Inner-Biblical Exegesis," in *Biblical and Other Studies*, ed. Alexander Altmann (Cambridge, Mass.: Harvard University Press, 1963), 29–46; and Aryeh Toeg, "A Halakhic Midrash in Num. xv:22–31," *Tarbiz* 43 (1973), 1–20 [Heb.] (see also Aryeh Toeg, *Lawgiving at Sinai* [Jerusalem: Magnes, 1977], esp. 41–46 [Heb.]).

2. The authorial unity of Isaiah 40–66 is debated in biblical studies. The summary I have given here diverges from the consensus position in that I view all of Isaiah 40–66 (along with Isaiah 35) as a unified literary corpus. For a detailed discussion of this issue, and the impact the study of inner-biblical allusion has on it, see the Appendix.

3. Given the anonymity of the author(s) of these chapters, it is not immediately clear what pronoun to use. One can speculate regarding not only the number but also the gender of the prophet; after all, females were known to prophesy in biblical Israel (one thinks of Miriam, Deborah and—only a generation before the exile—Hulda). In Isa 49.1–6 and 59.21, however, the prophet seems to make self-references, and it appears from these passages that the author of this literary unit is presented as a male (though this cannot be regarded as completely certain, since the identity of

the prophet overlaps with that of the nation in the former passage, and the pronouns in the latter are unambiguously masculine only in the vocalized text). Thus, I will, somewhat tentatively, use male pronouns when discussing Deutero-Isaiah. Incidentally, the frequent tendency of this prophet to liken YHWH to a mother does not indicate anything about the writer's gender, though it does tell us something about his attitude toward how we should imagine the divine. On the use of feminine metaphors and similes in Isaiah 40–66 see Mayer Gruber, *The Motherhood of God and Other Studies* (Atlanta: Scholars Press, 1992) and "Feminine Similes Applied to the LORD in Second Isaiah," *Beer Sheva* 2 (1985), 75–84 [Heb.]; Katheryn Pfisterer Darr, "Like Warrior, like Woman: Destruction and Deliverance in Isaiah 42:10–17," *CBQ* 49 (1987): 560–71; Marc Brettler, "Incompatible Metaphors for YHWH in Deutero-Isaiah," *JSOT* (forthcoming).

4. I should note that Deutero-Isaiah alludes for reasons that differ at times from those of the poet quoted above. Amichai attempts to humble not only himself but also his predecessors in the poem from which I drew. Deutero-Isaiah, we shall see, seeks to bolster his authority and that of the prophets who came before him. At the same time, both authors use allusion to assert their participation in Hebrew literary tradition. On Amichai's iconoclastic (or better, logoclastic) evocation of biblical texts, see Chana Kronfeld, *On the Margins of Modernism: Decentering Literary Dynamics* (Berkeley: University of California Press, 1996), 130–34 and 143–58.

5. Arguments that multiple compositional layers exist in Isaiah 40–66 (especially 56–66) appear, for example, in Westermann's work on Isaiah 40–66 (*Isaiah 40–66: A Commentary*, trans. D. Stalker [Philadelphia: Westminster Press, 1969]) and in the many publications on these chapters by Odil Steck (see especially the essays collected in *Studien zu Tritojesaja* [Berlin: de Gruyter, 1991] and *Gottesknecht und Zion: Gesammelte Aufsätze zu Deuterojesaja* [Tübingen: J. C. B. Mohr/Paul Siebeck, 1992], and also *Bereitete Heimkehr: Jesaja 35 als redaktionelle Brücke zwischen dem Ersten und dem Zweiten Jesaja* [Stuttgart: Katholisches Bibelwerk, 1985]). On the debate regarding redactional layers in these chapters as well as the related question of the length of units in Isaiah 40–66, see the literature reviews in Antti Laato, *The Servant of YHWH and Cyrus: A Reinterpretation of the Exilic Messianic Programme in Isaiah 40–55* (Stockholm: Almqvist and Wiksell, 1992), 3–16, and Menahem Haran, "The Literary Structure and Chronological Framework of the Prophecies of Is. XL–LXVI," *VTSup* 9 (1963), 127–31. These issues are also discussed by Wolfgang Lau, who favors the atomistic approach, in *Schriftgelehrte Prophetie in Jes 56–66: Eine Untersuchung zu den literarischen Bezügen in den letzten elf Kapiteln des Jesajabuches* (Berlin: de Gruyter, 1994), 1–21. Haran provides a particularly important defense of a more integrative and less atomistic reading ("Literary," 131–36), as does James Muilenburg in "The Book of Isaiah: Chapters 40–66," in *IB* 5, ed. G. A. Buttrick et al. (New York: Abingdon Press, 1956), 384–92, 415–18.

6. It is important to note that I do not intend to argue against source criticism

generally. The classic documentary hypothesis concerning the Pentateuch remains, to my mind, a highly plausible and solidly reasoned theory, in spite of attempts by fundamentalists and postmodern literary critics variously to rebut it or ignore it.

CHAPTER ONE

1. This book treats Deutero-Isaiah's use of one type of older biblical material: specific texts known to Deutero-Isaiah and purposefully utilized by him. Like all biblical writers, Deutero-Isaiah employed other sorts of older material as well. These include traditions that had appeared in many different texts or perhaps in no written text at all. The study of the latter sort of reuse is the subject of "tradition history," which differs from the study of "inner-biblical allusion and exegesis." The student of inner-biblical exegesis examines two texts (or sometimes more), both of which are probably written, and which are related to each other as source and reworking. The tradition historian, however, investigates a single text which is the result of a process of development, most of it oral. Alternatively, the tradition historian examines a number of texts and extrapolates back from them to an older tradition. But similarities among the texts examined by the tradition historian result not from the reliance of some texts on others, but from their use of common material.

A third sort of material which biblical writers might have used is formal or generic. A person composing a piece of writing in ancient Israel may have utilized (and perhaps changed) older conventions of expression, such as how one laments a personal problem or a national crisis, how one thanks God for recovery from danger, how one narrates the meeting of patriarch and matriarch, or how one discloses to one's fellows that one has been chosen by God to convey a message. The study of these conventions, their use, and their transformation is the realm of form criticism and certain types of literary criticism. These studies may, like the studies of tradition history and inner-biblical exegesis, compare biblical texts, but such comparison does not posit that one text is based on the others. Rather, all the texts exemplify some form; or one may embody a form while another presents a transformation of that form.

While I am concerned exclusively with Deutero-Isaiah's inner-biblical allusions and exegesis, tradition-historical and form-critical issues will have a role to play in my argument. In some passages it will be obvious that Deutero-Isaiah is using older material, but one may debate which sort of material it is. A major goal of this study will be the development of criteria to decide when a resemblance between Isaiah 40–66 and another text results from Deutero-Isaiah utilizing the other text and when it results from both texts utilizing older traditions or literary conventions.

2. Jay Clayton and Eric Rothstein, "Figures in the Corpus: Theories of Influence and Intertextuality," in *Influence and Intertextuality in Literary History*, ed. Jay Clayton and Eric Rothstein (Madison: University of Wisconsin Press, 1991), espe-

cially 3–4 and 21. Clayton and Rothstein distinguish between intertextuality and influence, but we shall see that influence and allusion belong together in opposition to intertextuality.

3. Ziva Ben-Porat, "Intertextuality," *Ha-Sifrut* 34 (1985), 170 [Heb.].

4. For the resemblances between intertextual approaches and reader-response criticism, see Clayton and Rothstein, 26.

5. Jonathan Culler, *The Pursuit of Signs: Semiotics, Literature, and Deconstruction* (Ithaca, N.Y.: Cornell University Press, 1981), 103. Cf. the quotation from Kristeva in Clayton and Rothstein, 21, and their remarks about Barthes on this issue, 22.

6. Ben-Porat goes further, maintaining that all texts *must* be read intertextually, for intertextuality is always at issue for any reader; it is the mechanism by which all texts are produced and understood. See Ben-Porat, "Intertextuality," 171.

7. While Clayton and Rothstein are perhaps the clearest and most insistent in describing this distinction, many others have noted it as well. See, e.g. (in addition to the citation from Culler above), James Chandler, "Romantic Allusiveness," *Critical Inquiry* 8 (1982), 464; Robert Alter, *The Pleasures of Reading in an Ideological Age* (New York: Norton, 1996 [1989]), 112–13; Richard Garner, *From Homer to Tragedy: The Art of Allusion in Greek Poetry* (London: Routledge, 1990), 228 n. 24; and Ben-Porat, "Intertextuality," 170, where she contrasts intertextuality from a "philological approach, which has abundantly investigated connections between texts under the headings of 'sources,' 'imitations,' 'garbled citations,' and the like." However, the terminology which Clayton and Rothstein suggest (and which I follow) is by no means universal. Thus, Ben-Porat contrasts "intertextuality" generally with what she calls "rhetorical intertextuality" ("Intertextuality," 171), which largely resembles traditional influence studies because it is concerned explicitly with "earlier" and "later" texts (see "Intertextuality," 175). John Guillory, in *Poetic Authority: Spenser, Milton and Literary History* (New York: Columbia University Press, 1983), 74, draws a distinction similar to the one described here, but in his terminology "intertextuality" denotes "the matter of echo" (which I would term "allusion"), while matters of "shared concerns" (a topic for intertextuality as the term is used here) he labels "contextual." Similarly, the work of Harold Bloom is explicitly concerned with influence, but it has been called an example of "intertextuality" (see Harold Bloom, *The Anxiety of Influence: A Theory of Poetry* [London: Oxford University Press, 1975 {1973}]; Clayton and Rothstein, 9; and Culler, 107–11). Richard Hays, in *Echoes of Scripture in the Letters of Paul* (New Haven, Conn.: Yale University Press, 1989), 14–15, glosses "the phenomenon of intertextuality" as "the imbedding of fragments of an earlier text within a later one"—i.e., Hays uses the term as Guillory uses it, though he also recognizes the broader, non-diachronic use of the term among critics such as Kristeva, Barthes, and Culler.

Not all critics posit such a strong polarity between intertextuality and allusion.

Recent Israeli critics attempt a synthesis, in which a theory of intertextuality moves away from generality and a focus on the commonplace, while allusion is viewed as a dynamic interaction of texts that mutually modify or criticize each other. See Chana Kronfeld, *On the Margins of Modernism: Decentering Literary Dynamics* (Berkeley: University of California Press, 1996), 121–23, 125, 129–30. Given the confusion between the two poles, however, I think it worthwhile to underscore the different aims, methods, and implications of intertextual study, on the one hand, and the investigation of allusion and influence, on the other.

8. See, e.g., Gail O'Day, who in "Jeremiah 9:22–23 and I Corinthians 1:26–31: A Study in Intertextuality," *JBL* 109 (1990), 259, subsumes the very different approaches to T. S. Eliot, Bloom, and Culler under the misleadingly broad term "intertextuality" and then goes on to identify both Fishbane's work and the approach of canon critics such as Brevard Childs as examples of intertextuality in biblical studies. While Fishbane and Childs share a broad concern for the relations among biblical texts, just as Bloom and, say, Culler or Barthes share an interest in connections among texts, the nature of these concerns differs markedly. (It may be suggested that Fishbane's approach is concerned with influence and allusion, while Childs's displays a certain synchronic bias which it shares, *mutatis mutandis*, with practitioners of intertextuality as defined here.)

9. See Clayton and Rothstein, 5, and cf. Culler, 108.

10. See Chandler, 464. Even a model of influence study which disavows any interest in historical context or the biography of the author (such as Bloom's, or Ben-Porat's "rhetorical intertextuality") is based on the distinction between earlier and later texts, and is hence diachronic.

11. So concludes Lyle Eslinger, "Inner-Biblical Exegesis and Inner-Biblical Allusion: The Question of Category," *VT* 42 (1992), 47–58. Confusingly, Eslinger uses the term "allusion" as a synonym for "intertextuality." See further my article, "Exegesis, Allusion and Intertextuality in the Hebrew Bible: A Response to Lyle Eslinger," in *VT* 56 (1996), 479–89.

12. See Clayton and Rothstein, 12–17, on the reasons for the decline of traditional influence studies since the late 1960's. Their essay (and the book in which it appears) is an excellent example of the advantages of a more eclectic approach in which both methods, or sometimes a combination, are viewed as valid and useful for different sorts of investigations or interests.

13. Michael Fishbane, in his *Biblical Interpretation in Ancient Israel* (Oxford: Oxford University Press, 1985), devotes considerable energy to this question. See his reflections regarding method, 17, and his basic statement regarding identifying cases of aggadic exegesis which have no explicit citation formulae, 285. Cf. the remarks of James Kugel, "The Bible's Earliest Interpreters," *Prooftexts* 7 (1987), 277–79.

14. Clayton and Rothstein, 31 n. 3.

15. Cf. Andrew D. Weiner, "Sidney/Spenser/Shakespeare: Influence/Intertextuality/Intention," in *Influence and Intertextuality*, ed. Jay Clayton and Eric Rothstein (Madison: University of Wisconsin Press, 1991), 246.

16. Earl Miner, s.v. "Allusion," in *Encyclopedia of Poetry and Poetics*, ed. Alex Preminger (Princeton, N.J.: Princeton University Press, 1965), 18. Miner gives a similar, though not identical, definition in a more recent edition: "a poet's deliberate incorporation of identifiable elements from other sources, preceding or contemporaneous, textual or extratextual" ("Allusion," in *The New Princeton Encyclopedia of Poetry and Poetics*, ed. A. Preminger and V. Brogan [Princeton, N.J.: Princeton University Press, 1993], 38–39). Cf. Alter, 112: "literary allusion . . . involves the evocation— through a wide spectrum of formal means—in one text of an antecedent literary text."

While Miner's definition requires that allusion is "tacit," Ben-Porat and Carmela Perri point out that sources can be mentioned explicitly in an allusion. Indeed, even critics who define allusion as covert often discuss examples where the poet specifies his or her source (see Ziva Ben-Porat, "The Poetics of Literary Allusion," *PTL: A Journal for Descriptive Poetics and Theory of Literature* 1 [1976], 127; cf. 109; Carmela Perri, "On Alluding," *Poetics* 7 [1978], 290; and Alter, 119–20). Overt allusions are less frequent in literature, but they do occur. For example, Aharon Meged's short story, "Indecent Act," contains an allusion to Goethe's *Faust,* but the source is made explicit as two characters discuss the correct translation of a line from that drama (Aharon Meged, "Indecent Act," in *Indecent Act: Three Stories* [Tel Aviv: Am Oved, 1986], 45– 46 [Heb.]). Alternatively, an author may indicate that the text contains allusions without identifying the sources by name. Thus the main character in Shmuel Yosef Agnon's story "Thus Far" ruminates on a number of biblical verses and rabbinic comments, each of which is overtly marked as an allusion by a citation formula such as כמו שאתה אומר ("as it says") or מלשון ("as in the line"), but he does not name the texts he cites (Shmuel Yosef Agnon, "Thus Far," in *Thus Far* [Jerusalem and Tel Aviv: Schocken Publishing House, 1952], 27 [Heb.]). In this case, the category of allusion overlaps with that of quotation. Explicit citation occurs rarely in ancient Greek lyric as well; see Garner, 2.

17. Many critics hold that a parallel qualifies as an allusion only if it was intended by the author (see Alter, 115–16). This approach to allusion is neither useful nor accurate, as Chandler explains in some detail, 476–82. Further, unconscious borrowing is likely in a highly traditional literature, whose authors are deeply familiar with earlier works and know large blocks of older material by heart. Moshe Seidel explains this phenomenon admirably: "The words a person reads and hears and repeats become his own, enter his verbal storehouse. When needed they become, even if he does not know it, the clothing for the thoughts to which he gives birth. Sacred literature, the inheritance of earlier generations, is incised on the heart of the prophets and sacred poets; it is their fount and the object of their musing, something they have contemplated many a day. Therefore the idea which appeared to them

through the holy spirit finds expression in the same linguistic forms and phrases that were impressed in their hearts, became habitual on their lips and were made a part of the prophets themselves" (Moshe Seidel, "Parallels Between the Book of Isaiah and the Book of Psalms," *Sinai* 38 [1955–56], 149, reprinted in Moshe Seidel, *Ḥiqrei Miqraʾ* [Jerusalem, 1978], 1 [Heb.]; cf. Dan Pagis, *Change and Tradition in the Secular Poetry: Spain and Italy* [Jerusalem: Keter, 1976], 70–71 [Heb.]). Even when an author borrows unconsciously, the alteration of the source's wording can provide new insight into the alluding text.

18. Perri, 295. Cf. Anthony Johnson, "Allusion in Poetry," *PTL: A Journal for Descriptive Poetics and Theory of Literature* 1 (1976), 579.

19. Geoffrey Hartman, ed., *The Selected Poetry and Prose of Wordsworth* (New York: Meridian, 1970), 398.

20. Merritt Hughes, ed., *Complete Poems and Major Prose by John Milton* (Indianapolis: Bobbs-Merrill, 1957), 170–71. I cannot help pointing out that Wordsworth alludes tacitly to a text that alludes overtly: Milton refers explicitly in line 2 to the myth of Alcestis, who was brought back from the grave to her husband, just as Milton's wife is brought back to him, though only for the single time during which he can see: at night, as he sleeps.

21. In her earlier article, "Allusion," though certain additional features are suggested in her discussion of certain types of rhetorical intertextuality in her later article, "Intertextuality."

22. Ben-Porat, "Allusion," 108. Ben-Porat notes that the term "allusion" is sometimes used to refer to the element that calls the other text to mind, but for the sake of clarity "allusion" should refer to the phenomenon as a whole, and "marker" to the verbal elements that call the source to mind. What Ben-Porat calls the marker is similar to what Miner calls "an echo of sufficiently familiar yet distinctive . . . elements," which is a necessary part of an allusion (see Miner [1965], 18).

23. See Perri, 305. Agnon again provides an example: his novel *Oreaḥ Naṭah Lalun* takes its title from the last words of Jer 14.8.

24. See Ben-Porat, "Allusion," 127; and cf. Chandler, 480. Similarly, Alter, *Pleasures*, 123, notes that the evoked text may be short (a line, a section) or much longer (a whole work or even a corpus).

25. Ben-Porat, "Allusion," 115 n. 10; cf. Perri, 295.

26. Perri summarizes this stage aptly, if technically: the marker "specifies some discrete, recoverable property(ies) belonging to the intention of this source text . . . the property(ies) evoked modifies the alluding text" (Perri, 295).

27. Ben-Porat, "Allusion," 111, 114. Perri describes a similar process in which the alluding text not only calls to mind the marked but also suggests "connotations" which further affect our reading of the alluding text. See Perri, 291–92, 296.

28. Erich Trunz, ed., *Goethes Werke* (Hamburg: Christian Wagner Verlag, 1949), 3: 107–8.

29. Louis Renza, s.v. "Influence," in *Critical Terms for Literary Study*, ed. Frank Lentricchia and Thomas McLaughlin (Chicago: University of Chicago Press, 1990), 186. Clayton and Rothstein, 3, provide a similar definition: "Strictly, influence should refer to relations built on dyads of transmission from one unity (author, work, tradition) to another."

30. On the relation of influence study and literary tradition see also René Wellek and Austin Warren, *Theory of Literature* (New York: Harcourt, Brace & World, 1956), 257–58, and Harold Bloom, *A Map of Misreading* (New York: Oxford University Press, 1975), 32.

31. Walter Jackson Bate, *The Burden of the Past and the English Poet* (Cambridge, Mass.: Harvard University Press, 1970); among many books by Bloom, note especially *The Anxiety of Influence* and *A Map of Misreading*.

32. Bloom, *Map*, 19; see also his remarks on p. 3, as well as his rejection of the approach of "those carrion-eaters of scholarship, the source hunters" (p. 17), and his differentiation of his work on influence from "the wearisome industry of source-hunting" (Bloom, *Anxiety*, 31). Cf. Clayton and Rothstein, 9.

33. Chandler, 462. On the distinction between allusion and influence generally, see also 485.

34. Indeed, Alter describes one type of allusion which overlaps with a particular class of influence: "whole to whole allusions" in which one text "is a reconstruction or rewriting of an antecedent text." See Alter, 132–34. Here the boundaries break down, but this blurring does not alter the fact that the study of each modality of relationship involves its own aims, emphases, and results.

35. A final note regarding the study of influence may be in order. Since the highly original and influential work of Bate and Bloom, the idea of poetic influence has become strongly associated with the anxiety of the influenced poet, with attempts (successful or not) to deny influence and hence to assert poetic originality, and with intergenerational strife among poets (described by Bloom in Oedipal terms). This model depicts an important side of influence, especially in certain periods (e.g., the Romantic; see Chandler, 462). However, it is by no means self-evident that twentieth-century models of originality and influence can be useful in describing premodern literature, as Weiner points out (Weiner, 245–46; cf. Renza, 188, and Clayton and Rothstein, 8–9). It is important to stress (as Bate himself does, at least when speaking of literature dating from earlier than the 1700's [see Bate, vii, 32, 61]) that not all poetry exhibits the sense of burden, the anxiety, the aversion to admitting its own traditionalism, which now are so associated with the term "influence." Such, for example, is the case with Pope (see Chandler, 463–64). T. S. Eliot reminds us that tradition for a poet "must be gained by great labor," a labor into which many poets throw themselves enthusiastically; and that the "best, and most individual parts of [a poet's] work may be those in which his ancestors, the dead poets, assert their immortality most vigorously" (Eliot, "Tradition and the Individual Talent," in *Selected Prose*

of T. S. Eliot, ed. Frank Kermode [London: Faber and Faber, 1975], 38). For some poets, influence provides a welcome invitation to originality. Wellek and Warren maintain that in the Middle Ages, "no author felt inferior or unoriginal because he used, adapted, and modified themes and images inherited by tradition and sanctioned by antiquity" (Wellek and Warren, 257); the same point is made by Hays regarding allusions to scripture in the letters of Paul (Hays, 19). This sort of conscious, confident openness to—even striving after—influence will prove a more relevant model for the study of ancient Israelite poetry.

36. Ben-Porat, "Allusion," 111; cf. 109. Essentially the same point is made by Perri, 296 and 300 number eight.

37. Cf. Chandler, 462.

38. Cf. Ben-Porat, "Allusion," 106 n. 3, where she uses the term "borrowing" for this sort of case. Pagis introduces a similar distinction: "Not every case of the use of earlier lines (שִׁבּוּץ) is meaningful. Many of the expressions or parts of verses [borrowed from an older work] appear in poetry solely as a linguistic usage. . . . It is possible to distinguish between several types: (1) neutral borrowings (שִׁבּוּצִים נייטרליים), in which the source is not felt and is not drawn into the poem, or does not even fit the poem; (2) meaningful borrowings (שִׁבּוּצִים בַּעֲלֵי מַשְׁמָעוּת) in which knowledge of the source and original context is part of the meaning of the passage . . . (3) borrowings . . . whose original content sheds new light on the content of the poem or contributes to the understanding of its internal structure" (Pagis, 70–71). The first category matches what I call "echo," while the second and third exemplify genuine allusion. Johnson, 580, also notes that some cases of dependence on an earlier text may have little meaningful component but are limited to purely formal elements: "The new poet's reworking of the original formal mold may totally neglect the semantic plane." However, he does not distinguish such cases as a separate category.

My distinction between allusion and echo also resembles that between the terms רמיזה and שיבוץ as they are used by *modern* Hebrew literary critics; see Chana Kronfeld, "Allusion: An Israeli Perspective," *Prooftexts* 5 (1985), 129–40 (cf. *Margins*, 117–88). These terms were used differently by medieval Hebrew literary theorists, for whom רמיזה was a type of thematic influence while שיבוץ encompassed both what I call echo and allusion; see Kronfeld, 138, and Pagis, 75. (Pagis, as cited above, uses the term שיבוץ in its medieval sense.)

39. Ben-Porat, "Allusion," 115 n. 11.

40. Yair Zakovitch, "Review of J. P. Fokkelman, *Narrative Art in Genesis*," *Shnaton: An Annual for Biblical and Ancient Near Eastern Studies* 4 (1980), 303 [Heb.].

41. A somewhat similar phrase appears elsewhere in Hebrew literature: תחלת המחשבה סוף המעשה in the translation of Judah Halevi's *Kuzari* (3.73) by Judah ibn Tibbon, but Zakovitch's borrowing is clearly from the more well-known Sabbath poem, whose wording he more exactly follows.

42. It is important to note how my use of the term "echo" differs from that of

Richard Hays in his excellent work on Paul's use of scripture. For Hays, echo and allusion are almost synonymous terms, but echo tends to be more faint: "I make no systematic distinction between the two terms. In general, throughout the following pages, *allusion* is used of obvious intertextual references, *echo* of subtler ones" (Hays, 29; note that Hays uses the term "intertextual" to include what I call influence and allusion). Hays states further that allusion is intentional on the part of the author, and that allusion assumes that the reader shares with the author a "portable library" to which the allusion is made. Echo does not depend on the author's intention. The interpreter of both echo and allusion in Hays's sense can move through all four of Ben-Porat's stages.

43. See, e.g., the entry "Exegesis" in Karl Beckson and Arthur Ganz, *Literary Terms: A Dictionary*, 3d ed. (New York: Farrar, Straus and Giroux, 1989), 89. Fabian Gudas, s.v. "Explication," in *The New Princeton Encyclopedia of Poetry and Poetics*, ed. A. Preminger and V. Brogan (Princeton, N.J.: Princeton University Press, 1993), 395–96, connects the term "exegesis," along with "analysis," "explanation," "interpretation," and "elucidation," with the term "explication."

44. Cf. Ben-Porat, "Intertextuality," 176. She does not discuss exegesis there but points out that a metatext which works at the level of metonymic rhetorical intertextuality (which is largely identical to what I call "allusion") relates to a source not transformatively but rather in a transferring manner, so that the older text hands over something to be used in the new. The new use of the material does not alter the original sign. This seems to me to set this phenomenon against exegesis, whose goal is a transformation or alteration of our perception of the sign in the text undergoing exegesis.

45. "Text" here is not confined to a work of commentary such as, say, Rashi's commentary on the Torah or an interpretive essay about a novel or poem or play. It can also include an interpretive comment (concerned with some earlier text) embedded in another type of text. Many of Fishbane's examples are of this sort: for example, narratives in Chronicles often suggest a reading of the Torah (or something very much like it) which is exegetical in the narrow sense proposed here, though Chronicles is not a commentary. For a brief and useful discussion of the difference between exegesis and commentary, see Steven Fraade, *From Tradition to Commentary: Torah and Its Interpretation in the Midrash Sifre to Deuteronomy* (Albany: SUNY Press, 1991), 1–3. Fraade describes commentary as a systematic and gradual set of interpretations of a text, while an exegesis can be a single interpretive remark, whether or not in a commentary. As Fraade notes, the Bible contains exegesis but no commentary.

46. A similar distinction occurs in Fraade, 5 and 175 n. 18. He contrasts commentaries such as *pesharim*, whose organization follows that of an older text, with texts that are "spiced" with citations and allusions, such as the Damascus Document or the New Testament Gospels. In the latter, "story takes precedence over Scripture as an organizing principle, even while heavily dependent on it."

47. See Ben-Porat, "Allusion," 114 n. 9.

48. Johnson, 581.

49. Cf. Fishbane, *Biblical*, 498–99.

50. See above, n. 35, and cf. Seidel, 150.

51. Cf. Renza, 186, who makes the same point about critics who study allusion, and Alter, 139. This culturally conservative effect looms large even in works that attempt (or purport) to reject the values of older texts. Kronfeld gives a fine example of this as she discusses allusion in the poetry of Yehuda Amichai and Nathan Zach. She notes "a fundamentally conservative moment in this new allusive poetry of anti-tradition. Both Zach and Amichai . . . can be described as coming *out of* the tradition: they are the harshest critics of the delusions of transcendent hope which tradition gives (Amichai) or of the illusion of meaning which its sacred language maintains (Zach). The one wishes to exalt the mundane and the secular, while deflating the traditional and sacred; the other wishes merely to thematize the tautological nature of all language and all thought. In this sense both place themselves *outside of* the tradition. But as reinterpreters and retellers of biblical, Talmudic, and liturgical allusions, in fact even as vociferous critics of the biblical God, they cannot help but identify themselves as *evolving out of* the same tradition which they so consistently fight. In this sense, Amichai and Zach are in the end familiar figures. They are the last in a long line of God's critics whom, like Job and Levi Yitzhak of Berdichev, the tradition has managed to pull into the mainstream" (Kronfeld, "Allusion," 158–59; updated version in Kronfeld, *Margins*, 139–40).

52. Cyrena Pondrom ("Influence? or Intertextuality? The Complicated Connection of Edith Sitwell with Gertrude Stein," in *Influence and Intertextuality*, ed. Clayton and Rothstein, 208) points out that an author may acknowledge influence for the sake of the older work, in order that the predecessor become better known or be seen as a prestigious (i.e., influential) text. Thus it may be the influenced writer, rather than the influence, with whom real literary power lies. For Pondrom, influence and especially assertions of influence are concerned with power and canon-formation; insofar as allusion can be an assertion of influence, the same may said about it.

53. E.g., in the cases of Amichai and Zach noted in n. 51. For example, Kronfeld examines biblical allusions in Amichai's poem "בכל חמרות הרחמים" and Zach's "כמו חול" (Kronfeld, *Margins*, 130–40, and "Allusion," 151–58). She shows that the poets allude to biblical texts in order to disagree with them: they reject some, highlight the inaccuracy of others, and ironically reverse a few. Through so doing they assert their distinct viewpoints. On the variety of relations between evoked text and allusion (ranging from consonance to dissonance, from homage to antagonism), see also Alter, 132.

54. So Seidel, "Parallels," 150.

55. Miner (1965), 18, and Kronfeld, "Allusion," 139 (cf. *Margins*, 117).

56. Perri, 301.

57. Sigmund Freud, *Jokes and Their Relation to the Unconscious*, trans. and ed. James Strachey (New York: Norton, 1963), 120, quoted in Perri, 301–2.

58. Johnson, 380. On this whole issue, see also Alter, 124.

59. If I may allude to a phrase coined by a well-known savant associated with intertextuality.

60. Cf. Fishbane, *Biblical*, especially 536–40. While my suggestions regarding inner-biblical exegesis here are at times opposed to his, both the line of questioning and many of the data used to find answers stem from his work.

61. In fact the exegetical work which the citation introduces in some such cases centers around resolving conflicts among the sources within the Pentateuch. See, e.g., Fishbane, *Biblical*, 134–38.

62. Fishbane, *Biblical*, 213.

63. Ibid., 209–10.

64. For a discussion of Ezekiel's references to comments made by his countrymen and their captors, see Moshe Greenberg, "The Citations in Ezekiel as a Background for the Prophecies," *BM* 17 (1972), 273–78 [Heb.].

65. See Fishbane, *Biblical*, 329–34.

66. A work may include portions of older works which are no longer available to us or whose existence may be debated; this is the case in the Pentateuch, which largely consists of a variety of older texts gathered into a new work. Since the older texts in such a case may not have been written or may no longer be extant, the analysis of this category to some extent belongs more to the study of tradition history than to inner-biblical allusion and exegesis.

67. Yair Zakovitch, *An Introduction to Inner-Biblical Interpretation* (Even-Yehuda: Reches, 1992), 28 [Heb.]; for further examples of interpolation, see 29–41, 89–92.

68. Fishbane is aware of the distinction between a narrow sense of the term exegesis and his broader use of the term (see Fishbane, *Biblical*, 321 and 415–17), but he fails to develop the distinction elsewhere in his book. On the term "inner-biblical exegesis," see Nahum Sarna, "Psalm 89: A Study in Inner Biblical Exegesis," in *Biblical and Other Studies*, ed. Alexander Altmann (Cambridge, Mass.: Harvard University Press, 1963), 29–46; Fishbane, *Biblical*, passim; and Zakovitch, *Introduction*, passim.

69. Cf. Fraade's distinction between exegesis and commentary (the latter includes the former, but the former need not occur in the latter), Fraade, 1–3.

70. See Fishbane, *Biblical*, 23–88, esp. 44–55, and also Zakovitch, *Introduction*, 20–27. In such cases, we are left with a single text. This differs from most cases of exegesis, in which the explicating text and the text being explicated are physically distinct. The explicative thrust of these scribal interpolations is nonetheless evident, which justifies including them in the category of exegesis.

71. Fishbane, *Biblical*, 70 n. 15.

72. See Fishbane, *Biblical*, 489–90.

73. Examples of influence which do not involve the formal category of inclusion can be found in literature as well. Goethe's *Iphigenie auf Tauris* depends on Euripides' drama, *Iphigenia at Aulis*, but Goethe's play does not repeat the actual wording of the source.

Cases of this sort straddle the line separating the study of inner-biblical allusion and exegesis on the one hand and tradition history on the other. Jubilees, for example, constitutes a retelling of Genesis, but some of the material it contains may be taken from other sources or traditions. An analogous phenomenon is found in literature. While Goethe's *Iphigenie* clearly goes back specifically to Euripides' drama, his *Faust* depends not only on Marlowe's play but on a variety of popular and literary traditions concerning the medieval magician of that name.

74. Cf. Renza, 186, and Bloom's notion that examples of influence fit into certain "revisionary ratios."

75. This category resembles the forms of relationship between sources and later texts which Ben-Porat, "Intertextuality," 175, calls "המשך" and "הרחבה."

76. Fishbane, *Biblical*, 476. In this example, the revision consists of an interpolation, a form discussed at greater length by Zakovitch, *Introduction*, 28–34.

77. A similar point has been made by Bernard Levinson, *Deuteronomy and the Hermeneutics of Legal Innovation* (New York: Oxford University Press, 1997). Levinson shows that Deuteronomy intends not merely to supplement but to replace the Covenant Code (see especially pp. 4, 15–17). Similarly, Levinson shows that the Chronicler preempts the Deuteronomist, presenting his work as textual original rather than as literary supplement (see pp. 154–55, esp. n. 21).

78. It is important to stress this point, because the only book-length studies of this phenomenon (Fishbane, *Biblical*, and Zakovitch, *Introduction*) stress the exegetical nature of many interpolations and new texts that are better described as revisionary. They do so, I suspect, in part due to their desire to emphasize the connections between the authors of the Hebrew Bible and the authors of rabbinic literature.

79. Cf. Levinson, *Deuteronomy*, 155. The fact that later redactors preserved the Covenant Code and the JE narratives alongside Deuteronomy does not suggest that the authors of the latter intended their source also to be preserved; the same point can be made about Chronicles' intentions regarding Samuel-Kings, which were not those of the canonizers.

80. Some texts may straddle the boundary between revision and exegesis I am drawing here. By the time the Book of Jubilees was written, Genesis was most likely well established as scripture. Jubilees presents a revision intended in all likelihood to exist alongside the already scriptural work while influencing our understanding of it. Indeed some of Jubilees' revisions appear as interpretations in midrashic texts (see, e.g., the examples cited in Zakovitch, *Introduction*, 133 n. 16).

81. Fishbane's stress on inner-biblical exegesis leads him to emphasize the connection between that phenomenon and rabbinic literature while underrating

the equally important connection between inner-biblical exegesis and the New Testament.

82. This category resembles a form of relationship between sources and later texts which Ben-Porat, "Intertextuality," 175, calls תגובה.

83. So according to the convincing explanation of Yochanan Muffs, "Between Justice and Mercy: The Prayer of the Prophets," in *Torah Nidreshet*, ed. Moshe Greenberg (Jerusalem: Am Oved and Jewish Theological Seminary, 1984), 47–57 [Heb.], translated in Yochanan Muffs, "Who Will Stand in the Breach: A Study of Prophetic Intercession," in *Love and Joy: Law, Language and Religion in Ancient Israel* (New York and Cambridge, Mass.: Jewish Theological Seminary and Harvard University Press, 1992), 16–24.

84. See Fishbane, *Biblical*, 343–47.

85. Muffs, "Mercy," 56–57, and "Breach," 23–24.

86. What was said above regarding the distinction between revision and exegesis applies to the distinction between polemic and exegesis: cases of polemic may later be seen as exegesis, but the categories differ conceptually and should be kept distinct.

87. Take, for example, the relationship between Deutero-Isaiah and the priestly creation account in Genesis 1 noted by Moshe Weinfeld, "God the Creator in Gen. 1 and in the Prophecy of Second Isaiah," *Tarbiz* 37 (1968), 120–32 (reprinted in *Likkutei Tarbiz: A Biblical Studies Reader*, ed. Moshe Weinfeld [Jerusalem: Magnes, 1979], 117–46) [Heb.]. Weinfeld demonstrates that Deutero-Isaiah disagreed with the earlier priestly writers of Genesis 1 on several points: Deutero-Isaiah had a less anthropomorphic view of God than the priestly writers, and he was less willing to tolerate the idea of pre-existent chaos. According to Fishbane, "The underlying cognitive concern [of Deutero-Isaiah] was not so much to undermine Gen. 1:1–2:4a as to maintain it in a newly understood way" (Fishbane, *Biblical*, 326)—that is, this is a case of exegesis (albeit a tendentious one). But it seems to me that we might more accurately see this as polemic (as Weinfeld does). Deutero-Isaiah's point was not to have people read Genesis 1 differently, but to have them believe his own ideas instead of those in Genesis 1. On the other hand, it is noteworthy that ultimately most readers, medieval and modern, in fact read Genesis 1 as if it described creation in the manner Deutero-Isaiah did. The polemic developed into a case of exegesis because later readers accepted both texts as canonical. For this reason Weinfeld had to spend half his article (Weinfeld, "Creator," 105–20) liberating Genesis 1 from Deutero-Isaiah's hegemony, arguing that Genesis 1 is neither as spiritual nor as nonanthropomorphic as most readers believe.

88. Fishbane, *Biblical*, 301–2.

89. Kugel, "Bible's," 280.

90. This occurs in cases of polemic in literature generally. See Kronfeld's discussion of Amichai and Zach in *Margins*, 130–40, and "Allusion," 151–58.

91. Fishbane, *Biblical*, 331.

CHAPTER TWO

1. The question of what can be considered a genuine allusion or source has played a major role in influence studies generally; see René Wellek and Austin Warren, *Theory of Literature* (New York: Harcourt, Brace and World, 1956), 258 and notes; Robert Alter, *The Pleasures of Reading in an Ideological Age* (New York: Norton, 1996 [1989]), 119; Jay Clayton and Eric Rothstein, "Figures in the Corpus: Theories of Influence and Intertextuality," in *Influence and Intertextuality in Literary History*, ed. Jay Clayton and Eric Rothstein (Madison: University of Wisconsin Press, 1991), 5–6; James Chandler, "Romantic Allusiveness," *Critical Inquiry* 8 (1982), 463–64, 480. Michael Fishbane discusses the issue as well in *Biblical Interpretation in Ancient Israel* (Oxford: Oxford University Press, 1985), 288–89. Biblical scholars (not a few of whom strive in vain for a scientific sort of precision) need to realize that indisputable assertions regarding the presence of allusion are not the goal of literary study; indeed, this branch of learning relishes that which is subtle and suggestive. Richard Garner articulates this point on the first page of his book *From Homer to Tragedy: The Art of Allusion in Greek Poetry* (London: Routledge, 1990): "Poetic allusions—this is part of their power to charm and to frustrate—cannot be proved or disproved. At first this elusiveness seems disastrous to the critic. Upon reflection, however, the problem seems less threatening: little that readers value in poetry responds reliably to the arid analysis of axiom and corollary, or even to the more pragmatic pins and tools of dissection that serve so well to examine the earthworm or affix the butterfly to the board once it can no longer fly."

2. That is, clusters of vocabulary, often centered around a particular topic, repeatedly used by prophets, scribes, and cult singers. On the issue of stock or formulaic vocabulary generally in ancient poetry, see Wilfred G. E. Watson, *Classical Hebrew Poetry: A Guide to Its Techniques* (Sheffield: Sheffield Academic Press, 1984), 70, 74–77, 81; for examples of formulaic language in similes, merismus, and hendiadys, see 318–28. On the use of formulaic language among prophets, see Robert Wilson, *Prophecy and Society in Ancient Israel* (Philadelphia: Fortress Press, 1980), 65–66.

3. For a brief discussion of the literary forms found in Isaiah 40–66 and their relation to other biblical texts, see Claus Westermann, *Isaiah 40–66: A Commentary*, trans. D. Stalker (Philadelphia: Westminster Press, 1969), 21–27, 300–305. For greater detail, see Joachim Begrich, *Studien zu Deuterojesaja*, 2d ed. (Munich: Kaiser Verlag: 1969), 13–66, and Hugo Greßmann, "Die literarische Analyse Deuterojesajas," *ZAW* 34 (1914), 263–97; and, for a form-critical discussion of 40–55 that is sensitive to more recent literary concerns, see especially Roy Melugin, *The Formation of Isaiah 40–55* (Berlin: de Gruyter, 1976), 13–74. Summaries of the history of scholarship on form and genre in Isaiah 40–66 are found in Antti Laato, *The Servant of YHWH and Cyrus: A Reinterpretation of the Exilic Messianic Programme in Isaiah 40–55* (Stockholm: Almqvist and Wiksell, 1992), 6–10.

4. Deutero-Isaiah's revision of an older form itself constitutes a transformation of older traditions, but the study of such transformations belongs to tradition history or form criticism. I am not primarily interested in this side of Deutero-Isaiah's use of older material, though I mention it at times when it sheds light on his inner-biblical exegesis. Westermann pays a great deal of attention (too much?) to this issue.

5. For example, Isa 56.8 repeats vocabulary and themes found in Isa 11.12. However, similar vocabulary appears in Deut 30.4, Mic 2.12, and Ps 147.2. This suggests that the shared terms constitute a case of stock vocabulary. As a result, one cannot assert with confidence that Deutero-Isaiah relied specifically on Isa 11.12 for this phrase, and the verse in question cannot be taken as a case of inner-biblical exegesis. The same can be said for the language in Isa 40.4–7, which shares vocabulary with Isa 1.30, 28.1, 34.4, 64.5, and Ps 90.5f. and 103.15f. It is impossible to suggest that Deutero-Isaiah depended on any particular text for his repeated use of the language; it is at least as likely that all the authors depended on stock language.

6. When two passages employ the same literary form, there is a high likelihood that they will both include stock vocabulary. For example, 41.8–16 and Psalm 35 share a fair number of words: תגיל בה׳, בק״ש יבושו ויכלמו, עז״ר, החזיק, ריב. However, one would be hasty to conclude that Deutero-Isaiah referred specifically to this psalm, because 41.8–16 seems to be related to the lament form. Similar language appears in several laments (and the declarations of praise that sometimes accompany them), such as Pss 70.2–5; 44.10, 16, 26; and 71.12–13. All this suggests that Deutero-Isaiah may have been utilizing stock lament vocabulary to effect a reversal of mood and a move away from lamentation toward consolation or celebration.

7. Isa 43.22–26 contain many words also found in Isa 1.10f.: חל״ב, עולות, זב״ח, חט״א, מנחה, and other related concepts and forms. The number of parallel terms is less impressive than it initially appears to be, however, because nearly all of the parallels concern the theme of sacrifice. Any author discussing that topic is likely to use certain words, so that the shared vocabulary does not suffice to point to the later text's dependence on the earlier. This may be the case even when the terms appear together only rarely. One might see 63.2 as an allusion to Lam 1.15 due to the shared terms דר״ך and גת, which occur together only once outside these texts (in Neh 13.15). But the occurrence of these words alongside one another may well have been quite common in spoken biblical Hebrew, given that "treading" (דר״ך) is what goes on in a "wine-press" (גת). That both Deutero-Isaiah and Lamentations take up the image in a metaphor concerning God's anger may well be coincidental.

8. See, among others, Friedrich Stummer, "Einige keilschriftliche Parallelen zu Jes. 60–66," *JBL* 45 (1926), 171–89; Shalom Paul, "Deutero-Isaiah and Cuneiform Royal Inscriptions," in *Essays in Memory of E. A. Speiser*, ed. William Hallo (New Haven, Conn.: American Oriental Society, 1968) (=*JAOS* 88 [1968]), 180–86; Israel Eph'al, "On the Linguistic and Cultural Background of Deutero-Isaiah," *Shenaton: An Annual for Biblical and Ancient Near Eastern Studies* 10 (1986–89), 31–35 [Heb.];

and Laato, 47–68, who stresses especially the use of royal and prophetic traditions connected with servants and Cyrus.

9. The themes and characteristic terms listed in examples one through seven appear in Akkadian inscriptions from periods throughout Mesopotamian history in both the north and the south, especially inscriptions lauding kings for restoring temples. Themes and terms in example eight are concentrated in neo-Assyrian royal oracles. It is interesting that in both Deutero-Isaiah and Jeremiah the elements found in the neo-Assyrian oracles occur together with the phrases found in the Akkadian inscriptions.

10. See Laato, 50–64; Stummer, 177–80; Paul, "Deutero-Isaiah," 181–86. For additional examples of number eight from Akkadian literature, see the convenient collection and translations in Edgar Conrad, *Fear Not Warrior: A Study of 'al Tîrā' Pericopes in the Hebrew Scriptures* (Chico, Calif.: Scholars Press, 1985), 58–61, 154–57. The wording found in number eight also occurs in Northwest Semitic texts (such as KAI 202 and KTU 2.30 [=UT 1013], lines 16–24) and elsewhere in the Hebrew Bible (e.g., Gen 15.1, 26.24, etc.).

11. Cf. Fishbane, *Biblical*, 285. Moshe Seidel attempted to find such a pattern in borrowings from Psalms in the Book of Isaiah. He pointed out that a word pair in the older text may occur in the later one in reverse order (Moshe Seidel, "Parallels Between the Book of Isaiah and the Book of Psalms," *Sinai* 38 [1955–56], 150). The value of this observation is limited, however, since coincidentally shared terms could very well appear in different order in two texts. Indeed, even stock parallel terms in Hebrew and Ugaritic sometimes appear with one term first and other times with the other first. (See Watson, 356f.; cf. 135.) Further, the inversion Seidel notes does not help us recognize which text is the source and which the borrower.

12. Cf. Richard Hays, *Echoes of Scripture in the Letters of Paul* (New Haven, Conn.: Yale University Press, 1989), 29–32. Hays suggests seven rules of thumb to aid in this pursuit: (1) *availability*—whether the author could have known the alleged source (this issue will present far greater difficulties in my study of Deutero-Isaiah than in Hays's study of Paul, since we know fairly well the nature of Paul's scripture but can only conjecture regarding Deutero-Isaiah's); (2) *volume*—the degree of explicit repetition of words or syntactic patterns; (3) *recurrence*—whether the author uses the passage elsewhere; (4) *thematic coherence*—whether the allusion fits into the tenor of the work as a whole; (5) *historical plausibility*—could the author have intended such an allusion, and (less importantly) could the audience have understood it; (6) *history of interpretation*—have others noticed it; (7) *satisfaction*—whether the proposed reading makes sense. Of course, some of Hays's rules are very loose (especially numbers four, five, and seven), and, slavishly applied, they could have a deadening effect; but when a sensitive critic (such as Hays) employs them, they can guide or caution the critic productively. In this study, an important eighth rule must always play a role: the critic must be reasonably sure that a similarity does not result from

common use of an Israelite or ancient Near Eastern literary topos (e.g., the lament genre or the royal oracle).

13. John Skinner notes such parallels throughout his commentary on Isaiah 40–66, *The Book of the Prophet Isaiah: Chapters XL–LXVI*, rev. ed. (Cambridge: Cambridge University Press, 1917). Umberto Cassuto identifies links between Deutero-Isaiah and Jeremiah in "On the Formal and Stylistic Relationship Between Deutero-Isaiah and Other Biblical Writers," in *Biblical and Oriental Studies*, trans. I. Abrahams (Magnes: Jerusalem, 1973), 1: 143–60. He also notes parallels between Deutero-Isaiah and other prophets, 160–77. Shalom Paul similarly describes Deutero-Isaiah's borrowings from Jeremiah in "Literary and Ideological Echoes of Jeremiah in Deutero-Isaiah," *Proceedings of the Fifth World Congress of Jewish Studies* (1969), 1: 109–21. A list of the relevant parallels appears in William Holladay, *Jeremiah 2: A Commentary on the Book of the Prophet Jeremiah Chapters 26–52* (Minneapolis: Fortress Press, 1989), 86–88.

14. See Wolfgang Lau, *Schriftgelehrte Prophetie in Jes 56–66: Eine Untersuchung zu den literarischen Bezügen in den letzten elf Kapiteln des Jesajabuches* (Berlin: Walter de Gruyter, 1994). He suggests that 56–66 contain several layers of tradition: an original Trito-Isaiah and four distinct groups of prophetic writers; the later ones often refer to the earlier, just as Trito-Isaiah refers to Deutero-Isaiah (on the characteristics of each group or "*Tradentenkreise*," see pp. 22–24, 118, 143, 203, and 262). This division of chapters 56–66 into several discrete corpora is unlikely. The alleged differences between the groups rest on types of thematic interest present in certain texts; thus Lau's divisions amount to a map of major themes in these chapters rather than the source-critical finding that he believes them to be. At times his divisions require carving up coherent texts into different levels of composition; that this style of analyzing prophetic texts is quite common does not make it any less speculative or unlikely (cf. my remarks in the Appendix, esp. pp. 217–18).

Many of the correspondences between Isaiah 56–66 and other biblical texts which Lau notes are genuine cases of allusion; others consist of too few elements to be considered real borrowings rather than coincidence or the common use of standard prophetic terminology. Oddly, Lau does not cite recent work on inner-biblical exegesis, and at times his work lacks methodological sophistication regarding the identification of genuine borrowings.

15. Cassuto, "Formal," 163–65, does describe some of these difficulties; see also 167.

16. On the provenance of Jeremiah 50–51, see the brief discussions in Otto Eissfeldt, *The Old Testament: An Introduction*, trans. Peter Ackroyd (New York: Harper and Row, 1965), 362–64, and Douglas Jones, *Jeremiah* (Grand Rapids, Mich.: Eerdmans, 1992), 34–35, 520–24. Even as conservative a critic as John Bright views most of this material as being later than the work of Jeremiah; see his remarks in his commentary, *Jeremiah* (Garden City, N.Y.: Doubleday, 1965), 359–60. Holladay ar-

gues in his commentary on these chapters for a more extensive Jeremian core; nonetheless, it seems better to err on the side of caution here by excluding them from consideration, especially since their connections with other parts of the Hebrew Bible make them doubtful cases of allusion anyway.

17. A convenient list of the parallels is found in Cassuto, "Formal," 152–54; Cassuto regards it as likely that Deutero-Isaiah is the source for Jeremiah 50–51 rather than the other way around.

18. For summaries of scholarship, see Robert Carroll, *Jeremiah* (London: SCM, 1986), 38–50; Holladay, 2: 10–14; and the still-useful précis by Eissfeldt, *Introduction*, 350–66. For a defense of a "maximalist" position (i.e., one that attributes a great deal of the book to Jeremiah himself or to scribes who knew his work directly) see especially Holladay, 2: 14–24 and passim, and Bright, lv–lxxxv and 284–87. For a defense of the minimalist position, see Carroll, *Jeremiah*, esp. 46–48.

19. See Sigmund Mowinckel, *Zur Komposition des Buches Jeremia*, Videnskapsselskapets Skrifter II, Hist.-Filos. Klasse No. 5, 1913 (Kristiania: Jacob Dwybad, 1914), esp. 16–54.

20. It is important to note that when I identified Deutero-Isaiah's allusions to Jeremiah, I was woefully—but fortunately—ignorant of Mowinckel's theories. If this had not been the case, my findings in this regard would be suspect. The material on which Deutero-Isaiah draws, incidentally, includes some material that Mowinckel dated later than Jeremiah; thus, even though the study of Deutero-Isaiah's allusions helps confirm Mowinckel's source-critical theories, it forces a revision of his dating of those sources. Deutero-Isaiah also alludes to four prose passages about whose attribution Mowinckel was hesitant; although Mowinckel tentatively assigns them to the Deuteronomistic block of material, they do not display characteristics of that block and must be regarded as stemming from an independent tradition. See further my article, "New Light on the Composition of Jeremiah," *CBQ* (forthcoming).

21. The same phenomenon is found within the Book of Jeremiah itself: at times the earlier prophet composed prophecies of consolation whose language resembles his own predictions of catastrophe. For example, Jeremiah had announced that God would banish "the sounds of joy and of happiness, the voices of the bride and groom from the cities of Judah and the streets of Jerusalem" (Jer 7.34; cf. 16.9, 25.10). But later he said, "Again will there be heard . . . in the cities of Judah and the streets of Jerusalem . . . the sounds of joy and of happiness, the voices of the bride and groom" (Jer 33.10–11). Similarly, Yochanan Muffs (in "As a Cloak Clings to Its Owner," in *Love and Joy: Law, Language and Religion in Ancient Israel* [New York: Jewish Theological Seminary and Harvard University Press, 1992], 52) points out that Jeremiah's buoyant remarks to the people in 33.7–9 are based on his rebuke in 13.11; they utilize similar vocabulary and images, but the later comment reverses the tone of the earlier one. A similar case is noted by R. Carroll (*Jeremiah*), who points out that 31.31–34 reverse 5.1–5 and 8.7. It seems likely that Deutero-Isaiah learned from Jeremiah this tendency

to construct prophecies of consolation with material gleaned from prophecies of condemnation; he extended it, as we shall see in the next chapter, to prophecies of doom from Isaiah as well.

22. Reading thus instead of the difficult MT, מֵרַחֵם. This emendation has been defended by Mayer Gruber, "'Can a Woman Forget Her Infant . . . ?'" *Tarbiz* 51 (1982), 491–92 [Heb.]. In addition to Gruber's already forceful arguments, we may note that אִם may stand behind the η of some LXX manuscripts.

23. One might respond to the prophet: yes, but mothers do sometimes abandon their children. Deutero-Isaiah anticipates this question in two ways. He likens YHWH to a mother who breast-feeds (עוּל refers specifically to an infant who is nursing); such a mother is physically unable to forget her child. Further, the prophet undercuts his metaphor immediately after he states it: YHWH as mother does not abandon—and even if mothers do abandon, YHWH is not that sort of mother. On this metaphor, see Marc Brettler, "Incompatible Metaphors for YHWH in Deutero-Isaiah," *JSOT* (forthcoming).

24. The subsequent verses of the passage in Deutero-Isaiah continue the trope of reversal. They evoke the prophecy of doom in Isa 6.10–12, repeating terms with which Isaiah predicted destruction and thus confirming that the dire prophecy has been fulfilled. But he effects a pithy reversal with one marker. In Isa 6.12, YHWH made His own people go far (וְרִחַק) from the land, which became devoid of inhabitants (מֵאֵין יוֹשֵׁב). Now, according to Isa 49.19, the invaders through whom YHWH carried out the disaster will go far away (וְרָחֲקוּ), and the land will once again be full of its erstwhile inhabitants (תֵּצְרִי מִיּוֹשֵׁב). This example contains sound play (on which see below), as Professor Marc Brettler pointed out to me: בְּנֵי in 49.20 may hearken back to יָבִין in 6.10; מְבַלְּעָיִךְ in 49.19 contains three consonants in common with לְבָעֵר in 6.13; and וְאֲשֵׁבָה in 49.20 recalls וְשָׁבָה in 6.13.

25. Other examples are equally pithy. In one case, Jeremiah says to Zion, "They called you (קָרְאוּ לָךְ) 'cut off,' 'That is Zion—no one cares for her (דּוֹרֵשׁ אֵין לָהּ)'" (Jer 30.17)." Deutero-Isaiah turns that phrase on its head: "They will call them (וְקָרְאוּ לָהֶם) 'the holy people, redeemed by YHWH'; and you [Zion] will be called, 'The one cared for (דְּרוּשָׁה), the city which has not been deserted' (Isa 62.12)."

26. While some commentators (e.g., Carroll, *Jeremiah*) claim that the passage in Jeremiah consists of several unrelated fragments and later additions, the unity of subject in these verses is clear: all relate to the downfall of the people, some bemoaning it (Jer 10.19–20), some giving reasons for it (Jer 10.21), some describing it (Jer 10.22), and some praying that it not become as severe as anticipated (Jer 10.23–24). On the unity of Jer 10.17–25 passim, see Holladay, 1: 339.

27. Holladay (2: 87) sees Isa 54.3 as a reversal of the reduction of Israel's numbers threatened in Jer 10.24 (of course 54.1 already reverses that motif), though he does not note the other correspondences between these passages.

28. Further, 52.13–53.12 also appear to allude to Jer 10.18–25. Parallel vocabulary

occurs throughout that passage and includes a case of the split-up pattern and cases of sound play reminiscent of the one found in this passage; the puns there are based on the words שֵׁמָ"ם and אָכֵן from Jeremiah. Deutero-Isaiah repeats Jeremiah's passage with variations, applying his prediction regarding the people's fate to the servant described there. Elements of reversal also appear, especially noticeable in the words לֹא הִשְׂכִּילוּ (Jer 10.21) and יַשְׂכִּיל (Isa 52.13), and in the different natures of the reports (שְׁמוּעָה) in each: in Jeremiah it is of an invading army from the north, and in Deutero-Isaiah it is of the surprising success of the servant.

29. Charles Torrey, who believes Isaiah 40–66 and 35 were written in Jerusalem near the end of the fifth century B.C.E., says of chapter 54: "This is one of the poems in which it is especially evident that no 'prophet of the Babylonian exile' is writing. Jerusalem is exhorted to expand on all sides, in confidence of increasing prosperity. These words would be a pitiful mockery if they were addressed to a city actually in ruins. On the contrary, it is plain from the poet's language that Jerusalem already is enjoying a considerable measure of material well-being." (Charles Torrey, *The Second Isaiah: A New Interpretation* [New York: Scribners, 1928], 423–24). As soon as one recognizes the allusion to Jeremiah, however, any difficulty in regarding this image of Jerusalem as stemming from the sixth century disappears. The prophet tells the personified city to enlarge her tent because an earlier prophet had told her that she would not be able to do so. The rhetoric here does not concern adding to already existing territory but reversing an older trope.

30. H. L. Ginsberg suggests some far-reaching emendations in the passage; these are cited in Paul, "Literary," 113 n. 51, and reflected in NJPS's footnotes. As Paul points out ("Literary," 114), they would produce even more parallel vocabulary with the passage in Jeremiah.

31. The allusion occurs over several verses which Westermann argues stem from separate strata. He claims that the prophet's utterance continues up until the words "God says"; from there on the text stems from a later hand. That the allusion runs over that boundary, and that both halves reflect a common stylistic technique of the prophet, show Westermann's dismembering of the last verses from the passage (which reflects his approach to the text generally) to be mistaken.

32. Another passage from Jeremiah 6 also provides Deutero-Isaiah with an opportunity for a reversal. In Jer 6.20, 22, Jeremiah proclaims YHWH's dissatisfaction with the sacrificial cult and the expensive items imported from afar used in it. He goes on to announce that a nation from afar will arrive to punish the people. In Isa 60.6–9, Deutero-Isaiah reverses both Jeremiah's rejection of the Israelites' sacrifices and the role he accorded to foreigners. Now, the prophet tells his audience, the Temple will be rebuilt, and nations from afar will donate expensive items to be used in worship there. The shared vocabulary appears in the same order in both texts.

33. Here, as in many other passages in Jeremiah, MT is no longer than the corresponding text in LXX. Most scholars regard the shorter LXX version of Jere-

miah's letter as more original; see e.g., Holladay. Therefore, a word which does not appear in LXX cannot be considered a marked item, because additional material in MT almost certainly was added after the exile. On the other hand, some of the material which appears in MT and not LXX may be original, in which case it is lacking in LXX because it was dropped from there or from its *Vorlage* (for example, due to haplography). Thus, while most "pluses" in MT indicate later additions, some "minuses" in LXX may result from deletions; see J. Gerald Janzen, *Studies in the Text of Jeremiah* (Cambridge, Mass.: Harvard University Press, 1973), 117–19. Each individual case must be examined carefully. It will be safest not to rely on a plus as a marked item demonstrating a borrowing unless its presence in the original LXX-*Vorlage* can be shown as likely on text-critical grounds.

34. The phrase is absent in LXX, and it is difficult to decide whether it was added to MT or dropped from LXX due to haplography (see Janzen, *Studies*, 103–4). However, the marked root יל״ד has already appeared immediately above, which makes the issue moot for our purposes.

35. This word is lacking in the LXX. Janzen sees it as an addition to the MT (*Studies*, 40), though I think its presence in 4QJerᵃ (see Janzen, *Studies*, 176) may argue for its original status. In any event, the word אֶרֶץ appears two other times in this passage, so that Deutero-Isaiah's use of it is clear.

36. The Hebrew phrase, כָּלוּ עֵינֵיהֶם, could also be understood to mean "their springs dried up"—a double entendre certainly intended by Jeremiah.

37. On the translation of נִדְהָם, see Holladay; or read "like a sleeping man" (כְּאִישׁ נִרְדָּם) with LXX.

38. The LXX reads ὡς ἀνὴρ (כְּגֶבֶר). The MT is preferable. Nonetheless, even if כְּגֶבֶר is the original text, the relationship of the marker (כַּגִּבּוֹר) to the marked would remain intact as a case of sound play (on which see immediately below).

39. See further on this image Katheryn Pfisterer Darr, "Like Warrior, Like Woman: Destruction and Deliverance in Isaiah 42:10–17," *CBQ* 49 (1987): 560–71, and Brettler, "Incompatible." Darr also argues effectively that these verses belong to a single literary unit rather than (as some scholars assert) to several distinct units that have been edited together secondarily.

40. See especially Isa 59.9–19, where Deutero-Isaiah alludes to Jer 14.7–9. Jeremiah confessed the nation's sins and called on God to save Israel for His own name's sake, but God rejected that prophet's plea. Deutero-Isaiah also confesses the nation's sinfulness (Isa 59.9–12), but he also supplies what was pointedly missing in the earlier text: a positive response from God. According to Deutero-Isaiah, YHWH will finally intervene, precisely for the reason that Jeremiah had already suggested: so that people all over the world will respect His name. Another case of response occurs in Isa 63.11–13. There Deutero-Isaiah alludes to Jer 2.6–8, where Jeremiah complained that the people did not recall that it was YHWH who brought them out of Egypt. Deutero-Isaiah announces that the people do recall that YHWH rescued them (see Radak and

Skinner on Isa 63.11). The later prophet asserts that what the people had failed to do earlier they finally do now, thus responding to the charge leveled against Israel in the earlier text. Additional cases of response occur elsewhere in the allusion. Finally, in Isa 52.13–53.12, Deutero-Isaiah describes the victory of the servant, which brings justice or forgiveness to the people. This passage alludes to Jer 10.23–25, in which the prophet prays for restoration. Thus the later passage also responds to the earlier one, supplying Jeremiah's prayer with a positive answer.

Similarly, Deutero-Isaiah often responds to actual complaints, laments, or skeptical attitudes of the exiles. Some Judeans seem to have despaired of YHWH's power to save or His inclination to listen to Israel's plea. Deutero-Isaiah insists to the contrary, "Look! YHWH's power to save has *not* withered, and His ears are *not* stopped up! Rather, it is your sins which have put up a division between you and your God" (Isa 59.1–2). Thus he asks Israel, "Why do you say, Jacob . . . 'My experience is hidden from YHWH, and my case passes by my God'?" (Isa 40.27). (Cf. Isa 49.14, 50.1, 50.2, and perhaps 49.24. In reacting to despondent statements of the exiles, Deutero-Isaiah was not unique; cf. Ezek 18.2, 37.11. For a discussion of Ezekiel's response to the exiles, see Moshe Greenberg, "The Citations in Ezekiel as a Background for the Prophecies," *BM* 17 [1972]. It is possible that in Isa 66.14 Deutero-Isaiah responds implicitly to the same exilic complaint to which Ezekiel responds explicitly in Ezek 37.11.)

41. Fishbane, *Biblical*, 497–98.

42. The abundant parallels between Jeremiah 30–31 and Isaiah 40–66 have been noted before, and some scholars suggest that the chapters from Jeremiah have in fact been influenced by Deutero-Isaiah. However, the presence of material in those chapters which refers to the northern kingdom shows that at least that section's kernel derives from early in the career of Jeremiah. There is no reason to doubt that additional material in these chapters stems from the same prophet's pronouncements. Jeremiah's mission was both to warn and to encourage, to break down and to build up; the concentration of the positive part of his message in these chapters does not indicate separate authorship. Further, the same thematic and stylistic characteristics which appear in Deutero-Isaiah's use of material from earlier sections of Jeremiah also appear in his use of 30–31. This makes clear that the similarities between 30–31 and Isaiah 40–66 result from Deutero-Isaiah's reliance on the Jeremiah collection, not the other way around. For a convincing defense of Jeremiah's authorship of 30–31, see Holladay, 2: 155–66, and, more briefly, Eissfeldt, *Introduction*, 361–62 (who regards most of the material as coming from Jeremiah but the redaction as exilic), and Bright, 284–87.

43. Thus the vocabulary item is borrowed from Jeremiah, but its use here may stem from the idea in Isaiah (Isaiah 6; 29.9f.; and cf. 9.1; 29.18f.; 32.3–4). The theme of the metaphorically blind nations does occur in Jer 5.21, where the people are described thus: עֵינַיִם לָהֶם וְלֹא יִרְאוּ.

44. Deutero-Isaiah refers to this passage in Jeremiah several other times.

Isa 42.16 briefly recapitulates the themes of Jeremiah 31, with which it shares terms such as דרך, הוליך, עור, and יל"ד and the theme of water in the wilderness. Cassuto hears the same source reused in 49.12, where we find a number of common items: יבאו מצפון, רנו, מים (Cassuto, "Formal," 150).

Another case occurs in chapter 55. Instead of Jeremiah's phrase, "with weeping they will come and because of supplications I will bring them in (אוביליס)," Deutero-Isaiah declares, "In happiness (בשמחה) you will go forth, and in peace you will be brought in (תובלון)" (Isa 55.12). Deutero-Isaiah repeats the prophecy but reverses its tone. Cassuto points out that Deutero-Isaiah changes "they will come" to "you will go" because he, unlike Jeremiah, is located in Babylonia, not the Land of Israel (Cassuto, "Formal," 150–51 n. 27). Further, Jeremiah refers to the exiles in the third person, because he does not directly address them; they were located far away. Deutero-Isaiah directly addresses his Judean audience in Babylon. The LXX for our verse in Jeremiah seems to be based on a Hebrew text reading יצאו rather than יבאו; while MT is to be preferred, it is again interesting to note that the LXX reading achieves the same revision that Deutero-Isaiah's allusion does.

Isa 35.4–10 contains a richly textured allusion to Jer 31.7–8, repeating the prophecy while reversing its tone. See the discussion in Chapter 6, pp. 162–63. (Scholars have long maintained that Isaiah 34–35 belong to the Deutero-Isaianic corpus; these chapters display typical features of Deutero-Isaiah's rhetoric in abundance [see references in Chapter 6, note 18]. To those features we can now add several aspects of Deutero-Isaianic allusion, since the allusion in Isa 35.4–10 contains several cases of sound play and the split-up pattern, and thus the study of Deutero-Isaianic allusion strengthens the case for attributing chapter 35 to Deutero-Isaiah. Only one possible allusion appears in Isaiah 34, however, and that one is not as strong a case. Isa 34.2 appears to reverse Jer 25.9. But the parallel is based on a single item of vocabulary [החרים], which is used with YHWH as subject only in these two verses and Isa 11.15], and thus a borrowing cannot be ascertained with confidence.)

45. For example, see Isa 40.9–10, which repeats Jer 31.16 with two variations: Deutero-Isaiah shifts the subject of the prediction from northern exiles to southern ones, and he reverses the somber tone of the older text. As the discussion of this example at the end of this chapter shows, this passage displays all the stylistic features which appear in Deutero-Isaiah's reuse of older material: the split-up pattern, sound play, word play, and identical word order. See also Jer 33.3f. and Isa 48.6, in which Deutero-Isaiah restates the earlier prediction while shifting its focus from comfort to the accuracy of YHWH's prophecies. Deutero-Isaiah picks up on the theme of "secret things" from Jer 33.3 to stress that YHWH, who predicted accurately in the past, can be trusted as He issues new prophecies now; indeed, Deutero-Isaiah's point is not merely that restoration is coming but that the world should acknowledge YHWH because his earlier prophecies have come true. Yochanan Muffs ("Cloak," in *Love and Joy*, 9–48) notes the dependence of Isa 61.1–4 on Jer 33.7–9 and Jer 13.11, which in

turn rely on Deut 26.19, though he points out only some of Deutero-Isaiah's markers. Finally, Isa 41.8–15, 43.1–7, and 44.1–3 all share a great deal of vocabulary with Jer 30.10–11 (as well as Jer 1.8); some of the earlier phrases seem to be split into parts, and examples of sound play may be evident. All the passages share a single oracular theme: God announces He is with Israel and will protect Israel. But all the parallel terms which connect these texts are part of the Assyrian/Northwest Semitic "fear not" tradition, so that it is impossible to claim with confidence that these passages in Deutero-Isaiah allude specifically to Jeremiah.

46. Omitting חֻקַּת, which is missing in LXX and seems out of place here. See Janzen, *Studies*, 49.

47. Holladay regards the last statement (Jer 31.35–36) as a fifth-century addition to Jeremiah (see Holladay, 2: 166–67, 199). His argument, atypically, is not particularly strong. I sense no discontinuity or contradiction between vv. 34 and 35 which suggests the need for source-critical division. That similar language appears in Trito-Isaiah shows only that the author of 56–66 depended on Jeremiah, and Holladay's reliance on Westermann's fifth-century dating of Isa 59.21 is ill-advised. That the passages in Isaiah 40–66 which rely on Jer 31.31–36 use vocabulary from throughout the passage, including vv. 35–36, further argues against Holladay's dating of these verses. Bright sees "no compelling reason" to deny the verses to Jeremiah and regards them as earlier than the prose additions to Jeremiah 30–31.

48. If we take the root as יצר (which is possible even with the *dāgēsh*; see GKB II § 26e(3e) and II § 26m). If the root is נצר, then translate "I guarded."

49. Heb. ברית עם, a famous crux. I believe Skinner is correct when he suggests that the sense is "the covenant in virtue of which Israel shall once more be restored as a nation," i.e., God tells the nation that He has created them as a people with a covenant; that covenant endures, and therefore they are assured of restoration. This sense, admittedly, is not a perfect semantic parallel to אור גוים (unless we translate that phrase as "a light among nations," which also would retain the sense of a unique property which inheres in Israel), but a perfect semantic parallel is not necessarily called for (as Laato notes, 85). The sense may be that by being granted the promises of the covenant, the people serve as a light to the nations who witness the redemptive activity of YHWH (cf. Yehezkel Kaufmann, *The Babylonian Captivity and Deutero-Isaiah*, trans. C. W. Efroymson [New York: Union of American Hebrew Congregations, 1970], 152). This is also the sense of Isa 42.1: through YHWH's election of Israel, YHWH's judgment and righteousness will become known to all the world (so Skinner).

50. The subject of the infinitives here may be either the people or God (cf. P. Joüon and T. Muraoka, *A Grammar of Biblical Hebrew* [Rome: Pontifical Biblical Institute, 1993], § 124s). Following Skinner and Kaufmann (*Babylonian*, 152), I regard the latter as more likely. Cf. Tryggve N. D. Mettinger, *A Farewell to the Servant Songs: A Critical Examination of an Exegetical Axiom* (Lund: CWK Gleerup, 1983), 35–37.

51. Several other elements of the royal tradition are present in Isaiah 42.1–9: קרא שם followed by בצדק; the idea of the עבד; יצר.

52. See, e.g., Ps 24.1–2 (where הארץ is paired through interlinear parallelism with ימים), 96.11; cf. Zech 9.10; Gen 1.28, 9.2; Exod 20.11; etc. Further, as if to emphasize this connection to those who may have missed it, הים appears immediately after this passage, in Isa 42.10 (where it is parallel to הארץ). On the phenomenon of parallel word pairs in biblical and other ancient Canaanite poetry, see Watson, 128–44, and James Kugel, *The Idea of Biblical Poetry: Parallelism and Its History* (New Haven, Conn.: Yale University Press, 1981), 27–40.

53. On the radical nature of the concept, see Gerhard von Rad, *Old Testament Theology*, trans. D. Stalker (Edinburgh: Oliver and Boyd, 1965), 2: 212–14, and Carroll, *Jeremiah*, 611, 614.

54. I regard the verses in question as being spoken to the nation Israel. Here as elsewhere (e.g., Isa 41.8–13), the עבד whom YHWH chooses and whose hand He takes is the people Israel. Cf. n. 107 to this chapter.

55. The tense and aspect of the verbs in Isa 42.6, starting from קראתיך, are ambiguous. MT does not point the last three as conversive, but the short prefix form of וְאַחְזֵק suggests a preterite, as does the affix form קראתיך. In such a case God is referring to his adopting the people as his own in the past, perhaps when he liberated the people from Egypt. However, if the affix form of קראתיך refers to a present action, then the following prefix forms may similarly denote current action which is incomplete; in that case we should translate, "I call you . . . I take your hand; I guard you and make you." Finally, we may take the last three verbs as simple future tenses (though this would really require emending to the regular prefix וְאַחְזֵק), and the first verb as a prophetic perfect. In this case, the events described have not yet occurred. In short, we do not know whether the covenant described here was made long ago, is (re)made now, or is soon to be made. Such ambiguity of tense and aspect, which blurs the boundaries between older events (ראשונות) and future events (חדשות) that re-enact the older ones, is surely intentional and occurs elsewhere in Deutero-Isaiah (for another example, see Isa 50.2–3 and the discussion in Michael Fishbane, *Text and Texture: Close Readings in Selected Biblical Texts* [New York: Schocken Books, 1979], 136–38).

56. Ezek 36.25–28, 37.25–28 also depend on Jer 31.31f. Like Deutero-Isaiah, Ezekiel pulls back slightly from the somewhat extraordinary claims of Jeremiah that there is a *new* covenant, obedience to which will be inevitable; rather, Ezekiel stresses the element of steadfastness. (On the differences between the passages in Ezekiel and Jeremiah, see Moshe Weinfeld, "Jeremiah and the Spiritual Metamorphosis of Israel," *ZAW* 88 [1976], 31–32.) Ezekiel, unlike Deutero-Isaiah, includes a reference to David in 37.24 (which occurs also in Jer 33.15). It is impossible to know whether Deutero-Isaiah knew of Ezekiel's transformation of Jeremiah's idea and adopted it himself with certain changes (e.g., regarding David), or whether Deutero-Isaiah and Ezekiel

similarly but independently utilized the statement of Jeremiah. The former may seem likely given Deutero-Isaiah's reference to the people as "servant," which resembles language found in Ezekiel but not Jeremiah. On the other hand, the servant language in both cases may simply be a reflex of the Mesopotamian royal tradition.

57. Von Rad explains, "What is outlined here [in Jeremiah 31] is the picture of a new man, a man who is able to obey perfectly because of a miraculous change in his nature" (*Old*, 213–14).

58. Examples abound; see, e.g., Psalm 29 or 114.

59. This passage, like Isa 42.5f., includes vocabulary reminiscent of the similar prophecies in Ezekiel: רוח (Ezek 36.26).

60. Several possible references to the idea of an inevitable covenant occur elsewhere in Deutero-Isaiah. Kaufmann (*Babylonian*, 187–88) suggests that Isa 60.21 ("all your people are righteous") predicts an end to sin in a manner similar to Jeremiah 31. However, if צַדִּיקִים there means "victorious" rather than "righteous," the connection with the ideas under consideration here would be broken. The end of Isa 63.11 also repeats the idea of an inevitable covenant. Neither of these verses, however, contains the same vocabulary which occurred in the original predictions in Jeremiah. The passage in Jeremiah 31 is quoted in one other instance: Isa 51.15, which repeats a line from Jer 31.35 verbatim: רֹגַע הַיָּם וַיֶּהֱמוּ גַּלָּיו ה' צְבָאוֹת שְׁמוֹ. Both passages connect the idea of God as creator to God as protector of Israel, Jeremiah quite emphatically and Deutero-Isaiah more vaguely (in Isa 51.16). Further, the words וָאָשִׂים דְּבָרַי בְּפִיךְ may also recall the idea of God's writing his torah in the people's hearts. Thus, this line is also an instance, however brief, of reprediction.

61. In addition to the following two examples, see especially Isa 60.7–13, which depends on Jer 3.16–18. This is a fine example of Deutero-Isaiah's stylistic tendencies: the markers appear in the same order as the marked terms and motifs, and Deutero-Isaiah engages in word play. While Deutero-Isaiah largely repeats the older prophecy, he drops some aspects of it (such as the address to the northern audience) and puts greater emphasis than Jeremiah on certain elements, such as the role of the foreigners who themselves bring (or send) gifts to Jerusalem.

62. Carroll, *Jeremiah*, claims that these verses are post-exilic, citing the reference to a seventy-year exile as a prophecy *ex eventu*. However, the words "seventy years" do not necessitate a post-exilic dating; they can be understood quite naturally as stemming from the beginning of the exile, when hope for a quick restoration was still prevalent. Jeremiah dashes these hopes with his prediction of an exile lasting two generations (=seventy years), insisting that those who went into exile would never see Judah again. Moreover, one expects that a prophecy *ex eventu* will be accurate. Jeremiah predicted that after seventy years Babylon would be defeated and the exile would end. However, the defeat of Babylon and the return occurred not seventy but about fifty years after the beginning of the exile in 587 B.C.E. (or about sixty years after the removal of the king and deportation of 597). What did happen about

seventy years after 587 was the rebuilding of the Temple. But that is not what this prophecy foresees.

63. I leave out several intervening words in MT which do not appear in the LXX. The textual variation does not affect my argument.

64. The relevance of this word as a marker may be questioned, because it is lacking in the LXX. Deutero-Isaiah may have used it simply because it works naturally as a parallel for שׁ״דר; and a later hand may have added it to MT Jeremiah because it also works naturally with התפללתם in the same verse. Even in that case, there remains sufficient vocabulary common to both texts to classify the relationship between these passages as a borrowing.

65. LXX ἐπιφανοῦμαι suggests that the Hebrew here originally read ונראיתי, and was changed to ונמצאתי under the influence of ומצאתם in the previous verse. If so, this word in Jer 29.14 is not a marked word; but the presence of the root in 29.13 indicates that בהמצאו in Isa 55.6 is a marker in any event.

66. This whole phrase, and everything that comes after it, is missing in LXX, casting serious doubt on the validity of these lines as marked. See Janzen, *Studies*, 48, who demonstrates that the material is more likely a later addition to MT, and Carroll, *Jeremiah*, who notes that the reference to a widespread Diaspora is odd in a letter to the exiles in Babylonia.

67. Holladay regards all the verses cited here (and also Jer 3.5, to which Isa 57.16 may allude as well) as part of the original recension of this long passage in Jeremiah, which was directed to the north. See Holladay, 1: 73. Cf. Bright, 25–27, who views even more material in chapter 3 as directed to the north.

68. On the former, see Fishbane, *Biblical*, 476. On the latter, see Yehezkel Kaufmann, *Toledot ha-Emunah ha-Yisraelit* (Tel Aviv: Mosad Bialik and Devir, 1937–56), 3: 523 and 487 n. 12 [Heb.].

69. See Holladay, 1: 62–63, 77–81.

70. The unit continues through Isa 57.21, but the use of the text in Jeremiah does not extend further than Isa 57.6. In spite of its length, the passage is a literary unity; see Skinner, 167, and Torrey, 429. Some scholars (e.g., Westermann) view the passage as pre-exilic because in form and content it resembles oracles of judgment uttered by Isaiah, Jeremiah, and others, and because it is clearly set in the Land of Israel (note the references to נחלים and hills with leafy trees). Its setting in the Land of Israel is no obstacle to its post-exilic date, however, if the passage was written by Deutero-Isaiah after he himself emigrated to the Land of Israel and criticized conditions he found there; see Menahem Haran, *Between RI'SHONÔT (Former Prophecies) and ḤADASHÔT (New Prophecies): A Literary-Historical Study of Prophecies in Isaiah XL–XLVII* (Jerusalem: Magnes, 1963), 85–86, 89–90 [Heb.]. Further, the passage includes examples of Deutero-Isaiah's poetic style, such as sound and word play in Isa 57.5, 6 (on which see Torrey, 193–95, 199–202) and repeated imperatives in Isa 57.14 (see Torrey, 195–96).

71. Some scholars see the צֹפִים and רֹעִים who are the object of criticism in Isa 56.10 as political leaders rather than prophets (Rashi, Westermann, Kaufmann [*Babylonian*, 168–69]). While רֹעִים could mean "prophets" or "leaders," צֹפִים more likely refers to a prophet; see Jer 6.17, Ezek 3.17, 33.2f. Hence I find more likely the view of ibn Ezra and Radak, who see this as a critique of false prophets. The word הֹזִים in Isa 56.10 may also suggest that the reference is to prophecy. הֹזִים, a hapax, may mean "to speak deliriously" (so Skinner) or "talk in one's sleep" (Torrey, Westermann, and note Targum's נְיְימִין, "people in a slumber"; LXX ἐνυπνιαζόμενοι means "those who see visions in their sleep," which usually translates חלם). Any of these senses constitutes a pun on חֹזִים, and they suggest a double complaint: The prophets/watchmen are derelict in their duty—they sleep on the watch rather than say what they ought; and they have dream visions, an unapproved type of divination (see Joseph Blenkinsopp, *A History of Prophecy in Israel*, rev. ed. [Louisville, Ky.: Westminster John Knox, 1996], 235). If 1QIsaᵃ is correct to read חֹוזִים, then we could state definitively that the critique refers to prophets (though in this case, the pun and implied critique of dream divination would be lost). This reading is also found in some biblical citations in rabbinic literature and in some MT manuscripts; see Moshe Goshen-Gottstein, ed., *The Hebrew University Bible: The Book of Isaiah* (Jerusalem: Magnes, 1995) ad loc.

72. This complaint about false prophets also echoes Jeremiah's complaint about false prophets in Jer 6.13 (=Jer 8.10), which Deutero-Isaiah utilizes extensively in Isa 57.17f., as we saw above.

73. Some commentators read וְ rather than כִּי, which would make the lines in Jeremiah and in Deutero-Isaiah completely identical. See Holladay and Carroll, *Jeremiah*.

74. The criticism of the prophets in Ezek 34.1–9 (esp. 5, 8) and in Ezek 39.17–18 also depends on Jeremiah 12 (see Cassuto, "Formal," 162), but Deutero-Isaiah does not seem to have utilized the Ezekiel passage.

74. The criticism of the prophets in Ezek 34.1–9 (esp. 5, 8) and in Ezek 39.17–18 also depends on Jeremiah 12 (see Cassuto, "Formal," 162), but Deutero-Isaiah does not seem to have utilized the Ezekiel passage.

75. This passage in Deutero-Isaiah also depends on several passages in Isaiah. The specific language of the criticism of the false prophets is taken from Isaiah 30 (see Chapter 3).

76. Unless the language at the beginning of Isa 57.2 is simply a description of death; see Skinner for such a reading.

77. Heb. יָדֵךְ חַיַּת—perhaps a reference to some idolatrous (phallic?—cf. Isa 57.8) object, "the renewal of your strength." The phrase seems to refer to something the people thought beneficial or enjoyable but which in fact brings about God's wrath.

78. Citing so common a term as a marked item may seem questionable—all the more so given that it is missing in LXX (though not Lucian). Its absence there may

result from LXX following the sense, according to which לוֹא is an exclamation, not a negation of the following clause. That the presence of the word in Deutero-Isaiah does result from its appearance in Jeremiah becomes clear when we realize that it appears together with אמ״ר and נואש in both: וְתֹאמְרִי נוֹאָשׁ לוֹא in Jeremiah, and לֹא אָמְרַת נוֹאָשׁ in Deutero-Isaiah.

79. In addition, the phrase וְתַחַת כָּל־עֵץ רַעֲנָן appears in Isa 57.5 and Jer 2.20, along with הַר־גָּבֹהַּ in Isa 57.7 and גִּבְעָה גְבֹהָה in Jer 2.20, but this parallel is not very impressive; תחת כל עץ רענן similarly appears along with גבעה [גבהה/רמה] in Deut 12.2, 1 Kgs 14.23, and Ezek 6.13.

80. In some of these passages Deutero-Isaiah refers to earlier prophecies as רֵאשֹׁנוֹת. For a discussion of the "rishonot" passages, see Menahem Haran, "The Literary Structure and Chronological Framework of the Prophecies in Isaiah XL–XLVIII," *VTSup* 9 (1963), 137–40, and the same author's *RIʾSHONÔT*, 23–28. Elsewhere Deutero-Isaiah uses the term רֵאשֹׁנוֹת in a number of other ways. For example, it can refer to YHWH's cosmogonic or redemptive acts in the past; see, e.g., Isa 43.18.

81. Fishbane notes several examples of this phenomenon (Fishbane, *Biblical*, 495–97).

82. The MT's יָרֹנּוּ makes no sense, and valiant attempts at forcing it to do so (e.g., ibn Ezra, NJPS) do not succeed. John McKenzie suggests יְרֻשׁוּ (*Second Isaiah* [Garden City, N.Y.: Doubleday, 1968]). This word fits the context, as ibn Ezra already recognizes in his paraphrase. (Klostermann's older suggestion of וָרֹק, cited in Torrey, Westermann, and BHS, also yields passable meaning but is more difficult paleographically.) Though McKenzie does not point this out, one can understand how in Aramaic/Jewish scripts שׁ could become ונ, so that an original ירשׁו could be copied as ירונו, which differs from the MT only in its *plene* orthography.

83. The LXX is missing the first half of Isa 61.7 (i.e., up to this point), which is the heart of the allusion. It is likely that the LXX dropped those words, however, because the sentence makes little sense without them.

84. Indeed, Gerhard von Rad ("כִּפְלַיִם in Jes. 40.2 = Äquivalent?" *ZAW* 79 [1967], 80–82) translates as "equivalent for all her sins." But the idea of double punishment unquestionably appears in Isa 61.7 and also in Isa 65.6–7; and when one recognizes the source of the idea in Jeremiah, it is no longer surprising that Deutero-Isaiah would make such an assertion. An analogous idea appears in a different (and more extreme) fashion in Lev 26.18, 21, where God promises sevenfold punishment for covenant infraction.

85. Paul ("Literary," 104) notes that these repeated references to the verse in Jeremiah reinforce the likelihood of a borrowing even in Isa 40.2, which contains less vocabulary from the source. A further reference to Jer 16.18 occurs in Isa 65.6–7, though this is not a case in which Deutero-Isaiah uses the earlier material to assert its fulfillment. The verses from Deutero-Isaiah read, "I shall pay them back (וְשִׁלַּמְתִּי)

for their sins and their fathers' alike . . . and I shall first (רִאשׁוֹנָה) mete out punishment (פְּעֻלָּתָם) on them." This statement not only repeats vocabulary from Jer 16.18, but also splits up Jeremiah's phrase וְשִׁלַּמְתִּי רִאשׁוֹנָה (which appears nowhere else in the Bible). This case constitutes a negative repredication, since Deutero-Isaiah warns that sinners may soon experience a double punishment similar to the one the nations underwent in Jeremiah's day. However, this case may be questionable, because רִאשׁוֹנָה does not appear in LXX texts of Jer 16.18 other than Origen, leading many critics to regard רִאשׁוֹנָה there as a gloss (see Bright and Holladay).

86. The second half of the verse is difficult. The MT reads כִּי־אֵיךְ אֶעֱשֶׂה מִפְּנֵי בַּת־עַמִּי. For other cases of מִפְּנֵי meaning "due to, because of," see BDB 818b. Targum renders, אֵיכְדֵין אֶעְבֵּיד מִן קֳדָם חוֹבֵי דִכְנִשְׁתָּא דְעַמִּי, and LXX reads, ὅτι ποιήσω ἀπὸ προσώπου πονηρίας θυγατρὸς λαοῦ μου. These lead Bright and Carroll to suggest that a word like רָעַת has fallen out, which would yield the translation, "How [else] can I act because of the evil deeds of the daughter of my people?" Holladay's suggestion that we read אֵיד instead of אֵיךְ would undermine the argument I am making here, since אֵיךְ is one of the marked items demonstrating Deutero-Isaiah's reliance on Jeremiah. But his reconstruction of the verse is somewhat too involved to be fully convincing. Further, retaining the question introduced by the word אֵיךְ in the MT harmonizes better with the similar question found in Jer 9.8.

87. A difficult phrase (הִנֵּה צְרַפְתִּיךְ וְלֹא בְכָסֶף). Westermann simply emends, deleting the negative particle and substituting a kāph for the bêt to form a text translated as, "I refine you like silver." This reading seems logical, since the people *have* in fact been refined as silver is refined: through their suffering, they have become better material. However, the emendation finds no support in the versions (a single medieval MT manuscript reads כְּכֶסֶף, while another omits וְלֹא [see Goshen-Gottstein], but these probably result from scribal errors and in any event neither agrees with Westermann's two-part emendation). Christopher North (*The Second Isaiah: Introduction, Translation and Commentary to Chapters XL–LV* [Oxford: Oxford University Press, 1964]) argues that the *bêt* can mean "for the sake of," yielding the sense, "I have assayed you, but not for the sake of silver accrued through the process." Though North does not note this, LXX supports his suggestion, as it reads, οὐχ ἕνεκεν ἀργυρίου. North further suggests, but apparently rejects, another reading of the verse: understand צְרַפְתִּיךְ in Isa 48.10 as meaning "to purchase," like Akkadian ṣarāpu (CAD 16: 105). Thus, the sentence would mean, "I bought you, but not for money," an idea which also appears in Isa 52.3. בְחַרְתִּיךְ would retain its normal meaning of "choose" (see next note), and the sense of the verse would be that God acquired the people as his own by redeeming them from their affliction. This hints back to the Exodus while referring to their present exile as well. If this is the case, we have an elaborate example of Deutero-Isaiah's punning use of vocabulary borrowed from his source. For a fourth suggestion, see Kaufmann, *Babylonian*, 225 n. 68.

88. I understand this word as an Aramaism whose meaning is identical to בְּחַנְתִּיךְ (so BDB). One would arrive at the same translation by reading בְּחַנְתִּיךְ with 1QIsaᵃ, some medieval MT manuscripts, and several biblical citations in rabbinic manuscripts (see Goshen-Gottstein). Either way, the parallel with Jeremiah remains strong. Even if one reads בְּחַרְתִּיךְ with MT and understands it to mean "I chose you," the word would still work as a marker, in which case it would be a case of sound play.

89. It is clear from Isa 48.9 and the second half of this verse that God's name or glory is the implied subject of this verb (יֵחָל); LXX adds τὸ ἐμὸν ὄνομα, probably for clarity, but perhaps because its Hebrew text in fact included the word שְׁמִי (which does occur in one medieval MT manuscript; see Goshen-Gottstein). Alternatively, read a first-person niphal from the root חל״ל with 1QIsaᵃ, 4QIsaᶜ, and 4QIsaᵈ (אֵיחַל = "how can I be dishonored?"; see Goshen-Gottstein's comment *apud* E. Y. Kutscher, *The Language and Linguistic Background of the Isaiah Scroll* [Leiden: Brill, 1974], 242). The Qumran reading may confirm the suggestion of H. D. Chajes (*apud* Cassuto, "Formal," 166 n. 93) that the text originally read אָחֵל but was changed to the third person due to a *tiqqun sofrim*.

90. The word הִנֵּה is used differently in the two passages as well, and thus its presence constitutes a case of word play. In Jeremiah, it is a grammatical indicator of imminent action, while in Deutero-Isaiah it is an exclamation. To underscore its use as a marker, I include the word "behold" in my translation of both texts.

91. A clear example occurs in Isa 51.19, which combines vocabulary from Jer 4.20 and 15.2, 5. The specific disasters Jeremiah foresaw (חֶרֶב, שֶׁבֶר, and the absence of anyone to comfort the afflicted) are described as realities in Deutero-Isaiah (cf. Paul, "Literary," 116–17). Isa 58.12 and 61.4 may represent a confirmation of Jer 25.9 and 49.13. Jeremiah announced there that God would bring the Babylonians to make the land and its inhabitants an "eternal ruin" (חָרְבוֹת עוֹלָם). These words appear elsewhere in the Bible only in the verses from Deutero-Isaiah. Deutero-Isaiah's declaration that the ruins will now be rebuilt would not contradict Jeremiah, since the earlier prophet predicts an end to the affliction in Jer 25.12f. But other clear markers which connect these texts do not appear, so that the matter must be left in doubt. Finally, Isa 51.7 seems to represent as an accomplished reality what Jeremiah had predicted in Jer 31.32, though similar vocabulary appears in other exilic texts (Ezek 26.36–37), so that the status of this case as a borrowing is questionable.

92. On the use of the term, and the similarities between such linkages in biblical and post-biblical texts, see Fishbane, *Biblical*, 350–52.

93. Not all typologies are cases of inner-biblical allusion or exegesis in the strict sense; in fact, most are not. For example, if an author describes a redemptive act of YHWH as imitating or re-enacting the creation of the world, he posits a typological link between creation and that act, but he is not necessarily utilizing a particular text that describes creation. He may be relying instead on widespread traditions. Thus when Exodus 15 depicts the crossing of the Reed Sea as a repetition of the cosmogonic

act of YHWH who defeated Yam/Sea, a typological link has been asserted: the defeat of Yam is the prototype, the splitting of the Reed Sea the imitation. This typology is not a case of inner-biblical exegesis, because Exodus 15 does not depend on any discrete text which tells the story of the fight between YHWH and Yam. On the other hand, when there are signs that an author does depend on a specific text for the description of the prototypical event, person, or place, the typological linkage is a case of inner-biblical allusion or exegesis. Thus, when Jeremiah describes the upcoming disaster as an undoing of creation (Jer 4.23–26), he uses enough vocabulary from the P creation account to make clear that he is relying on a particular text, not only a widespread tradition (see Fishbane, *Biblical*, 321, and Holladay). Of course, deciding in a particular case whether a typology is based on a tradition (and belongs to the study of tradition history) or a text (and constitutes a case of inner-biblical allusion or exegesis) is often quite difficult, and such a distinction may not interest the student of typology in any event. Here, however, I shall limit my study to typological linkages which are also cases of inner-biblical exegesis or allusion.

Isaiah 40–66 includes many other cases of typology based on widespread traditions rather than on a specific text. For a discussion of Deutero-Isaiah's reliance on Exodus traditions as a prototype for the return from Babylon, see Bernhard Anderson, "Exodus Typology in Second Isaiah," in *Israel's Prophetic Heritage: Essays in Honor of James Muilenburg*, ed. B. W. Anderson and W. Harrelson (New York: Harper, 1962), 177–95; for an outstanding discussion of his use of those traditions in concert with his transformation of covenant traditions, see Bernhard Anderson, "Exodus and Covenant in Second Isaiah and Prophetic Tradition," in *Magnalia Dei, the Mighty Acts of God: Essays on the Bible and Archaeology in Memory of G. Ernest Wright*, ed. F. M. Cross, W. Lemke, and P. Miller (Garden City, N.Y.: Doubleday, 1976), 339–60. See also Shemaryahu Talmon, "The 'Desert Motif' in the Bible and Qumran Literature," in A. Altmann, ed., *Biblical Motifs: Origins and Transformations* (Cambridge, Mass.: Harvard University Press, 1966), 54.

94. LXX (except for Origen and Lucian) does not include אדם or "beast," but as both Carroll (*Jeremiah*) and Janzen (*Studies*, 118) point out, this is due to homoioteleuton, and MT preserves the older text.

95. Cf. the similar pattern in the use of Jer 10.20 in Isa 54.2 cited above.

96. Paul, "Literary," 111.

97. The linkage between Nebuchadnezzar and Cyrus may occur in Isa 41.25 as well, where YHWH declares that He has raised up a savior from the north, who turns out to be Cyrus (Isa 44.24–45.1). This passage reverses the theme of the enemy from the north in Jeremiah (see, e.g., Jer 1.14, 4.6, 6.1, 6.22, 10.22, 13.19), who turns out to be Nebuchadnezzar (see Jer 25.9).

98. "Planting the heavens" strikes some readers as odd, and Torrey and others emend to לנטות. But the phrase is not as odd as it seems, as Skinner points out: נט"ע can mean "establish," forming a sensible parallel to יס"ד.

99. As Radak points out.

100. Some of the same borrowed vocabulary appears again in Isa 59.21. The nationalization of the prophetic role and the stress on the permanence of the relation between YHWH and Israel found in Isa 51.16 also appear there. The idea that the people serve as a witness to the nations appears elsewhere in Deutero-Isaiah (e.g., Isa 43.10), sometimes in language resembling Jeremiah's dedication scene; see Isa 55.4–5.

101. This is H. L. Ginsberg's emendation for the MT's difficult צִוָּה, mentioned *apud* Paul, "Literary," 115, and standing behind the note NJPS.

102. As Paul points out ("Literary," 115 n. 58), the root is used of cutting down a tree several times: Deut 20.19, 20.

103. On this translation of the verse, see Paul, "Literary," 115 n. 56 and references there.

104. So LXX; MT, "Your."

105. One additional marker/marked may be present: the root נטע appears in Isa 51.16 and Jer 11.17, but 11.17 probably belongs to the preceding pericope in Jeremiah.

106. Both of these passages are very difficult text-critically and might have been translated differently. However, the correspondences remain even if we reconstruct the texts in other ways. For example, if we accept MT and read צעה (whatever that may mean) rather than העץ in Isa 51.14, then Deutero-Isaiah employs sound play to allude back to עץ in Jer 11.19. Similarly, one may follow Ginsberg and translate לחמו as "its sap" (from לֵחַ with enclitic *mēm*) rather than "its fruit," in both Jer 11.19 and Isa 51.14 (see NJPS notes to each passage), but the parallel would remain intact. If one follows Holladay by reading these consonants in Jeremiah to mean "his opponent" (לְחֻמוֹ), the parallel in Deutero-Isaiah (whether translated "fruit" or "sap") would refer back to Jeremiah via sound play.

107. This is hardly the place to enter into the debate regarding the identification of the servant in the so-called servant songs—if, indeed, it is legitimate at all to speak of those passages as a special corpus within Isaiah 40–66. For a discussion, see especially the careful considerations in the monograph by Mettinger, who sees no reason to separate the servant songs from their context, and who finds no reason to identify the servant figures in Deutero-Isaiah with anyone other than the nation Israel. We shall see that Jeremiah relates to the servant in precisely the same way that Jeremiah relates to Israel in the passages just examined.

108. Further, the servant songs share a great deal of vocabulary with the dedication scene in Jeremiah 1, but most of those parallels involve language from the ancient Near Eastern royal traditions, so that they cannot suffice to show that Deutero-Isaiah modeled the servant figure on Jeremiah.

The connection between Jeremiah and the servant was noted already in the tenth century by Saadia Gaon (according to ibn Ezra on Isa 52.13), and more recently by Otto Eissfeldt, *Der Gottesknecht bei Deuterojesaja* (Halle: Max Niemeyer, 1933), 16–18, and Sheldon Blank, "Studies in Deutero-Isaiah," *HUCA* 15 (1940), 27–30. These scholars note prophetic themes in passages describing servant figures and highlight the special place that Jeremiah plays in them. They do not discuss the pointed differences between the servant songs and the Jeremiah passages noted below. That Deutero-Isaiah patterns servant figures after the character Jeremiah does not mean (contra Saadia) that he attempts to identify the servant as Jeremiah. We have seen that Deutero-Isaiah patterns the nation after Jeremiah as well, but clearly such patterning does not imply that Deutero-Isaiah believes the nation *is* Jeremiah.

109. For comprehensive lists, see Westermann, *Isaiah*, 227–28, and Laato, 127.

110. Heb. אֲדֹנָי ה׳ פָּתַח לִי אֹזֶן. The phrase refers to a prophet's hearing a message from God; cf. the similar wording in 1 Sam 9.15 and 2 Sam 7.27. See also Radak, according to whom the verse describes a prophecy coming to the prophet. Indeed, Westermann argues that 4–5a represent a kind of prophetic call. Already the rabbis seemed to have sensed this; see *Pesiq. Rab. Kah.*, Par. *Naḥamu* § 4 (ed. Bernard Mandelbaum, *Pesikta de Rav Kahana* [New York: Jewish Theological Seminary, 1987], 269–70) and Rashi on Isa 50.5.

111. Isa 52.13–53.12 utilizes the lament and prayer in Jer 10.19–25; this allusion was discussed earlier in this chapter. The people's fate in Jeremiah 10 provides the pattern, lexically and existentially, for what happens to the servant in Deutero-Isaiah. The lament bemoans the people's suffering; in Deutero-Isaiah the servant receives the punishment described in Jeremiah. In both, the people go astray like sheep (though in Jeremiah this is apparently the punishment, and in Deutero-Isaiah it sounds like the sin). Thus the song in Isa 52.13–53.12 relies on several texts from Jeremiah, connecting the servant at once with Jeremiah (by depending on Jeremiah 11) and with the people as portrayed by Jeremiah (by depending on Jeremiah 10).

112. For a further example of echo, compare Isa 40.19–22, 41.6–7, and 44.9–14 with Jer 10.1–16 (this is discussed in detail by Cassuto, "Formal," 144–49). Deutero-Isaiah simply repeats Jeremiah's criticism of the production and worship of idols without employing the older material for some new end. The only difference between Deutero-Isaiah's and his predecessor's approaches to the subject lies in the much stronger element of humor in Deutero-Isaiah's depiction of the idolater.

113. Note that the passage is directed toward northern exiles. On the dating of the passage, see Holladay, 2: 155–58, 188; Bright, 284–85; Eissfeldt, *Introduction*, 361.

114. A comparable phenomenon in poetic texts generally has been noted by E. Z. Melammed, "Break Up of Stereotype Phrases as an Artistic Device in Biblical Poetry," *Scripta Hierosolymitana* VIII (1961), 115–53; see also by E. Z. Melammed, "EN ΔIA ΔYOIN in the Bible," *Tarbiz* 16 (1944–45), 179–85 (reprinted in Weinfeld, *Likkutei*, 201–19) [Heb.]. Melammed shows that compound linguistic stereotypes, such as two-part names and cases of hendiadys, are often broken up in biblical poetry so that the first part appears in an "A" verset and the second in the "B" verset. See, e.g., the division of the name מסה ומריבה in Deut 33.8, or the split-up of the hendiadys חסד ואמת in Isa 16.5 and Mic 7.20. The technique Melammed noticed occurred elsewhere

in Northwest Semitic literature; note the split-up of the name Kōtar wa-Ḥasīs in the Baal Epic, I AB vi 49 (UT 62.48–49 = KTU 1.6.v.49–50). (Ugaritic examples involving hendiadys are listed in Watson, 329.) I am pointing out a different phenomenon: in Deutero-Isaiah we see not the breakup of words that often occur together but of words that appear as a unit only in Deutero-Isaiah's source. Further, Deutero-Isaiah does not usually recast the two halves as parallel terms in an "A" and a "B" verset; indeed, since almost none of the borrowed phrases he splits up are examples of hendiadys or two-part names, they do not work as parallel terms. Nonetheless, it is conceivable that Deutero-Isaiah imitated a widespread Northwest Semitic poetic technique, making it the basis for a new technique in his extended project of allusion.

115. The split-up pattern may occur in a few cases outside of Deutero-Isaiah. See, for a possible example, the expansion of Zeph 3.3–4 in Ezek 22.25–28· (discussed in Fishbane, *Biblical*, 462–63), which inevitably involves several splittings of phrases from the source. Another possible case may be found in Jer 33.14–15 (see ibid., 471–72), where the phrase וַהֲקִמֹתִי לְדָוִד from an earlier oracle in Jer 23.5 reappears in two parts separated by several clauses. The division of a phrase from a source into two parts is likely to occur now and again when later authors reformulate their sources. But it is not clear that other authors repeatedly used such divisions as a literary technique. On the other hand, the frequency of this phenomenon in Deutero-Isaiah's use of older vocabulary is, to my knowledge, unique in the Hebrew Bible. Only of this author can we assert that splitting a phrase from a source into two was a technique purposefully used as part of his project of allusion.

116. Sound play in inner-biblical allusion and exegesis is not limited to Deutero-Isaiah, but it is particularly characteristic of his work. For other cases, see Job 15.14 in relation to Ps 8.5 (noted by Fishbane, *Biblical*, 286 n. 7); the reference in Ps 4.7 to Num 6.25 (ibid., 330 n. 37); multiple examples in Mal 1.6–2.9 based on Num 6.23–27 (ibid., 333); Prov 16.4–7 and 19.9–17, again based on the priestly benediction (referred to but not discussed ibid., 347 n. 79); and Ezek 22.28 in relation to Zeph 3.4 (ibid., 462, though the pun is not noted).

117. For further examples, see Torrey, 195–96; Kaufmann, *Babylonian*, 80–87; and Lawrence Boadt, "Intentional Allusion in Second Isaiah," *CBQ* 45 (1983), 353–63.

118. Again, word play based on homonymy, though especially common in Deutero-Isaiah's allusions, appears rarely elsewhere. See the use of Gen 49.11 in Zech 9.11 (Fishbane, *Biblical*, 501–2).

119. Torrey, 199–202. Cf. Kaufmann, *Babylonian*, 78.

120. For a tally of each technique's occurrences, see pp. 159–60, 192–93.

121. For a detailed discussion, see pp. 194–195.

122. See Fishbane, *Biblical*, 17. On the use of what may be called cumulative evidence in identifying allusions, see also Steven Weitzman, "Allusion, Artifice, and Exile in the Hymn of Tobit," *JBL* 115 (1996), 58.

CHAPTER THREE

1. Yehezkel Kaufmann maintains that almost all the material in 1–33, including even 24–27, is Isaiah's work. He agrees with others that 34–35 belong to Deutero-Isaiah and that 36–39 are secondary prose additions (though he believes that the prophecies attributed to Isaiah there may be genuine). See *Toledot ha-Emunah ha-Yisraelit* (Tel Aviv: Mosad Bialik and Devir, 1937–56), 3: 147–256, esp. 147–57, 163–73 [Heb.]; for a summary of his position, see *The Religion of Israel*, translated and abridged by Moshe Greenberg (Chicago: University of Chicago Press, 1960), 378–85. John Hayes and Stuart Irvine argue for a nearly identical thesis in *Isaiah, the Eighth Century Prophet* (Nashville, Tenn.: Abingdon Press, 1987). The analyses these scholars offer are more textually grounded and less reliant on hair-splitting source-critical divisions than those of most who work on Isaiah. Kaufmann, Hayes, and Irvine demonstrate that many allegedly late passages can be understood reasonably in an eighth-century context. Indeed, many of their readings are less strained than those according to which passages contain or consist of later additions. On the other hand, their arguments regarding chapters 24–27 are implausible, and they fail to take into account the clear elements of LBH which appear in those chapters (though not, to the best of my knowledge, in many other passages in 1–34); see H. L. Ginsberg, "Introduction," in *The Book of Isaiah: A New Translation* (Philadelphia: Jewish Publication Society, 1972), 14. Ginsberg's survey of the book, 16–20, represents a circumspect variation of Kaufmann's position. He attributes the bulk of material to the eighth century while recognizing that several passages are late.

2. For example, Hermann Barth, *Die Jesaja-Worte in der Josiazeit* (Neukirchen-Vluyn: Neukirchener Verlag, 1977), identifies various passages throughout the book as resulting from a seventh-century redaction that reshaped the older Isaiah traditions. See also Gerald Sheppard, "The Anti-Assyrian Redaction and the Canonical Context of Isaiah 1–39," *JBL* 104 (1985), 193–216. For summaries of other views that attempt to identify whole sections, shorter passages, occasional verses, or individual words as later additions, see Otto Eissfeldt, *The Old Testament: An Introduction*, trans. Peter Ackroyd (New York: Harper and Row, 1965), 306–30; Hayes and Irvine, 390–99.

On attempts to date material to the post-exilic era, see Barth, 286–94; Marvin Sweeney, *Isaiah 1–4 and the Post-Exilic Understanding of the Isaianic Tradition* (Berlin: Walter de Gruyter, 1988), esp. 1–11, 123–33, 163–85; R. E. Clements, "The Prophecies of Isaiah and the Fall of Jerusalem in 587 B.C.," *VT* 30 (1980), 421–36; and many of the commentaries, as well as the summaries in Eissfeldt and Hayes-Irvine mentioned above.

These highly complex reconstructions of the book's compositional history can only be, at best, speculative. They seem strained in comparison with the more elegant and soundly reasoned arguments of Kaufmann.

3. In addition to the commentaries, it is important to note Umberto Cassuto, "On the Formal and Stylistic Relationship Between Deutero-Isaiah and Other Biblical Writers," in *Biblical and Oriental Studies*, trans. I. Abrahams (Jerusalem: Magnes, 1973), 160–77; Armond Kaminka, *Meḥqarim* (Tel Aviv: Devir, 1938), 1: 19–30, 52–56, 159–64; and the scholars cited in the next note.

4. See especially R. E. Clements, "Beyond Tradition History: Deutero-Isaianic Development of First Isaiah's Themes," *JSOT* 31 (1985), 95–113; Odil Steck, *Bereitete Heimkehr: Jesaja 35 als redaktionelle Brücke zwischen dem ersten und zweiten Jesaja* (Stuttgart: Katholisches Bibelwerk, 1985); H. G. M. Williamson, *The Book Called Isaiah: Deutero-Isaiah's Role in Composition and Redaction* (Oxford: Oxford University Press, 1994). For summaries of the "Unity of Isaiah" school (which has strong links to canon criticism), see Rolf Rendtorff, "The Book of Isaiah: A Complex Unity. Synchronic and Diachronic Reading," in *New Visions of Isaiah*, ed. Roy Melugin and Marvin Sweeney (Sheffield: Sheffield Academic Press, 1996), 32–49, and other essays in that volume, in particular the overview by Melugin (13–29); Christopher Seitz, *Zion's Final Destiny: The Development of the Book of Isaiah, a Reassessment of Isaiah 36–39* (Minneapolis: Fortress Press, 1991), 26–35; and David Carr, "Reaching for Unity in Isaiah," *JSOT* 57 (1993), 61–81.

5. For a lengthier discussion of this issue, see my essay "Allusions and Illusions: The Unity of the Book of Isaiah in Light of Deutero-Isaiah's Use of Prophetic Tradition," in *New Visions*, ed. Melugin and Sweeney, 156–86.

6. I noted that this category occurs frequently within the Book of Jeremiah; it also occurs occasionally within Deutero-Isaiah's other sources. For example, Isa 11.12f. reverses the negative message of Isa 5.26, and Isa 32.2–6 reverse Isa 5.20–21 and Isa 29.10. Hosea 3 reverses the negative vocabulary in Hosea 1–2.

7. As I pointed out above, we cannot be sure that the historical Isaiah composed each utterance in the first part of the book. Nonetheless, for convenience, I will refer to the authors of these passages which Deutero-Isaiah utilized as "Isaiah."

8. The text here is difficult. I take the phrase אֲשֶׁר עַל־רֹאשׁ גֵּיא־שְׁמָנִים to refer to the inhabitants of the city of Samaria, which was located on a hill above a valley. My translation is only one of several possible renderings. The point regarding the parallel between these verses and Deutero-Isaiah is not affected by the text-critical issues.

9. Because MT has an adjective (חָזָק) rather than a noun (חֹזֶק or חֵזֶק), the *bêt* must be seen as a *bêt essentiae*. LXX seems to have read the word as a noun, however, and translates ἰδοὺ κύριος μετὰ ἰσχύος ἔρχεται (though see the comment ad loc. in Moshe Goshen-Gottstein, ed., *The Hebrew University Bible: The Book of Isaiah* [Jerusalem: Magnes, 1995]). Similarly, 1QIsaᵃ has בחוזק. These would yield the translation, "the Lord YHWH is coming with strength." Nonetheless, in view of the dependence on Isaiah 28, MT is to be preferred: Deutero-Isaiah's point may be precisely that in the past He utilized a strong person to punish Israel, but now He

Himself is the strong one who will redeem Israel. On the other hand, even if one prefers 1QIsaᵃ and LXX, the marker remains clear.

10. See Christopher Seitz, "The Divine Council: Temporal Transition and New Prophecies in the Book of Isaiah," *JBL* 109 (1990), 242, who points out some of the common themes and the words צִיץ and נָבֵל, and Williamson, 77–79, who notes גִיא as well.

11. Further, I have translated גֵּיא in Isa 28.1 and 28.4 as "valley," which is what גֵּיא means in Isa 40.4. However, if ibn Ezra is correct that the word in Isa 28.1 means "haughty" (see his second suggestion, following Sa'adia), then this pair of marked and marker represents a case of word play. Similarly, if we read גֵאָי in Isa 28.1 with 1QIsaᵃ (from the root meaning "pride"; see the comparison to Sa'adia in Goshen-Gottstein), the parallel remains strong as a case of sound play.

12. This same passage from Deutero-Isaiah reverses another prophecy, Ezek 21.2–12. Some of the markers in that allusion are common, but other items suggest the parallels are not coincidental. One clause appears in precisely the same form in both texts: "And all flesh will see." (This clause does not appear outside of Ezekiel and Deutero-Isaiah.) Further, the phrase is subject to the split-up pattern: in Ezekiel, the word כִּי follows this clause immediately, while in Deutero-Isaiah the word כִּי is separated from the clause by one intervening word. Word play occurs as well: in both texts, a plural form of a word beginning פָּנֵ- occurs immediately before the word דָרַד, but in Ezekiel, the word is a noun meaning "face," while in Deutero-Isaiah it is a verb meaning "set up, prepare." Ezekiel faces Jerusalem (Ezek 21.2, 21.7; see Rashi and Radak) and predicts utter disaster. When all the world sees how YHWH punishes His nation, they will realize how mighty He is and how pathetic the nation is. Deutero-Isaiah's message, too, is directed towards Jerusalem (Isa 40.2). Like his predecessor, Deutero-Isaiah announces that all the world will acknowledge what God does, but this time the action is salvific. The reversal becomes particularly acute in the clause that Deutero-Isaiah borrows verbatim from his source, since "all flesh will see" something terrible in the older text and something wonderful in the later one. Deutero-Isaiah reformulates other individual items in consistent ways. In Ezekiel, "hands" and "wind/spirit" are figures of human frailty and suffering: the people's hands go slack and their spirit languishes in consequence of YHWH's brutal punishment. But in Deutero-Isaiah these words betoken YHWH's power, on which the people can rely. Deutero-Isaiah's reference to YHWH's hand may also be understood quite literally in light of the source, for there God announced His intention to unsheathe His sword. In both texts, then, it was God's hand that effected the destructive punishment.

13. Even this prophecy of doom in Mic 3.12, however, holds some promise of restoration. Micah's comment that Zion will be plowed under like a field is not exclusively a figure of devastation. By plowing a field under, one destroys the old crop

in order to plant a new one. The field is temporarily overturned so that it will be covered with vegetation once again. Thus Micah (like his contemporary Isaiah and like Jeremiah a century later) foresaw both the devastation of Judah and the re-emergence of life there, though he stresses the former and merely intimates the latter.

14. Additional cases in which Deutero-Isaiah reverses material from older proph-ets occur, though fewer cases than are found in Deutero-Isaiah's allusions to Jere-miah. Isa 49.24–26 (like Isa 40.1–8, discussed in note 12 above) reverse Ezek 21.2–12, employing word play as they do so (צַדִּיק is "righteous one" in Ezek 21.8 but "victor" in Isa 49.24). Hosea 1–2 are the subject of a complex reworking that involves reversal; the allusion is discussed at the end of this chapter.

Isaiah 6 is the subject of numerous reversals. Isa 49.19–20 reverse Isa 6.10–12 (see Chapter 2, note 19; cf. Williamson, 53–54, who further notes the similarity of Isa 49.19–20 to Isa 5.8). A similar reversal of Isaiah 6 may appear in Isaiah 54; see Williamson, 54. The proclamation of doom in 6.12 may be the basis of the comfort-ing language in 62.4. Finally, when Deutero-Isaiah announces that the blind will see, the deaf will hear, and those in darkness will be set free (Isa 42.7, 42.16, 49.6, 52.8, 61.1), he may be reversing a theme from Isa 6.9–10 and 29.9. The reversal of the blindness theme from Isa 6.9 is especially clear in 40.21–28, as Craig Evans points out in *To See and Not Perceive: Isaiah 6.9–10 in Early Jewish and Christian Interpretation* (Sheffield: Sheffield Academic Press, 1989), 45 and 186 n. 166. Deutero-Isaiah de-scribes idolaters as blind in 44.9–19, which include several markers pointing back to Isa 6.9–13: blindness and obduracy language; מֵאֵין אָדָם (6.11) // מֵאָדָם (44.11); וְהָיָה לְבָעֵר (6.13) // וְהָיָה לְאָדָם לְבָעֵר (44.15, a case of the split-up pattern); אַלּוֹן (6.13 // 44.14). The allusion involves a large change in the use of the vocabulary: in chapter 6, the Judeans were blind because God punished them for their sinfulness, but here the idolaters are blind in that they fail to see how foolish they are. In chapter 6, the prophet prevented the nation from knowing, while in chapter 44 the prophet makes fun of the idolaters who don't know. Further, Clements ("Beyond," 107–8) suggests that 44.26 is based on Isa 6.11–12. The parallels are weak, but in light of the use of 6.11–13 earlier in chapter 44, Clements's proposal has merit.

Other passages in Isaiah are reversed as well. The passage in Isa 40.28–31 may reverse the negative trope of 5.27. The comments in Isa 49.22 and 62.10 reverse Isa 5.24–29 (for a discussion that notes some but not all of the parallels between 5 and 49, see Williamson, 65–66). In Isa 65.1–3, 24, YHWH reverses His earlier refusal to see and hear, which He had announced in Isa 1.12, 15. The connection in this case, however, is tenuous, because the issue at hand—whether YHWH will listen to the people or not—is not uncommon in the prophets and the psalms; see especially Jer 7.17, 11.11–14, and 14.11–13. Several additional cases involving elements of reversal will be noted in other sections below.

15. Some commentators date this passage to the post-exilic era, which would

mean that Deutero-Isaiah could not have known it. R. E. Clements, *Isaiah 1–39* (Grand Rapids, Mich.: Eerdmans, 1980), asserts that the passage "expresses a picture of the future exaltation of Jerusalem and Mount Zion, not one that was currently thought to exist. . . . Quite certainly, therefore, we must ascribe the prophecy to a time after the destruction of Jerusalem in 587." But Clements's claim that the Jerusalem described does not currently exist finds no textual support. The passage refers neither to the rebuilding of the city nor to the reconstruction of the "House of YHWH," so that there is no reason to believe either was destroyed.

Barth (291–92) argues that the positive view of the nations in this passage as well as in Isa 19.18–25 can only have been possible at a time of relative calm in Judah and warfare among the nations, viz., the beginning of the fourth century. For Barth (as for so many biblicists), certain ideas can only have been thought at a particular moment. In fact, we should ask why it is implausible that an eighth-century thinker would have hoped for peace in Israel and among the nations. Even if such an idea were surprising, this would not make it impossible. Isaiah conceived of notions which were unexpected, even bizarre. Therein lies the genius of any original thinker. To deny that an idea could have been thought of in a given age, as Barth and so many biblicists do, is to deny the possibility of intellectual creativity—the absence of which is perhaps more acute among biblicists than poets. In addition, we should note that the absence of LBH in these two passages speaks against Barth's extremely late dating; and it is easier to see the reference to Assyria in Isa 19.23–25 as a reference to Assyria rather than (as Barth would suggest) a reference to Persia.

Sweeney (*Isaiah*, 165–74) notes the similarity of the passage to Isa 51.4–6 and claims that Isa 2.2–4 must be the later passage. He suggests only two reasons for this. First, Deutero-Isaiah depicts YHWH as returning to Jerusalem, while in 2.2–4 He is "already" there. In fact, 2.2–4 more likely present YHWH as never having left, since these verses mention neither His exit nor His return. Second, Sweeney notes that visions in which nations come to Jerusalem occur in other post-exilic texts, such as Trito-Isaiah and Zechariah. But this hardly means that *any* such vision must stem from the same era. Sweeney dates the passage to the final years of Cyrus's reign, arguing that its bright outlook and vision of universal peace fit that era of universal peace well. Could not such a vision date just as easily to a time of turbulence, when a writer longed for the universal peace that was lacking? Or, if the thinker was original enough, to any other time whatsoever?

It is difficult to date this passage with precision. Its appearance in two eighth-century prophetic collections may bolster an eighth-century dating. The vision displays several characteristic features of Isaiah's utterances: the focus on Zion's centrality, the concern for peace and just relations among the powers, and the anticipation of a generally unrealistic state of affairs. On the integral place of the vision in Isaiah's thought, see further Kaufmann, *Toledot*, 3: 199–200 (where he also criticizes the view that the universalism of the passage would be impossible for an eighth-century thinker) and 3: 221–22. In any event, there is no reason to view it as post-exilic or to doubt that Deutero-Isaiah could have known it.

16. Another possible marker deserves notice. The noun אוֹר ("light") in Isa 51.4 may hint back at the verb וְנָהֲרוּ ("flow") in the source. That verb came to have the sense of "shine, glimmer" by Deutero-Isaiah's day, and it recalls the noun נְהוֹר ("light") in Aramaic, a language familiar to the exiles in Babylonia. Thus to Deutero-Isaiah (if not to an eighth-century audience), the verb in Isaiah 2/Micah 4 suggests illumination, a connection that was abetted by the link between "light" and "teaching" or "God's word" in many biblical texts (on which see Avi Hurvitz, *Wisdom Language in Biblical Psalmody* [Jerusalem: Magnes, 1991], 110–13 [Heb.]). This connotation of וְנָהֲרוּ plays an even more prominent role in Deutero-Isaiah's allusion to this text in Isa 60.1–7, as we shall see shortly.

17. Ezekiel, the other Judean who prophesied in Babylon, also grappled with this problem. He announced that he had witnessed the divine presence (כבוד) leaving its abode in the Jerusalem temple and arriving in the exilic community in Mesopotamia (Ezekiel 9–11 and 1, on which see Joseph Blenkinsopp, *A History of Prophecy in Israel*, rev. ed. [Louisville, Ky.: Westminster John Knox, 1996], 168–69). The transfer of the כבוד explained how an exile could see and hear YHWH so far from Zion. Concerns such as these, we should recall, remained strong long afterwards. The first section of *Mekilta d'Rabbi Yishmael* (*Bo'*, section before *Par. A*, ed. Horovitz and Rabin [Jerusalem: Wahrmann, 1970], 1–6) deals precisely with the question: can there be prophecy outside the Land of Israel?

18. The use of the word אֵילֵי in this sense signifies that rams will be used in sacrifice. In addition, the word may retain its other sense, "leaders" (which is found in Exod 15.15), in order to imply that foreign kings will serve Israel. That idea occurs also in Isa 49.23 and later in this chapter in verse 11.

19. According to this translation, the animals are the subject of the *qal* verb יַעֲלוּ. Alternatively, one could see the animals as the implied object of a *hiphil* verb יַעֲלוּ, whose subject is understood to be the foreigners, yielding the translation, "they will offer acceptable offerings."

20. For examples in Hebrew and Ugaritic, see Mitchell Dahood, "Ugaritic-Hebrew Parallel Pairs," in *Ras Shamra Parallels: The Texts from Ugarit and the Hebrew Bible*, ed. Loren Fisher (Rome: Pontifical Biblical Institute, 1972–75), 1: 203.

21. Gerhard von Rad, "The City on the Hill," in *The Problem of the Hexateuch and Other Essays*, trans. E. Trueman Dicken (London: SCM Press, 1984), 238–39.

22. Pierre Grelot, "Un parallèle Babylonien d'Isaïe LX et du psaume LXXII," *VT* 7 (1957), 319, notices that the ritual aspect of Isaiah 60 is more pronounced than that of Isaiah 2.

23. "Here"—i.e., Babylon. The statement implies that YHWH Himself (the "I" who speaks the verse) has been in exile along with the people (cf. Rashi). In verse 8,

watchmen in Jerusalem see YHWH returning to the city. Alternatively, the phrase may simply "express a strong sense of incongruity between what is and what ought to be" (John Skinner, *The Book of the Prophet Isaiah: Chapters XL–LXVI*, rev. ed. [Cambridge: Cambridge University Press, 1917]). The text in this verse contains difficulties (see the discussion in Skinner and the judicious remarks of Richard Clifford, *Fair Spoken and Persuading: An Interpretation of Second Isaiah* [New York: Paulist Press, 1984]), but they do not affect our issue. On my translation of מה לי, cf. the commentary of Joseph ibn Caspi.

24. Cf. the similar tendency to amplify figures from the source in the allusion to Jer 31.7–9 in Isa 35.4–10; the allusion to Ps 72.7 in Isa 60.19–20; the allusion to Ps 102.25–27 in Isa 51.6–8.

25. Menahem Haran, *Between RĪŠHONÔT (Former Prophecies) and ḤADA-SHÔT (New Prophecies): A Literary-Historical Study of Prophecies in Isaiah XL–XLVII* (Jerusalem: Magnes, 1963), 97–98 [Heb.]. The section in brackets summarizes material from p. 96. Haran concludes on the basis of other elements in Isa 40–66 and Isa 35 that Deutero-Isaiah expected the rebuilt Jerusalem in its entirety to be a Temple-city (pp. 100 and 97 n. 43). The idea that Jerusalem will be a Temple-city is found nowhere else in the Bible. Haran notes an analogous idea in rabbinic literature, but he points out that the rabbinic idea differs from Deutero-Isaiah's in that it still allows many types of impurity forbidden in the Temple to remain in Jerusalem (see Haran, *RĪŠHONÔT*, 99–100). Since 1963, when Haran wrote his book, a much closer parallel to Deutero-Isaiah's notion has come to light: the Temple Scroll, which, like Deutero-Isaiah, extends P's ritual rules for the Tabernacle or Temple to the entire city. The Temple Scroll "considers all of Jerusalem as a temple-city and requires a corresponding state of purity [in it]. In a sense, for the [Qumran] sect, the Temple and Jerusalem are one and the same" (Devorah Dimant, "Qumran Sectarian Literature," in *Jewish Writings of the Second Temple Period*, ed. Michael Stone [Philadelphia: Fortress Press, 1984], 520, and cf. 528).

26. A case involving Hosea will be discussed below. Further, reprediction of Zeph 2.13–15 occurs in Isa 47.5–11; this example includes sound play and precise quotation.

Several examples of reprediction based on Isaiah are of interest. In Isa 35.1–8, Deutero-Isaiah repeats Isaiah's vision of a better future from 32.1–6. (On the inclusion of Isaiah 35 in the Deutero-Isaianic corpus, see Chapter 6, note 18.) Both prophets look forward to the blind seeing, the dumb talking, the thirsty drinking. But the meaning of these figures changes. In Isaiah, the blind, deaf, and lame symbolize the nobility which acts ignobly, the rulers who rule unjustly. In the future, people will act more appropriately: judges will judge, and eyes will see. Water in Isaiah 32 suggests the well of torah, of law. Deutero-Isaiah transforms these political figures into salvific ones. His blind are captives who will now see their restoration; his lame, those will walk to the freedom they have been denied. The desert motif no longer represents the current political order in Judah but stands for the exile. Water is a figure not of torah but of redemption. Furthermore, Deutero-Isaiah uses these tropes literally as well as figuratively; for him the desert refers to the real desert which the exiles will traverse on their way home. Water means the actual stuff the thirsty travelers will drink.

A further case of reprediction occurs in Isa 53.1–12, which refer back to Isa 11.1–10. Finally, Deutero-Isaiah's descriptions of the end of the nation's blindness may constitute not only a reversal of 6.9 but also a confirmation of Isaiah's predictions in 29.18f. and 32.3–4, according to which the people would see again.

Finally, Isa 66.12–24 repeat the prediction of Isa 30.27–33 while utilizing the split-up pattern, word play, and several cases of sound play. This allusion is especially instructive because, according to my reading, it is spread across several verses that some commentators attribute to diverse hands. John McKenzie (*Second Isaiah* [Garden City, N.Y.: Doubleday, 1968]), Claus Westermann (*Isaiah 40–66: A Commentary*, trans. D. Stalker [Philadelphia: Westminster Press, 1969]), and (less decidedly) Skinner view 66.23–24 as a later addition, and Westermann sees 66.15 as part of an older theophany text into which the prophet's lines have been placed. While the text of 66 is full of sudden shifts of subject, excising verses 15 and 23–24 does not solve the problems that allegedly suggest a composite document; the sources which Westermann posits, for example, are still full of apparent incongruities. Why, then, do these scholars attribute the last verses of the chapter (and of the book as it now exists) to another author? They seem unable to understand that the same writer who looked forward to the positive future described in parts of chapter 66 can also anticipate divine retribution. But if there is any inconsistency here, it exists only for the moderns, not for a sixth-century thinker. The commentators would be happier if the Book of Isaiah ended at the buoyant proclamation in 66.22 rather than with the gruesome picture in 66.24. Indeed, McKenzie says as much, and Westermann bemoans the incompatibility of 66.23–24 with the New Testament (apparently forgetting passages such as Rev 8.6–9, 11). Their discomfort with 66.23–24 leads them to attribute them to a later, and lesser, hand. But the verses follow naturally from what precedes them. They complete the thoughts expressed earlier in the chapter and in the last part of 40–66—viz., that there are good and evil people among both the Judeans and the nations; the evil will be punished. Against the excision of the last two verses and verse 15, see Charles Torrey, *The Second Isaiah: A New Interpretation* (New York: Scribners, 1928) and Yehezkel Kaufmann, *The Babylonian Captivity and Deutero-Isaiah*, trans. C. W. Efroymson (New York: Union of American Hebrew Congregations, 1970), 185–86, and cf. James Muilenburg, "The Book of Isaiah: Chapters 40–66," in *IB* 5, ed. G. A. Buttrick et al. (New York: Abingdon Press, 1956).

27. Chapter 11 consists of two parts, verses 1–9 and 10–16. Some scholars date the second half or both halves to the post-exilic (or, at the earliest, the exilic) period. Clements (*Isaiah*), for example, argues that 1–9 must have been written after 587 because the term גֵּזַע יִשַׁי ("stump of Jesse") indicates that the Davidic dynasty has

lost its throne (i.e., the "tree" of the Davidides has been cut down and only a stump remains). However, the semantic range of גזע is not limited to "stump." As Hayes and Irvine point out (212), in Isa 40.24 this word refers to the part of a live tree which comes out of the ground. Thus the term's semantic range includes "trunk" as well as "stump." (This sense of the word continues in later Hebrew; note *m. B. Bat.* 4.5, where context requires "trunk," and see the commentary by Obadiah of Bertinoro ad loc. in the standard editions of the Mishna.) Thus Clements fails to demonstrate that verses 1–9 must have been written after 587. Barth (59–62) admits the Isaian authorship of 11.1–5 but judges 6–9 to be independent and later. However, verses 6–9 continue the description of the peaceful future described in 1–5 and contain no disjunction suggesting a late interpolation (contra, e.g., Odil Steck, " 'Ein kleiner Knabe kann sie leiten,' Beobachtungen zum Tierfrieden in Jesaja 11,6–8 und 65,25," in *Alttestamentlicher Glaube und biblische Theologie: Festschrift für Horst Dietrich Preuß*, ed. J. Hausmann and H. J. Zobel [Stuttgart: Kohlhammer, 1992], esp. 105–8; Steck's view that 11.1–16 contain four sources depends on a discovery of multiple disjunctions in a text that coheres quite well).

The arguments for the lateness of verses 10–16 initially appear to be more serious. Barth holds that the formula וְהָיָה בַּיּוֹם הַהוּא indicates an interpolation (58), but, as Hayes and Irvine point out (216), the phrase can also introduce a new section within a composition by a single author. Skinner, Clements, and Barth (58–59) see the references to the return of exiles as necessarily dating after 587; further, for these critics, the description of exiles in Egypt, Pathros, Cush, and other lands (Isa 11.11) must be dated well into the post-exilic era. But northerners had already been exiled in Isaiah's day; and even before 722 the Assyrian policy of deportation was well known and feared throughout the ancient Near East. It is for that reason that, even before the fall of Samaria, eighth-century prophets anticipated that Israelites would become refugees in Egypt and Assyria (see Amos 9.3, 11.5; Hosea 8.13). Thus the reference to exiles in and around Egypt is not surprising in an eighth-century document. Indeed, the list of locations in 11.11b corresponds in content and order to an eighth-century topographical list of Esarhaddon and is likely to stem from that time (see Moshe Weinfeld, *Deuteronomy 1–11* [New York: Doubleday, 1991], 48). The description of exiles in "four corners of the earth" (11.12) is hardly surprising in an era when peoples feared the Assyrians, who notoriously labeled themselves the rulers of *arba'i kibrāti erṣēti*.

In short, there are no good reasons to see any parts of chapter 11 as exilic or post-exilic. Indeed, many elements of the chapter, especially in verses 10–16, reflect typical eighth-century concerns. Moreover, verses 11–16 emphasize the return of victims of Assyrian deportation but contain no explicit reference to Babylonian exiles (see Antti Laato, *The Servant of YHWH and Cyrus: A Reinterpretation of the Exilic Messianic Programme in Isaiah 40–55* [Stockholm: Almqvist and Wiksell, 1992], 116–17). This points strongly to a dating before 597. Finally, the phrase וְאָסַף נִדְחֵי יִשְׂרָאֵל is unlikely in the post-exilic period, when כָּנַס replaced אָסַף (see Mark Rooker, *Biblical Hebrew in Transition: The Language of the Book of Ezekiel* [Sheffield: Sheffield Academic Press, 1990], 156).

28. On the translation of the preceding two verses, see notes 48–50 in Chapter 2.

29. Most of the markers in the first half of the song (42.1–4) occur in the same order as the marked items:

רוח (4x) [11.2] // רוחי [42.1]

ישפוט [11.3] // משפט [42.1]

ולא למשמע [11.3] // ולא יַשמיע [42.2]

The servant's humility [42.3] // The king's favor to the humble and poor [11.4]

והאמונה [11.5] // לאמת [42.3]

People look towards the servant/the king [42.4 // 11.10]

Some additional terms occur slightly out of order. In the source, the word ומשפט (11.4) occurs before the idea of humility and the word אמונה, while in the allusion the word משפט appears a second time after the idea of humility and the word אמת (42.4). Further, the word ארץ appears before אמונה in the source (Isa 11.4) but immediately after אמת in the allusion (42.4). The root יצ״א is the first item in the source and the second in the allusion.

In the second half of the song (42.5–9), Deutero-Isaiah returns to the beginning of the source as he again borrows vocabulary and motifs, many of which appear in the same order as the source:

רוח (4x) [11.2] // ורוח [42.5]

עיניו [11.3] // עינים [42.6]

The lowly set free [42.6] // The lowly judged rightly [11.4]

כבוד [11.10] // וכבודי [42.8]

Further, the root יצ״א and the word משפט appear at the outset of both the source and the second half of the song. Additional markers, however, appear out of order.

30. The theme of תורה which Deutero-Isaiah adds here may come from Isa 2.3, a text closely related to chapter 11. Cf. Laato, 80–81, for further parallels between Isa 2.1–4 and 42.1–9. Although the parallels which Laato notes are not particularly strong, the idea that Isa 2.3 served as a source for 42 seems likely in light of Deutero-Isaiah's several other allusions to 2.1–4.

31. See Joachim Begrich, *Studien zu Deuterojesaja* (Munich: Chr. Kaiser, 1969), 105; Bernhard Anderson, "Exodus and Covenant in Second Isaiah and Prophetic Tradition," in *Magnalia Dei, the Mighty Acts of God: Essays on the Bible and Archaeology in Memory of G. Ernest Wright*, ed. F. M. Cross, W. E. Lemke, and P. D. Miller (Garden City, N.Y.: Doubleday, 1976), 343; Claus Westermann, *Isaiah 40–66: A Commentary*, trans. D. Stalker (Philadelphia, Westminster Press, 1969), 362–63.

32. On these, see Blenkinsopp, *History*, 154; Peter Ackroyd, *Exile and Restoration*

(Philadelphia: Westminster Press, 1968), 124–25; on this hope in exilic literature, see J. Coppens, "L'Espérance Messianique Royale à la Veille et au Lendemain de l'Exil," in *Studia Biblica et Semitica Theodoro Christiano Vriezen Dedicata*, ed. W. van Unnik and A. van der Woude (Wageningen: Veenan & Zonen, 1966), 46–61, esp. 54–59.

33. See Chapter 2, n. 107. The single exception may be 52.13–53.12, but Tryggve N. D. Mettinger, *A Farewell to the Servant Songs: A Critical Examination of an Exegetical Axiom* (Lund: Gleerup, 1983), 38–43, produces a very strong argument that the servant in 52.13–53.12 is in fact the nation Israel.

34. Thus the Jeremian idea of the people as a light of nations is grafted into the Isaianic idea of a Davidide who will give teaching to the whole world. Further, the phrase אור גוים here may be influenced by Deutero-Isaiah's punning reuse of ונהרו אליו כל גוים in Isaiah 2.

35. The transfer of the royal promises to the whole nation occurs in other passages from Deutero-Isaiah and has been noticed before (see Mettinger, 44; Begrich, 105; Ackroyd, 124–25; Anderson, "Typology," 191; and the lengthier discussion in Kaufmann, *Babylonian*, 189, who nevertheless does not believe that Deutero-Isaiah gainsaid the restoration of the Davidic house). This theme is especially clear in the allusions to chapter 11. On Isa 55.3, which plays a crucial role in the articulation of this theme, see the discussion in Chapter 4.

36. For the former, see Skinner. For the latter, see Laato, 79.

37. One might object that the allusion I am positing here extends over two distinct passages, since 61.1 clearly begins a new pericope. However, Kaufmann has shown that Deutero-Isaiah continued to treat certain themes or to use words from an immediately preceding section as he composed successive passages (see *Babylonian*, 78–87). Similarly, the allusion to chapter 11 which occurs in chapter 60 spills over into the beginning of chapter 61.

38. See Jer 23.5 and 33.15 and the third-century Phoenician inscription of Yatan-baal from Cyprus (*KAI* 43: 11). The phrasing in these texts is not identical to the phrasing in Isaiah (Jeremiah and the Phoenician text use צמח rather than נצר), but they show that likening a king to a branch may have been common. The comparison of a king to an eternal branch or shoot also occurs repeatedly in the inscriptions of Esarhaddon, a seventh-century king of Assyria, though the language used there occurs in nonroyal prayers for progeny as well; see the references in *CAD* 8: 423, s.v. "*kisittu*" #3.

39. The word נגשׁיך in v. 17 may echo Isa 9.3, a passage closely related in content to chapter 11. That verse was alluded to earlier at the beginning of chapter 60 (see Michael Fishbane, *Biblical Interpretation in Ancient Israel* [Oxford: Oxford University Press, 1985], 497–98).

40. Allusions to chapter 11 occur in three other passages. Both Isa 49.22 and 62.10 depend on Isa 11.11–16. (Although some of the shared items appear in other biblical

passages, such as Jer 4.10, 50.2, and 51.11, other markers connect Isaiah 49 and 62 with chapter 11 exclusively, and the allusions are made clear by a case of sound play and of the split-up pattern.) Isa 65.25 includes a word-for-word borrowing from 11.6 (as has long been noted; see, e.g., Steck, " 'kleiner,' " 108–9). All these passages repeat aspects of Isaiah's prediction without referring to a restored monarchy. Williamson (66–67) claims that the similarities between Isa 11.12f. and Isa 49.22 show that the former were written by Deutero-Isaiah himself. However, the presence of typical features of Deutero-Isaianic allusion in the passage's parallels in 49 and 62 indicates that the similarity results from Deutero-Isaiah's borrowing from, rather than interpolating into, chapter 11.

41. Deutero-Isaiah alludes to Isa 30.9–14 again in 42.18–25. The former passage is translated later in this chapter. For a translation of parts of Isaiah 56–57, see Chapter 2.

42. Reading מְקֶדֶם rather than MT's מְקֶדֶם.

43. Reading שִׁקּוּצַיִךְ rather than MT's קִבּוּצַיִךְ.

44. Note that the passage in Isaiah preceding the one Deutero-Isaiah alludes to here concerns the holy mountain (Isa 2.2), so that these words may also act as markers.

45. Some of these parallels have also been noted by Williamson (39), who points out that the words רם and נשׂא occur together outside the Book of Isaiah only in Prov 30.13.

46. So, e.g., Westermann. See especially *Isaiah*, 325.

47. See Skinner, especially pp. 168, 171, and Brooks Schramm, *The Opponents of Third Isaiah: Reconstructing the Cultic History of the Restoration* (Sheffield: Sheffield Academic Press, 1995), 127–33, 157, and 179.

48. Kaufmann, *Babylonian*, 170.

49. Does לַמֶּלֶךְ refer to a deity, perhaps a chthonic one? Note the reference to child sacrifice four verses earlier. Cf. Westermann.

50. This element reflects the tendency of Deutero-Isaiah to portray YHWH as voluntarily accepting human roles out of His love for His people. This is also evident in a use of the word הִנֵּנִי ("here I am"), which is unique to Deutero-Isaiah. As Rabbi Yehiel Poupko pointed out to me, only in the last part of the Book of Isaiah does YHWH call "here I am" to His people (52.6, 58.9, 65.1); elsewhere in the Bible this word is used by humans responding to a divine call (e.g., Gen 22.1, 11; Exod 3.4).

51. Similarly, in this passage Deutero-Isaiah mitigates the negative aspects of Jeremiah 12 even as he repeats them, as I noted in Chapter 2.

52. So according to the second reading of Isa 57.18 proposed by ibn Ezra and the first proposed by Skinner.

53. To wit:

רָם וְנִשָׂא [57.15 // 6.1]
קד"שׁ [57.13, 15 // 6.2]

עֲוֹנֶךְ [6.7] // בַּעֲוֹן [57.17]

וְשָׁב וְרָפָא לוֹ [6.10] // שׁוֹבֵב . . . וְאֶרְפָּאֵהוּ [57.17–18]

שְׂפָתֶיךָ [6.7] // שְׂפָתָיִם [57.18]

Several stylistic patterns appear in the markers pointing back to chapter 6. Isaiah's וְשָׁב וְרָפָא לוֹ is subject to both the split-up pattern and sound play: וְשָׁב becomes שׁוֹבֵב, and the root רפ״א appears in the following verses. The trisagion in Isa 6.2 yields three occurrences of the root קד״שׁ in Isa 57.13–15; this constitutes an elaborate case of the split-up pattern.

54. Deutero-Isaiah borrows from Isaiah what might be called vertical imagery and a particular notion of humility elsewhere as well. Isaiah often contrasts anything high and lofty—a mountain, a person, an empire—with what is low and humble, favoring the latter and looking forward to a day when their respective places will be reversed: in addition to 2.5–21, see 2.2, 6.1, and the excellent discussion of Kaufmann, *Toledot*, 3: 202–4: only YHWH's throne is and deserves to be called high and elevated; anyone or anything else which attempts to become great is guilty of self-deification. Deutero-Isaiah utilizes these themes in 40.4 and in his descriptions of a servant. The servant matches Isaiah's ideal conception of a person or nation: he is humble (42.3, 53.3, 7; cf. 49.7, 50.6); he does not harm even those who are easily taken advantage of (42.4); he accepts YHWH, even when despairing (49.4; cf. 50.10); he causes the mighty to stand up and notice, to be surprised, to acknowledge YHWH (49.7, 52.15); in spite of his lowly place he is ultimately raised up and exalted (52.13, 53.12). By creating the figure of the servant (whether he represents the people Israel or serves as the exemplar of the ideal individual), Deutero-Isaiah repeats Isaiah's idea regarding the place of humility for an individual or a nation.

55. In Isa 65.12–13 and 66.17–24, Deutero-Isaiah repeats Isa 1.28–30, specifying like his source that the evildoers will receive the punishment. Another instance may occur in 56.12, where Deutero-Isaiah criticizes the people who revel and drink while ignoring the righteous and the real message of God. This rebuke recalls Isaiah's complaint about the drunkards in Isa 5.11f. Both the source and the allusion contain a description of sheep wandering without a shepherd (5.17, 56.11). The first-person quotation of the revelers' words in 56.12 further recalls Isa 22.13, but there are few lexical parallels between the passages, so these similarities with material from Isaiah cannot be described with any certainty as borrowings.

56. This phenomenon resembles what some scholars refer to as "Fortschreibung der Prophetie." See Wolfgang Lau, *Schriftgelehrte Prophetie in Jes 56–66* (Berlin: Walter de Gruyter, 1994), 8; R. Albertz, "Das Deuterojesaja-Buch als Fortschreibung der Jesaja-Prophetie," in *Die hebräische Bibel und ihre zweifache Nachgeschichte: Festschrift für Rolf Rendtorff*, ed. E. Blum, C. Macholz, and E. Stegemann (Neukirchen-Vluyn: Neukirchener, 1990), 241. Cf. Fishbane, *Biblical*, esp. 458–99.

57. On the case of confirmation, see the discussion of Isa 51.17–22 later in this

chapter. Other texts not mentioned here also combine reprediction with historical recontextualization. Isa 47.5–11 utilize Zeph 2.13–15, reassigning Zephaniah's prediction regarding Nineveh to Babylon. Isa 46.5–12 update Isaiah's ill-fated prediction from 14.24–25. Isa 60.1–5 recall Isaiah's descriptions of the darkness in which the people wander and the light they are soon to enjoy, which appeared in Isa 5.30 and Isa 8.22–9.5. The allusion contains several cases of sound play. Isaiah predicted restoration for the northerners, which was to result from the downfall of the Assyrians (9.3–4) and the ascendancy of a Davidic ruler who was recently born or enthroned. Alas, as with so many prophecies of Isaiah, the predictions contained here never came to fruition. Deutero-Isaiah borrows his predecessor's vocabulary not to utter the same prediction (which would no longer be meaningful), but to make a new one whose background is the collapse of the Babylonian empire: he revises rather than repeats, and hence he may implicitly interpret. He passes over all reference to a Davidic king along with the descriptions of the northerners. Deutero-Isaiah also describes the nexus between Israel and the gentiles in a new way. In Isaiah, the nation that walked in darkness and saw a great light was Israel. In Deutero-Isaiah, other nations walk in darkness, and Israel is the light to which they come.

Some scholars would deny that the source actually predates Deutero-Isaiah. Clements (*Isaiah*) characterizes 5.30 as an exilic interpretation of the preceding eighth-century passage. But there is no ground for dating the verse to the exile, even if 5.30 is separate from the preceding passage (for evidence of the disjunction, see Barth, 192–93). Clements further avers that the "picture of appalling distress and anguish" in 8.22 must refer to "the aftermath of the Babylonian destruction of Jerusalem." Clements's attempt to limit the reference to the events of 587 is unwarranted; the language of the verse, which is quite general, describes many other situations equally well. Most critics, however, date these verses to an earlier period. Skinner sees the end of chapter 8 as describing the Assyrian takeover of parts of the northern kingdom mentioned in 8.23, which occurred in c. 733 and is described in 2 Kgs 15.29.

58. Though Mettinger presents important arguments that even here the servant is the nation (38–43).

59. Some of these parallels were noted by Bernard Gosse, "Isaïe 52,13–53,12 et Isaïe 6," *RB* 98 (1991), 537–43, who suggests tentatively that chapter 53 may have influenced chapter 6 (see p. 543). As we shall see, the parallels reflect several typical features of Deutero-Isaianic allusion, which shows that chapter 6 is the source and 53 the borrowing. See also Williamson, 39–41.

60. So Tg, rather than MT's "you." See the discussions in Skinner and Torrey.

61. Read יִכ for MT's ןֵכ; so Torrey.

62. So NJPS.

63. Deutero-Isaiah may borrow from Isaiah 6 in Isaiah 40 as well; see Williamson, 37–38. However, Isaiah 40 contains elements of the prophetic call genre and of the

heavenly council scene (on the former, see especially Norman Habel, "The Form and Significance of the Call Narrative," *ZAW* 77 [1965], 314–16, and Begrich, 61; on the latter, see F. M. Cross, "The Council of YHWH in Second Isaiah," *JNES* 12 [1953], 274–77; on both, see the careful remarks of Roy Melugin, *The Formation of Isaiah 40–55* [Berlin: Walter de Gruyter, 1976], 82–86, and the sensitive reading of Stephen Geller, "Were the Prophets Poets?" *Prooftexts* 3 [1983], 217–18). Consequently, it is possible that the similarities result from a common use of set vocabulary associated with particular genres. On the other hand, since we know that Deutero-Isaiah often used Isaiah 6, and since Williamson shows that the linkages between Isaiah 6 and 40 are particularly close, the likelihood of a genuine allusion is strong. The allusion links the prophet of chapter 6 and the nation in chapter 40, and hence represents typology similar to that seen in Deutero-Isaiah's allusions to Jeremiah.

64. Gosse, 538, notes an additional link in which the verbal correspondence is less precise: the people are told not to understand or know (ע"בי, ד"עי) in 6.9; the servant will "have insight" (ישׂכיל) in 52.13. As Gosse notes, שׂכ"ל often appears alongside ד"עי and בי"ן (e.g., 41.20, 44.18), which strengthens the connection he suggests between 6.9 and 52.13.

65. Gosse stresses this element of reversal: the servant makes possible that which was impossible earlier, and hence the passage permits the contravening of chapter 6's pessimism (538–39).

66. As noted by Herbert Wolf, "The Relationship Between Isaiah's Final Servant Song (52:13–53:12) and Chapters 1–6," in *A Tribute to Gleason Archer*, ed. Walter Kaiser and Ronald Youngblood (Chicago: Moody, 1986), 252–53. Wolf further notes שׂב"ע in 1.11 and 53.11.

67. See Wolf, 254–56.

68. As noted already by H. L. Ginsberg, "The Arm of YHWH in Isaiah 51–63 and the Text of Isaiah 53:10–11," *JBL* 77 (1958), 156. The phrase from Ps 91.16, אֹרֶךְ יָמִים אַשְׂבִּיעֵהוּ ("I shall satisfy him for the length of his days"), lies behind Deutero-Isaiah's comment about the servant in Isa 53.10–11, יַאֲרִיךְ יָמִים . . . יִשְׂבָּע ("his days will be lengthened . . . he will be satisfied"). The reuse of this phrase involves the split-up pattern. The texts share additional roots as well: וְאַרְאֵהוּ ("I will show him") in Ps 91.16 parallels יִרְאֶה ("he will see") in Isa 53.10 and again in 53.11, while וְאֶעֱנֵהוּ ("I will answer him") in Ps 91.15 forms the basis for נַעֲנֶה ("he humbled himself") in 53.7; this latter parallel is a case of sound play.

69. Another case of typological linkage occurs in Isa 50.10–11, which refer back to Isa 5.30 and 8.22–9.1 (to which, as we have seen, he also alludes in 60.1–5). The servant in chapter 50, like the people in 9.1, goes about in darkness. In a bitter reversal that depends on a case of sound play, those who reject the servant (or reject the prophecy?) are told that they, too, will experience אוּר (*'ur*, "fire," 50.11) as a punishment, rather than אוֹר (*'or*, "light," 9.1). The allusion creates a typological connection between the servant in Deutero-Isaiah and the nation in Isaiah. The phrasing of 50.11

also echoes Isa 2.5 (reversing it in a bitter way): "Come let us go in the light of YHWH." It is significant that whenever Deutero-Isaiah alludes to the light imagery from Isaiah 9 or the redemption imagery from Isaiah 11, he usually hints at Isaiah 2 as well; so in 60.1–5 and 42.1–9.

70. D. Jones, "The Tradition of the Oracles of Isaiah of Jerusalem," *ZAW* 67 (1955), 245–46; Brevard Childs, *Introduction to the Old Testament as Scripture* (Philadelphia: Fortress Press, 1979), 329; Christopher Seitz, "Isaiah 1–66: Making Sense of the Whole," in *Reading and Preaching the Book of Isaiah*, ed. C. Seitz (Philadelphia: Fortress Press, 1988), 110. A similar view appeared already in Martin Buber, *The Prophetic Faith*, trans. Carlyle Witton-Davies (New York: Macmillan, 1949), 204. Buber suggests, however, that the "new things" prophesied by Deutero-Isaiah represent an "unfolding" (akin to what I term "reprediction") of Isaiah's message of salvation in the "former things."

71. See Haran, *RĪSHONÔT*, 23–28. Williamson (67–77) also recognizes that Deutero-Isaiah employs the term in several ways. Further, he suggests that Deutero-Isaiah's varied uses of the term depend on Isa 8.23, but the linkages between Isaiah 8 and the relevant texts in Deutero-Isaiah are too few and too broad to be significant.

72. The two examples I discuss in the body stem from Isaiah ben Amoṣ. Confirmations based on other prophets are rare. Isa 48.11 recalls Ezek 20.9, 24, 22 and thus reminds the audience of an older prediction that has come to fruition. Hos 2.19 is confirmed by Isa 54.8, 10 in an extended allusion discussed below. Besides the two cases of confirmation discussed in the body, an additional example occurs in Isa 59.11, in which the people repeat God's statement of disappointment in Isa 5.7, implicitly acknowledging that the punishment resulting from that disappointment has come to pass.

73. Williamson, 90–91. Williamson further argues that the sense of תורה in Deutero-Isaiah as teaching rather than law results from Isaianic influence.

74. Reading imperatives (שִׂכְרוּ, נְעוּ) with LXX rather than MT's affix forms (נָעוּ, שָׁכְרוּ). Cf. Skinner and Clements, *Isaiah*.

75. The words in parentheses are often regarded as glosses; so Skinner, Clements, and Fishbane (*Biblical*, 50). These scholars deem the gloss a misreading of the verse which "transformed a national oracle of condemnation into a rebuke of false prophets" (Fishbane). However, the point of mentioning prophets may be to announce that *God* is misleading the prophets, or that He is using the prophets to mislead the people (as the parallel with 6.10 suggests): it is by means of the prophets that YHWH makes the people blind so that they can receive even greater punishment. (See the convincing, if disturbing, exegesis of Matitiahu Tsevat, "The Throne Vision of Isaiah," in *The Meaning of the Book of Job and Other Biblical Studies* [New York: Ktav, 1980], 165–66, 170–71.) If this is so, the explanatory notes I have put in parentheses, whether or not added by a later hand, match the message of the passage, which remains an oracle of national condemnation. (On the distinction between glosses

and explanatory notes, see Yair Zakovitch, *An Introduction to Inner-Biblical Inter-pretation* [Even-Yehuda: Reches, 1992], 28 [Heb.].)

76. Omitting the repeated word כוס, which is an explanatory note for the obscure older word קבעת.

77. On these allusions, see note 14 above and the discussion of Isa 57.16 on p. 91.

78. Several other passages in Deutero-Isaiah refer to the nation Israel as blind, deaf, or dwelling in darkness (42.18–20, 42.25, 43.8, 49.8, 59.10). Deutero-Isaiah's use of this theme may have been influenced by Isaiah's frequent reference to the nation's blindness (see especially Isa 6.9–10, and cf. 9.1, 29.9 and 18f., 32.3–4), as several scholars have suggested. If this is so, then Deutero-Isaiah's use of the theme belongs under the category of fulfillment. However, the connection to the blindness motifs in Isaiah and Deutero-Isaiah can be, and has been, overstressed. Williamson, 49–51, sees the influence of Isa 6.9–10 in these passages, but many of the parallels he notes are too broad or involve too few vocabulary items to be considered allusions. Further, Deutero-Isaiah's references to the people as dwelling in darkness usually appear alongside portrayals of the people as imprisoned in the exile or alongside motifs from royal ideologies, such as YHWH as liberator. Thus the parallels between the two prophets here may depend on their common use of standard motifs. Indeed, similar descriptions of the nation appear elsewhere in the Hebrew Bible (see especially Jer 5.21, though Williamson, 50, argues that the blindness motif in Deutero-Isaiah is closer to Isaiah than to Jeremiah). For a discussion of related texts in the Book of Isaiah and elsewhere, see Craig Evans, *To See and Not Perceive: Isaiah 6.9–10 in Early Jewish and Christian Interpretation* (Sheffield: Sheffield Academic Press, 1989), 19–52.

If Deutero-Isaiah's use of the motif indeed depends on Isaiah's, it is interesting that Deutero-Isaiah avoids mentioning the origin Isaiah posited for the people's blindness in chapter 6—viz., YHWH's covering their eyes. Possible exceptions to this tendency may include Isa 59.7–10 and Isa 63.17, but even they are quite subtle. Deutero-Isaiah does not want to recall Isaiah's image of God as striking the nation with blindness to prevent their repentance. In this respect, he resembles later inter-preters of Isaiah, on which see the traditional commentaries to Isa 6.9–10.

79. Or, "my man" (Heb. אִישִׁי).

80. Or, "my master," "my husband."

81. Further, the text itself effects a confirmation: as Buber notes (208), in Hos 2.19, God promised to return to Israel, and in Isa 54.8, 10 God announces that He has done so.

82. On the tendency of some Israelites to equate YHWH and Baal or to view YHWH as a baal, see H. W. Wolff, *Hosea*, trans. G. Stansell (Philadelphia: Fortress Press, 1974), 49–50; Frank Moore Cross, *Canaanite Myth and Hebrew Epic: Essays in the History of the Religion of Israel* (Cambridge, Mass.: Harvard University Press, 1973), 191; Jeffrey Tigay, "Israelite Religion: The Onomastic and Epigraphic Evi-dence," in *Ancient Israelite Religion: Essays in Honor of Frank Moore Cross*, ed. P. D.

Miller, P. D. Hanson, and S. D. McBride (Philadelphia: Fortress Press, 1987), 163; John Day, s.v. "Baal," in *The Anchor Bible Dictionary*, ed. David Noel Freedman et al. (New York: Doubleday, 1992), 3: 548.

83. See Day, 547–48; M. D. Cassuto, s.v. "Baal," in *Encyclopaedia Biblica* (Jerusalem: Mossad Bialik, 1950–88), 2: 285. Schramm argues (111, 128–32) that the syncretistic cult of YHWH continued into the post-exilic period; nevertheless, evidence of the cult of Baal among Jews in the exile and Persian era is lacking.

84. Deutero-Isaiah alludes again to Hosea 1–2 in 62.4–5. Like the longer allusion in Isaiah 54, this passage shares with Hosea the theme of naming Israel. It also refers to the land of Israel as being בעולה (married to YHWH) once again, thus pointing back to the Hosea passage while using the root בע"ל in a positive rather than negative manner.

Deutero-Isaiah may allude to Hosea in other passages, but some of these cases are questionable. According to H. L. Ginsberg ("Introduction," 21b), Isa 43.10–11 contain an allusion to Hos 13.4. Hosea complains that the people have failed to recognize that YHWH is the only redeemer; Deutero-Isaiah affirms that YHWH really is the redeemer, and hence that the people will be saved. The shared items are relatively common, however, so that one cannot consider this a definite case of allusion. Isa 43.27 refers to the patriarchs in a negative fashion. Ginsberg ("Introduction," 21a) points out that this reference reflects a tradition also found in Hos 12.3–5. Deutero-Isaiah does not borrow specific vocabulary or even plot elements from that passage. Hence it is possible that Deutero-Isaiah knows of this view of the patriarchs from some wider tradition. On the use of the divorce theme in Isa 50.1, which resembles Hosea in some ways, see my discussion of the allusion to Deut 24.1–3 in Chapter 5.

85. Isa 51.1 contains a motif and vocabulary item also found in Ezek 33.24, but this parallel may result from their common use of an otherwise unattested pattern. Isa 54.10 and Ezek 34.25 and 37.26 all depend on Hosea 1–2, but the passages in Deutero-Isaiah and Ezekiel share one phrase not found in the common source, ברית שלום. Thus it is possible that Deutero-Isaiah relied not only on Hosea but also on Ezekiel. (It is clear that Deutero-Isaiah did not depend on Ezekiel exclusively, since some of the vocabulary and motifs he borrowed from Hosea do not appear in Ezekiel.)

Many other parallels between Ezekiel and Deutero-Isaiah exist, but, as Cassuto notes in listing them ("Formal," 160–71), they are not likely to be cases of allusion or echo. The two prophets were separated by a single generation, and both were active in the Judean community in Babylon. In some cases, similarities between their books reflect the two prophets' shared historical circumstances and concerns; in others, the parallels result from the prophets' common use of Jeremiah.

86. See Cassuto, "Formal," 174–76. Many of these cases, however, are rather weak, containing little vocabulary or consisting of words that appear together elsewhere in the Bible. Further, several examples stem from chapter 3.14–20 of Zephaniah, which many critics regard as exilic. Cf. Cassuto, "Formal," 176.

87. For examples of this vocabulary, see the (perhaps overly) exhaustive lists in Leon Liebreich, "The Composition of the Book of Isaiah," *JQR* 46 (1955–56), 276–77, and *JQR* 47 (1956–57), 127, and Rachel Margalioth, *The Indivisible Isaiah* (Jerusalem: Sura Institute and New York: Yeshiva University, 1964), esp. 216–18; for themes the chapters share, see Sweeney, *Isaiah*, 21–24 and references there. Most of these parallels consist simply of individual words that fail to display patterns of reuse or transformation. (Indeed, much of this vocabulary results from the shared themes of sacrifice, sin, and punishment, which are hardly uncommon and necessarily suggest certain words, as Anthony Tomasino notes, "Isaiah 1.1–24 and 63–66 and the Composition of the Isaianic Corpus," *JSOT* 57 [1993], 82 n. 4. Those parallels are of little significance, and they cannot by themselves demonstrate that one text is based on the other.) For a discussion of the implication of these parallels regarding the composition history of the Book of Isaiah, see my article, "Allusions and Illusions," 178–83, and also David Carr, "Reading Isaiah from Beginning to End," in *New Visions*, ed. Melugin and Sweeney, 182–217.

88. See above, note 14.

89. Williamson (59–60), who also notes the parallel, asks whether Jeremiah 18 rather than Isaiah 29 might have served as Deutero-Isaiah's source. He argues persuasively that the connection with Isaiah 29 is much closer.

90. Many other cases of parallels that lack significant thematic revision have been proposed (especially by scholars interested in the alleged redactional unity of the Book of Isaiah), but few contain enough items to be convincing. A single example of this tendency will suffice: Steck sees a connection between 56.7–8 and various Isaianic verses such as 1.11 and 11.11 ("Zu jüngsten Untersuchungen von Jes 56,1–8; 63,7–66,24," in *Studien zu Tritojesaja* [Berlin: Walter de Gruyter, 1991], 247–48). But the vocabulary items shared between 56.7 and 1.11 are all concerned with sacrifice and hence result from the common topic rather than from any compositional connection between the verses (whether redactional or allusive). Isa 56.8 and 11.11 both make use of a widespread vocabulary cluster (cf. Deut 30.4, Mic 2.12, and Ps 147.2), and thus there is no reason to suspect that one is related specifically to the other.

91. See above, note 4 to this chapter.

92. This conclusion has important ramifications for recent work on the unity of the Book of Isaiah, on which see my article "Allusions and Illusions" and Carr, "Reading." Cf. also my article "The Scroll of Isaiah as Jewish Scripture, or, Why Jews Don't Read Books," in *Society of Biblical Literature 1996 Seminar Papers* (Atlanta: Scholars Press, 1996), esp. 228–29 n. 10.

93. By "statement," I mean a verse or set of verses used by Deutero-Isaiah in at least one particular allusion. Thus, I am counting Isa 1.12–15 separately from Isa 1.28–29, because he alludes to each statement separately and because they are discrete subunits of a single longer composition; similarly, I count Jer 31.1–9 and 31.31–36 separately, because the allusions to each occur in different passages and because they

are discrete subunits. Long units which Deutero-Isaiah utilizes repeatedly as units (such as Isaiah 6 or Jeremiah 3) I count as a single case. One might define "statement" differently, but this does not affect my argument, since I am interested in a ratio, not an absolute number; what matters is that I have used the same criteria for defining statements from each source.

94. The complete list is as follows. I put the doubtful cases in parentheses.

Jer 1.9–10 // Isa 51.16

Jer 2.6–8 // Isa 63.11–12

Jer 2.23–25 // Isa 57.10

Jer 2.32 // Isa 49.14–18

(Jer 3.1 // Isa 50.1)

Jer 3.12–14, 21–22 // Isa 57.16

Jer 3.16–18 // Isa 60.7–13

(Jer 4.13 // Isa 66.15)

Jer 4.20 // Isa 51.19

Jer 4.22–25 // Isa 41.23–29, (Isa 60.18–22)

(Jer 6.7 // Isa 60.18, 65.3)

Jer 6.13–14 // Isa 57.17–21

Jer 6.20, 22 // Isa 60.6–9

(Jer 7.13 // Isa 65.12)

Jer 9.6 // Isa 48.10–11

(Jer 9.8 // Isa 57.6)

(Jer 10.1–16 // Isa 40.19–22, 41.6–7, 44.9–14)

Jer 10.17–25 // Isa 54.1–5, 52.13–53.12

Jer 11.18–21 // Isa 51.12–14, 53.3–18

Jer 12.7–13 // Isa 56.9–57.5

Jer 14.2–9, 12 // Isa 42.10–16, 59.9–19

Jer 15.2, 5 // Isa 51.19

(Jer 15.13 // Isa 65.13)

Jer 16.16–18 // Isa 40.2, 61.7, 65.6–7

Jer 20.7–13 // Isa 50.4, 9

(Jer 25.9, 49.13 // Isa 34.2, 58.12)

Jer 27.5–6 // Isa 45.12–13

Jer 29.4–6 // Isa 65.18–23

Jer 29.10–14 // Isa 55.6–12

(Jer 30.10–11, 1.8 // Isa 41.8–15, 43.1–7, 44.1–3)

Jer 30.17 // Isa 62.12

(Jer 30.24 // Isa 55.11)

Jer 31.1–9 // Isa 35.4–10, 41.14–16, 43.5–9, 55.12

Jer 31.16 // Isa 40.9–10

Jer 31.31–36 // Isa 42.5–9, 51.15, 54.10, 59.21

Jer 33.3 // Isa 48.6

Jer 33.7–9 // Isa 61.1–4

(Jer 48.3 // Isa 51.19, 59.7, 60.18)

(Jer 49.23 // Isa 57.20)

95. The complete list follows. I put the doubtful cases in parentheses.

(1.5–6 // 53.4–5)

(1.12, 15 // 65.1–3, 24)

1.28–29 // 65.12–13, 66.17, 24

2.1–4 // 51.3–5, 60.5–7

2.5–21 // 57.5–20

5.7 // 59.11

(5.11 // 56.12)

5.26 // 49.22, 62.10

(5.27 // 40.28–31)

5.30 // 50.10–11, 60.1–5

6 // (40.1–8), (40.21–28), 44.9–14, 49.19–20, 52.13–53.12, (54.1–3, 14), 57.5–20, (62.4), (63.17)

(8.16–18 // 50.4–9)

8.22–9.1 // 50.10–11, 60.1–5

11.1–10 // 42.1–9, (53.1–12), 60.17–61.1, (65.1–2), 65.25

11.10–12.3 // 49.22, 62.10

14.24–25 // 46.9–13

(22.13f. // 56.12)

28.1–2 // 40.6–10

29.9–10 // 51.17–22

29.16 // 45.9–10

30.9–12 // 42.23–24, 56.10–57.6

30.28–33 // 66.12, 24

32.2–6 // 35.1–8

Most of these cases are mentioned in this chapter, either in the body of the text or in footnotes. In addition, Fishbane (in *Biblical*) includes 9.3 // 60.17 (discussed on p. 497), 10.22 // 66.12, 14 (p. 489), and 12.6 // 60.14 (p. 498 n. 103), though I count these as doubtful cases. I do not include here cases mentioned by other scholars which are so broad or involve so few significant parallels as to be coincidental or the result of common use of standard vocabulary clusters—e.g., 30.7 // 51.9–10 (discussed by Williamson, 83–86); 9.1 // 42.16 (ibid., 72–73); various references to 8.16–17 (ibid., 108–11).

96. By "passage" I mean a set of verses over which the markers pointing back to the source are spread. These can be short (e.g., 40.2, which alludes to Jer 16.16–18, or 45.9–10, which allude to Isa 29.16) or long (e.g., 42.10–16, which allude to Jer 14.1–20, or 42.1–9, which allude to Isaiah 11). If a passage alludes to more than one passage in the source, I am counting it as a single case (e.g., 57.5–20, which allude to Isa 2.5–21 and Isaiah 6; and 51.12–16, which allude to Jer 1.9–10, 11.19, and 31.35). Again, one could define "passage" differently or count cases of allusion in some other way, but I am interested in the relative frequency rather than absolute numbers; what matters is a consistent method.

CHAPTER FOUR

1. Otto Eissfeldt discusses this problem aptly ("The Promises of Grace to David in Isaiah 55:1–5," in *Israel's Prophetic Heritage*, ed. B. Anderson and W. Harrelson [New York: Harper, 1962], 196–97): "In my opinion, the similarities between certain psalms and the words of Second Isaiah can and are to be accounted for by the fact that both have drawn upon a common source. With this in mind, one should be very cautious about designating particular psalms of our Psalter as prototypes of particular verses of Second Isaiah, e.g., the 'enthronement psalms' as model of those poems in Isa. 50–55 reminiscent of them." Eissfeldt further points out (as does Claus Westermann, e.g., in his commentary to Isa 40.22 in *Isaiah 40–66: A Commentary*, trans. D. Stalker [Philadelphia: Westminster Press, 1969]) that "the psalms preserved for us in the Old Testament represent only a minute portion of the much richer poetic materials once possessed by Israel," so that it is also likely that certain psalms not known to us served as sources for Deutero-Isaiah.

2. In light of Ugaritic literature, it is clear that this tradition was not only a Hebrew one. As many have noticed, the psalms often draw on the same vocabulary clusters found in Canaanite hymns and epics. Thus Psalms 18, 29, 46, and others describe YHWH's theophany using language earlier found in Ugaritic descriptions of Baal's manifestations (including terms such as נתן קול ישב ה׳/בעל, בע״ר, גע״ר, במתי, ארץ, and various words meaning "break," "shatter," and "thunder"). See especially Frank Moore Cross, *Canaanite Myth and Hebrew Epic: Essays in the History of the Religion of Israel* (Cambridge, Mass.: Harvard University Press, 1973), 147–63 (and on vocabulary regarding the god El, such as כונן and קנה, 69).

3. See Hugo Greßmann, "Die literarische Analyse Deuterojesajas," *ZAW* 34 (1914), 283, 293–96. Joachim Begrich, in his *Studien zu Deuterojesaja* (Munich: Chr. Kaiser, 1969), 67, disagrees, arguing that actual psalm forms are rare in Deutero-Isaiah. He nonetheless acknowledges the strong influence of psalms on the prophet, who created new literary forms based on psalm forms such as laments and songs of thanks. See Begrich, 16–20, 61–65, 66.

4. For example, the words יוֹרְדֵי הַיָּם וּמְלֹאוֹ in Isa 42.10, which recall a line appearing in Pss 96.11 and 98.7, יִרְעַם הַיָּם וּמְלֹאוֹ. See further parallels noted by H. L. Ginsberg, "A Strand in the Cord of Hebraic Hymnody," *ErIsr* 9 (Albright Volume; 1969), 45–50. Ginsberg argues that Deutero-Isaiah did utilize Psalms 96 and 98 specifically, but his arguments are less than definitive, and he does not adequately discuss other possible reasons for the parallels.

5. See Westermann's commentary.

6. Because the traditions upon which ancient Hebrew poets drew are often shared with other Canaanite languages, one must further make sure that parallels between Deutero-Isaiah and a psalm do not result from their common use of a vocabulary cluster known from Ugaritic texts as well. Isa 51.9–10 recall Ps 89.6–14, Ps 87.12–20 and other texts, but it is not clear that Deutero-Isaiah knew those psalms specifically; all these texts display vocabulary relating to the defeat of Yam/Sea, and those same vocabulary items appear in several Ugaritic texts, on which see, e.g., Cross, *Canaanite*, 112–20.

7. This may be the case with the parallels between Isaiah 42 and Psalms 96 and 98 mentioned in the previous paragraph. Even if one argues that the similarities result from borrowing, it is not clear who borrowed from whom. If Sigmund Mowinckel is right that Psalms 96–98 are royal psalms from the First Temple period, then they influenced Deutero-Isaiah, as Ginsberg argues (in "Strand," and see further his article "The Arm of YHWH in Isaiah 51–63 and the Text of Isaiah 53:10–11," *JBL* 77 [1958], 152–56). But Moshe Weinfeld ("Universalism and Particularism in the Period of the Return to Zion," *Tarbiz* 33 [1964], 235 n. 41; reprinted in *Likkutei Tarbiz: A Biblical Studies Reader*, ed. Moshe Weinfeld [Jerusalem: Magnes, 1979], 42–57 [Heb.]) rejects the First Temple dating and holds that these psalms are from the period of the return to Zion. In that case, it is possible that Deutero-Isaiah influenced the psalmists; or that the authors of all these texts rely on common traditions that were especially strong in the exile. See further Marc Brettler, *God Is King: Understanding an Israelite Metaphor* (Sheffield: Sheffield Academic Press, 1989), 148 and 191 n. 41.

8. Armond Kaminka, "Expressions of Moses and Psalms in Isaiah," in *Meḥqarim* (Tel Aviv: Devir, 1938), 1: 159–63; Moshe Seidel, "Parallels Between the Book of Isaiah and the Book of Psalms," *Sinai* 38 (1955–56), passim [Heb.] (and see also Ginsberg, "Strand" and "Arm"). The studies by Kaminka and Seidel include lists of borrowings but almost no discussion of the use to which the source has been put or the transfor-

mations of the earlier language. Nor do they discuss the difficulties of distinguishing borrowings from coincidental similarities of vocabulary. Nonetheless, they provide a useful starting point for the student of inner-biblical exegesis and allusion.

Yehezkel Kaufmann, *Toledot ha-Emunah ha-Yisraelit* (Tel Aviv: Mosad Bialik and Devir, 1937–1956), discusses points of contact between Deutero-Isaiah and various psalms especially in II: 717–18, 723–25. Skinner does so throughout his commentary on Isa 40–66 (*The Book of the Prophet Isaiah: Chapters XL–LXVI*, rev. ed. [Cambridge: Cambridge University Press, 1917).

Moses Buttenweiser noted manifold points of contact between Deutero-Isaiah and Psalms 68, 85, 93, 96, 97, 98, 107, and 126; see *The Psalms Chronologically Treated with a New Translation* (Chicago: University of Chicago Press, 1938), 213–16, 257–343. Buttenweiser's claim that Deutero-Isaiah actually wrote these psalms is hardly likely; see Brettler, *God*, 148 and 191 n. 41.

9. In particular, Psalms 103, 107, and 147 include a remarkable number of parallels with passages throughout Deutero-Isaiah (on which see Seidel, "Parallels," passim; Kaufmann, *Toledot*, II: 717, 725; and Ginsberg, "Strand," 48–50). However, it is likely that all three psalms are post-exilic.

Avi Hurvitz demonstrates conclusively on a linguistic basis that Psalm 103 is post-exilic; see *The Transition Period in Biblical Hebrew: A Study in Post-Exilic Hebrew and Its Implications for the Dating of Psalms* (Jerusalem: Mossad Bialik, 1972), 107–30 [Heb.]. Additional linguistic evidence to support this dating is provided by Elisha Qimron, "Concerning the Language of the Second Temple Period in the Book of Psalms," *BM* 23 (1977), 144–45 [Heb.].

Ps 107.3 refers in the past tense to the ingathering of exiles from many directions: וּמֵאֲרָצוֹת קִבְּצָם מִמִּזְרָח וּמִמַּעֲרָב מִצָּפוֹן וּמִיָּם. A *prediction* regarding the ingathering of exiles could be pre-exilic, since prophets had anticipated both an exile and a return since the eighth century at the latest. But this psalm's reference to the ingathering as an accomplished fact almost certainly dates from after 538 B.C.E. One might argue that the line is a prediction couched in the prophetic perfect, but the prophetic perfect does not appear in Psalms (see GKC § 106n). Moreover, Hurvitz cites several words in Ps 107 which are probable indicators of LBH: מַעֲרָב in v. 3 (which appears in exilic and post-exilic texts but not in pre-exilic ones), שׁת"ק in v. 30, and מָחוֹז in v. 30 (see Hurvitz, *Transition*, 173 and references there). See further Qimron, 145–46.

The reference to the building of Jerusalem and the ingathering of exiles in Ps 147.2 need not be post-exilic or even exilic, since pre-exilic writers already anticipated not only the destruction of Jerusalem (e.g., Micah 3.12) and the exile but also a return from exile and a renewal of life in Judah (indeed, this is implicit in Micah's metaphor). The post-exilic dating of Psalm 147 becomes clear, however, from two strong indicators of LBH: the word יְכַנֵּס in v. 2, which is the LBH replacement of the words יְקַבֵּץ / יֶאֱסֹף found in pre-exilic texts (see Mark Rooker, *Biblical Hebrew in Transition:*

The Language of the Book of Ezekiel [Sheffield: Sheffield Academic Press, 1990], 156; Hurvitz, *Transition*, 175 n. 308); and the root שׁב״ח in v. 12, which is limited to LBH and later forms of Hebrew (see Hurvitz, *Transition*, 88–91).

10. Westermann suggests that at times Deutero-Isaiah composes a passage so that it mirrors the form of a psalm of lament. In these cases, the three elements of an individual lament (the charge against God, the first-person lament, and the description of enemies) occur, but each is reversed or given a response. See his commentary on 49.14–26 and 51.9–11. Kaufmann (*Toledot*, II: 717 n. 105) argues that stock psalm-phrases appear in Deutero-Isaiah, but that the prophet consistently uses them in a new way. Certain descriptions of YHWH's might in Psalms always refer to the past, but in Deutero-Isaiah they refer to the present or the future. For example, both Ps 74.13 and Isa 51.9 mention God's arm (זְרוֹעַ ה׳). The psalmists recall its power over the sea in the past (either at the creation of the world or at the Exodus), but Deutero-Isaiah at once recalls its past victories over the sea and predicts similar victories in the near future. In fact, Kaufmann argues (*Toledot*, II: 717–18, 724–25), Deutero-Isaiah and other prophets often use traditional motifs that referred to nature, creation, or past events in psalms, but as they do so, they endow them with national or es-chatological meaning. (Greßmann makes a similar point, 284.)

These examples of Deutero-Isaiah's use of older material are not cases of literary allusion, and hence they go somewhat beyond the scope of this study. Nonetheless, like the allusions which I discuss, they give witness to the prophet's transformations of older biblical material. Greßmann aptly summarizes Deutero-Isaiah's use of these forms: his hymns relate not so much to "den Lobpreis Gottes, sondern auf das spezifisch Prophetische, die Wirkung auf den Menschen. Die Hymnen dienen ihm nur als Begleitmotive; sie sollen die prophetische Verkündigung unterstützen, die Gottesworte glaubhaft machen. . . . Man muß sie überdies scharf von den Hymnen des Psalters unterscheiden. Die lyrisch-geistlichen Hymnen sind in der Regel selb-ständig, die prophetischen niemals. Jene besingen die Taten Gottes in der Ver-gangenheit, diese dagegen meist die der Zukunft" (Greßmann, 294–95).

11. Seidel ("Parallels," 343) asserts that Deutero-Isaiah borrowed again from Ps 37.26–29 in Isa 61.7–9, which is a strong possibility. His suggestion (343) and that of Kaminka (43) that Isa 58.10–14 borrow from Ps 37.4–6, 34 is much less likely.

One might object that Psalm 37 is a wisdom psalm, and that wisdom psalms are uniformly post-exilic, so that Deutero-Isaiah cannot have borrowed from it. How-ever, Hurvitz demonstrates that some wisdom psalms are pre-exilic, even though most are post-exilic (Avi Hurvitz, *Wisdom Language in Biblical Psalmody* [Jerusalem: Magnes, 1991], 129–31 [Heb.]). Hurvitz finds elements of LBH to be "*completely lacking*" in Ps 37 (131, emphasis his; on the psalm as a wisdom text, see *Wisdom*, 75–93).

12. Some might wonder whether Psalm 132 predates Deutero-Isaiah, since psalms

from the last of the five divisions of the Psalter (Psalms 107–50) are generally thought to be late (see the references in Hurvitz, *Transition*, 172). But this characterization of the last part of the Psalter is imprecise. Nahum Sarna points out that in all likelihood the fourth and fifth books of the Psalter were originally a single book; the doxology that creates a division between Psalms 106 and 107 was probably added secondarily so that the Psalter would have the same number of books as the Pentateuch (see Nahum Sarna, s.v. "Psalms, Book of," in *Encyclopedia Judaica* [Jerusalem: Keter, 1971], 13: 1308–09). Book 4/5 includes within it diverse earlier collections (Sarna, 1310), and some of these collections include pre-exilic and exilic material. Thus the presence in Book 4/5 of a psalm that could have been known to Deutero-Isaiah need not seem surprising.

Moreover, Psalm 132 contains internal evidence of a pre-exilic dating. Artur Weiser points out, "Since the sacred Ark is mentioned in vv. 7f. and since the intercession in v. 10 and the promise in vv. 17f. are intended for the king, the psalm must originate in the pre-exilic period" (*The Psalms: A Commentary*, trans. Herbert Hartwell [Philadelphia: Westminster Press, 1962], 779). Further, so far as I can tell, none of the morphological, syntactic, or lexical features of LBH identified by Hurvitz, Qimron, or Rooker appears in the psalm.

13. My translation follows the LXX, which has only one verb: δοθῆναι τοῖς πενθοῦσιν Σιων δόξαν ἀντὶ σποδοῦ. The MT has two verbs, one of which lacks an object: לָשׂוּם לַאֲבֵלֵי צִיּוֹן לָתֵת לָהֶם פְּאֵר תַּחַת אֵפֶר (so also 1QIsaᵃ). It is possible that the LXX reflects an older text that had either לָשׂוּם or לָתֵת (evidence for this reading may appear in some biblical citations in rabbinic manuscripts, which omit לָתֵת לָהֶם; see Moshe Goshen-Gottstein, *The Hebrew University Bible: The Book of Isaiah* [Jerusalem: Magnes, 1995]), while the MT and 1QIsaᵃ provide a conflated reading that includes both these synonyms. Alternatively, an object of the first verb found in the MT may have fallen out (Charles Torrey, in his *The Second Isaiah: A New Interpretation* [New York: Scribners, 1928], speculates that the original reading was לָשׂוּם לֵב לַאֲבֵלֵי צִיּוֹן לָתֵת לָהֶם), and the LXX may have smoothed out the translation by omitting the now-useless verb (cf. Goshen-Gottstein's remark on the LXX as a condensation of its *Vorlage*). It is impossible to decide between the two explanations.

14. Reading יָרֵשׁוּ instead of the MT's יִירָשׁוּ, which is difficult; for the text-critical discussion, see Chap. 2, nn. 82 and 83. On the other hand, if the attempts to preserve the MT are correct, the word יָרֵנּוּ is an additional marker, since יְרַנֵּנוּ is the last word of Psalm 132.9.

15. Further, verses 10–11 ("I greatly rejoice . . .") may be spoken by the city. The speaker of those verses is bedecked with jewelry; in Isa 49.14–18 YHWH predicted that Zion would wear jewels. Great wealth from the nations is brought to the subject of verses 10–11 here; in Isa 60.1–7 the wealth of nations was brought to Zion. For the idea that vv. 10–11 are spoken by Jerusalem, see Targum and Radak. Alternatively, it is

possible that the speaker in this verse is the nation, which ultimately benefits from that wealth and is served by foreign kings according to this passage (v. 5) as well as 49.7, 23. See ibn Ezra as well as Radak's second reading.

16. Thus the split-up pattern results in the same syntactic revision of the source which we saw in Isa 54.1–3's allusion to Jer 10.18–25; cf. the allusion in Isa 45.12–13 to Jer 27.5–6.

17. So Targum, ibn Ezra, Radak, and Skinner.

18. So Torrey. Isa 61.1–3 repeat much of the central phrasing of the first three servant songs. For a review of the evidence suggesting that this passage is a fifth servant song, see Skinner (who ultimately rejects the possibility).

19. See Cross, 233.

20. Much of the vocabulary shared by Psalm 72 and Isaiah 60 appears frequently in the Hebrew Bible, and several of the themes they share (in particular, that of the foreigners who bring tribute from throughout the world and abase themselves) are characteristic of royal and temple texts in the ancient Near East. Both themes appear in an inscription of the Babylonian king Marduk-apla-iddina discussed by René Follet, "Une nouvelle inscription de Merodach-Baladan II," *Bib* 35 (1954), 413–28. As a result, Pierre Grelot argues that the similarity between Psalm 72 and Isaiah 60 most likely results not from one text's reliance on the other but from common use of an ancient Near Eastern literary pattern (Pierre Grelot, "Un parallèle Babylonien d'Isaïe LX et du Psaume LXXII," *VT* 7 (1957), 319–21). But the parallels display the split-up pattern and fine case of sound play (Deutero-Isaiah's וּתְאַשּׁוּר [*ut°ashur*, "juniper"] recalls the psalm's יְאַשְּׁרוּהוּ [*y°ash°ruhu*, "they will proclaim him happy"]). Their presence suggests a closer relationship between Psalm 72 and Deutero-Isaiah.

Two additional aspects of the use of Psalm 72 in Isaiah 60 are of special interest. First, Deutero-Isaiah amplifies certain rhetorical figures from the source, as I note below, p. 164. Second, Ps 72.5 includes the words דּוֹר דּוֹרִים, while Isa 60.15 says, דּוֹר וָדוֹר. Semantically, these phrases are equivalent, but the later text includes the *wāw*-copulative. As Hurvitz points out (*Transition*, 70–73, and cf. S. R. Driver, *Introduction to the Literature of the Old Testament* [New York: Meridian, 1956], 538), in pre-exilic Hebrew, the idea "every X" is usually expressed by the syntagma "X X," (see, e.g., Exod 3.15), and only rarely "X וֹ X" (e.g., Deut 32.7). However, in post-exilic Hebrew, one finds the syntagma "X וֹ X" exclusively; and the later the text, the more likely one finds the syntagma "כֹל X וֹ X." In this passage, Deutero-Isaiah has borrowed the phrase from the pre-exilic psalm but added the *wāw*, which is normal in later texts. On the other hand, he has not added the word כֹל, which becomes normal in even later texts such as Ps 145.13, Esth 9.28, or 2 Chr 28.25.

21. Reading וּדְרָכִים, with Torrey, instead of MT's וְהָדוּרִים, 1QIsaᵃ's והררים, or 1QIsaᵇ's הרורים, all of which yield the sense "mountains," high places, so that the following verb would be translated "make flat." Goshen-Gottstein regards 1QIsaᵃ (which matches LXX) as most likely, noting the parallel with 40.4, etc. However, the

piel and hiphil of יש״ר usually take a word such as "road" or "way" as an object. The debate does not affect the analysis of the allusion.

22. In Masoretic Hebrew, this *kaf* is a fricative, since it has no *dāgēsh* while the *qōf* is a stop. It is likely, however, that in the pronunciation of biblical times both were realized as stops, creating an even greater similarity between them.

23. Further, the parallel between the psalm's הַוָּסְרוּ and the allusion's word for "make straight" represents yet another case of sound play. The resemblance remains intact whether we read אֲיַשֵּׁר with *Qere* (as I have done in my translation) or אוֹשֵׁר with *Ketib* and 1QIsa[b]. (The latter represents a hiphil of יש״ר, either as a shortened prefix [אוֹשֵׁר] or as a regular prefix [אוֹשֵׁר], or it may represent a piel [אֲוַשֵּׁר].) The marked item can be the basis even for the odd reading in 1QIsa[a], יאוֹשֵׁר (on which see E. Y. Kutscher, *The Language and Linguistic Background of the Isaiah Scroll (1QIsa[a])* [Leiden: E. J. Brill, 1974], 222).

24. See Nahum Sarna, "Psalm 89: A Study in Inner-Biblical Exegesis," in *Biblical and Other Studies*, ed. Alexander Altmann (Cambridge, Mass.: Harvard University Press, 1963).

25. Eissfeldt, "Promises," 202–7; see also Yehezkel Kaufmann, *The Babylonian Captivity and Deutero-Isaiah*, trans. C. W. Efroymson (New York: Union of American Hebrew Congregations, 1970), 188–89. Eissfeldt is hesitant regarding which text, if any, served as Deutero-Isaiah's source, but suggests that the parallels with Psalm 89 are impressive enough at least to suggest that Deutero-Isaiah may have known that psalm in particular. See his cautious remarks, "Promises," 199–200.

26. This is also the conclusion of Bernhard Anderson ("Exodus Typology in Second Isaiah," in *Israel's Prophetic Heritage: Essays in Honor of James Muilenburg*, ed. B. W. Anderson and W. Harrelson [New York: Harper, 1962], 191), who notes that "the berit olam is not made with a member of the house of David but with Israel (55.3)." In his later essay ("Exodus and Covenant in Second Isaiah and Prophetic Tradition," in *Magnalia Dei, the Mighty Acts of God: Essays on the Bible and Archaeology in Memory of G. Ernest Wright*, ed. F. M. Cross, W. E. Lemke, and P. D. Miller [Garden City, N.Y.: Doubleday, 1976], 343), Anderson points out the paradoxical nature of this shift. The prophet emphasizes the everlasting Davidic covenant, but ignores David, just as he stresses the Exodus event, but not the contingent Sinaitic covenant related to it.

27. See, e.g., exilic texts such as Jer 33.14–16 and Ezekiel 37, as well as post-exilic texts such as Zech 3.8, 6.12, 4.6–10 and Hag 1.12–15, 2.21–23. For a discussion, see Peter Ackroyd, *Exile and Restoration: A Study of Hebrew Thought of the Sixth Century B.C.* (Philadelphia: Westminster Press, 1968), 124–25, and Joseph Blenkinsopp, *A History of Prophecy in Israel*, 2d ed. (Louisville, Ky.: Westminster John Knox, 1996), 154.

28. For a different view, see Kaufmann, *Babylonian*, 236 n. 138 (cf. Eissfeldt, "Promises," 203, and Westermann's comment to Isa 60.17). But a comparison of Deutero-Isaiah and his sources reveals a pointed silence on the exilic prophet's part as

far as the Davidic family goes. He says nothing about the future of the monarchy because, in all likelihood, he believes that there is nothing to say—to wit, the monarchy has no future.

29. Eissfeldt, "Promises," 207.

30. Similarly, Deutero-Isaiah composed texts that respond to laments and confessions found in the Book of Jeremiah (e.g., Jer 14.2–9 // Isa 42.10–16; Jer 2.6–8 // Isa 63.11–13; Jer 7.13, 27 // Isa 65.12, 24). Further, in passages such as Isa 40.27 and Isa 49.14 he responds to utterances of dejected exiles, some of which may have come from laments unknown to us. See Moshe Greenberg, "The Citations in Ezekiel as a Background for the Prophecies," *BM* 17 (1972) [Heb.], and Westermann's commentary to Isa 40.27, 49.14, and 62.1.

31. For example, Isa 41.10–13 announces that those who pursue Israel will be put to shame, using many of the same words with which the speaker in Psalm 35 asked that his enemies be humiliated. Most of these terms also appear in Ps 70.2–6 (which is identical to Ps 40.14–18), and some appear in Ps 44.10–26. Deutero-Isaiah may be using stock vocabulary quite independently of these psalms, so that we cannot classify this as a case of allusion. Nevertheless, his use of the lament tradition and its vocabulary involves the same transformation from prayer to prophecy which we see in his allusions to specific texts.

32. One might argue against this for two reasons. First, the personal lament and prayer in Psalm 22 contains some, though not all, of these items: רח״ק (Ps 22.1, 12, 20); הושיע (22, and cf. 1); פלט (5, 8); מל״ט (6); מבטן (10, 11); צדקה (32). Further, many of the items shared by Isaiah 46 and Psalm 71 stem from either the lament tradition or the royal tradition better known to us from Mesopotamian royal inscriptions. Thus, terms like רחוק and הושיע appear in several laments, and the womb image appears in royal texts (as well as Jeremiah 1). If the author of the psalm and Deutero-Isaiah independently used both traditions, then the parallels noted above do not result from allusion. I nonetheless regard the likelihood of a borrowing from Psalm 71 as high for three reasons. First, additional vocabulary such as עד זקנה and עד שׂיבה does not appear in Psalm 22 or other laments. Second, the presence of the split-up pattern and a case of sound play is a strong indication of Deutero-Isaianic allusion. Finally, the consistent thematic pattern of response extends not only to the common lament vocabulary (which might result from Deutero-Isaiah's use of stock language) but also to the additional terms. At the same time, this example lays bare the particular difficulty of asserting the presence of allusion to a psalm.

33. Cf. Mayer Gruber, *The Motherhood of God and Other Studies* (Atlanta: Scholars Press, 1992) and "Feminine Similes Applied to the LORD in Second Isaiah," *Beer Sheva* 2 (1985), 75–84 [Heb.], though he does not discuss this passage.

34. Thus Deutero-Isaiah at once compares YHWH to a mother and notes that even this figure of YHWH's grace (like all metaphors describing the divinity) is

insufficient. See the sensitive reading of this passage in Marc Brettler, "Incompatible Metaphors for YHWH in Deutero-Isaiah," *JSOT* (forthcoming).

Other probable cases of response to a specific psalm include Isa 43.22–44.3, which rework Psalm 51. For a list of the shared items see Seidel, "Parallels," 277–78 (and note further the appearance in both texts of a verb from the root חל״ל, which constitutes a case of word play). The psalm is a confession, and in Deutero-Isaiah YHWH seems to respond positively to it. Although much of the shared vocabulary centers around the themes of sacrifice and sin, some identical phrases that appear infrequently elsewhere in the Hebrew Bible increase the probability of a borrowing. Cf. מחה פשע (which occurs elsewhere only in Isa 44.22) in Isa 43.25 and Ps 51.3, and למען תצדק parallel to שפ״ט in Isa 44.26 and Ps 51.6.

Another possible case of response occurs in Isa 50.2–3, which share themes with Ps 74.11–16. The psalmist asks YHWH why He, who was mighty enough in the past to destroy the sea and to blot out light, fails to act now. Deutero-Isaiah has YHWH proclaim that He is indeed capable of saving the nation, because He was mighty enough to destroy the sea and blot out light. However, the passages share few vocabulary items, and the themes of Exodus and creation which they share are very common, so that this case is very questionable.

Isa 52.3 ("You were sold off for nothing, and you will be redeemed for free") recalls the national lament of Ps 44.13 ("You sold off your people for no fortune"). It is difficult to ascertain whether Deutero-Isaiah knew this idea from Ps 44.13 specifically or from other exilic texts or popular sayings. Deutero-Isaiah confirms that the complaint was accurate but asserts that the people therefore still belong to YHWH, who can redeem them at will. Thus he responds to the lament not by denying it but by taking it literally: since YHWH in the psalm received no payment, the nation still belongs to Him.

35. Other vocabulary items in Isa 40.12–18 appear in Ps 89.7, 38. While it is likely that Deutero-Isaiah knew Psalm 89 (see the discussion of Isa 55.3–4 above), most of the words which these two passages share pertain to the theme of YHWH's incomparability, so that one cannot use them to build a case for Deutero-Isaiah's dependence on Psalm 89 in this passage.

36. Moshe Weinfeld, "God the Creator in Gen. 1 and in the Prophecy of Second Isaiah," *Tarbiz* 37 (1968), esp. 120–26. For a more extensive discussion, see Chapter 5 below.

37. Matitiahu Tsevat, "God and the Gods in Assembly," in *The Meaning of the Book of Job and Other Biblical Studies* (New York: Ktav, 1980), 131–47.

38. Deutero-Isaiah may borrow from Psalm 82 again in Isa 44.18, where the exact phrasing of the psalm's fifth verse, לֹא יָדְעוּ וְלֹא יָבִינוּ, appears. Seidel, "Parallels," 278, points out that by recognizing the source one can explain why the verbs in Isa 44.18 are plural, even though the subject in the previous verse is singular: the source, which

has plural verbs, is retained verbatim. Incongruities of this sort are a normal feature of ancient Near Eastern allusion. Rooker, 61–62, cites other cases (in Ezekiel, Ezra, and an Assyrian inscription) where "incongruity results from the author's lifting material from his source without harmonizing the older material to his text." Robert Alter observes a similar incongruity in the wording of Josh 2.4, which alludes to Exod 2.2 and retains its singular pronoun even when speaking of a plurality of persons; see *The Pleasures of Reading in an Ideological Age* (New York: Norton, 1996 [1989]), 118. Seidel, "Parallels," 352, finds another example of this phenomenon in Isa 65.9, where the feminine direct object marker in וִירֵשׁוּהָ is odd, since the object is the masculine noun הָרַי. He claims the source is Ps 69.36–37, where וִירֵשׁוּהָ makes sense. However, there are not enough markers in Isaiah 65 to allow one to assert with full confidence that Psalm 69 serves as a source.

39. So MT, which has a *wāw*-conversive form (וַיַּאֲכִילֵהוּ); the next verb must then be taken as a *yaqtul*-preterite. The LXX is similar, translating both with aorist verbs. Alternatively, one might read וְיַאֲכִילֵהוּ, which would yield the translation "He will feed them . . . I shall feed them." In the former case, the psalmist refers to God's benefactions for the people in the desert after the Exodus; in the latter, he patterns future benefactions on the earlier ones. Ibn Ezra's suggestion that the first verb refers to the past and the second to the future is less likely.

40. Some commentators and translators (e.g., Richard J. Clifford, *Fair Spoken and Persuading: An Interpretation of Second Isaiah* [New York: Paulist Press, 1984], NJPS) read these phrases as a present or future conditional: "If only you would pay attention to My commands, your well-being would be like a river." Such a translation avoids the problem of an apparently bleak section in the middle of this prophecy of salvation (on which see the next note). However, the protasis contains לוּ followed by a perfect, which most likely refers to a wished-for event that failed to occur in the past—i.e., a past subjunctive (see GKC § 106e, 151e); the apodosis contains *wāw*-conversive forms, which also are most likely to refer to events in the past (GKC § 111x, which notes that our verse is a possible exception, though the weight of the evidence there in fact suggests that one must translate the verse as a past subjunctive).

41. The regretful tone of verses 18–19 (from "thus says YHWH your redeemer" to "like its granules") leads some commentators to regard them as an interpolation added to the prophecy of salvation in which they are found; see, e.g., Westermann, who notes the resemblance between these verses and Psalm 81 and suggests that they were added, perhaps under the psalm's influence, in the post-exilic period. Three factors argue against such a view.

First, as Skinner notes, "the second Isaiah was capable of a great variety of emotions; and it is not inconceivable that in looking back over Israel's past history, and deploring the unbelief of the mass of his contemporaries, he should reflect on the different reception his message of hope would now have had if the nation had been responsive to the teaching of its God."

Second, in this section as in several others, Deutero-Isaiah describes the sins of the past and their consequences: because your ancestors did not obey the law, the promise vouchsafed to Abraham that his descendants would be as numerous as the sand did not come true. The point of such a declaration is not so much to reprove the people as to explain the apparent failure of YHWH's promises. That failure reflects no lack of loyalty or power on YHWH's part, since the people's own deeds have brought on the current situation. Ironically, by stressing the nation's past sins, Deutero-Isaiah demonstrates that the people need not despair: they still belong to YHWH, and He will reverse the situation now that His anger has run its course. (Cf. Yehoshua Gitay, *Prophecy and Persuasion: A Study of Isaiah 40–48* [Bonn: Linguistica Biblica, 1981], 222.)

Third, the markers which point back to Psalm 81 occur throughout this passage, not only in the verses allegedly added later. Thus the allusion itself makes clear that verses 18–19 are an integral part of the unit. Here, as elsewhere, Westermann's atomizing approach fails to take into account the organic nature of lengthy units.

42. Cf. both essays by Anderson ("Typology" and "Covenant").

43. Cf. Anderson, "Covenant," 341.

44. The ambiguity in Ps 81.15 of the word כמעט, which Deutero-Isaiah exploits in his allusion-cum-commentary, may have been noted by the LXX as well. When this word clearly means "quickly," LXX renders it ἐν τάχει (so in Ps 2.12); when it clearly means "as a trifle," it is translated παρὰ μικρὸν (see LXX Ps 72.2 [=MT Ps 73.2]) or παρὰ βραχὺ (LXX Ps 93.17 [=MT Ps 94.17] and elsewhere). None of these straightforward options appears in LXX Ps 80.15 (=MT Ps 81.15), where the word כמעט is translated with the ambiguous phrase ἐν τῷ μηδενὶ. Very few commentators or translators of Psalm 81 note the alternative that is suggested by Deutero-Isaiah and perhaps LXX; an exception is Martin Buber, who renders, "Wie leicht zwänge ihre Feinde ich nieder" (*Das Buch der Preisungen* [Köln: Jakob Hegner, 1963]).

Other cases in which Deutero-Isaiah repeats the message of a psalm occur elsewhere. In Isa 51.6–8, Deutero-Isaiah reuses the imagery and language of Ps 102.25–27; see Seidel, "Parallels," 335. Only in these two passages is the earth said to wear out like a garment; only in these two (and Ps 72.5, which also served as a source for Deutero-Isaiah) does the plural דורים appear. In both Isaiah 51 and Psalm 102 an author contrasts the figure of the worn-out earth with God and His eternal promises, which never wear thin. The allusion displays the typical Deutero-Isaianic tendency to extend a figure: the psalmist speaks of the earth wearing away like a garment and the heaven coming to an end; as Deutero-Isaiah repeats these tropes, he includes moths in the garment simile and adds that the inhabitants of the earth can die like lice. (A similar use of the image from Psalm 102 appears in Isa 50.9.)

Seidel, "Parallels," 279–80, argues that Isa 45.19–24 borrow the calls for universal praise of God from Ps 22.24, 28–30, but this claim is questionable due to the stereotypical nature of a call to praise. If indeed the verses in Deutero-Isaiah borrow from the psalm, it is not clear that recognizing the source alters one's reading of the later text, so that this is a case of echo.

Similarly, as noted already by Ginsberg ("Arm," 156), Isa 53.10–11 are based on Ps 91.16; this borrowing involves the split-up pattern and sound play. Again, however, Deutero-Isaiah merely repeats the older language without utilizing it strategically, so that this is a case of echo, not a genuine allusion.

45. Examples of Deutero-Isaiah's borrowing from the Book of Lamentations also appear in Kaufmann, *Toledot*, III: 592–93, and Norman Gottwald, *Studies in the Book of Lamentations* (London: SCM Press, 1962), 44–45.

46. See, e.g., Westermann, *Isaiah*, 19, 24, 59, 373.

47. As Gottwald, 44, already recognizes. Further, the Book of Lamentations may partake in a wider tradition of poems bemoaning the fate of cities destroyed by invaders, a tradition known from Sumerian and Akkadian texts. F. W. Dobbs-Allsopp describes the elements of the city-lament genre in Mesopotamia and Israel in *Weep, O Daughter of Zion: A Study of the City-Lament Genre in the Hebrew Bible* (Rome: Pontifical Biblical Institute, 1993), 167–82. None of the markers in Deutero-Isaiah's allusions to the Book of Lamentations appear in Allsopp's list of the genre's features, and thus we are justified in concluding that Deutero-Isaiah borrowed from the Book of Lamentations specifically rather than relying on a common ancient Near Eastern tradition. Further, scholars debate whether similarities between Israelite and Mesopotamian city laments are in fact to be attributed to the use of a common literary tradition or to the similarity of the situations poets in each culture faced. Among many studies, see William Gwaltney, "The Biblical Book of Lamentations in the Context of Near Eastern Literature," in *Scripture in Context II*, ed. William Hallo, J. Moyer, and L. Perdue (Winona Lake, Ind.: Eisenbrauns, 1983), 191–211, who attempts to trace specific connections between the biblical book and Mesopotamian prototypes; but see also the more skeptical view of Paul Ferris, *The Genre of Communal Lament in the Bible and the Ancient Near East* (Atlanta: Scholars Press, 1992), esp. 164–67.

48. Some might further object that the Book of Lamentations may not in fact stem from the early exilic period (see the summary of this position in Eissfeldt, "Introduction," 504, who does not find such arguments persuasive). If so, then Deutero-Isaiah could not have known these poems. Kaufmann, *Toledot*, III: 591–94, however, argues convincingly that the poems in Lamentations were most likely written at the outset of the exile, immediately after the destruction of the Temple.

49. The vocabulary may also recall Deutero-Isaiah's contention in Isa 40.28–31 that YHWH never tires, which is part of his polemic against the priestly creation account.

50. Omitting the repeated word כֹּס, which is a gloss for the obscure older word קֻבַּעַת. See, e.g., H. L. Ginsberg, "Ugaritic Texts and Textual Criticism," *JBL* 62 (1943),

111, and Christopher North, *The Second Isaiah: Introduction, Translation and Commentary to Chapters XL–LV* (Oxford: Oxford University Press, 1964).

51. This clause (אֵין־מְנַהֵל לָהּ מִכָּל־בָּנִים יָלָדָה) reverses another text in Lamentations: "She has none to comfort her from among all her lovers (אֵין־לָהּ מְנַחֵם מִכָּל־אֹהֲבֶיהָ)" (Lam 1.2). The substitution of מְנַהֵל (*mᵉnaheil*) for the source's מְנַחֵם (*mᵉnaḥeim*) is a case of sound play. The similarity results not only from the same verbal form but also from the proximity of both the marker and the marked item to אֵין and לָהּ (cf. a similar type of sound play, e.g., in the allusion to Jer 31.16 in Isa 40.9, discussed at the end of Chapter 2). Because the root נחם appears later in Isaiah 51, this borrowing includes the split-up pattern. (The LXX, Peshitta, and Tg Jonathan in Isa 51.18 read אֵין־מְנַחֵם לָהּ, which would be even closer to Lam 1.2 [though without sound play], but the MT is to be preferred. MT's מנהל provides a better parallel for the next phrase, "take by the hand," as North points out. Further, MT bemoans the fact that drunken Zion has no offspring to lead her and thus refers to a notion apparently current among Canaanites. A list of filial responsibilities in the Ugaritic epic of Aqhat makes clear that children in Canaanite culture had the responsibility to lead a drunk parent [see UT 2 Aqht I: 31–32 = KTA 1.17.I.30–31; translated by H. L. Ginsberg in ANET 150a, and cf. Ginsberg, "Ugaritic"]. I suspect that the LXX and Tg Jon read מנחם rather than מנהל because they are influenced by Lamentations to begin with.)

52. Cf. Umberto Cassuto, "On the Formal and Stylistic Relationship Between Deutero-Isaiah and Other Biblical Writers," in *Biblical and Oriental Studies*, trans. I. Abrahams (Jerusalem: Magnes, 1973), 169 n. 104.

53. In fact, 1QIsaᵃ and a single medieval MT manuscript do read ינחמך (see Goshen-Gottstein), which represents an attempt to solve the oddity of MT. Others might simply emend to מה (cf. Joseph ibn Caspi). Nonetheless, MT's *lectio difficilior* is to be preferred. Attempting to make sense out of the *lectio difficilior*, some commentators suggest that מי here should be rendered "how," which would mitigate the oddness of the text, allowing the translation, "How shall I comfort you?" Such a sense of the word מי seems to occur in Amos 7.2, 5; for this reading see Torrey on Isa 51.12 and 51.19 and Skinner on 51.19. Even if we follow the suggestion of Skinner and Torrey, the lack of parallelism between the third person in the first half of the verse and the first person here remains odd and requires explanation. (For another unsatisfying solution, see ibn Ezra and Radak, who gloss במי אנחמך, which similarly damages the verse's parallelism.)

54. It occurs, for example, in the allusion to Ps 89.5 in Isa 44.18. Cf. Seidel, "Parallels," 278 and 352. For other biblical and Mesopotamian examples, see Rooker, 61–62, and note the fine case described by Alter, *Pleasures*, 118.

55. Gottwald's list of parallels (44–45) contains some cases that may indeed result from borrowing: Lam 1.9 // Isa 47.7; Lam 1.1 // Isa 47.8; Lam 3.30 // Isa 50.6.

Kaufmann (*Toledot* III: 592 n.7) discusses an important case that Gottwald does not point out. Lam 4.15 describes the revulsion the nations feel toward the defeated Judeans: " 'Get away! Unclean!' they [the nations] shouted [of the Judeans]. 'Get away! Get away! Don't touch!' (סוּרוּ טָמֵא קָרְאוּ לָמוֹ סוּרוּ סוּרוּ אַל־תִּגָּעוּ). . . . They said among the nations, 'They shall not dwell there anymore!' " This verse may have provided the pattern for Isa 52.11, in which the prophet bids the people to leave Babylon: "Get away! Get away! Depart from there! Don't touch an unclean thing" (סוּרוּ סוּרוּ צְאוּ מִשָּׁם טָמֵא אַל־תִּגָּעוּ). One might doubt this case, since the root נג"ע and טמ"א appear together often in priestly literature (e.g., Lev 15.23, 27; 22.4; Num 19.22; Hag 2.13), and since טמא and קר"א appear together in Lev 13.45. The repetitive phrase סוּרוּ סוּרוּ in both makes them seem more similar. The line in Deutero-Isaiah also splits in half Lamentations' line, סוּרוּ סוּרוּ אַל־תִּגְּעוּ; this typical feature of Deutero-Isaianic allusion further supports the identification of this parallel as a borrowing. The reversal is an especially fine one, since the identity of the unclean people has switched: in Lamentations the Judeans are the unclean ones whom foreigners shun, while in Deutero-Isaiah the Babylonians are the unclean ones whom the Judeans shun.

Wolfgang Lau, *Schriftgelehrte Prophetie in Jes 56–66* (Berlin: Walter de Gruyter, 1994), 207–8, argues that Isa 59.3 quotes Lam 4.14 (so already Gottwald), but this suggestion is not fully persuasive, since only one phrase is parallel. He points out the rare grammatical form in both, which tightens the link between them (though only if the Masoretic tradition here is genuine).

Finally, one wonders whether the opening sentence of Deutero-Isaiah's prophecy, with its repetition of the imperative נַחֲמוּ ("comfort"), responds to the repeated cry of Lamentations, אֵין מְנַחֵם ("there is none to comfort"—1.2, 9, 16, 21; cf. 2.13, etc.). In any event, it is taken up that way very effectively by the Jewish lectionary cycle, in which Isaiah 40 is read several days after the Book of Lamentations. Kaufmann (*Toledot*, III: 592) points out that the comforters in Lamentations whose absence is bemoaned are the foreign nations, the erstwhile allies of the Judeans. But in Deutero-Isaiah YHWH (and, we should add, members of the heavenly court) are the comforters.

CHAPTER FIVE

1. Much the same can be said of his use of other biblical texts as well. He knew traditions ascribed to Jeremiah, for example, but surely not the Book of Jeremiah as it appears in either the Masoretic text or the Septuagint. Those editions of Jeremiah include biographical material and prose passages that seem not to have been known to Deutero-Isaiah. Similarly, the Isaian collection known to Deutero-Isaiah did not yet encompass the late additions found in 14.1–23 or chapters 24–27. Deutero-Isaiah depended on psalms but not our Book of Psalms.

2. Regarding the exodus motif, see the sensitive essays by Bernhard Anderson,

"Exodus Typology in Second Isaiah," in *Israel's Prophetic Heritage: Essays in Honor of James Muilenburg*, ed. B. Anderson and W. Harrelson (New York: Harper, 1962), 177–95, and "Exodus and Covenant in Second Isaiah and Prophetic Tradition," in *Magnalia Dei, the Mighty Acts of God: Essays on the Bible and Archaeology in Memory of G. Ernest Wright*, ed. W. E. Lemke, F. M. Cross, and P. D. Miller (Garden City, N.Y.: Doubleday, 1976), 339–60. See further Michael Fishbane, *Biblical Interpretation in Ancient Israel* (Oxford: Oxford University Press, 1985), 364. Regarding the prophet's transformation of the wandering and desert motifs from the Pentateuch and elsewhere, see Shemaryahu Talmon, "The 'Desert Motif' in the Bible and Qumran Literature," in *Biblical Motifs: Origins and Transformations*, ed. Alexander Altmann (Cambridge, Mass.: Harvard University Press, 1966), 54; Talmon notes that Deutero-Isaiah emphasizes the "divine benevolence" theme within the desert motif at the expense of the "purification" and *rite de passage* aspect of that motif, since the exilic community (unlike the community that left Egypt) had already been purified of its dross by the exile itself. As a result, "the desert motif could be wedded with the theme of the Davidic covenant, and with the vision of the restituted Jerusalem." Regarding the typological use of the name Jacob in Deutero-Isaiah, see Joseph Blenkinsopp, *A History of Prophecy in Israel*, 2d ed. (Louisville, Ky.: Westminster John Knox, 1996), 190.

3. Cf. Fishbane, *Biblical*, 375, who notes a link between Genesis 12.1–3 and Isaiah 51.2.

4. Several cases in which Deutero-Isaiah depended on texts from the Pentateuch have been noted and discussed by Armond Kaminka (who already recognizes the problem of distinguishing between allusions to a specific Pentateuchal text and the use of widespread traditions) in *Meḥqarim* (Tel Aviv: Devir, 1938), 1: 159–63 [Heb.], and by Fishbane, *Biblical*, e.g., 128, 142, 364, 374–75, 477–79. Moshe Weinfeld, *Deuteronomy 1–11* (New York: Doubleday, 1991), 82, notes possible cases of the Book of Deuteronomy's influence on Deutero-Isaiah, but most of these are examples of Deuteronomic phrasing or ideology that come not from a specific verse but from the Deuteronomic stream of tradition; in fact, most of the phrases or ideas in Deutero-Isaiah Weinfeld cites could have been based as easily on Deuteronomic sections of Jeremiah or Ezekiel.

5. Perhaps one should read the hiphil וַיַּאֲכֶל here: "And He feeds [Israel]." The LXX reads a hiphil and adds an indirect object: ἐψώμισεν αὐτούς. Similarly, Tg reads וְאוֹכִילִינוּן; the presence of a *wāw* (indicating an o-class vowel) rather than a *yōd* (which would indicate an i-class vowel) demonstrates that the word is an *'aphēl* rather than a *pᵉal* verb.

6. See Kaminka, 159, and Fishbane, *Biblical* 477.

7. Fishbane, *Biblical*, 478–79.

8. Deutero-Isaiah utilizes this poem also in Isa 48.20–21, which includes several vocabulary items pointing to Deut 32.1–5:

הַשְׁמִיעוּ (48.20) // הַאֲזִינוּ . . . וְתִשְׁמַע (32.1);

הַזִּיל (48.21) // תִּזַּל (32.2);

הַצּוּר (48.21) // מָצוֹר, צוּר (32.4).

One wonders further whether the word מַיִם in Isa 48.21 hints back at מוּמָם in Deut 32.5. These vocabulary items occur in the same order in each text. The word הַשְׁמִיעוּ depends on both וְתִשְׁמַע and הַאֲזִינוּ in Deut 32.1: it repeats the root of the former and the grammatical construction (and hence sound) of the latter. The use of the terms differs: in Deuteronomy the word נז"ל refers to revelation, while in Deutero-Isaiah it refers to sustenance in a desert. In Deuteronomy צור is God, but in Deutero-Isaiah it literally means "a rock" (though one may find the hint of a metaphor concerning prophecy and guidance, which are the concerns of the last half of Isaiah 48). Aside from these transformations of the marked items, the older text has not been strategically reemployed; this is a case of echo rather than full-fledged allusion.

9. My translation of עוֹלָם follows Jeffrey Tigay, *Deuteronomy* (Philadelphia: Jewish Publication Society, 1996). T. H. Gaster emends the text to read "who humbled (מְעַנֶּה) divine beings of old and subdued (מִחַתֵּת) the ancient powers" ("An Ancient Eulogy on Israel: Deuteronomy 33:3–5, 26–29," *JBL* 66 [1947], 60–61). If this emendation reconstructs the text accurately, then Deutero-Isaiah's allusion also serves as a corrective to its source: the powers whom YHWH defeated were not really divine beings, since YHWH alone is God (Isa 45.14, 18, 21 [this last verse also contains the marker מִקֶּדֶם]). In this case, the use of עוֹלָם is innovative, since this word is transferred from the primordial rebels to YHWH. The allusion clarifies that eternal power belongs only to YHWH; He alone knew from ancient times what would occur.

10. One might argue that Deutero-Isaiah bases himself here on a general Israelite practice, and that the terminology was known from that widespread practice. Given Deutero-Isaiah's familiarity with Deuteronomy (including material from outside the book's editorial framework), however, it seems likely that he knew the text in its context in the Book of Deuteronomy. Even if he knew the legal ruling from some other context (e.g., if the Deuteronomic law code was not yet part of a Book of Deuteronomy), one can still justifiably term the connection between the law and Isa 50.1 an allusion.

11. On the phrasing of Hos 1.9 as a divorce formula, see J. Rabinowitz, s.v. "*Gerushin*," in *Encyclopaedia Biblica* (Jerusalem: Mossad Bialik, 1950–88), 2: 551–54 [Heb.].

12. Deutero-Isaiah may allude to another Deuteronomic law, which appears in Deut 23.2, in Isa 56.3. But the two texts share no actual wording, so that it is difficult to assert that Deutero-Isaiah had the specific passage in mind. Cf. Fishbane's discussion, *Biblical*, 118 n. 36, and the interesting reading of John Skinner in his commentary to Isaiah ad loc. (John Skinner, *The Book of the Prophet Isaiah: Chapters XL–LXVI*, rev. ed. [Cambridge: Cambridge University Press, 1917]).

13. See the list of curses appearing in ancient Near Eastern treaties in Dennis

McCarthy, *Treaty and Covenant* (Rome: Biblical Institute Press, 1981), 173, and cf. the various treaties in ANET. The only possible parallel stems from the vassal treaty of Esarhaddon, which mentions walking in blindness but does not include the image of a person floundering in the afternoon: "May it be dark (*liṣlimma*) in your eyes! Walk about in darkness (*ina iklitte itallaka*)!" (Lines 423–24. The Akkadian text and a translation appear in D. J. Wiseman, "The Vassal Treaties of Esarhaddon," *Iraq* 20 [1958], 59–60; see also the translation by Erica Reiner in ANET, 538b, and *CAD* 1: 32.)

14. Another possible allusion to Deuteronomy involves a thematic category found ·in Deutero-Isaiah's use of prophetic literature. As Fishbane notes (*Biblical*, 364), "In contrast to the original exodus, which occurred in an atmosphere of anxiety and haste (בחפזון, cf. Exod. 12:11; Deut. 16:3), the people are now told 'לא בחפזון not in haste will you leave, nor will you go in flight' (Isa. 52:11–12). By this explicit reversal, the prophet avers that in the new exodus disquietude will be replaced by calm. The new exodus will therefore not simply be a manifestation of an older prototype, but will have qualitative distinctions of its own." It is difficult to be sure whether Deutero-Isaiah alludes to Exod 12.11, Deut 16.3, or a widespread tradition about the flight from Egypt, though he shares one vocabulary item with Deut 16.3 that does not appear in Exod 12.11: the verb יצ״א. On the other hand, John McKenzie (*Second Isaiah* [Garden City: Doubleday, 1968]) points out that these verses in Deutero-Isaiah share with the Book of Exodus two additional themes. In the Book of Exodus the escaping Israelites took vessels from the Egyptians (see Exod 12.35); now they will take nothing with them—except their own temple vessels (Isa 52.11). Further, 52.12b repeats a theme from the wandering tradition, viz., that God goes in front of them and behind them (Exod 14.19). This may suggest a stronger connection with sources comprising the Book of Exodus. We cannot know whether the prophet refers to one of these texts, to both, or to parallel traditions known to him from some other source. In any event, it is noteworthy that Deutero-Isaiah endeavors to create a contrast between the old Exodus and the new, in favor of the latter. This reuse (whether of a text or a tradition), then, resembles his allusion to Jer 31.7–9 in Isa 35.4–10. There, as Deutero-Isaiah relies on Jeremiah's description of the return of exiles, he jettisons any negative language and stresses that the return will be joyful and orderly.

J. Gerald Janzen suggests that Deutero-Isaiah alludes to Deut 6.4 ("An Echo of the Shema in Isaiah 51.1–3," *JSOT* 43 [1989], 69–82). The alleged borrowing contains only a single marker (the word אחד), however, and Janzen's argument relies on novel readings of both passages. The case for this allusion is not strong.

15. Klaus Baltzer, "Schriftauslegung bei Deuterojesaja?—Jes 43,22–28 als Beispiel," in *Die Väter Israels*, ed. Manfred Görg (Stuttgart: Katholisches Bibelwerk, 1989), 11–16.

16. Antti Laato, *The Servant of YHWH and Cyrus: A Reinterpretation of the Exilic*

Messianic Programme in Isaiah 40–55 (Stockholm: Almqvist and Wiksell, 1992), 94–95, suggests another case in which Deutero-Isaiah alludes to the Jacob story. Isa 43.1–7 share a fair amount of vocabulary with Gen 28.13–15, but some of the words are common, and the crucial ones (אל תירא, כי אתך אני, אני ה׳) all belong to the vocabulary cluster associated with royal oracles in the ancient Near East. They appear in the Assyrian royal oracles, in many other oracles to the patriarchs in Genesis, and in prophetic commissioning stories such as Jeremiah 1, as well as in Jeremiah 30 (see Chap. 2, p. 33). Consequently, we cannot identify the parallel between Isaiah 43 and Genesis 28 as a borrowing.

17. See, e.g., the comments of Baruch Levine, *Leviticus* (Philadelphia: Jewish Publication Society, 1989), on this passage, and also his Appendix 10, pp. 270–74.

18. On the largely benign conditions of the exiles in Babylonia, see the discussion in Yehezkel Kaufmann, *The Babylonian Captivity and Deutero-Isaiah*, trans. C. W. Efroymson (New York: Union of American Hebrew Congregations, 1970), 3–9; J. M. Miller and J. Hayes, *A History of Ancient Israel and Judah* (Philadelphia: Westminster Press, 1986), 429–35.

19. Other typological allusions to Pentateuchal material appear elsewhere. As Isa 48.18–21 create an analogy between the new and old Exodus, they seem to rely not only on general exodus traditions but on Exod 17.2–6, as Professor Shalom Paul pointed out to me (private communication): not only are the terms יצ״א, צמ״א, צור, and מַיִם shared (as well as a word meaning "river"), but sound play occurs also: the word בָּחֳרָבוֹת (*bo-ḥorabot* "in dry places") in Isa 48.21 points back to the geographic name בְּחֹרֵב (*bᵊ-ḥoreib*, "in Sinai") in Exod 17.6.

20. In Old Babylonian, the term is *andurāru*; in neo-Assyrian, the form *durāru* occurs. See *CAD* I/2: 115–17; Julius Lewy, "The Biblical Institution of *dᵊrôr* in the Light of Akkadian Documents," *ErIsr* 5 (1958), 21*–31*.

21. Cf. Lewy, 29. The דרור proclaimed by Zedekiah in Jeremiah 34 does not seem to have been a regularly scheduled one that occurred every fifty years; the text in Jeremiah clearly refers back to the laws of Deuteronomy 15 (which are not concerned with the jubilee), not to Leviticus 25 (which is); see also William Holladay, *Jeremiah 2: A Commentary on the Book of the Prophet Jeremiah 26–52* (Minneapolis: Fortress Press, 1989), 239, 240. Thus the term דרור used in Jeremiah is a legal term meaning "release from slavery by royal decree," like the Akkadian *andurāru*, but it is not used in the more narrow sense it has in Leviticus, where a דרור takes place automatically every fifty years. Sarna argues that Zedekiah's proclamation took place during a sabbatical year (see "Zedekiah's Emancipation of Slaves and the Sabbatical Year," in *Orient and Occident: Essays Presented to Cyrus H. Gordon*, ed. Harry Hoffner, Jr. [Neukirchen: Neukirchener, 1973], 147–49), but even if this is so, there is no indication that the proclamation occurred in a jubilee year.

22. Ezek 46.17, which seems to assume a דרור that follows a regular cycle, also depends on Leviticus 25.

23. So Fishbane, *Biblical*, 483.

24. Moshe Weinfeld, "God the Creator in Genesis 1 and in the Prophecy of Second Isaiah," *Tarbiz* 37 (1968), 105–32 (reprinted in *Likkutei Tarbiz: A Biblical Studies Reader*, ed. Moshe Weinfeld [Jerusalem: Magnes, 1979], 117–46) [Heb.].

25. For this reading of Gen 1.1–3, see Weinfeld, "Creator," 121–22. See also some of the commentaries, including Rashbam (though he assumes that heaven and earth had been created earlier as chaotic things to which God now brings order, while Weinfeld stresses that the biblical text is silent regarding the origin of the chaos).

26. A hendiady, signifying "all the world."

27. Another hendiady, signifying "everything."

28. Weinfeld, "Creator," 123–24.

29. Weinfeld, "Creator," 124–25. For this reading of Genesis 1.26, see the detailed and convincing discussion on pp. 113–16.

30. So *ketib* (מִי אִתִּי); the *qere* reads "unaccompanied" (מֵאִתִּי), which makes the same point.

31. Weinfeld, "Creator," 125–26. On the existence of a heavenly council in the background of the P creation account, see pp. 115–16. The objections to this view brought up by Claus Westermann in *Genesis 1–11*, trans. John Scullion (Minneapolis: Augsburg Press, 1984), 144–45, had already been countered in Weinfeld, 116 n. 66. For the idea that Gen 1.26 refers to the ministering angels, see also traditional commentaries (Rashi, Seforno), midrashic texts (e.g., Gen Rab 8.3 and 8.5 [in *Midrash Bereshit Rabba*, ed. J. Theodor and C. Albeck {Jerusalem: Wahrmann, 1965}, 1: 58–60]), and Tg PsJon.

32. Weinfeld, "Creator," 126.

33. Contra Fishbane's understanding of this material. See the discussion in Chap. 1, n. 87.

34. Throughout this chapter I use the term "priestly" in a broad sense, to include material from both PT (such as Genesis 1) and HS (such as Numbers 18 and Exod 31.17; on the attribution of these to HS, see Israel Knohl, *The Sanctuary of Silence: The Priestly Torah and the Holiness School* [Minneapolis: Fortress Press, 1995], 15–16, 53–54, 67).

35. Ezekiel 44 is even more restrictive, limiting the priesthood to members of the Zadokite family alone. See the discussion in Fishbane, *Biblical*, 138–42. For a discussion of these issues in the Numbers passage, see especially Jacob Milgrom, *Numbers* (Philadelphia: Jewish Publication Society, 1989), 341–44, 423–24.

36. Elsewhere in priestly literature the term refers to anyone not allowed to approach the sanctuary—i.e., those who were neither Aaronides nor Levites (so in Num 3.10, 38). See Milgrom, 342–43, 424.

37. It is likely that the prophet has in mind eunuchs in the service of the Babylonian or Persian court, whether Judean or foreign. Kaufmann, *Babylonian*, 167–68, believes the eunuchs referred to are Judean exiles maimed for service at these foreign

royal courts, who were "cut off" from their people in the sense that they would have no descendants; the nation in the future would not include their seed. Non-Judean advisers to royalty in these courts seem to have been especially attracted to the monotheism of the Judean exiles' religion; see Moshe Weinfeld, "Universalism and Particularism in the Period of the Return to Zion," *Tarbiz* 33 (1964), 231–32; reprinted in *Likkutei*, ed. Weinfeld, 42–57.

38. Heb., יָד וָשֵׁם. The first term may be a euphemistic reference to what eunuchs lack (cf. BDB 390b #4g). The second term is often used of progeny (see BDB 1028a #2c), which eunuchs are consequently incapable of siring.

39. So 1QIsaᵃ, LXX, and medieval manuscripts according to Eliezer of Beaugency; cf. Moshe Goshen-Gottstein, ed., *The Hebrew University Bible: The Book of Isaiah* (Jerusalem: Magnes, 1995).

40. This term (יִכָּרֵת, "be cut off") may also be used to hint at the experience of eunuchs.

41. The Hebrew is וּבְנֵי הַנֵּכָר, the same term used in Ezek 44.9. This passage in Deutero-Isaiah shares several other terms with Ezekiel 44, all of which also occur in Numbers 18. It is clear that both Ezekiel 44 and Isaiah 56 depend on Numbers 18, but it is less clear that Deutero-Isaiah relied specifically on Ezekiel 44. Nonetheless, the identical vocabulary and concerns demonstrate that both prophets were adding their voices to a debate concerning "a live post-exilic issue," as Fishbane shows (*Biblical*, 138).

42. Some critics claim to find several redactional layers in these few verses (e.g., Seizo Sekine, *Die tritojesajanische Sammlung (Jes 56–66) redaktiongeschichtlich untersucht* [Berlin: Walter de Gruyter, 1989], 37–41; cf. Odil H. Steck, "Zu jüngsten . . . 56,1–8," in *Studien zu Tritojesaja* [Berlin: Walter de Gruyter, 1991], 244 and notes). This is a fine example of the tendency to create several garbled fragments from a text that makes sense as it stands. On the dating of this passage, see Menahem Haran, who shows that it was most likely written before the Second Temple was rebuilt (*Between RIʾSHONÔT [Former Prophecies] and ḤADASHÔT [New Prophecies]: A Literary-Historical Study of Prophecies in Isaiah XL–XLVII* [Jerusalem: Magnes, 1963], 91–92, 101–2 [Heb.]).

43. Already the priestly writers allow offerings from foreigners at the Israelite sanctuary; see Num 15.14–16 and Lev 22.18–25 (and cf. 1 Kings 8.41–43, which looks forward to God granting prayers offered by foreigners at the Temple). Deutero-Isaiah also allows foreigners to rejoice at the Temple in Isa 56.7 (וְשִׂמַּחְתִּים בְּבֵית תְּפִלָּתִי), but this does not give foreigners a priestly status; as Deut 12.7 shows, rejoicing at the Temple was a national, not an exclusively priestly, activity. Rather, Isa 56.7 accords to foreigners who observe the covenant the status of regular Israelites.

In Isaiah 56, as in Isa 61.5–6, foreigners who observe the covenant seem to be assigned a role in the future similar to that of Israelites in the past: they can rejoice at the holy mountain, and their offerings are accepted there. Such a state of affairs harmonizes with Deutero-Isaiah's notion in 61.5–6 that all Israelites in the future will have the role which had been limited to Aaronides and Levites in the past, but that notion is not explicit in chapter 56.

44. Even as a technical term, the term שרת has several meanings. See the brief remarks of Milgrom, 16 n. 5, and BDB 1058a #2.

45. As noted by Weinfeld, "Universalism," 240–41; the absence of the verb in 1QIsaᵃ is also noted by Roy Wells, Jr., "'Isaiah' as an Exponent of Torah: Isaiah 56:1–8," in *New Visions of Isaiah*, ed. Roy Melugin and Marvin Sweeney (Sheffield: Sheffield Academic Press, 1996), 147–48. Weinfeld points out that LXX translates לשרתו with a verb usually used for עב"ד, which may reflect discomfort at associating the technical term שר"ת with foreigners and eunuchs; further, LXX translates נלוים with the term normally used for the root גור, which reflects the translators' attempt to read the passage as referring to what became the institution of conversion.

46. A similar, though not necessarily identical, law appears in Deut 23.2. Several commentators hold that Deutero-Isaiah rejects the law from Deuteronomy (Westermann, McKenzie, and see also Brooks Schramm, *The Opponents of Third Isaiah: Reconstructing the Cultic History of the Restoration* [Sheffield: Sheffield Academic Press, 1995], 124). A closer reading of the text shows this not to be the case. Skinner, following W. R. Smith, notes that the law in Deuteronomy was directed not against victims of mutilation at the Babylonian or Persian courts and harems, but against those who voluntarily mutilated themselves. "If this be so," Skinner writes, "the present passage [Isa 56.3] need not be regarded as superseding the Deuteronomic law; it may only be a protest against its extension to cases which it did not contemplate [viz., to] the unfortunate victims of Oriental tyranny." According to Skinner, Deutero-Isaiah does not so much oppose Deuteronomy here as clarify the older text—we see here a case of inner-biblical exegesis rather than inner-biblical polemic. Cf. the similar view of Kaufmann, *Babylonian*, 168–69.

47. As Ezra 4.1–5 demonstrate, this viewpoint already existed at the time of the return to Zion. See Weinfeld, "Universalism," 238.

48. For additional discussion of this debate, see Weinfeld, "Universalism," esp. 237–38, and Fishbane, *Biblical*, 114–29, esp. 128.

49. Weinfeld, "Universalism," 239, defends this understanding (i.e., that the word "them" refers to the nations); see also Skinner. Westermann and McKenzie, unfortunately, assume this translation without discussing the other possibility.

50. A similar viewpoint is expressed in Deut 4.37.

51. Connecting בְּכָל־צָרָתָם from v. 9 to the last three words of v. 8 (with the LXX and against the MT), and reading צָר rather than the MT's צָר (again with the LXX). This reading, defended in Skinner and McKenzie, is much more likely than those of the MT. The MT's *qere* reading ("He [לֹו] was afflicted in their affliction, and the messenger of His presence saved them") reflects the exegesis found in rabbinic texts such as Mekilta d'Rabbi Yishmael (*Bōʾ*, section before *Par. A*, ed. Horovitz and Rabin

[Jerusalem: Wahrmann, 1970], 51) and Exod Rab 2.5 (ed. Avigdor Shinan, *Midrash Shemot Rabbah Chapters I–XIV* [Jerusalem: Dvir, 1984], 111). The MT's *ketib* reading ("He was not [לֹא] afflicted in their affliction, and the messenger of His presence saved them") is also unlikely, since a "messenger of His presence" is nowhere else attested in the Bible. For a different reconstruction of the text (which is also superior to the MT but more speculative than the one I have subscribed to), see Torrey.

52. Since his polemics against priestly texts encompass both PT (Genesis 1) and HS (Exod 31.17, Numbers 18), it appears that HS had already edited and supplemented PT by this time. (On the relation between PT and HS, see Knohl.) But we cannot know whether something resembling the whole Pentateuch, including material from J, E, PT, HS, and D, had been redacted.

I should note one other allusion, which indicates Deutero-Isaiah knew a redacted version of JE. Isa 40.1–4 share several items with Exod 32.14–15: נח"ם (32.14 // 40.1), דב"ר (32.14 // 40.2), עמ' (32.14 // 40.1), פנ"ה (32.15 // 40.3), הר (32.15 // 40.4), יד (32.15 // 40.2, in both cases associated with a word signifying "two"). Because much of this vocabulary is common, one can doubt whether this is a genuine case of echo (in any event, it is not an allusion). If, however, the dense clustering of shared terms is not a coincidence, it follows that Deutero-Isaiah knew a text in which two originally discrete sources had already been combined: the calf narrative in Exod 32.1–8, 15–24 is interrupted in 32.9–14 by a story that has nothing to do with the calf narrative and displays vocabulary distinct from what surrounds it. The interruption probably belongs to J, while the longer calf narrative in all likelihood stems from an Elohistic strand. (See especially S. R. Driver, *The Book of Exodus* [Cambridge: Cambridge University Press, 1911]. See also J. Carpenter and G. Harford-Battersby, *The Hexateuch According to the Revised Version* [London: Longmans, Green, 1900], 2: 130–31, and Erhard Blum, *Studien zur Komposition des Pentateuch* [Berlin: Walter de Gruyter, 1990], 73–74, both of whom would include verses 7–8 with 9–14, a source-critical decision that strikes me as unlikely but does not affect my point.) In this case, Deutero-Isaiah knew a redacted version of JE, which is not surprising in the exilic period. If Carpenter and Harford-Battersby are correct that 32.15aβ–b stem from a priestly redactor, then Deutero-Isaiah may have known a text that incorporated P as well as JE, but no conclusions can be reached on the basis of this highly speculative suggestion; indeed, as Driver notes, the only P element there is the word העדת (rather than all of 32.15aβ–b), and thus we cannot know whether the gloss already existed in Deutero-Isaiah's text.

53. See Paul Hanson, *The Dawn of Apocalyptic*, rev. ed. (Philadelphia: Fortress Press, 1975), 17–20, 25–26, and passim.

54. See especially Schramm, 85–86, 108–11, 174–82. See also Wells, 152, and Alexander Rofé, "Isaiah 66.1–4: Judean Sects in the Persian Period as Viewed by Trito-Isaiah," in *Biblical and Related Studies Presented to Samuel Iwry*, ed. A. Kort and S. Morschauser (Winona Lake, Ind.: Eisenbrauns, 1985), 212–17.

55. This allusion was noted by Wells, 143–45. On the attribution of Exodus 31.12–16 to both PT and HS see Driver, *Exodus*, and Knohl, 14–16, 66–67.

56. Lev 24.8 describes the rules regarding the Sabbath sacrifices (but not the Sabbath itself) as an eternal covenant. Other passages concerning the Sabbath do not use this language at all.

CHAPTER SIX

1. Indeed, in the thinking of many biblical authors, both before and after the disaster, exile and punishment had to be experienced in order for the redemption to come (see Peter Ackroyd, *Exile and Restoration: A Study of Hebrew Thought of the Sixth Century B.C.* [Philadelphia: Westminster Press, 1968], 243–44). By confirming that the foretold punishment had come to pass, Deutero-Isaiah implies that redemption is finally possible.

2. On the notion of cognitive dissonance in the prophetic tradition, see Robert Carroll, "Prophecy and Dissonance: A Theoretical Approach to Prophetic Tradition," *ZAW* 92 (1980), 108–19, esp. 111 and 118.

3. The same happened to his polemic against anthropomorphic conceptions of God; only after Maimonides' time did Deutero-Isaiah's view become the norm in Judaism.

4. Even the idea of a heavenly redeemer (which appears in some strands of ancient Judaism, including, most of all, Christianity) largely develops out of notions of a human Messiah's exaltation. See John Collins, *The Scepter and the Star: The Messiahs of the Dead Sea Scrolls and Other Ancient Literature* (New York: Doubleday, 1995), 136–89.

5. Bernard A. Levinson, "The Human Voice in Divine Revelation: The Problem of Authority in Biblical Law," in *Innovations in Religious Traditions: Essays in the Interpretation of Religious Change*, ed. Michael Williams, Collet Cox, and Martin Jaffee (Berlin: Walter de Gruyter, 1992), 45.

6. See Bernard Levinson, *Deuteronomy and the Hermeneutics of Legal Innovation* (New York: Oxford University Press, 1997), passim, esp. 4, 15–17. The quote appears on p. 4.

7. The prophet of comfort was especially in need of this sort of affirmation, since the exiles had been instructed to doubt prophets who predicted renewal; see Ezekiel 13 and Jeremiah 29.

8. So also Wolfgang Lau, *Schriftgelehrte Prophetie in Jes 56–66* (Berlin: Walter de Gruyter, 1994), 317. This tendency among allusive authors has often been noted by literary theorists, e.g., Anthony Johnson, "Allusion in Poetry," *PTL* 1 (1976), 581.

9. A few literary theorists have noted that allusions and acknowledgments of influence are often made for the sake of the borrowed, not just for that of the borrower. See Louis Renza, s.v. "Influence," in *Critical Terms for Literary Study*, ed.

Frank Lentricchia and Thomas McLaughlin (Chicago: University of Chicago Press, 1990), 186; Cyrena Pondrom, "Influence? or Intertextuality? The Complicated Connection of Edith Sitwell with Gertrude Stein," in *Influence and Intertextuality in Literary History*, ed. Jay Clayton and Eric Rothstein (Madison: University of Wisconsin Press, 1991), 208; and Gian Biagio Conte, *The Rhetoric of Imitation: Genre and Poetic Memory in Virgil and Other Latin Poets*, ed. Charles Segal (Ithaca, N.Y.: Cornell University Press, 1986), 69.

10. The work of James Muilenburg, Yehoshua Gitay, and Richard Clifford is especially useful in encouraging scholars to understand the prophet's use of language to persuade and encourage. See Muilenburg, "The Book of Isaiah: Chapters 40–66," in *IB*, ed. Arthur Buttrick et al. (New York: Abingdon Press, 1956), 5: 381–419, 422–773; Gitay, *Prophecy and Persuasion: A Study of Isaiah 40–48* (Bonn: Linguistica Biblica, 1981); Clifford, *Fair Spoken and Persuading: An Interpretation of Second Isaiah* (New York: Paulist Press, 1984).

11. At the end of Chapter 2, I examine an allusion in Isa 40.9–10 that contains all these techniques. For a fuller description of these techniques and their relationship to other elements of Deutero-Isaiah's poetic style on the one hand and other authors' inner-biblical allusions on the other, see the discussion there.

12. For this point, I am indebted to my student Jennie Kiffmeyer.

13. See my description of the techniques at the end of Chapter 2 and also the last paragraph of the Appendix.

14. I am indebted to Professor Chana Kronfeld for encouraging me to contemplate this phenomenon.

15. While the semantic aspect of biblical parallelism is widely stressed, non-semantic parallels (including equivalences of syntax, accent, and phonology) deserve greater attention. See Adele Berlin, *The Dynamics of Biblical Parallelism* (Bloomington: Indiana University Press, 1985), 103–25, and Benjamin Hrushovski, "Note on the Systems of Hebrew Versification," in *The Penguin Book of Hebrew Verse*, ed. T. Carmi (New York: Viking Press, 1981), 58–60, and cf. Benjamin Hrushovski, s.v. "Prosody, Hebrew," in *Encyclopaedia Judaica* (Jerusalem: Keter, 1971), 13: 1200–1203.

16. See James Kugel, *The Idea of Biblical Poetry: Parallelism and Its History* (New Haven, Conn.: Yale University Press, 1981), 1–58, and Robert Alter, *The Art of Biblical Poetry* (New York: Basic Books, 1985), 3–25 and 62–84.

17. The pattern in which the first half of a line contains a number and the second contains that number + 1 occurs with great frequency in biblical and Ugaritic poetry; see Wilfred G. E. Watson, *Classical Hebrew Poetry: A Guide to Its Techniques* (Sheffield: Sheffield Academic Press, 1984), 144–49.

18. Chapters 34–35 are widely recognized to belong to the same corpus as 40–66 due to the similarities of theme, vocabulary, and style which link them. See, e.g., Heinrich Graetz, who argues persuasively that 35 is part of Deutero-Isaiah but 34 is not ("Isaiah XXXIV and XXXV," *JQR* [OS] 4 [1891], 1–8); Yehezkel Kaufmann, *The*

Babylonian Captivity and Deutero-Isaiah, trans. C. W. Efroymson (New York: Union of American Hebrew Congregations, 1970), 184–85, who regards them as the latest prophecies of the collection; Charles Torrey, *The Second Isaiah: A New Interpretation* (New York: Scribners, 1928), 103–4, who regards them as the earliest. It is significant that the characteristic literary features of Deutero-Isaiah which Torrey describes, 183–204, appear frequently in chapters 34–35. To these similarities we may now add that chapter 35 exhibits many of the characteristic features of Deutero-Isaiah's project of allusion and borrowing, on both thematic and stylistic levels. Chapter 35 also alludes to Isa 32.1–6.

19. In place of MT's בם עור ופסח, LXX seems to be based on a *Vorlage* reading במועד פסח, which links this passage with the Exodus. But the following words make clear that Jeremiah is describing not the timing of the event but rather the range of participants, which includes those who normally would have difficulty on such a journey. Thus the reading reflected in LXX may be a simple *Schreibfehler* (בם עור ופסח > במועד פסח) resulting from the similarity between the letters *rêsh* and *dālet* and metathesis of the *waw* and *ʿayin*.

20. Heb. וּבְתַחֲנוּנִים; I understand the *bêt* to indicate "by means of." LXX reads ἐν παρακλήσει, which seems to assume a Hebrew text reading וּבְתַנְחוּמִים. Further, LXX seems to have read יָצְאוּ (ἐξῆλθον), rather than יָבֹאוּ earlier in the verse. This seems initially to make more sense: "They went out weeping and will come back comforted." But MT is probably to be preferred, for reasons discussed in n. 23 below.

21. See Chap. 2, n. 11, for a discussion of Seidel's law.

22. We do not know how Deutero-Isaiah pronounced Hebrew (perhaps these words were realized as ['ōbīlēm] and ['awīlīm]), but the similarity affecting all the consonants remains, regardless. In both words the glottal stop is followed by a labial, then the letter *lāmed*, and then the letter *mēm*.

23. The allusion is a fine example of reprediction with historical recontextualization. Jeremiah directed this message to northern exiles, as the continuation of Jer 31.9 indicates: "For I have been to Israel as a father, and Ephraim is my eldest son." Deutero-Isaiah shifts the reference of the prediction to his own contemporaries from the south. (However, it is possible that Jeremiah added 31.7–9a later to an original core directed to the northern kingdom which included 9b; in that case, these verses may be directed to southern exiles. See William Holladay, *Jeremiah 2: A Commentary on the Book of the Prophet Jeremiah 26–52* [Minneapolis: Fortress Press, 1989], 156, 161–62.)

Other adjustments occur as well. Jeremiah's tone is oddly mournful considering his positive message: the exiles will return with weeping and by means of supplications. Jeremiah may have stressed the need for repentance not to avoid the disaster (which had already taken place in the north and which Jeremiah came to regard as inevitable for the south) but to bring the punishment to its end. (For this reason the MT text of Jeremiah ["by means of supplication"] is to be preferred over the LXX ["with comfort"], contra, e.g., Robert Carroll, *Jeremiah* [London: SCM, 1986]. At the same time, it is interesting to note that the LXX, by shifting תַּחֲנוּנִים to תַּנְחוּמִים, effects the same revision of tone which Deutero-Isaiah did. Incidentally, the oddly mournful view of the return we see in MT of Jer 31.9 appears clearly in Jer 50.4 as well.) But Deutero-Isaiah is not interested in recalling sorrow and proposing repentance; he focuses more exclusively on comfort. As if he speaks to an audience who have Jeremiah's less joyful prediction in mind, he says to the "anxious," "Do not fear." Alluding to Jeremiah's "With weeping they will come," he states, "In song they will come." His assurance that "sorrow and sighing will flee" (Isa 35.10) may also respond to the tone of the earlier prediction. Thus the allusion treats the older text like a question to which a response must be given.

24. A word on Deutero-Isaiah's stress on a straight path through the desert is appropriate. In ancient times, one traveling from Mesopotamia to Canaan could not take the direct route, which moves due west through an impenetrable desert. Rather, one would move north and west along the Euphrates, then south parallel to the Lebanon mountains. In this chapter YHWH tells the people that they will be able to march straight (and hence quickly) to their homeland through the desert, because water and a safe roadway will suddenly materialize there.

25. Reading בַּלַּיְלָה (which is not in MT) along with 1QIsaᵃ; so also Targum and the LXX.

26. The allusion encompasses the entirety of Isaiah 60, utilizing language and ideas from all of Psalm 72. For a defense of the parallel as a genuine case of allusion, see Chap. 4, n. 20.

27. For a discussion of standard parallel word pairs in biblical and Ugaritic poetry, with many examples and additional bibliography, see Watson, 128–44; Kugel, *Idea*, 27–40.

28. See, e.g., Ps 80.12, Isa 19.5, Jonah 2.4, Job 14.11. The words יָם and נָהָר parallel each other frequently in Ugaritic as well; see Mitchell Dahood, "Ugaritic-Hebrew Parallel Pairs," in *Ras Shamra Parallels: The Texts from Ugarit and the Hebrew Bible*, ed. Loren Fisher (Rome: Pontifical Biblical Institute, 1972–75), 1: 203.

29. E.g., Ps 24.1–2, Ps 96.11.

30. See Job 34.35, Isa 44.18.

31. On the importance of allusions in incipits, see Conte, 70–71, 76–78.

32. On the delimitation of Isa 40.1–11, see Muilenburg; Gitay, *Prophecy*, 63f.; and David Carr, "Isaiah 40:1–11 in the Context of the Macrostructure of Second Isaiah," in *Discourse Analysis of Biblical Literature*, ed. Walter Bodine (Atlanta: Scholars Press, 1995), 52–65. Carr (who provides a helpful review of literature on the extent of the opening unit of Deutero-Isaiah) sees verses 1–8 as God's call to the prophet and 9–11 as the prophet's call to his audience. In this case, verses 1–11 contain two introductions rather than one. The role of these two preludes remains as described above: they present the salient aspects of the work as a whole.

33. See Armond Kaminka, *Meḥqarim* (Tel Aviv: Devir, 1938), 1: 159 [Heb.], and Michael Fishbane, *Biblical Interpretation in Ancient Israel* (Oxford: Oxford University Press, 1985), 477.

34. See my article, "New Light on the Composition of Jeremiah," *CBQ* (forthcoming).

35. The redactors of the Pentateuch, working around the same time as or shortly after Deutero-Isaiah, accomplish the same goal in a different way as they incorporate diverse and at times contradictory texts into a single document. One might contrast this unifying course with the slightly later work of the Chronicler, who is more selective in his retelling of the nation's history—e.g., ignoring material relevant to the northern kingdom.

36. Interestingly, the single possible case of Deutero-Isaiah polemicizing against a prophet involves Ezekiel 44; see the discussion in Chapter 5.

37. See my brief remarks at the beginning of Chapter 2 and a more extensive analysis in my article "New Light on the Composition of Jeremiah."

38. See Hugo Greßmann, "Die literarische Analyse Deuterojesajas," *ZAW* 34 (1914), 295.

39. More specifically, with the Holiness School; see Israel Knohl, *The Sanctuary of Silence: The Priestly Torah and the Holiness School* (Minneapolis: Fortress Press, 1995), 14–19.

40. Very few clusters of wisdom vocabulary occur in Isaiah 35, 40–66. One of the only exceptions is 59.3b–8, and even these verses do not seem to quote any known passage from wisdom literature. See John Skinner, *The Book of the Prophet Isaiah: Chapters XL–LXVI*, rev. ed. (Cambridge: Cambridge University Press, 1917), and Claus Westermann, *Isaiah 40–66: A Commentary*, trans. D. Stalker (Philadelphia: Westminster Press, 1969).

41. Deutero-Isaiah's distance from wisdom traditions stands in stark contrast with Isaiah's strong connection to them, on which see Yehezkel Kaufmann, *Toledot ha-Emunah ha-Yisraelit* (Tel Aviv: Mosad Bialik and Devir, 1937–56), 3: 245–48, and J. William Whedbee, *Isaiah and Wisdom* (Nashville, Tenn.: Abingdon Press, 1971), esp. 149–53.

42. See, e.g., the summary in Joseph Blenkinsopp, *A History of Prophecy in Israel*, 2d ed. (Louisville: Westminster John Knox, 1996), 21–22.

43. See the helpful discussion of Shmuel Safrai, "Oral Torah," in *The Literature of the Sages, Vol. I*, ed. S. Safrai (Philadelphia: Fortress Press, 1987), 75–76. Safrai notes not only that large pericopes were committed to memory by specialized memorizers, but also that study in the rabbinic academies was often based on the memorizers' recitation rather than on reading from a written text. On the oral transmission and publication of rabbinic texts, see also G. Stemberger and H. L. Strack, *Introduction to the Talmud and Midrash*, trans. M. Bockmuehl (Edinburgh: T. & T. Clark, 1991), esp. 45; on the oral publication of the Mishna, see Saul Lieberman, "The Publication of

the Mishnah," in *Hellenism in Jewish Palestine* (New York: Jewish Theological Seminary, 1962), 93, 97–98.

44. Cf. Lau, 12.

45. So argues Klaus Baltzer regarding Deutero-Isaiah's reference to Jacob stories from Genesis: "Die Kompliziertheit des Auslegungsvorganges spricht für schriftliche, an den Texten orientierte Abfassung" ("Schriftauslegung bei Deuterojesaja?—Jes 43,22 als Beispiel," in *Die Väter Israels*, ed. M. Görg [Stuttgart: Katholisches Bibelwerk, 1988], 16). Baltzer's reasoning also applies to Deutero-Isaiah's allusions to other texts.

46. See Merritt Hughes, ed., *Complete Poems and Major Prose by John Milton* (Indianapolis: Bobbs-Merrill, 1957), 1021–22, 1036–37.

47. Yehoshua Gitay maintains that the distinction between oral and written literature is anachronistic when applied to ancient texts; see his article "Deutero-Isaiah: Oral or Written?" *JBL* 99 (1980), 185–97, esp. 191: "In modern culture, it is rather easy to distinguish between written and oral literature. . . . In ancient times this was not the situation since even written material was written to be heard. . . . Even if a class of educated people knew how to read, the majority did not share this knowledge, and not less important, copies of written material in the pre-printing period were limited in number for physical reasons. Hence the material had to be distributed by reading in public. . . . As a matter of fact the custom of reading aloud has to be understood in light of the mentality of reading. That is, the process of reading was actually a process of listening." Gitay argues that to classify Deutero-Isaiah as a writing prophet or a speaking prophet is to introduce a misleading distinction; his conclusions are just as important for a discussion of the nature of Deutero-Isaiah's sources. This point is especially relevant to a discussion of allusion, as Richard Garner points out (*From Homer to Tragedy: The Art of Allusion in Greek Poetry* [London: Routledge, 1990], 18): "In any case, recognition of allusions depends on the audience knowing that [older] poetry, having it in their heads, regardless of how they learned it" (i.e., regardless of whether they read it in written form or heard its oral presentation).

48. See Kaminka, 1: 159, and Fishbane, *Biblical*, 477.

49. Thus allusions in Deutero-Isaiah differ from references to older and authoritative works introduced by citation formulas—for example, in midrash, in pesher, or in biblical verses such as 2 Kgs 14.6. The examples in Deutero-Isaiah even differ from literary allusions in which the source is specified or the presence of an allusion is made explicit; see the examples from the works of the Israeli writers S. Y. Agnon and Aharon Meged that I cite (explicitly) in Chap. 1, n. 16.

50. Cf. the similar conclusion of Lau, 13, 31, and 317 n. 8; and recall the important distinctions made by James Kugel, "The Bible's Earliest Interpreters," *Prooftexts* 7 (1987), 280.

51. Some scholars challenge this thesis; see Ephraim Urbach, "When Did Prophecy Cease?" *Tarbiz* 17 (1946), 1–11, reprinted in *Likkutei Tarbiz: A Biblical Studies Reader*, ed. Moshe Weinfeld (Jerusalem: Magnes, 1979), 58–68 [Heb.]; David Aune,

Prophecy in Early Christianity and the Ancient Mediterranean World (Grand Rapids, Mich.: Eerdmans, 1983), 103–52, esp. 103–6; Thomas Overholt, "The End of Prophecy: No Players Without a Program," *JSOT* 42 (1988), 103–15; Frederick Greenspahn, "Why Prophecy Ceased," *JBL* 108 (1989), 37–49. While these scholars force us to attend to relevant texts and issues that were not fully explored in earlier scholarship, they do not successfully rebut the view that Jews in the Second Temple period viewed prophecy as having ceased. See my detailed discussion in "Did Prophecy Cease?" *JBL* 115 (1996), 31–47.

Incidentally, while Jews in the Second Temple period maintained that prophecy had ceased, they did not believe that it had ceased forever. Throughout the Judaisms of the ancient world we find the view that the dormant institution of prophecy would return at the advent of the eschaton; see 1 Macc 4.46 and 14.41; 1QS 9:11; 2 Apoc Bar 85.3; Acts 2.14–36; *Num. Rab.* 15.10; *b. San.* 93a–b. See further "Did Prophecy Cease?" 36–39, and cf. the sources collected by Peter Schäfer, *Die Vorstellung vom Heiligen Geist in der rabbinischen Literatur* (Munich: Kösel-Verlag, 1972), 112–15 and 143–44.

52. Similarly, the prophets in the northwestern Mesopotamian kingdom of Mari addressed messages to the king. While messages to other strata of the population may have existed as well (see Abraham Malamat, "A Forerunner of Biblical Prophecy: The Mari Documents," in *Ancient Israelite Religion: Essays in Honor of Frank Moore Cross*, ed. P. D. Hanson, P. D. Miller, and S. D. McBride [Philadelphia: Fortress Press, 1987], 36–37), the large number of prophetic letters to or concerning the king demonstrates the close relationship between prophecy and royalty in Mari. The same is true of the neo-Assyrian royal oracles, on which see Robert R. Wilson, *Prophecy and Society in Ancient Israel* (Philadelphia: Fortress Press, 1980), 115–19. On the connection between prophecy and kingship in Israel and Judah, see Frank Moore Cross, *Canaanite Myth and Hebrew Epic: Essays in the History of the Religion of Israel* (Cambridge: Harvard University Press, 1973), 223–29.

53. See Cross, *Canaanite*, 343; D. Petersen, *Late Israelite Prophecy: Studies in Deutero-Prophetic Literature and in Chronicles* (Missoula, Mont.: Scholars Press, 1977), 2–6; Clifford, 18.

54. My reasoning here follows that of J. Z. Smith in a number of his essays, especially "Wisdom and Apocalyptic," "The Influence of Symbols upon Social Change: A Place on Which to Stand," and "Map Is Not Territory," in his collection *Map Is Not Territory* (Leiden: Brill, 1978), 67–87, 129–46 and 289–309, and "A Pearl of Great Price and a Cargo of Yams: A Study in Situational Incongruity," in his collection *Imagining Religion from Babylon to Jonestown* (Chicago: University of Chicago Press, 1982), 90–101.

55. This notion of exile as more than a geographic category is developed with particular acuity by Smith.

56. Perhaps for this reason, some rabbinic sources date the end of prophecy not to the time of Malachi or Alexander (so *b. San.* 11a and parallels; *S. 'Olam Rab.* 86b)

but to the destruction of the *First* Temple: so *y. Ta'an* 2.1, *b. Yoma* 21b, *b. B. Bat.* 12a, *Pesiq. Rab. Kah.* 13.14 (ed. Bernard Mandelbaum [New York: Jewish Theological Seminary, 1987], 238). According to this view, the prophecies of Haggai, Zechariah, and Malachi had been deposited with Jeremiah before the First Temple fell. See the discussion and additional references in Urbach, 3, and note also his remarks, 8 and 11. On the strong connection between prophecy and temple in rabbinic and targum literature, see Schäfer, 73–78 and 135–40.

A further contributory factor in the decline of prophecy may have been attenuated support for prophets resulting from the failure of many pre-exilic oracles to come true, especially those concerning the restoration of a Jewish kingdom. See Wilson, 306–7.

57. One can question whether Zechariah participated in the activities of the council (as a pre-exilic prophet like Isaiah did) or merely observed them. According to the MT of Zech 3.5, the prophet himself entered the deliberations, ordering that a diadem be placed on the high priest's head. But in the LXX, the Peshitta, and the Vulgate, these words are spoken by the angel; the prophet's role is limited to watching the council's activity.

58. So also Blenkinsopp, *History*, 208–9.

59. The Book of Chronicles gives a similar impression. Chronicles, of course, does not relate the history of the post-exilic period. But William Schniedewind shows that the Chronicler's portrayal of pre-exilic Levites as enjoying an attenuated form of prophetic inspiration reflects post-exilic realities. See *The Word of God in Transition: From Prophet to Exegete in the Second Temple Period* (Sheffield: Sheffield Academic Press, 1995).

60. For examples, see Petersen, 25–26; Blenkinsopp, *History*, 227–35; many cases of this kind involve inner-biblical exegesis and revision on the scribal level, on which see Fishbane, *Biblical*, 23–88.

61. Pseudepigraphy is hardly unique to the post-exilic era (this is clear from Deuteronomy and the priestly laws in Leviticus and Numbers ascribed to Moses or Aaron). But the high proportion of pseudepigraphs in the late Second Temple period discloses a consciousness that direct revelation has departed. Many visionary or aural revelations are described by pre-exilic and early post-exilic figures without recourse to pseudepigraphy, but by the late Second Temple period all such experiences are reported pseudepigraphically. See also Urbach, 6. Aune points out (109) that pseudepigraphs were only rarely attributed to prophets, a point which further underscores the gap between prophecy and Second Temple period revelatory literature.

62. Schniedewind, e.g., 112–17.

63. For examples, see Blenkinsopp, *History*, 209; Petersen, 33–38; Carroll, "Prophecy," 118; Fishbane, *Biblical*, 481, 513.

64. Cf. 1QpHab 2.1–10. See Michael Fishbane, "Use, Authority and Interpretation of Mikra at Qumran," in *Mikra: Reading and Interpretation of the Hebrew Bible in*

Ancient Judaism and Early Christianity, ed. Martin Jan Mulder (Philadelphia: Fortress Press, 1988), 361–62; Steven Fraade, *From Tradition to Commentary: Torah and Its Interpretation in the Midrash Sifre to Deuteronomy* (Albany: SUNY Press, 1991), 3–4; Joseph Blenkinsopp, "Prophecy and Priesthood in Josephus," *JJS* 25 (1974), 247 (and note his additional references in n. 32).

65. See Fraade, 5, 9, 13.

66. Julius Wellhausen, *Prolegomena to the History of Israel*, trans. Black and Menzies (New York: Meridian, 1957 [1885]), 403–4. Cf. Martin Buber, *The Prophetic Faith*, trans. Carlyle Witton-Davies (New York: Harper and Row, 1949), 204–5, who sees Deutero-Isaiah as occupying a "singular intermediate position between the full prophetic immediacy of receiving and uttering, and the acquired status of an interpreter who explains words handed down."

67. See especially the works of Christopher Seitz ("Isaiah 1–66: Making Sense of the Whole," in *Reading and Preaching the Book of Isaiah*, ed. C. Seitz [Philadelphia: Fortress Press, 1988]; "The Divine Council: Temporal Transition and New Prophecies in the Book of Isaiah," *JBL* 109 [1990]; and *Zion's Final Destiny: The Development of the Book of Isaiah, a Reassessment of Isaiah 36–39* [Minneapolis: Fortress Press, 1991]), and note also Wilson, 291.

68. See especially the end of Chapter 3 above.

69. Isaiah is called a prophet by the Deuteronomistic narrator (e.g., in 2 Kgs 20.14) and in the narrative material appended to the words of Isaiah (e.g., Isa 37.2), but in the sections that profess to report the prophet's words, neither the prophet himself nor the editors term Isaiah a נביא. Hosea is not termed a נביא (except, perhaps, in Hos 9.7–8; whether נביא in those verses refers to Hosea cannot be known, given their extraordinary philological difficulties). From Amos 3.7 one may sense that Amos is among the נביאים, but this is a title he elsewhere disavows (Amos 7.14).

70. So also Lau, who stresses that the authors of 56–66 were prophets, not mere exegetes (13). This is also the conclusion of Joachim Begrich (*Studien zu Deuterojesaja* [Munich: Chr. Kaiser, 1969], 153): "Gegenüber den Versuchen, Deuterojesaja als Dichter im allgemeinem oder als Hymnensänger im besonderen oder als Literat oder Rhetor aufzufassen, glauben wir, daß er als Prophet genommen werden muß. . . . In Übereinstimmung mit diesem hochgespannten Selbstbewußtsein steht, daß die Worte Deuterojesajas vorwiegend als Wortlaut YHWHs selbst auftreten."

71. Isa 42.5; 43.1; 43.14, 16; 44.2, 6, 24; 45.1, 11, 14, 18; 48.17; 49.7, 8; 49.22, 25; 50.1; 51.22; 52.3, 4; 56.1, 4; 57.15; 65.8; 65.13; 66.1, 12.

72. Isa 41.14; 43.10, 12; 49.18; 52.5; 54.17; 55.8; 56.8; 59.20; 66.2, 17, 22.

73. Chapters 56–66, and perhaps 49–55 and 35, were written in the Land of Israel, but I think that in a phenomenological sense they too can be termed "exilic." Their author composed in a world still in need of rectification, a cosmos that was still amiss because the magnificent restoration anticipated in the earlier chapters had still not fully come to fruition. That is, all of 40–66 are "exilic" in the sense used by J. Z. Smith.

74. In Exodus 3, Isaiah 6, Jeremiah 1, and Ezekiel 1–3. Some scholars doubt whether Isaiah 6 is in fact an initiation, since it follows five chapters of prophecy (see Kaufmann, *Toledot* 3: 207; J. Hays and S. Irvine, *Isaiah: Eighth Century Prophet* [Nashville, Tenn.: Abingdon Press, 1987], 108–9; and Matitiahu Tsevat, "The Throne Vision of Isaiah," in *The Meaning of the Book of Job and Other Biblical Studies* [New York: Ktav, 1980], 155–56), and it may represent more a renewal than an initiation. Nonetheless, it contains the elements of an initiation and can be compared to the others form-critically.

75. That Isaiah 40 contains elements of the call-scene without actually being such a scene has been noted several times before. See, e.g., Skinner, 5; Cross, "The Council of YHWH in Second Isaiah," *JNES* 12 (1953), 274–77; Westermann, *Isaiah*, 32, 42–43; Roy Melugin, *The Formation of Isaiah 40–55* (Berlin: Walter de Gruyter, 1976), 82–86; Carr, "Isaiah," 59–63. Norman Habel summarizes the discussion well: "In short, it seems apparent that the literary *Gattung* of the call narrative has been utilized to some extent by second Isaiah at least in Is 40_{1-8} and probably in 40_{1-11}" ("The Form and Significance of the Call Narratives," *ZAW* 75 [1965], 316).

76. In attributing the query to the prophet, I read the preceding word as a first-person verb with LXX and 1QIsa[a] instead of MT's third-person verb. For a detailed text-critical defense of this reading, see Carr, "Isaiah," 66–69.

77. My readings follow the especially fine analysis by Stephen Geller, "Were the Prophets Poets?" *Prooftexts* 3 (1983), 215–18.

78. These words are also addressed to the recipients of a divine message in non-Israelite prophecies from the ancient Near East; for several Assyrian cases, see E. Conrad, *Fear Not Warrior* (Chico, Calif: Scholars Press, 1985), 58–60, 154–57, and, for an example involving Aramaic seers, KAI 202 (=*ANET* 655b).

79. Though this phrase occurs often later in Deutero-Isaiah (e.g., 41.10).

80. Some scholars suggest that the absence of information about Deutero-Isaiah in his writings also reflects Deutero-Isaiah's anxiety concerning his prophetic status (see Begrich, 154 and 158, and cf. Wilson, 291, and Torrey, 182). We know a fair amount about Isaiah, Jeremiah, Hosea, and Amos, because they make some personal remarks along with prophetic statements (e.g., Jer 20.7–12; Isa 8.16–18), and their books include biographical information. Deutero-Isaiah, however, exclusively focuses on his message. He does not allow his own person to appear, and he almost never speaks in the first person (the exceptions include 40.6 [as in 1QIsa[a] and LXX], 48.16, 49.1–6, and 61.2; see also 59.21, where YHWH seems to address the prophet directly; some claim that servant passages include information on the prophet, but these passages are very general in comparison with what we are told of earlier prophets). It appears, then, that Deutero-Isaiah functions exclusively as YHWH's mouthpiece; and he is hesitant to include any information about himself or to utter his own words (significantly, Habel ["Form," 313] describes a similar characteristic in the commissioning of Ezekiel, who like Deutero-Isaiah was an exilic prophet).

Against this line of reasoning, however, it should be noted that we know just as little about Micah, who certainly is a classical prophet.

81. Holladay, 2: 35–70.

82. "The anonymous man tells his hearers [in Isa 50.4] that he, born late in time, was called by God Himself to be Isaiah's *limmud*, whose office it was to unseal and to reveal the words handed down by Isaiah to the *limmudim*. Isaiah's message of salvation was not exhausted, we must understand, in the songs and sayings preserved in writing; secret knowledge proceeded from him to be uncovered by God's will before the late disciple." Buber, 204.

83. H. G. M. Williamson, *The Book Called Isaiah: Deutero-Isaiah's Role in Composition and Redaction* (Oxford: Oxford University Press, 1994), 108–9. See further 111ff., where the witness theme throughout Deutero-Isaiah is traced back to Isaiah.

84. For a more detailed critique of the "unity of Isaiah" school, see my article "Allusions and Illusions: The Unity of the Book of Isaiah in Light of Deutero-Isaiah's Use of Prophetic Tradition," in *New Visions of Isaiah*, ed. Roy Melugin and Marvin Sweeney (Sheffield: Sheffield Academic Press, 1996), 156–86. See also my comment in "The Scroll of Isaiah as Jewish Scripture, or, Why Jews Don't Read Books," in *Society of Biblical Literature 1996 Seminar Papers* (Atlanta: Scholars Press, 1996), 228–29 n. 10.

85. For example, Isa 40.27 shares only one term with Isa 8.16–17, and a second common term appears in 40.31; these parallels are too scant to suggest that the relationship between the verses is a borrowing. Similarly, 54.8 shares with 8.17 only a single phrase (הסתיר פנים), and this phrase appears in the Hebrew Bible twenty-eight other times (in various prophets, in the Pentateuch, in Psalms, and in wisdom literature); clearly Deutero-Isaiah was using a common phrase, not the specific text from Isaiah. The case for a genuine borrowing in Isa 50.4–9 is stronger, since it displays a larger number of parallels with Isa 8.16–18: למודים (50.4) // למודי (8.16); פני (8.18); נתן לי ה' (50.4) // א־דני ה' נתן לי (8.17); המסתיר (50.6) // הסתיר (50.6) // פניו (8.17). But here Deutero-Isaiah exploits Isaiah 8's terminology to describe his relationship with earlier prophets and writers generally.

86. Cf. the similar conclusion of Lau, 318–20.

87. On the crucial distinction between scripture and canon, see John Barton, *Oracles of God: Perception of Ancient Prophecy in Israel After the Exile* (London: Darton, Longman and Todd, 1986), 44, 75, and esp. 91–92.

88. Levinson, *Deuteronomy*, 4, 15–17, and 154–55 (esp. n. 21).

89. Levinson, "Human," 45.

APPENDIX

1. This point can be, and has been, exaggerated, however. Note the critical tone of passages such as Isa 42.18–25, 43.22–28, and 48.12–21. These passages are typical in style and vocabulary of Deutero-Isaiah, and there is no reason to view them as

interpolations. See my detailed treatments of allusive style in each passage in Chapters 3, 4, and 5.

2. At least one exception exists: Isa 44.9–20 display fewer features of poetry than most of these chapters.

3. The clearest summary of this consensus position is found in John Skinner's commentary, *The Book of the Prophet Isaiah: Chapters XL–LXVI*, rev. ed. (Cambridge: Cambridge University Press, 1917), xiv–xv and xxix–xxxi. For a review of scholarship, see the sympathetic treatments of Otto Eissfeldt, *The Old Testament: An Introduction*, trans. Peter Ackroyd (New York: Harper and Row, 1965), 341–46; Paul Hanson, *The Dawn of Apocalyptic*, rev. ed. (Philadelphia: Fortress Press, 1979), 32–46; Brooks Schramm, *The Opponents of Third Isaiah: Reconstructing the Cultic History of the Restoration* (Sheffield: Sheffield Academic Press, 1995), 11–40, 50–52. A helpful review of scholarship also appears in Menahem Haran, *Between RI'SHONÔT (Former Prophecies) and ḤADASHÔT (New Prophecies): A Literary-Historical Study of Prophecies in Isaiah XL–XLVII* (Jerusalem: Magnes, 1963), 76–78, although Haran himself does not subscribe to this consensus position.

4. For a review of scholarship advocating this position at the end of the nineteenth century, see Haran, *RI'SHONÔT*, 74–75.

5. Yehezkel Kaufmann's discussion is found in *The Babylonian Captivity and Deutero-Isaiah*, trans. C. W. Efroymson (New York: Union of American Hebrew Congregations, 1970), 68–87; Haran's appears in *RI'SHONÔT*, 79–92, 101–2. Even the more detailed discussions, such as those in Hanson and Schramm, fail to cite these works.

6. Hanson, 34–37.

7. See especially Charles Torrey, *The Second Isaiah: A New Interpretation* (New York: Scribners, 1928), 193–202; Kaufmann, *Babylonian*, 78–87.

8. Torrey, 189–90. See further James Muilenburg, "The Book of Isaiah: Chapters 40–66," in *IB*, ed. G. A. Buttrick et al. (New York: Abingdon Press, 1956), 5: 388–90.

9. See Torrey, 193–94, and Kaufmann, *Babylonian*, 80–87. Cf. the detailed discussion in Lawrence Boadt, "Intentional Alliteration in Second Isaiah," *CBQ* 45 (1983), 353–63.

10. Many other examples of sound play in Isa 40–66 and 35 are given in Torrey, 192–95; Kaufmann, *Babylonian*, 84–87.

11. Torrey, 199–202; Kaufmann, *Babylonian*, 84–87. Copious examples could be cited (for example, in 52.2); the best example may be 56.1, where צדקה appears twice, once in a hendiady meaning "justice" and once in a hendiady meaning "victory."

12. Cf. A. Murtonen, who defends the unity of Isaiah 40–66 on linguistic (as opposed to stylistic) grounds in "Third Isaiah—Yes or No?" *Abr-Nahrain* 19 (1980–81), 20–42; see especially 36–38.

13. Haran, *RI'SHONÔT*, 81 n. 20 and 89–90.

14. Bernhard Duhm, one of the first scholars to propose the existence of Trito-

Isaiah (see the summary in Schramm, 1 n. 1), also asserted that the first four of these passages constitute a separate compositional level within 40–55. Duhm claimed that those passages, which he termed the "Servant Songs," were written later than Deutero-Isaiah and that they differed from Deutero-Isaiah's work especially in that they portray an innocent individual as servant, while Deutero-Isaiah uses the term "servant" to refer to the sinful nation as a whole. Duhm's thesis has been widely accepted in modern biblical scholarship, though some scholars argue that the passages in question actually predate Deutero-Isaiah. Other scholars agree that the passages are a distinct unit but defend Deutero-Isaiah's authorship of them. For a review of the literature, see Eissfeldt, *Introduction*, 333–36. More recently, several scholars have questioned whether these passages can be separated from their context at all. Tryggve N. D. Mettinger, in his important and detailed monograph on this issue, shows that the songs do not differ from the rest of Deutero-Isaiah in their language or their form (*A Farewell to the Servant Songs: A Critical Examination of an Exegetical Axiom* [Lund: Gleerup, 1983], 14–17). He notes further that the songs have a role to play in the compositional structure of the book; that is, they fit into the flow of chapters 40–55 (26–28). Finally, Mettinger demonstrates that the servant figure in these songs in fact is the same servant figure as elsewhere in 40–55: the nation Israel (29–43). In light of Mettinger's work, I can only agree with his conclusion (45): "Duhm's theory concerning the four 'Servant Songs' has enjoyed almost a century of eminence; its success has been as formidable as it has been undeserved. . . . It is quite astonishing that so little attention has been paid by scholars to the *criteria* upon which it was based. The leap from newly launched hypothesis to generally accepted axiom was indeed a short one."

See further Antti Laato, who stresses that Duhm's "Servant Songs" do not differ in language or theme from other servant passages in Deutero-Isaiah (*The Servant of YHWH and Cyrus: A Reinterpretation of the Exilic Messianic Programme in Isaiah 40–55* [Stockholm: Almqvist and Wiksell, 1992], 30–36; cf. 39–46). Kaufmann presents a strong argument against seeing the servant of the songs as an individual (*Babylonian*, 129–34, 148). Torrey (135–43) also presents arguments in favor of the national interpretation of the servant figure and against severing the songs from their context.

15. See Haran, *RPSHONÔT*, 84. In 40.9, God may address Zion directly, depending on how one understands the phrase מְבַשֶּׂרֶת צִיּוֹן; see the readings of Radak, Torrey, and Richard J. Clifford, *Fair Spoken and Persuading: An Interpretation of Second Isaiah* (New York: Paulist Press, 1984).

16. See Haran, *RPSHONÔT*, 48–49.

17. Torrey, 184–85.

18. Mayer Gruber, "The Motherhood of God in Second Isaiah," in *The Motherhood of God and Other Studies* (Atlanta: Scholars Press, 1992), 3–15, esp. 7 (reprinted from *RB* 90 [1983], 351–59); and the same author's "Feminine Similes Applied to the LORD in Second Isaiah," *Beer Sheva* 2 (1985), 75–84 [Heb.].

19. See Haran, *RI'SHONÔT*, 81–84.

20. The one possible exception to this is Isa 40.9, in which YHWH may address the city directly (see above, note 19); even here, the address is quite brief.

21. Similarly, Shalom Paul has noted that language reminiscent of Babylonian royal inscriptions is found throughout the book, but the bulk of examples occur in chapters 40–48. See his essay "Deutero-Isaiah and Cuneiform Royal Inscriptions," in *Essays in Memory of E. A. Speiser*, ed. William Hallo (New Haven, Conn.: American Oriental Society, 1968) (=*JAOS* 88 [1968]), 180–86. (For a discussion of these parallels, see the beginning of Chapter 2 and my references there.) Further, David Carr ("Isaiah 40:1–11 in the Context of the Macrostructure of Second Isaiah," in *Discourse Analysis of Biblical Literature*, ed. Walter Bodine [Atlanta: Scholars Press, 1995], 63 n. 12) notes that certain themes central to 40–48 appear rarely from chapter 49 on: the new Exodus and God's glory that is expressed through it, and the reliability of God's word. Starting in chapter 49, the prophet focuses instead on the restoration of Judah. The presence of elements of divine call in 49.1–6, noted briefly by Carr, also suggests that chapter 49 rather than 56 marks the beginning of a subsection.

22. See *RI'SHONÔT*, 84; on the dating of this section, see his careful and convincing arguments, 91–95, 101–2. In this respect Haran differs from (and improves on) Kaufmann, who believes that the whole work was composed in the exile.

23. For a review of scholarship, see Haran, *RI'SHONÔT*, 75 n. 5.

24. Fritz Maass, "Tritojesaja?" in *Das ferne und nahe Wort: Festschrift Leonhard Rost*, ed. F. Maass (Berlin: Töpelmann, 1967), 153–63. A somewhat more complicated variation of this viewpoint is found in Murtonen, 38–41.

25. Kaufmann's analysis of the unlikely assumptions underlying the work of those who separate chapters 56–66 is especially helpful; see *Babylonian*, 88–89.

26. On all three of these, see Schramm, 31, 34–35.

27. See Hanson, e.g., 47, 59–60, 104–5, 143. For the terms "baroque" and "grotesque" specifically, see 47, 59, and 60.

28. See, e.g., Hanson, 11–12, 150–51. In the former type of eschatology, hope focuses on historical events, political entities, and human figures. In the latter, which is divorced from clear reference to history on earth, hope focuses on a cosmic realm and a divine warrior.

29. E.g., Hanson, 106–7; 113, 119–20; 143–44; 150; 162–63. See also Schramm, 35–36.

30. See James Kugel, *The Idea of Biblical Poetry: Parallelism and Its History* (New Haven, Conn.: Yale University Press, 1981), 292–302, and Wilfred G. E. Watson, *Classical Hebrew Poetry: A Guide to Its Techniques* (Sheffield: Sheffield Academic Press, 1984), 98 and (on syllable counting, the method that Hanson employs) 104–5.

31. Further, Hanson's idea that this alleged development discloses a chronological order is flawed. It is possible for us to note a *schematic* order in the movement from a more prophetic to a more apocalyptic eschatology. But representatives of the dif-

ferent positions could have lived at the same time; indeed, representatives of the "earlier" position could have lived long after the "later" viewpoint came into being.

32. Robert Carroll sees in chaps. 56–66 the work of followers of Deutero-Isaiah who were disappointed by the failure of his prophecies (see "Prophecy and Dissonance: A Theoretical Approach to the Prophetic Tradition," *ZAW* 92 [1980], 108–19). As Carroll accurately points out ("Second Isaiah and the Failure of Prophecy," *ST* 32 [1978], 120), the "glorious and miraculous return of all the exiles to the homeland" predicted by Deutero-Isaiah never took place, at least not on the scale he anticipated. Similarly, Deutero-Isaiah's "triumphalism was misplaced, the transformation of nature did not materialize, the survivors of the nations did not acknowledge YHWH, nor did the salvation of YHWH last forever" ("Second," 121). Carroll claims that "the oracles of Third Isaiah certainly seem to be a series of desperate measures designed to retrieve the expectations created by the proclamation of Second Isaiah by explaining the causes for the delay of national salvation" ("Dissonance," 118). The disappointment Carroll senses in chaps. 56–66 is real, but there is no reason to attribute it exclusively to followers of Deutero-Isaiah. The author of chaps. 40–55 himself may well have felt that disappointment, and he may have composed new oracles as a result.

33. On the other hand, Haran's point that the major shift of focus and setting occurs in chapter 49 may strongly bolster the claim that the sections before and after chapter 56 were written by a single author.

34. Heinrich Graetz, "Isaiah XXXIV and XXXV," *JQR* (OS) 4 (1891), 1–8.

35. See especially Marvin Pope, "Isaiah 34 in Relation to Isaiah 35, 40–66," *JBL* 71 (1952), 235–43.

36. Torrey, 184–85.

37. In a few of these allusions the split-up pattern occurs more than once (see, for example, the allusion to Jer 31.7–9 in Isa 35.4–10), but the figures I list here provide a count of the number of allusions in which the split-up pattern appears, not the total of split-up phrases. The same is true for the figures regarding the other techniques cited in the next several sentences; thus sound play occurs twice in Isa 66.12–24, which allude to Isa 30.27–33, but that example is counted only once.

38. The extent to which these features are evenly distributed is worthy of note; they are not predominantly found in any one section of the book. Chapters 40–55 account for 57 percent of the chapters in what I call Deutero-Isaiah, and they contain 56 percent of the cases of the split-up pattern, 67 percent of the sound plays, and 69 percent of the word plays. Chapters 55–66 account for 39 percent of the chapters in this corpus, and they contain 40 percent of the split-ups, 28 percent of the sound plays, and 19 percent of the word plays. Chapter 35 accounts for 4 percent of the chapters in Deutero-Isaiah and contains 3 percent, 5 percent, and 1 percent of these features respectively. (All figures are rounded to the nearest percent.)

39. Similar reasoning appears in Steven Weitzman, "Allusion, Artifice, and Exile

in the Hymn of Tobit," *JBL* 115 (1996), 51. Weitzman shows that allusions in the hymn in Tobit 13 reflect an allusive strategy found in other allusions within Tobit. On this basis Weitzman argues against viewing the hymn as a later interpolation.

40. Or perhaps at 49.14. See Haran, *RPSHONÔT*, 81–84. Cf. also Joseph Blenkinsopp, *A History of Prophecy in Israel*, 2d ed. (Louisville, Ky.: Westminster John Knox, 1996), 211 and 223 n. 82, though he does not fully recognize the significance of the thematic divide at chapter 48.

41. See especially the summary of Odil Steck's work in his *Studien zu Tritojesaja* (Berlin: Walter de Gruyter, 1991), 269–79. For a critique of this whole model of how prophetic books were composed, see especially the important, if neglected, comments in Yehezkel Kaufmann, *Toledot ha-Emunah ha-Yisraelit* (Jerusalem and Tel Aviv: Bialik and Devir, 1937–56), 3: 20–32 [Heb.].

42. That is, Claus Westermann (*Isaiah 40–66: A Commentary*, trans. D. Stalker [Philadelphia: Westminster Press, 1969]) views the "true" Trito-Isaiah as being nearly a contemporary of, and extraordinarily similar to, Deutero-Isaiah, while other parts of Isaiah 56–66 were written by subsequent figures. Even if one accepts Westermann's divisions within 56–66, it would seem easier to acknowledge that the author who knew Deutero-Isaiah and wrote in his style was Deutero-Isaiah himself.

43. These allusions are discussed above in Chapters 5, 3, and 2.

44. On the other hand, I must acknowledge that especially chapters 60–62 are particularly rich in typical Deutero-Isaianic allusion, while, for example, chapters 63 and 64 have fewer allusions, and those that do occur do not display as many stylistic or thematic features as occur in the preceding three chapters.

45. See, for example, Lau's comments in *Schriftgelehrte Prophetie in Jes 56–66* (Berlin: Walter de Gruyter, 1994), esp. 324.

46. John Day, "A Case of Inner Scriptural Interpretation: The Dependence of Isaiah xxvi.13–xxvii.11 on Hosea xiii.4–xiv.10 (Eng. 9) and Its Relevance to Some Theories of the Redaction of the 'Isaiah Apocalypse,' " *JTS* NS 31 (1980), 309–19, and Marvin Sweeney, "Textual Citations in Isaiah 24–27: Toward an Understanding of the Redactional Function of Chapters 24–27 in the Book of Isaiah," *JBL* 107 (1988), 39–52.

47. A single case of the split-up pattern may be present in Day's first example, and sound play may be present in his seventh, but these exceptions are sufficiently sporadic within the context of the many allusions these scholars note that we may term them coincidences. Further, Day's seventh example involves so few parallels that it is questionable whether it should be considered an allusion at all.

48. Day notes this on p. 317.

49. See Sweeney's summary in "Textual," esp. 51.

50. See, e.g., Odil Steck, "Zu jüngsten . . . 56, 1–8," in *Studien zu Tritojesaja* (Berlin: Walter de Gruyter, 1991), 244–46. These alleged allusions or redactional connections consist of concordance-like listings of parallels whose compositional significance is unclear, given the commonplace nature of the vocabulary and the

absence of a studied reuse of the older passages. On Walter Zimmerli's unfortunate attempt to argue that Trito-Isaiah appropriates and spiritualizes passages from Deutero-Isaiah ("Zur Sprache Tritojesajas," in his *Gottes Offenbarung: Gesammelte Aufsätze zum Alten Testament* [Munich: Chr. Kaiser, 1963], 217–33), see Michael Fishbane, *Biblical Interpretation in Ancient Israel* (Oxford: Oxford University Press, 1985), 288–89.

BIBLIOGRAPHY

Ackroyd, Peter. *Exile and Restoration: A Study of Hebrew Thought of the Sixth Century B.C.* Philadelphia: Westminster Press, 1968.

Agnon, Shmuel Yosef. *Thus Far.* Jerusalem and Tel Aviv: Schocken Publishing House, 1952. [Hebrew.]

Albertz, R. "Das Deuterojesaja-Buch als Fortschreibung der Jesaja-Prophetie." In *Die hebräische Bibel und ihre zweifache Nachgeschichte: Festschrift für Rolf Rendtorff,* ed. C. Macholz, E. Blum, and E. Stegemann, 241–56. Neukirchen-Vluyn: Neukirchener Verlag, 1990.

Alter, Robert. *The Art of Biblical Poetry.* New York: Basic Books, 1985.

——. *The Pleasures of Reading in an Ideological Age.* New York: Norton, 1996 [1989].

Amichai, Yehuda. *Even a Fist Was Once an Open Hand and Fingers.* Tel Aviv and Jerusalem: Schocken Publishing House, 1989. [Hebrew.].

Anderson, Bernhard. "Exodus and Covenant in Second Isaiah and Prophetic Tradition." In *Magnalia Dei, the Mighty Acts of God: Essays on the Bible and Archaeology in Memory of G. Ernest Wright,* ed. W. E. Lemke, F. M. Cross, and P. D. Miller, 339–60. Garden City, N.Y.: Doubleday, 1976.

——. "Exodus Typology in Second Isaiah." In *Israel's Prophetic Heritage: Essays in Honor of James Muilenburg,* ed. B. W. Anderson and W. Harrelson, 177–95. New York: Harper & Row, 1962.

The Assyrian Dictionary of the Oriental Institute of the University of Chicago. Multiple vols. Chicago: The Oriental Institute, 1956–.

Aune, David E. *Prophecy in Early Christianity and the Ancient Mediterranean World*. Grand Rapids, Mich.: William B. Eerdmans, 1983.

Baltzer, K. "Schriftauslegung bei Deuterojesaja?—Jes 43,22–28 als Beispiel." In *Die Väter Israels*, ed. M. Görg, 11–16. Stuttgart: Katholisches Bibelwerk, 1988.

Barth, Hermann. *Die Jesaja-Worte in der Josiazeit*. WMANT. Neukirchen: Neukirchener Verlag, 1977.

Barton, John. *Oracles of God: Perception of Ancient Prophecy in Israel After the Exile*. London: Darton, Longman and Todd, 1986.

Bate, Walter Jackson. *The Burden of the Past and the English Poet*. Cambridge, Mass.: Harvard University Press, 1970.

Beckson, Karl, and Arthur Ganz. *Literary Terms: A Dictionary*. 3d ed. New York: Farrar, Straus and Giroux, 1989.

Begrich, Joachim. *Studien zu Deuterojesaja*. TBü. Munich: Chr. Kaiser, 1969 [1938].

Ben Yehudah, E., and H. Tur-Sinai. *Thesaurus Totius Hebraitatis*. 8 vols. Jerusalem and Tel Aviv: Ben Yehudah Society, 1908–9. [Hebrew.]

Ben-Porat, Ziva. "Intertextuality." *Ha-Sifrut* 34 (1985): 170–78. [Hebrew.]

——. "The Poetics of Literary Allusion." *PTL: A Journal for Descriptive Poetics and Theory of Literature* 1 (1976): 105–28.

Bergsträsser, G. *Hebräische Grammatik mit Benutzung der von E. Kautzsch bearbeiteten 28. Auflage von Wilhelm Gesenius' hebräischer Grammatik*, trans. Mordechai Ben Asher and Josua Blau. 2d ed. Jerusalem: Magnes Press, 1982. [Hebrew.]

Berlin, Adele. *The Dynamics of Biblical Parallelism*. Bloomington: Indiana University Press, 1985.

Blank, Sheldon. "Studies in Deutero-Isaiah." *HUCA* 15 (1940): 1–46.

Blenkinsopp, Joseph. *A History of Prophecy in Israel*. 2d ed. Louisville, Ky.: Westminster John Knox, 1996.

——. "Prophecy and Priesthood in Josephus." *JJS* 25 (1974): 239–62.

Bloom, Harold. *The Anxiety of Influence: A Theory of Poetry*. London: Oxford University Press, 1975 [1973].

——. *A Map of Misreading*. Oxford: Oxford University Press, 1975.

Blum, Erhard. *Studien zur Komposition des Pentateuch*. BZAW. Berlin: Walter de Gruyter, 1990.

Boadt, Lawrence. "Intentional Alliteration in Second Isaiah." *CBQ* 45 (1983): 353–63.

Brettler, Marc. *God Is King: Understanding an Israelite Metaphor*. JSOTSup. Sheffield: Sheffield Academic Press, 1989.

——. "Incompatible Metaphors for YHWH in Deutero-Isaiah." *JSOT* (forthcoming).

Bright, John. *Jeremiah*. AB. Garden City, N.Y.: Doubleday, 1965.

Brown, F., S. R. Driver, and C. Briggs. *A Hebrew and English Lexicon of the Old Testament*. Oxford: Oxford University Press, 1907.

Buber, Martin. *Das Buch der Preisungen*. Cologne: Jakob Hegner, 1963.

——. *The Prophetic Faith*, trans. Carlyle Witton-Davies. New York: Harper and Row, Harper Torchbooks/Cloister Library, 1960 [1949].

Burrows, Millar, ed. *The Isaiah Manuscript and the Habakkuk Commentary*. In *The Dead Sea Scrolls of Saint Mark's Monastery*. New Haven, Conn.: American Schools of Oriental Research, 1950.

Buttenweiser, Moses. *The Psalms Chronologically Treated with a New Translation*. Chicago: University of Chicago Press, 1938.

Carpenter, J., and G. Harford-Battersby. *The Hexateuch According to the Revised Version*. London: Longmans, Green, 1900.

Carr, David. "Isaiah 40:1–11 in the Context of the Macrostructure of Second Isaiah." In *Discourse Analysis of Biblical Literature*, ed. Walter Bodine, 51–73. Atlanta: Scholars Press, 1995.

——. "Reaching for Unity in Isaiah." *JSOT* 57 (1993): 61–81.

——. "Reading Isaiah from Beginning to End." In *New Visions of the Book of Isaiah*, ed. Roy Melugin and Marvin Sweeney, 188–218. JSOTSup. Sheffield: Sheffield Academic Press, 1996.

Carroll, Robert. *Jeremiah*. London: SCM, 1986.

——. "Prophecy and Dissonance: A Theoretical Approach to Prophetic Tradition." *ZAW* 92 (1980): 108–19.

——. "Second Isaiah and the Failure of Prophecy." *ST* 32 (1978): 119–31.

Cassuto, M. D. (Umberto). "Baal." In *Encyclopaedia Biblica*. 9 vols. 2: 285. Jerusalem: Mossad Bialik, 1950–88. [Hebrew.]

——. "On the Formal and Stylistic Relationship Between Deutero-Isaiah and Other Biblical Writers." In *Biblical and Oriental Studies*. 2 vols. Trans. I. Abrahams. 1: 141–77. Jerusalem: Magnes Press, 1973.

Chandler, James. "Romantic Allusiveness." *Critical Inquiry* 8 (1982): 461–87.

Childs, Brevard S. *Introduction to the Old Testament as Scripture*. Philadelphia: Fortress Press, 1979.

Clayton, Jay, and Eric Rothstein. "Figures in the Corpus: Theories of Influence and Intertextuality." In *Influence and Intertextuality in Literary History*, ed. Jay Clayton and Eric Rothstein, 3–36. Madison: University of Wisconsin Press, 1991.

Clements, R. E. "Beyond Tradition History: Deutero-Isaianic Development of First Isaiah's Themes." *JSOT* 31 (1985): 95–113.

——. *Isaiah 1–39*. NCB. Grand Rapids, Mich.: Eerdmans, 1980.

——. "The Prophecies of Isaiah and the Fall of Jerusalem in 587 B.C.E." *VT* 30 (1980): 421–36.

——. "The Unity of the Book of Isaiah." *Int* 36 (1982): 117–29.

Clifford, Richard J. *Fair Spoken and Persuading: An Interpretation of Second Isaiah*. New York: Paulist Press, 1984.

Cogan, Mordechai. "Tofet." In *Encyclopaedia Biblica.* 9 vols. 8: 923–24. Jerusalem: Mossad Bialik, 1950–88. [Hebrew.]

Cohen, Menahem, ed. *Mikra'ot Gedolot 'Haketer': Isaiah.* Ramat Gan: Bar Ilan, 1996.

Cohen, Shaye J. D. *From the Maccabees to the Mishna.* Library of Early Christianity. Philadelphia: Westminster Press, 1987.

Collins, John J. *The Scepter and the Star: The Messiahs of the Dead Sea Scrolls and Other Ancient Literature.* ABRL. New York: Doubleday, 1995.

Conrad, E. "The 'Fear Not' Oracles in Second Isaiah." *VT* 34 (1984): 129–52.

——. *Fear Not Warrior: A Study of 'al Tîrā' Pericopes in the Hebrew Scriptures.* BJS. Chico, Calif.: Scholars Press, 1985.

——. "Second Isaiah and the Priestly Oracle of Salvation." *ZAW* 93 (1981): 225–46.

Conte, Gian Biagio. *The Rhetoric of Imitation: Genre and Poetic Memory in Virgil and Other Latin Poets,* ed. Charles Segal. Ithaca, N.Y.: Cornell University Press, 1986.

Cooke, G. A. *A Critical and Exegetical Commentary on the Book of Ezekiel.* ICC. Edinburgh: T & T Clark, 1936.

Cross, Frank Moore. *Canaanite Myth and Hebrew Epic: Essays in the History of the Religion of Israel.* Cambridge, Mass.: Harvard University Press, 1973.

——. "The Council of YHWH in Second Isaiah." *JNES* 12 (1953): 274–77.

Culler, Jonathan. *The Pursuit of Signs: Semiotics, Literature, and Deconstruction.* Ithaca, N.Y.: Cornell University Press, 1981.

Dahood, Mitchell. "Ugaritic-Hebrew Parallel Pairs." In *Ras Shamra Parallels: The Texts from Ugarit and the Hebrew Bible.* 2 vols. Ed. Loren Fisher. 1: 71–382; 2: 3–39. Rome: Pontifical Biblical Institute, 1972–75.

Darr, Katheryn Pfisterer. "Like Warrior, Like Woman: Destruction and Deliverance in Isaiah 42:10–17." *CBQ* 49 (1987): 560–71.

Day, John. "Baal." In *Anchor Bible Dictionary.* 6 vols. 3: 547–48. New York: Doubleday, 1992.

——. "A Case of Inner Scriptural Interpretation: The Dependence of Isaiah XXVI. 13–XXVII. 11 on Hosea XIII. 4–XIV.10 (Eng. 9) and Its Relevance to Some Theories of the Redaction of the 'Isaiah Apocalypse.'" *JTS* NS 31 (1980): 309–19.

Dietrich, N., O. Loretz, and A. Sanmartín. *Die keilalphabetischen Texte aus Ugarit.* AOAT. Neukirchen: Neukirchener Verlag, 1976.

Dimant, Devorah. "Qumran Sectarian Literature." In *Jewish Writings of the Second Temple Period,* ed. Michael Stone, 483–550. CRINT. Philadelphia: Fortress Press, 1984.

Dobbs-Allsopp, F. W. *Weep, O Daughter of Zion: A Study of the City-Lament Genre in the Hebrew Bible.* Biblica et Orientalia. Rome: Pontifical Biblical Institute, 1993.

Donner, H. and W. Röllig, eds. *Kanaanäische und aramäische Inschriften.* 3 vols. Wiesbaden: Harrassowitz, 1973–79.

Driver, S. R. *The Book of Exodus*. CBSC. Cambridge: Cambridge University Press, 1911.

———. *Introduction to the Literature of the Old Testament*. New York: Meridian Books, 1956 [1897].

Eissfeldt, Otto. *Der Gottesknecht bei Deuterojesaja*. Halle: Max Niemeyer, 1933.

———. *The Old Testament: An Introduction*, trans. Peter R. Ackroyd. New York: Harper and Row, 1965.

———. "The Promises of Grace to David in Isaiah 55:1–5." In *Israel's Prophetic Heritage*, ed. B. Anderson and W. Harrelson, 196–207. New York: Harper and Row, 1962.

Eliezer of Beaugency. Commentary on Isaiah, quoted from Menahem Cohen, *Mikra'ot Gedolot 'Haketer': Isaiah*.

Eliot, T. S. *Selected Poems*. London: Faber & Faber, 1954.

———. "Tradition and the Individual Talent." In *Selected Prose of T.S. Eliot*, ed. Frank Kermode, 37–44. London: Faber & Faber, 1975.

Elliger, K., W. Rudolph, et al., eds. *Biblia Hebraica Stuttgartensia*. Stuttgart: Deutsche Bibelgesellschaft, 1967.

Eph'al, Israel. "On the Linguistic and Cultural Background of Deutero-Isaiah." *Shenaton: An Annual for Biblical and Near Eastern Studies* 10 (1986–89): 31–35. [Hebrew.]

Epstein, J. N., and E. Z. Melammed, eds. *Mekilta De-Rabbi Šimon*. Jerusalem: Beit Hillel, 1955. [Hebrew.]

Eslinger, Lyle. "Inner-Biblical Exegesis and Inner-Biblical Allusion: The Question of Category." *VT* 42 (1992): 47–58.

Evans, Craig. *To See and Not Perceive: Isaiah 6.9–10 in Early Jewish and Christian Interpretation*. JSOTSup. Sheffield: Sheffield Academic Press, 1989.

Ferris, Paul. *The Genre of Communal Lament in the Bible and the Ancient Near East*. SBLDS. Atlanta: Scholars Press, 1992.

Fishbane, Michael. *Biblical Interpretation in Ancient Israel*. Oxford: Oxford University Press, 1985.

———. "Biblical Prophecy as a Religious Phenomenon." In *Jewish Spirituality from the Bible Through the Middle Ages*, ed. Arthur Green, 62–81. World Spirituality. New York: Crossroad, 1988.

———. *Text and Texture: Close Readings in Selected Biblical Texts*. New York: Schocken Books, 1979.

———. "Use, Authority and Interpretation of Mikra at Qumran." In *Mikra: Reading and Interpretation of the Hebrew Bible in Ancient Judaism and Early Christianity*, ed. Martin Jan Mulder, 339–77. CRINT. Philadelphia: Fortress Press, 1984.

Fohrer, Georg. "Jesaja 1 als Zusammenfassung der Verkündigung Jesajas." *ZAW* 74 (1962): 251–68.

Follet, René. "Une nouvelle inscription de Merodach-Baladan II." *Bib* 35 (1954): 413–28.

Fraade, Steven. *From Tradition to Commentary: Torah and Its Interpretation in the Midrash Sifre to Deuteronomy*. SUNY Series in Judaica. Albany: SUNY Press, 1991.

Freud, Sigmund. *Jokes and Their Relation to the Unconscious*, trans. James Strachey. New York: W. W. Norton, 1963.

Friedländer, M., ed. and trans. *The Commentary of Ibn Ezra on Isaiah*. New York: Feldheim, n.d. [1873].

Garner, Richard. *From Homer to Tragedy: The Art of Allusion in Greek Poetry*. London: Routledge, 1990.

Gaster, T. H. "An Ancient Eulogy on Israel: Deuteronomy 33:3–5, 26–29." *JBL* 66 (1947): 53–62.

Geller, Stephen. "Were the Prophets Poets?" *Prooftexts* 3 (1983): 211–21.

Ginsberg, H. L. "The Arm of YHWH in Isaiah 51–63 and the Text of Isaiah 53:10–11." *JBL* 77 (1958): 152–56.

——. "A Strand in the Cord of Hebraic Hymnody." *ErIsr* 9 (1969): 45–50.

——. "Ugaritic Texts and Textual Criticism." *JBL* 62 (1943): 109–15.

——, ed. *The Book of Isaiah: A New Translation*. Philadelphia: Jewish Publication Society, 1972.

Gitay, Yehoshua. "Deutero-Isaiah: Oral or Written?" *JBL* 99 (1980): 185–97.

——. *Prophecy and Persuasion: A Study of Isaiah 40–48*. LB. Bonn: Linguistica Biblica, 1981.

Gordon, Cyrus Herzl. *Ugaritic Textbook*. AnOr. Rome: Pontifical Biblical Institute, 1965.

Goshen-Gottstein, Moshe, ed. *The Hebrew University Bible: The Book of Isaiah*. Jerusalem: Magnes Press, 1995.

Gosse, Bernard. "Isaïe 52,13–53,12 et Isaïe 6." *RB* 98 (1991): 537–43.

Gottwald, Norman. *Studies in the Book of Lamentations*. SBT. London: SCM Press, 1962.

Graetz, H. "Isaiah XXXIV and XXXV." *JQR* (OS) 4 (1891): 1–8.

Gray, George Buchanan. *A Critical and Exegetical Commentary on the Book of Isaiah*. ICC. New York: Scribners, 1912.

Greenberg, Moshe. "The Citations in Ezekiel as a Background for the Prophecies." Heb. *BM* 17 (1972): 273–78. [Hebrew.]

Greenfield, Jonas. "The Zakir Inscription and the Danklied." *Proceedings of the Fifth World Congress of Jewish Studies* (1969): 1: 181–82.

Greenspahn, Frederick. "Why Prophecy Ceased." *JBL* 108 (1989): 37–49.

Grelot, Pierre. "Un parallèle Babylonien d'Isaïe LX et du psaume LXXII." *VT* 7 (1957): 319–21.

Greßmann, Hugo. "Die literarische Analyse Deuterojesajas." *ZAW* 34 (1914): 263–97.

Gruber, Mayer. "Feminine Similes Applied to the LORD in Second Isaiah." *Beer Sheva* 2 (1985): 75–84. [Hebrew.]

——. "'Can a Woman Forget Her Infant . . . ?'" *Tarbiz* 51 (1982): 491–92. [Hebrew.]

——. *The Motherhood of God and Other Studies*. South Florida Studies in the History of Judaism. Atlanta: Scholars Press, 1992.

Gudas, Fabian. "Explication." In *The New Princeton Encyclopedia of Poetry and Poetics*, ed. A. Preminger and V. Brogan, 395–96. Princeton, N.J.: Princeton University Press, 1993.

Guillory, J. *Poetic Authority: Spenser, Milton, and Literary History*. New York: Columbia University Press, 1983.

Gwaltney, William. "The Biblical Book of Lamentations in the Context of Near Eastern Literature." In *Scripture in Context II*, ed. J. Moyer, W. Hallo, and L. Perdue, 191–211. Winona Lake, Ind.: Eisenbrauns, 1983.

Habel, Norman. "The Form and Significance of the Call Narratives." *ZAW* 77 (1965): 297–323.

Hanson, Paul D. *The Dawn of Apocalyptic*. Philadelphia: Fortress Press, 1975.

Haran, Menahem. *Between Rľ SHONÔT (Former Prophecies) and ḤADASHÔT (New Prophecies): A Literary-Historical Study of Prophecies in Isaiah XL–XLVIII*. Jerusalem: Magnes Press, 1963. [Hebrew.]

——. "The Literary Structure and Chronological Framework of the Prophecies of Is. XL–LXVI." *VTSup* 9 (1963): 127–55.

Hartman, Geoffrey, ed. *The Selected Poetry and Prose of Wordsworth*. New York: Meridian Books, 1970.

Hayes, J., and S. Irvine. *Isaiah: Eighth Century Prophet*. Nashville, Tenn.: Abingdon Press, 1987.

Hays, Richard B. *Echoes of Scripture in the Letters of Paul*. New Haven, Conn.: Yale University Press, 1989.

Holladay, William. *Jeremiah 1: A Commentary on the Book of the Prophet Jeremiah 1–25*. Hermeneia. Philadelphia: Fortress Press, 1986.

——. *Jeremiah 2: A Commentary on the Book of the Prophet Jeremiah 26–52*. Hermeneia. Minneapolis: Fortress Press, 1989.

Horovitz, H. and Rabin, I., eds. *Mechilta D'Rabbi Ismael cum Variis Lectionibus et Adnotationibus*. Jerusalem: Wahrmann, 1970. [Hebrew.]

Hrushovski, Benjamin. "Note on the Systems of Hebrew Versification." In *The Penguin Book of Hebrew Verse*, ed. T. Carmi, 57–72. New York: Viking Press, 1981.

——. "Prosody, Hebrew." In *Encyclopaedia Judaica*, 13: 1195–1240. Jerusalem: Keter, 1971.

Hughes, Merritt, ed. *Complete Poems and Major Prose by John Milton*. Indianapolis: Bobbs-Merrill, 1957.

Hurvitz, Avi. *The Transition Period in Biblical Hebrew: A Study in Post-Exilic Hebrew and Its Implications for the Dating of Psalms.* Jerusalem: Mossad Bialik, 1972. [Hebrew.]

——. *Wisdom Language in Biblical Psalmody.* Jerusalem: Magnes Press, 1991. [Hebrew.]

Ibn Caspi, Joseph. Commentary on Isaiah. In Menahem Cohen, *Mikra'ot Gedolot 'Haketer': Isaiah.*

Ibn Ezra, Abraham. Commentary on Isaiah. In Menahem Cohen, *Mikra'ot Gedolot 'Haketer': Isaiah,* and M. Friedländer, *The Commentary of Ibn Ezra on Isaiah.*

Janzen, J. Gerald. "An Echo of the Shema in Isaiah 51.1–3." *JSOT* 43 (1989): 69–82.

——. *Studies in the Text of Jeremiah.* Cambridge, Mass.: Harvard University Press, 1973.

Johnson, Anthony. "Allusion in Poetry." *PTL: A Journal for Descriptive Poetics and Theory of Literature* 1 (1976): 579–87.

Jones, D. "The Tradition of the Oracles of Isaiah of Jerusalem." *ZAW* 67 (1955): 226–46.

Joüon, Paul, and T. Muraoka. *A Grammar of Biblical Hebrew.* Rome: Pontifical Biblical Institute, 1993.

Kaminka, Armond. *Meḥqarim.* 2 vols. Tel Aviv: Devir, 1938. [Hebrew.]

Kaufmann, Yehezkel. *The Babylonian Captivity and Deutero-Isaiah,* trans. C. W. Efroymson. New York: Union of American Hebrew Congregations, 1970.

——. *The Religion of Israel: From Its Beginnings to the Babylonian Exile,* trans. and abridged by Moshe Greenberg. Chicago: University of Chicago Press, 1960.

——. *Toledot ha-Emunah ha-Yisraelit (History of the Religion of Israel).* 4 vols. Jerusalem and Tel Aviv: Bialik and Devir, 1937–56. [Hebrew.]

Kautzsch, E. *Gesenius' Hebrew Grammar,* trans. A. E. Cowley. 2d ed. Oxford: Oxford University Press, 1910.

Knohl, Israel. *The Sanctuary of Silence: The Priestly Torah and the Holiness School.* Minneapolis: Fortress Press, 1995.

Kronfeld, Chana. "Allusion: An Israeli Perspective." *Prooftexts* 5 (1985): 137–63.

——. *On the Margins of Modernism: Decentering Literary Dynamics.* Contraversions. Berkeley: University of California Press, 1996.

Kugel, James. "The Bible's Earliest Interpreters." *Prooftexts* 7 (1987): 269–83.

——. *The Idea of Biblical Poetry: Parallelism and Its History.* New Haven, Conn.: Yale University Press, 1981.

Kutscher, E. Y. *The Language and Linguistic Background of the Isaiah Scroll (1QIsaᵃ).* Leiden: E. J. Brill, 1974.

Laato, Antti. *The Servant of YHWH and Cyrus: A Reinterpretation of the Exilic Messianic Programme in Isaiah 40–55.* ConBOT. Stockholm: Almqvist and Wiksell, 1992.

Lau, Wolfgang. *Schriftgelehrte Prophetie in Jes 56–66*. BZAW. Berlin: Walter de Gruyter, 1994.

Levine, Baruch. *Leviticus*. JPSTC. Philadelphia: Jewish Publication Society, 1989.

Levinson, Bernard A. *Deuteronomy and the Hermeneutics of Legal Innovation*. New York: Oxford University Press, 1997.

———. "The Human Voice in Divine Revelation: The Problem of Authority in Biblical Law." In *Innovations in Religious Traditions: Essays in the Interpretation of Religious Change*, ed. Michael Williams, Collet Cox, and Martin Jaffee, 29–45. Berlin: Walter de Gruyter, 1992.

Lewy, Julius. "The Biblical Institution of *dᵉrôr* in the Light of Akkadian Documents." *ErIsr* 5 (Mazar Volume) (1958): 21*–31*.

Liddell, H. G., et al. *An Intermediate Greek-English Lexicon Founded upon the Seventh Edition of Liddell and Scott's Greek-English Lexicon*. Oxford: Oxford University Press, 1889.

Lieberman, Saul. "The Publication of the Mishnah." In *Hellenism in Jewish Palestine*. New York: Jewish Theological Seminary, 1962.

Liebreich, Leon. "The Composition of the Book of Isaiah." *JQR* 46 (1956): 259–78.

———. "The Composition of the Book of Isaiah." *JQR* 47 (1957): 114–38.

Maass, Fritz. "Tritojesaja?" In *Das ferne und nahe Wort: Festschrift Leonhard Rost*, ed. F. Maass, 153–63. BZAW. Berlin: Töpelmann, 1967.

McCarthy, Dennis. *Treaty and Covenant*. AnBib. Rome: Biblical Institute Press, 1981.

McKenzie, John. *Second Isaiah*. AB. Garden City, N.Y.: Doubleday, 1968.

Malamat, Abraham. "A Forerunner of Biblical Prophecy: The Mari Documents." In *Ancient Israelite Religion: Essays in Honor of Frank Moore Cross*, eds. P. D. Hanson, P. D. Miller, and S. D. McBride, 33–52. Philadelphia: Fortress Press, 1987.

Mandelbaum, Bernard. *Pesikta de Rav Kahana*. 2 vols. New York: Jewish Theological Seminary, 1987. [Hebrew.]

Margalioth, Rachel. *The Indivisible Isaiah*. Jerusalem and New York: Sura Institute and Yeshiva University, 1964.

Meged, Aharon. *Indecent Act: Three Stories*. Tel Aviv: Am Oved, 1986. [Hebrew.]

Melammed, E. Z. "Break-up of Stereotype Phrases as an Artistic Device in Biblical Poetry." *Scripta Hierosolymitana* 8 (1961): 115–53.

———. "EN ΔIA ΔYOIN in the Bible." *Tarbiz* 16 (1944–45): 179–85. [Hebrew.]

Melugin, Roy. *The Formation of Isaiah 40–55*. BZAW. Berlin: Walter de Gruyter, 1976.

———. "Introduction." In *New Visions of Isaiah*, ed. Roy Melugin and Marvin Sweeney, 13–29. Sheffield: Sheffield Academic Press, 1996.

Mettinger, Tryggve N. D. *A Farewell to the Servant Songs: A Critical Examination of an Exegetical Axiom*. Lund: Gleerup, 1983.

Milgrom, Jacob. *Numbers*. JPSTC. Philadelphia: Jewish Publication Society, 1989.

Miller, J. M., and J. Hayes. *A History of Ancient Israel and Judah*. Philadelphia: Westminster Press, 1986.

Miner, Earl. "Allusion." In *Encyclopedia of Poetry and Poetics*, ed. Alex Preminger, 18. Princeton, N.J.: Princeton University Press, 1965.

——. "Allusion." In *The New Princeton Encyclopedia of Poetry and Poetics*, ed. A. Preminger and V. Brogan, 38–39. Princeton, N.J.: Princeton University Press, 1993.

Miqra'ot Gedolot: Nach. 4 vols. Jerusalem: Schocken Publishing House, 1946 [1862–66].

Miqra'ot Gedolot: Torah. 2 vols. Tel Aviv: Schocken Publishing House, 1959 [1859].

Mowinckel, S. "Zur Komposition des Buches Jeremia." *Videnkabs-Selskabet. Hist-filos*. 11 (1913): 220–78. Kristiania: Jacob Dwybad, 1914.

Muffs, Yochanan. "Between Justice and Mercy: The Prayer of the Prophets." In *Torah Nidreshet*, ed. Moshe Greenberg, 39–87. Jerusalem: Am Oved and Jewish Theological Seminary, 1984. [Hebrew.]

——. *Love and Joy: Law, Language and Religion in Ancient Israel*. New York and Cambridge, Mass.: Jewish Theological Seminary and Harvard University Press, 1992.

Muilenburg, James. "The Book of Isaiah: Chapters 40–66." In *IB*, ed. G. A. Buttrick et al., 5: 381–419, 422–773. New York: Abingdon Press, 1956.

Murtonen, A. "Third Isaiah—Yes or No?" *Abr-Nahrain* 19 (1980–81): 20–42.

Obadiah of Bertinoro. Commentary on the Mishna, quoted from standard editions of the Mishna. Warsaw, 1862.

O'Day, Gail. "Jeremiah 9:22–23 and I Corinthians 1:26–31: A Study in Intertextuality." *JBL* 109 (1990): 259–67.

Overholt, Thomas. "The End of Prophecy: No Players Without a Program." *JSOT* 42 (1988): 103–15.

Pagis, Dan. *Change and Tradition in the Secular Poetry: Spain and Italy*. Jerusalem: Keter, 1976. [Hebrew.]

Paul, Shalom. "Deutero-Isaiah and Cuneiform Royal Inscriptions." In *Essays in Memory of E. A. Speiser* (=*JAOS* 88 [1968]), ed. William Hallo, 180–86. New Haven, Conn.: American Oriental Society, 1968.

——. "Literary and Ideological Echoes of Jeremiah in Deutero-Isaiah." *Proceedings of the Fifth World Congress of Jewish Studies* (1969): 1: 102–20.

Perri, Carmela. "On Alluding." *Poetics* 7 (1978): 289–307.

Petersen, D. *Late Israelite Prophecy: Studies in Deutero-Prophetic Literature and in Chronicles*. Missoula, Mont.: Scholars Press, 1977.

Pondrom, Cyrena. "Influence? or Intertextuality? The Complicated Connection of Edith Sitwell with Gertrude Stein." In *Influence and Intertextuality in Literary History*, ed. Jay Clayton and Eric Rothstein, 204–20. Madison: University of Wisconsin Press, 1991.

Pope, Marvin. "Isaiah 34 in Relation to Isaiah 35, 40–66." *JBL* 71 (1952): 235–43.

Pritchard, James B., ed. *Ancient Near Eastern Texts Relating to the Old Testament.* 3d ed. Princeton, N.J.: Princeton University Press, 1969.

Qimron, Elisha. "Concerning the Language of the Second Temple Period in the Book of Psalms." *BM* 23 (1977): 139–50. [Hebrew.]

Rabinowitz, J. "*Gerushin.*" In *Encyclopaedia Biblica.* 9 vols. 2: 551–54. Jerusalem: Mossad Bialik, 1950–88. [Hebrew.]

Rahlfs, Alfred, ed. *Septuaginta.* Stuttgart: Deutsche Bibelgesellschaft, 1979 [1935].

Radak (Rabbi David Qimḥi). Biblical commentaries. In Menahem Cohen, *Mikra'ot Gedolot 'Haketer': Isaiah,* and from standard editions of the *Miqra'ot Gedolot.*

Rashbam (Rabbi Shmuel ben Meir). *Commentary on the Torah,* ed. D. Rosin. Breslau, 1882. [Hebrew.]

Rashi (Rabbi Shlemo ben Isaac). Biblical commentaries. In Menahem Cohen, *Mikra'ot Gedolot 'Haketer': Isaiah,* and from standard editions of the *Miqra'ot Gedolot.*

Rendtorff, Rolf. "The Book of Isaiah: A Complex Unity. Synchronic and Dia-chronic Reading." In *New Visions of Isaiah,* ed. Roy Melugin and Marvin Sweeney, 32–49. Sheffield: Sheffield Academic Press, 1996.

——. "Jesaja 6 im Rahmen der Komposition des Jesajabuches." In *The Book of Isaiah,* ed. J. Vermeylen, 73–82. BETL. Leuven: University Press, 1981.

——. "Zur Komposition des Buches Jesaja." *VT* 34 (1984): 295–320.

Renza, Louis. "Influence." In *Critical Terms for Literary Study,* ed. Frank Lentricchia and Thomas McLaughlin, 186–202. Chicago: University of Chicago Press, 1990.

Rofé, Alexander. "Isaiah 66.1–4: Judean Sects in the Persian Period as Viewed by Trito-Isaiah." In *Biblical and Related Studies Presented to Samuel Iwry,* ed. A. Kort and S. Morschauser, 205–17. Winona Lake, Ind.: Eisenbrauns, 1985.

——. "Isaiah 55:6–11: The Problems of the Fulfillment of Prophecies and Trito-Isaiah." *Proceedings of the Sixth World Congress of Jewish Studies* (1977): 1: 213–21. [Hebrew.]

Rooker, Mark. *Biblical Hebrew in Transition: The Language of the Book of Ezekiel.* JSOTSup. Sheffield: Sheffield Academic Press, 1990.

Safrai, Shmuel. "Oral Torah." In *The Literature of the Sages, Volume One,* ed. Shmuel Safrai, 35–119. CRINT. Philadelphia: Fortress Press, 1987.

Sarna, Nahum. "The Abortive Insurrection in Zedekiah's Day." *ErIsr* 14 (H. L. Ginsberg Volume) (1978): 89*–96*.

——. "Psalm 89: A Study in Inner-Biblical Exegesis." In *Biblical and Other Studies,* ed. Alexander Altmann, 29–46. Lown Institute at Brandeis University Texts and Studies. Cambridge, Mass.: Harvard University Press, 1963.

——. "Psalms, Book of." In *Encyclopedia Judaica,* 13: 1303–22. Jerusalem: Keter, 1971.

——. "Zedekiah's Emancipation of Slaves and the Sabbatical Year." In *Orient and Occident: Essays Presented to Cyrus H. Gordon*, ed. Harry Hoffner, Jr., 143–49. AOAT. Neukirchen: Neukirchener Verlag, 1973.

Schäfer, Peter. *Die Vorstellung vom Heiligen Geist in der rabbinischen Literatur*. SANT. Munich: Kösel-Verlag, 1972.

Schmitz, P. "Tophet." In *Anchor Bible Dictionary*. 6 vols. 6: 600–601. New York: Doubleday, 1992.

Schniedewind, William. *The Word of God in Transition: From Prophets to Inspired Messengers in the Second Temple Period*. JSOTSup. Sheffield: Sheffield Academic Press, 1995.

Schramm, Brooks. *The Opponents of Third Isaiah: Reconstructing the Cultic History of the Restoration*. JSOTSup. Sheffield: Sheffield Academic Press, 1995.

Seeligmann, I. L. "Voraussetzungen der Midraschexegese." *SVT* 1 (1953): 150–81.

Seidel, Moshe. *Ḥiqrei Miqra'*. Jerusalem, 1978. [Hebrew.]

——. "Parallels Between the Book of Isaiah and the Book of Psalms." *Sinai* 38 (1955–56): 149–72, 229–42, 272–80, 333–55. [Hebrew.]

Seitz, Christopher. "The Divine Council: Temporal Transition and New Prophecies in the Book of Isaiah." *JBL* 109 (1990): 229–47.

——. "Isaiah 1–66: Making Sense of the Whole." In *Reading and Preaching the Book of Isaiah*, ed. C. Seitz, 105–26. Philadelphia: Fortress Press, 1988.

——. *Zion's Final Destiny: The Development of the Book of Isaiah, a Reassessment of Isaiah 36–39*. Minneapolis: Fortress Press, 1991.

Sekine, Seizo. *Die tritojesajanische Sammlung (Jes 56–66) redaktionsgeschichtlich untersucht*. BZAW. Berlin: Walter de Gruyter, 1989.

Shaw, Harry. *A Dictionary of Literary Terms*. San Francisco: McGraw-Hill, 1972.

Sheppard, G. "The Anti-Assyrian Redaction and the Canonical Context of Isaiah 1–39." *JBL* 104 (1985): 193–216.

Shinan, Avigdor, ed. *Midrash Shemot Rabbah Chapters I–XIV*. Jerusalem: Dvir, 1984. [Hebrew.]

Skinner, John. *The Book of the Prophet Isaiah: Chapters I–XXXIX*. CBSC. Cambridge: Cambridge University Press, 1896.

——. *The Book of the Prophet Isaiah: Chapters XL–LXVI*. Rev. ed. CBSC. Cambridge: Cambridge University Press, 1917.

Smith, J. Z. *Imagining Religion from Babylon to Jonestown*. Chicago: University of Chicago Press, 1982.

——. *Map Is Not Territory*. Leiden: Brill, 1978.

Sommer, Benjamin. "Allusions and Illusions: The Unity of the Book of Isaiah in Light of Deutero-Isaiah's Use of Prophetic Tradition." In *New Visions of the Book of Isaiah*, ed. Roy Melugin and Marvin Sweeney, 156–86. JSOTSup. Sheffield: Sheffield Academic Press, 1996.

——. "Did Prophecy Cease? Evaluating a Re-evaluation." *JBL* 115 (1996): 31–47.

——. "New Light on the Composition of Jeremiah." *CBQ* (forthcoming).

——. "The Scroll of Isaiah as Jewish Scripture, or, Why Jews Don't Read Books." In *Society of Biblical Literature 1996 Seminar Papers*, 225–42. Atlanta: Scholars Press, 1996.

Sperber, Alexander, ed. *The Bible in Aramaic: The Latter Prophets According to Targum Jonathan.* Leiden: Brill, 1962.

Steck, Odil H. *Bereitete Heimkehr: Jesaja 35 als redaktionelle Brücke zwischen dem ersten und zweiten Jesaja.* SBS. Stuttgart: Katholisches Bibelwerk, 1985.

——. *Gottesknecht und Zion: Gesammelte Aufsätze zu Deuterojesaja.* Tübingen: J. C. B. Mohr/Paul Siebeck, 1992.

——. " 'Ein kleiner Knabe kann sie leiten': Beobachtungen zum Tierfrieden in Jesaja 11,6–8 und 65,25." In *Alttestamentlicher Glaube und biblische Theologie: Festschrift für Horst Dietrich Preuß*, ed. J. Hausmann and H. J. Zobel, 104–13. Stuttgart: Kohlhammer, 1992.

——. *Studien zu Tritojesaja.* BZAW. Berlin: Walter de Gruyter, 1991.

Stemberger, G., and H. L. Strack. *Introduction to the Talmud and Midrash*, trans. M. Bockmuehl. Edinburgh: T. & T. Clark, 1991.

Stummer, Friedrich. "Einige keilschriftliche Parallelen zu Jes. 40–66." *JBL* 45 (1926): 171–89.

Sturrock, John, ed. *Structuralism and Since: From Lévi-Strauss to Derrida.* Oxford: Oxford University Press, 1979.

Sukenik, E. L., ed. *The Dead Sea Scrolls of the Hebrew University.* Jerusalem: Mossad Bialik and the Hebrew University, 1954. [Hebrew.]

Sweeney, M. *Isaiah 1–4 and the Post-Exilic Understanding of the Isaianic Tradition.* BZAW. Berlin: Walter de Gruyter, 1988.

——. "The Unity of the Book of Isaiah in the History of Modern Critical Research." Paper read at the Society of Biblical Literature meeting, 1990.

——. "Textual Citations in Isaiah 24–27." *JBL* 107 (1988): 39–52.

Talmon, Shemaryahu. "The 'Desert Motif' in the Bible and Qumran Literature." In *Biblical Motifs: Origins and Transformations*, ed. Alexander Altmann, 31–63. Lown Institute at Brandeis University Text and Studies. Cambridge, Mass.: Harvard University Press, 1966.

Tanakh: A New Translation of the Holy Scriptures—The New JPS Translation According to the Traditional Hebrew Text. Philadelphia: Jewish Publication Society, 1985.

Theodor, J., and C. Albeck, eds. *Midrash Bereshit Rabba.* 3 vols. Jerusalem: Wahrmann, 1965. [Hebrew.]

Tigay, Jeffrey. *Deuteronomy.* JPSTC. Philadelphia: Jewish Publication Society, 1996.

——. "Israelite Religion: The Onomastic and Epigraphic Evidence." In *Ancient Israelite Religion: Essays in Honor of Frank Moore Cross*, ed. P. D. Hanson, P. D. Miller, and S. D. McBride, 157–94. Philadelphia: Fortress Press, 1987.

Toeg, Aryeh. *Lawgiving at Sinai*. Jerusalem: Magnes Press, 1977. [Hebrew.]

———. "A Halakhic Midrash: Num. xv:22–31. *Tarbiz* 43 (1973): 1–20. [Hebrew.]

Tomasino, Anthony. "Isaiah 1.1–2.4 and 63–66 and the Composition of the Isaianic Corpus." *JSOT* 57 (1993): 81–98.

Torrey, Charles. *The Second Isaiah: A New Interpretation*. New York: Scribners, 1928.

Tov, Emmanuel. "The Literary History of the Book of Jeremiah in Light of Its Textual History." In *Empirical Models for Biblical Criticism*, ed. J. Tigay, 211–38. Philadelphia: University of Pennsylvania Press, 1985.

Trunz, Erich, ed. *Goethes Werke*. Hamburg: Christian Wagner Verlag, 1949.

Tsevat, Matitiahu. "God and the Gods in Assembly." In *The Meaning of the Book of Job and Other Biblical Studies*, 155–76. New York: Ktav, 1980.

———. "The Throne Vision of Isaiah." In *The Meaning of the Book of Job and Other Biblical Studies*. New York: Ktav, 1980.

Urbach, Ephraim. "When Did Prophecy Cease?" *Tarbiz* 17 (1946): 1–11. [Hebrew.]

von Rad, Gerhard. "כְּפָלַיִם in Jes. 40.2 = Äquivalent?" *ZAW* 79 (1967): 80–82.

———. "The City on the Hill." In *The Problem of the Hexateuch and Other Essays*, trans. E. Trueman Dicken. London: SCM, 1984.

———. *Old Testament Theology*. 2 vols. Trans. D. M. G. Stalker. Edinburgh: Oliver and Boyd, 1965.

Watson, Wilfred G. E. *Classical Hebrew Poetry: A Guide to Its Techniques*. JSOTSup. Sheffield: Sheffield Academic Press, 1984.

Weiner, Andrew D. "Sidney/Spenser/Shakespeare: Influence/Intertextuality/Intention." In *Influence and Intertextuality*, ed. Jay Clayton and Eric Rothstein, 245–70. Madison: University of Wisconsin Press, 1991.

Weinfeld, Moshe. *Deuteronomy 1–11*. AB. New York: Doubleday, 1991.

———. "God the Creator in Gen. 1 and in the Prophecy of Second Isaiah." *Tarbiz* 37 (1968): 105–32. [Hebrew.]

———. "Jeremiah and the Spiritual Metamorphosis of Israel." *ZAW* 88 (1976): 15–56.

———. "Universalism and Particularism in the Period of the Return to Zion." *Tarbiz* 33 (1964): 228–42. [Hebrew.]

———, ed. *Likkutei Tarbiz: A Biblical Studies Reader*. Jerusalem: Magnes Press, 1979. [Hebrew.]

Weiser, Artur. *The Psalms: A Commentary*, trans. Herbert Hartwell. OTL. Philadelphia: Westminster Press, 1962.

Weitzman, Steven. "Allusion, Artifice, and Exile in the Hymn of Tobit." *JBL* 115 (1996): 49–61.

Wellek, René, and Austin Warren. *Theory of Literature*. 3d ed. New York: Harcourt, Brace and World, Harvest Books, 1956.

Wellhausen, Julius. *Prolegomena to the History of Ancient Israel*, trans. Black and Menzies. New York: Meridian Books, 1957 [1885].

Wells, Roy Jr. "'Isaiah' as an Exponent of Torah: Isaiah 56:1–8." In *New Visions of the Book of Isaiah*, ed. Roy Melugin and Marvin Sweeney, 140–55. JSOTSup. Sheffield: Sheffield Academic Press, 1996.

Westermann, Claus. *Genesis 1–11*, trans. J. Scullion. Minneapolis: Augsburg Press, 1984.

——. *Isaiah 40–66: A Commentary*, trans. D. Stalker. OTL. Philadelphia: Westminster Press, 1969.

Wevers, John. *Ezekiel*. Century Bible. London: Nelson, 1969.

Whedbee, J. William. *Isaiah and Wisdom*. Nashville, Tenn.: Abingdon Press, 1971.

Williamson, H. G. M. *The Book Called Isaiah: Deutero-Isaiah's Role in Composition and Redaction*. Oxford: Oxford University Press, 1994.

Wilson, Robert R. *Prophecy and Society in Ancient Israel*. Philadelphia: Fortress Press, 1980.

Wiseman, D. J. "The Vassal Treaties of Esarhaddon." *Iraq* 20 (1958): 1–100.

Wolf, H. "The Relationship Between Isaiah's Final Servant Song and Chapters 1–6." In *A Tribute to Gleason Archer*, ed. W. Kaiser and Ronald Youngblood, 251–59. Chicago: Moody, 1986.

Wolff, Hans Walter. *Hosea*, trans. G. Stansell. Hermeneia. Philadelphia: Fortress Press, 1974.

Zakovitch, Yair. *An Introduction to Inner-Biblical Interpretation*. Even-Yehuda: Reches, 1992. [Hebrew.]

——. "Review of J. P. Fokkelman, *Narrative Art in Genesis*." *Shnaton: An Annual for Biblical and Ancient Near Eastern Studies* 4 (1980): 302–8. [Hebrew.]

Ziegler, Joseph, ed. *Ieremias, Baruch, Threni, Epistula Ieremiae*. Vol. XV of *Septuaginta: Vetus Testamentum Graecum*. Göttingen: Vandenhoeck & Ruprecht, 1957.

——, ed. *Isaias*. Vol. XIV of *Septuaginta: Vetus Testamentum Graecum*. Göttingen: Vandenhoeck & Ruprecht, 1939.

Zimmerli, W. *Ezekiel*. 2 vols. Trans. R. Clements. Philadelphia: Fortress Press, 1979.

——. "Zur Sprache Tritojesajas." In *Gottes Offenbarung: Gesammelte Aufsätze zum Alten Testament*, 217–33. TBü. Munich: Chr. Kaiser, 1963.

CHART OF ALLUSIONS
IN ISAIAH 34–35, 40–66

The following chart lists all the cases I have identified as allusions or echoes in Isaiah 34–35 and 40–66. Doubtful cases are given in parentheses (and, for a few very doubtful cases, double parentheses). For allusions or echoes discussed in this book, I list the page on which the main discussion of each occurs; for those that are not discussed in the body of the text but are mentioned briefly in a note, I list the chapter and note number. For allusions or echoes that are not mentioned specifically in this book, I list one or more salient features.

LOCATION OF ALLUSION	SOURCE OF ALLUSION			
	Isaiah	Jeremiah	Psalms	Other
Isaiah 34.1		⊐— (Jer 25.9) (Ch2n44)		
2				
3				
4				
5				
6				
7				
8				
9				
10				

(continued)

LOCATION OF ALLUSION	Isaiah	Jeremiah	Psalms	Other
Isaiah 35.1				
2				
3	Isa 32.1–6 (Ch3n26)			
4				
5				
6		Jer 31.7–9 (p. 162)		
7				
8				
9				
10				
Isaiah 40.1				Exod 32.14–15 (Ch5n52)
2		Jer 16.16–18 (p. 57)		
3				Ezek 21.2–12 (Ch3n12)
4	(Isa 6) (Ch3n63)			
5				
6	Isa 28.1–5 (p. 75)			
7				
8				
9		Jer 31.16 (p. 68)		
10				
11				
12				
13				
14				
15				
16				
17				
18				
19		(Jer 10.1–16) (Ch2n112)		
20			(Ps 82.5–8) (p. 123)	
21				
22				
23	Isa 6.9–10 (Ch3n14)			
24				
25				
26				
27				

(continued)

	Isaiah	*Jeremiah*	*Psalms*	*Other*

(Isaiah 40 continued)

Isaiah 40.28				Gen 2.2,
29				Exod 31.17
30	(Isa 5.27)			(p. 144)
31	(Ch3n14)			

Isaiah 41.1				
2				
3				
4				
5				
6		(Jer 10.1–16)		
7		(Ch2n112)		
8				
9				
10		(Jer 30.10–11)		
11		(p. 34;	((Ps 35))	
12		Ch2n45)	(Ch4n31)	
13				
14				
15				
16				
17				
18				
19				
20				
21				
22				
23				
24				
25		Jer 4.22–25		
26		(p. 67)		
27				
28				
29				

(continued)

	Isaiah	*Jeremiah*	*Psalms*	*Other*

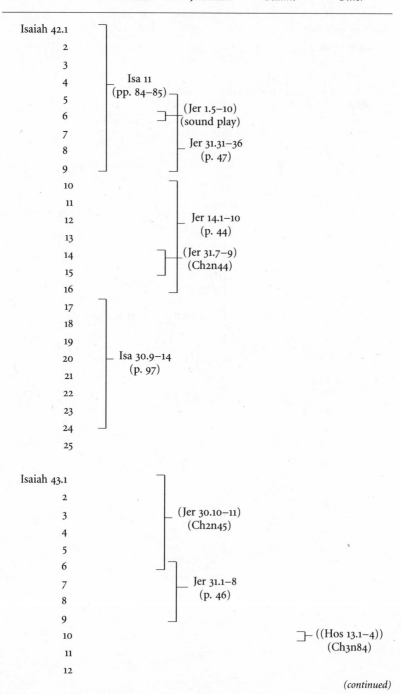

Isaiah 42.1
2
3
4   Isa 11
5   (pp. 84–85)
6   (Jer 1.5–10)
7   (sound play)
8   Jer 31.31–36
9   (p. 47)
10
11
12   Jer 14.1–10
13   (p. 44)
14   (Jer 31.7–9)
15   (Ch2n44)
16
17
18
19
20   Isa 30.9–14
21   (p. 97)
22
23
24
25

Isaiah 43.1
2
3   (Jer 30.10–11)
4   (Ch2n45)
5
6
7   Jer 31.1–8
8   (p. 46)
9
10   ((Hos 13.1–4))
11   (Ch3n84)
12

(continued)

LOCATION OF ALLUSION	SOURCE OF ALLUSION			
	Isaiah	*Jeremiah*	*Psalms*	*Other*

(Isaiah 43 continued)

Isaiah 43.13				
14				
15				
16				
17				
18		(Jer 16.14) (typology)		
19				
20				
21			Ps 51 (Ch5n34)	Gen 30–32 (p. 140)
22				
23				
24				
25				
26				
27				((Hos 12)) (Ch3n84)
28				
Isaiah 44.1		(Jer 30.10–11) (Ch2n45)		
2				
3				
4				
5				
6				
7				
8				
9	Isa 6.9–13 (p. 104)	(Jer 10.1–16) (Ch2n112)		
10				
11				
12				
13				
14				
15				
16				
17				
18				
19				
20				

(continued)

Location of Allusion	Isaiah	Jeremiah	Psalms	Other
(Isaiah 44 continued)				
Isaiah 44.21				
22				
23				
24				Gen 1 (p. 144)
25				
26				
27				
28				
Isaiah 45.1				
2			Ps 72; Ps 2 (p. 115)	
3				Gen 1 (p. 143)
4				
5				
6				
7				
8				
9				
10				
11	Isa 29.14–21 (p. 104)	Jer 27.5–6 (p. 60)		
12				
13		((Jer 15.13))		
14				
15				
16				Deut 33.26–29 (p. 136)
17				
18				Gen 1 (pp. 142–43)
19				
20			(Ps 22.24–30) (Ch4n44)	
21				
22				
23				
24				
25				

(continued)

	Isaiah	Jeremiah	Psalms	Other
		SOURCE OF ALLUSION		

Isaiah 46.1
2
3
4
5
6
7
8
9
10
11
12
13

Isa 14.24–25 (Ch3n57) — spanning verses 10–13

Ps 71.2–19 (p. 120) — spanning verses 3–13

Gen 1 (pp. 143–44) — at verse 6

Isaiah 47.1
2
3
4
5
6
7
8
9
10
11
12
13
14
15

((Jer 30.14)) — at verse 9

Zeph 2.13–15 (Ch3n26) — spanning verses 6–10

Isaiah 48.1
2
3
4
5
6
7
8

Jer 33.3 (reprediction; sound play; split-up) — at verses 6–8

(continued)

	Isaiah	*Jeremiah*	*Psalms*	*Other*

(Isaiah 48 continued)

Isaiah 48.9

10	⊐⊢ (Isa 1.25)	⊐⊢ Jer 9.6–8		
11		(p. 58)		⊐⊢ (Ezek 20)
12				(p. 104)
13				
14				
15			Ps 81.6–17	
16			(p. 125)	
17				
18				
19				
20				
21				Deut 32.1–5
22				(Ch5n8)

Isaiah 49.1   ⊐⊢ (Jer 1)

2				
3				
4				
5				
6				
7				
8				
9				
10				
11				
12				
13			Ps 72; Ps 2	
14			(p. 115)	
15		Jer 2.32		
16		(p. 37)		
17				
18				
19	Isa 6.10–12			
20	(Ch2n24)			
21				
22	Isa 11.10–			
23	12.3			
24	(Ch3n40)			

(continued)

	SOURCE OF ALLUSION			
	Isaiah	*Jeremiah*	*Psalms*	*Other*

(Isaiah 49 continued)

Isaiah 49.25

| 26 | | ⊐⊢ (Jer 3.1, 3.8) (p. 137) | | ⊐⊢ Ezek 21.2–12 (Ch5n14) |

Isaiah 50.1

		⊐⊢ (Jer 7.13, 27)		⊐⊢ Deut 24.1–3 (Hos 2.4)
2			(Ps 74.11–16)	(p. 137)
3			(Ch5n34)	

4				
5		Jer 20.7–13		
6	(Isa 8.16–18)	also 1.7–9,		
7	(Ch6n85)	18.20, 15.16		⊐⊢ (Lam 3.30)
8		etc. (p. 64)		

9				
10	⌐ (Isa 2.5) Isa 5.30,			
11	8.22–9.1 (Ch3n69)			

Isaiah 51.1

				⊐⊢ ((Ezek 33.24)) (Ch3n85)
2				((Gen 22.15–17))
3				
4	Isa 2.1–4			Micah 4.1–4
5	(p. 79)			(p. 79)
6			⌐ Ps 102.25–27	
			(Ch4n44; p. 164)	
7		⊐⊢ (Jer 31.32)	⊐⊢ Ps 37.31	
8		(Ch2n91)	(p. 112)	

9				
10				
11		⌐		
12		Jer 11.19–21		
13		(p. 63)		
14		⊐⊢ Jer 31.35 (Reprediction)		
15		⊐⊢ Jer 1.9–10		
16		(p. 62)		

17				
18	Isa 29.9–10 ⊐⊢ Jer 15.2–5			Lam 2.13–19
19	(p. 99)	Jer 4.20		(pp. 128–29)
20		(Ch2n91)		
21				

(continued)

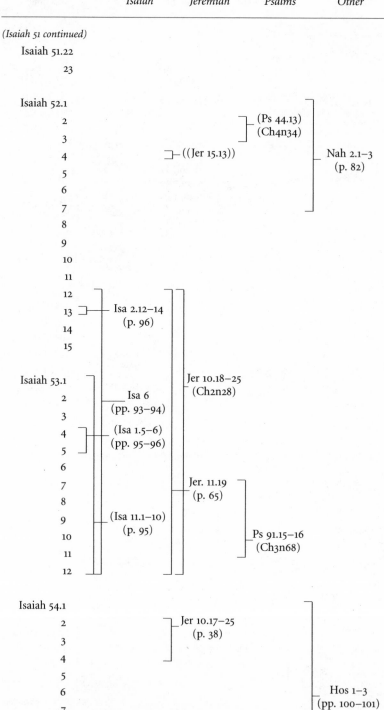

(Isaiah 51 continued)

Isaiah 51.22

    23

Isaiah 52.1

    2   (Ps 44.13)

    3   (Ch4n34)

    4   ((Jer 15.13))   Nah 2.1–3

    5   (p. 82)

    6

    7

    8

    9

    10

    11

    12

    13   Isa 2.12–14

    14   (p. 96)

    15

Isaiah 53.1   Jer 10.18–25

    2   Isa 6   (Ch2n28)

    3   (pp. 93–94)

    4   (Isa 1.5–6)

    5   (pp. 95–96)

    6

    7   Jer. 11.19

    8   (p. 65)

    9   (Isa 11.1–10)

    10   (p. 95)   Ps 91.15–16

    11   (Ch3n68)

    12

Isaiah 54.1

    2   Jer 10.17–25

    3   (p. 38)

    4

    5

    6   Hos 1–3

    7   (pp. 100–101)

(Isaiah 54 continues)

LOCATION OF ALLUSION	Isaiah	Jeremiah	Psalms	Other
(Isaiah 54 continued)				
Isaiah 54.8				
9				
10				(Ezek 34.25, 37.26)
11		Jer 31.33–35		
12		(p. 49)		
13				
14				
15				
16				
17				
Isaiah 55.1			Ps 89 or	
2			2 Sam 7	
3			(p. 118)	
4		(Jer 1)		
5		(typology)		
6				
7		Jer 29.10–14		
8		(pp. 50–51)		
9				
10				
11				
12		Jer 31.8		
13		((Jer 30.24))		
		(Ch2n44)		
Isaiah 56.1				
2				Deut 23.2–5 (p. 147)
3				Exod 31.12–16 (p. 150)
4				Num 18 (p. 146)
5				Lev 21.16–23 (p. 147)
6				
7				
8				
9				

(continued)

	Isaiah	*Jeremiah*	*Psalms*	*Other*

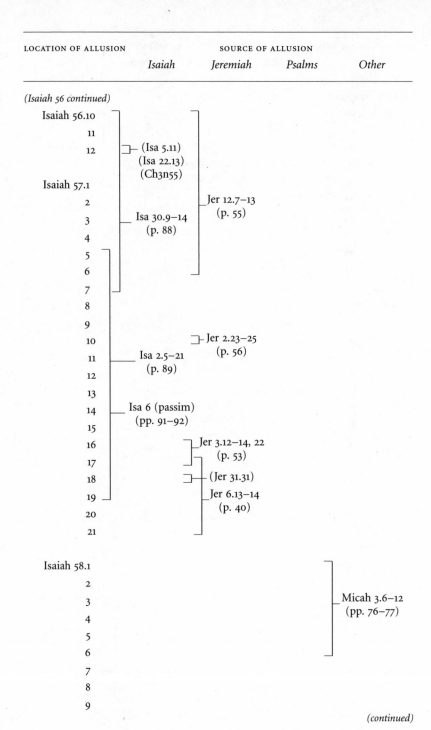

(Isaiah 56 continued)

Isaiah 56.10
11
12   (Isa 5.11)
            (Isa 22.13)
            (Ch3n55)

Isaiah 57.1
2   Jer 12.7–13
3   Isa 30.9–14   (p. 55)
4   (p. 88)
5
6
7
8
9
10   Jer 2.23–25
11   Isa 2.5–21   (p. 56)
12   (p. 89)
13
14   Isa 6 (passim)
15   (pp. 91–92)
16   Jer 3.12–14, 22
17   (p. 53)
18   (Jer 31.31)
19   Jer 6.13–14
20   (p. 40)
21

Isaiah 58.1
2
3   Micah 3.6–12
4   (pp. 76–77)
5
6
7
8
9

(continued)

(Isaiah 58 continued)

Isaiah 58.10
11   ((37))
12   (Jer 25.9/49.13)   Deut 32.9–13
13   (Ch2n91)   (pp. 134–35)
14

Isaiah 59.1
2
3   (Lam 4.14)
4
5
6
7
8   Deut 28.29
9   (p. 139)
10
11   Isa 5.7
12   (Ch3n72)
13   Jer 14.7–9, 12
14   (Ch3n40)
15
16
17
18
19
20
21   Jer 31.31 (1.9)
              (p. 50)

Isaiah 60.1
2   Isa 5.30,
3   8.22–9.5   Micah 4.1–4
4   (Ch3nn39, 57)   (p. 79)
5   Isa 2.1–4
6   (p. 79)   (Ezek 26.10)
7   Jer 6.20, 22   (p. 104)
8   (Ch2n32)
9

(Isaiah 60 continues)

(Isaiah 60 continued)

Location	Isaiah	Jeremiah	Psalms	Other
Isaiah 60.10		Jer 3.16–18 (Ch2n61)		
11				
12			Ps 72 (pp. 115, 164)	
13				
14				
15				
16				
17	(Isa 9.3) (Ch3n39)			
18		(Jer 6.7) (reversal)		
19	Isa 11 (p. 87)	(Jer 4.23–26) (reversal)	Ps 37.26–29 (p. 111)	
20				
21		(Jer 31.31) (reprediction)		
22				
Isaiah 61.1		Jer 33.7–9 (Jer 13.11) (Ch2n45)		Lev 25.10 (p. 141)
2				
3				
4		Jer 25.9 (Ch2n91)		Num 18 (p. 145)
5				
6				
7		Jer 16.16–18 (p. 57)		
8				
9				
10			Ps 132.9–18 (pp. 112–13)	
11				
Isaiah 62.1				
2				
3				
4	Isa 6.12 (reversal)			Hos 1–3 (Ch3n84)
5				
6				Lam 2.18–19 (p. 128)
7				
8				
9				

(continued)

LOCATION OF ALLUSION	Isaiah	Jeremiah	Psalms	Other
(Isaiah 62 continued)				
Isaiah 62.10	⅂‒ Isa 5.26, 11.10–16 (Ch3n40)			
11		⅂‒ Jer 31.16 (split-up)		
12		⅂‒ Jer 30.17 (Ch2n25)		
Isaiah 63.1				
2				
3				
4				
5				
6				
7				
8				⅂(Exod 23.20,
9				23) (p. 148)
10				
11		⅂Jer 2.6–8		
12		(Ch2n40)		
13				
14				
15		⅂(Jer 31.19)		
16		echo		
17	⅂‒(Isa 6.9–13)			
18				
19				
Isaiah 64.1				
2				
3				
4				
5				
6				
7				
8				
9				
10				
11				

(continued)

LOCATION OF ALLUSION	*Isaiah*	*Jeremiah*	*Psalms*	*Other*
Isaiah 65.1	(Isa 1.12, 15)			
2	(Ch3n14)			
3				
4				
5				
6		Jer 16.16–18		
7		(Ch3n85)		
8				
9				
10				
11				
12	Isa 1.28–30	(Jer 7.13)		
13	(Ch3n55)	(response)		
14				
15				
16				
17				
18				
19				
20		Jer 29.4–6		
21		(p. 42)		
22				
23				
24				
25	Isa 11.6–9, 1.12, 15 (Ch3n40)	(Jer 7.13) (response)		
Isaiah 66.1				
2				
3				
4				
5				
6				
7				
8				
9				
10				
11				

(continued)

(Isaiah 66 continued)

Isaiah 66.12
13
14
15
16
17
18
19
20
21
22
23
24

(Jer 4.13)
(reprediction)

Isa 30.27–33
(Ch3n26)

Isa 1.28–29
(Ch3n55)

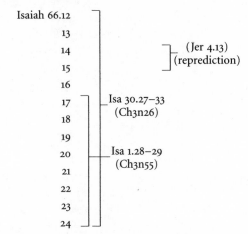

INDEX OF BIBLICAL CITATIONS

In this and the following index an "f" after a number indicates a separate reference on the next page, and an "ff" indicates separate references on the next two pages. A continuous discussion over two or more pages is indicated by a span of page numbers, e.g., "57–59." *Passim* is used for a cluster of references in close but not consecutive sequence.

32.4	274n8
32.5	274n8
32.7	264n20
32.9–13	134–35, 171
33	137
33.8	237n114
33.26–29	136

JOSHUA

Book of	25, 169
2.4	268n38
9.6–14	25

JUDGES

Book of	25, 169

1 SAMUEL

Book of	22–27 *passim*, 169, 215n79
2.1, 21	v
2.8a	109
9.15	237n110

2 SAMUEL

Book of	22–27 *passim*, 169, 215n79
7	115–18 *passim*
7.8	119
7.27	237n110
13.13	102

1 KINGS

Book of	22–27 *passim*, 169, 179, 215n79
2.3	21
8.41–43	278n43
14.23	232n79

2 KINGS

Book of	22–27 *passim*, 169, 179, 215n79
14.6	21, 25, 286n49
15.29	252n57
20.12–19	28
20.14	289n69

ISAIAH

Book of	219n11, 250nn45, 50, 257nn87–92 *passim*
ben Amos	69, 73f, 97, 104–5, 119, 131, 168, 172, 176–81 *passim*, 254n72
1	96, 104
1–33	5, 239n1
1–39	73f
1.2	164
1.5–6	95, 258n95
1.6	96
1.10, 11	218n7
1.11	253n66, 257n90
1.12, 15	242n14, 258n95
1.12–15	257n93
1.25	58
1.28–29	257n93, 258n95
1.28–30	251n55
1.30	218n5
2	74, 81, 87–92 *passim*, 96, 244nn16, 22, 249n34, 254n69
2.1–4	165, 178, 248n30, 258n95
2.2	250n44, 251n54
2.2–4	79, 243n15
2.3	248n30
2.5	254n69
2.5–21	251n54, 258n95, 259n96
2.6–21	89, 164
2.9, 11, 12, 13	91
2.9–10	91
2.10, 21	90
2.11, 12	91
2.12–14	91, 96
2.18	90f
2.20	90
2.21	91
5	242n14
5.7	254n72, 258n95
5.8	242n14
5.11	258n95
5.11, 12	251n55
5.17	251n55
5.20–21	240n6

43.16–21	133	46	119–20, 266n32
43.18	232n80	46.3–13	120–21
43.20	190	46.4	121
43.22	140	46.5	144
43.22–23	140	46.5–12	154, 252n57
43.22–26	218n7	46.9–13	258n95
43.22–28	140f, 169, 291n1	47.3	102
43.22–44.3	267n34	47.5–11	245n26, 252n57
43.23	140	47.7	271n55
43.24	140	47.8	271n55
43.25	267n34	48	190, 193, 274n8,
43.27	256n84		296n40
44	104, 242n14	48.3	57, 97
44.1–3	34, 227n45, 258n94	48.6	226n45, 258n94
44.2, 6, 24	289n71	48.9	234n89
44.6–7	57, 97	48.10	233n87
44.9–14	104, 237n112,	48.10–11	58–59, 258n94
	258nn94, 95	48.11	104, 189, 254n72
44.9–19	242n14	48.12–21	125, 291n1
44.9–20	292n2	48.15	189
44.11	242n14	48.16	290n80
44.14	242n14	48.17	289n71
44.15	242n14	48.17–19	169
44.18	253n64, 267n38,	48.18–19	268n41
	271n54, 284n30	48.18–21	276n19
44.22	267n34	48.19	189
44.24	144, 169	48.20	274n8
44.24–45.1	235n97	48.20–21	273n8
44.24–45.8	116, 154	48.21	189, 274n8, 276n19
44.26	190, 242n14, 267n34	49	62, 189f, 242n14,
44.28–45.8	115, 173		250n40, 294n21,
45	137		295n33
45.1	117	49–55	190, 289n73
45.1, 11, 14, 18	289n71	49–66	190, 294n21
45.1–2	116	49.1–6	203n3, 290n80,
45.3	116		294n21
45.4, 5	116	49.4	251n54
45.6–7	143, 169	49.6	64, 189, 242n14
45.9–10	258n95, 259n96	49.7	251n54
45.9–15	104	49.7, 8	289n71
45.10	190	49.7, 23	264n15
45.12–13	60–61, 154, 258n94,	49.7–23	115, 173
	266n16	49.8	110, 255n78
45.14, 18, 21	274n9	49.12	226n44
45.14–19	136	49.14	127, 190, 225n40,
45.18–19	143, 169		266n30, 296n40
45.19–24	269n44	49.14–15	190

53.9, 12	65f		289nn70, 73, 294n25,
53.10	65f, 253n68		295nn32, 38, 296n42
53.10–11	270n44	56.1	70, 150, 292n11
53.11	65f, 95, 253nn66, 68	56.1, 4	289n71
53.11–12	95	56.1–7	188
53.14	95	56.1–8	147, 150
53.15	95	56.2, 4, 6	169
54	102f, 189, 223n29,	56.3	274n12, 279n46
	242n14, 256n84	56.4–5	150
54.1	103, 222n27	56.4–7	146–47, 169
54.1, 4–8, 10–11, 13–14	101–2	56.5	150
54.1–3	266n16	56.7	188, 257n90, 278n43
54.1–3, 5	39	56.7–8	257n90
54.1–3, 14	258n95	56.8	187, 218n5, 257n90,
54.1–5	258n94		289n72
54.1–13	100	56.9	55
54.2	39, 68, 235n95	56.9–57.5	258n94
54.3	40, 222n27	56.9–57.6	54f
54.4	102	56.9–57.13	90
54.5	104	56.10	88, 231n71
54.7, 8, 11	102	56.10–57.6	88, 194, 258n95
54.8	70, 291n85	56.11	55, 88, 251n55
54.8, 10	254n72, 255n81	56.12	251n55, 258n95
54.9	133	57	53, 56, 89–92 *passim*,
54.10	49f, 164, 256n85,		169
	258n94	57.1	55
54.10, 13	49	57.2	56, 88, 231n76
54.13	103	57.3–4	90
54.15	70	57.3–13	187
54.17	289n72	57.3–15	89–90, 164
55	118, 193, 226n44	57.5	91, 232n79
55.1–5	117, 154	57.5–6	230n70
55.3	249n35, 265n26	57.5–20	258n95, 259n96
55.4	119	57.6	56, 66, 88, 230n70,
55.4–5	236n100		258n94
55.6	230n65	57.6–7	189
55.6–12	51ff, 258n94	57.7	91, 232n79
55.8	289n72	57.8	231n77
55.11	52, 66, 258n94	57.9	90f
55.12	226n44, 258n94	57.10	56, 258n94
56	147, 169, 190, 193,	57.11	90f
	278nn41, 43, 279n43,	57.12–13	56
	294n21, 295n33	57.13	90f, 250n53
56–57	250n41	57.13–15	251n53
56–66	5, 35, 150, 160, 187–94	57.14	189, 230n70
	passim, 204n5,	57.14, 15	55
	220n14, 227n47,	57.14–20	193

INDEX OF SECONDARY SOURCES

235n93, 236n106, 237n113, 276n21, 283n23, 291n81

Horovitz-Rabin, 279n51

Hrushovski, B., 282n15

Hughes, M., 209n20, 286n46

Hurvitz, A., 244n16, 261n9, 262nn9, 11, 263n12, 264n20

Ibn Caspi, J., 245n23, 271n53

ibn Ezra, A., 231n71, 232n82, 236n108, 241n11, 250n52, 264nn15, 17, 268n39, 271n53

Irvine, S., 239nn1, 2, 247n27, 290n74

Janzen, G., 224nn33–35, 227n46, 230n66, 235n94, 275n14

Johnson, A., 18f, 209n18, 211n38, 213n48, 214n58, 281n8

Jones, D., 220n16, 254n70

Joüon, P., 227n50

Kaminka, A., 110, 240n3, 260n8, 262n11, 273nn4, 6, 285n33, 286n48

Kaufmann, Y., 90, 110, 127, 188–91 passim, 227nn49, 50, 229n60, 230n68, 231n71, 233n87, 238nn117, 119, 239nn1, 2, 243n15, 246n26, 249nn35, 37, 251n54, 261n8, 262n10, 265nn25, 28, 270nn45, 48, 272n55, 276n18, 277n37, 279n46, 282n18, 285n41, 290n74, 292nn5–11 passim, 293n14, 294nn22, 25, 296n41

Kautzsch, E., 261n9, 268n40

Kiffmeyer, J., 282n12

Kimḥi, D. (Radak), 63, 224n40, 231n71, 236n99, 237n110, 241n12, 263n15, 264nn15, 17, 271n53, 293n15

Klostermann, 232n82

Knohl, I., 277n34, 280n52, 281n55, 285n39

Kristeva, J., 7, 206n5

Kronfeld, C., 204n4, 207n7, 211n38, 213nn51–55 passim, 216n90, 282n14

Kugel, J., 30, 161, 207n13, 216n89, 228n52, 282n16, 284n27, 286n50, 294n30

Kutscher, E. Y., 234n89, 265n23

Laato, A., 204n5, 217n3, 219nn8, 10, 227n49, 237n109, 247n27, 248n30, 249n36, 275n16, 293n14

Lau, W., 35, 193f, 204n5, 220n14, 251n56, 272n55, 281n8, 286nn44, 50, 289n70, 291n86, 296n45

Levine, B., 276n17

Levinson, B., 155, 182, 215nn77, 79, 281nn5, 6, 291nn88, 89

Lewy, J., 276nn20, 21

Lieberman, S., 285n43

Liebreich, L., 257n87

Maass, F., 190, 294n24

Malamat, A., 287n52

Mandelbaum, B., 288n56

Margalioth, R., 257n87

Marlowe, C., 215n73

Marvell, A., 171

McCarthy, D., 274–75n13

McKenzie, J., 232n82, 246n26, 275n14, 279nn46–51 passim

Meged, A., 11–13, 30, 208n16, 286n49

Melammed, E. Z., 237n114

Melugin, R., 217n3, 240n4, 253n63

Mettinger, T., 227n50, 236n107, 249nn33, 35, 252n58, 293n14

Milgrom, J., 277nn35, 36, 279n44

Miller, J. M., 276n18

Milton, J., 11–17 passim, 171

Miner, E., 10, 208n16, 209n22, 213n55

Mowinckel, S., 36, 221nn19, 20, 260n7

Muffs, Y., 216nn83, 85, 221n21, 226n45

Muilenberg, 204n5, 246n26, 281n10, 284n32

Muraoka, T., 227n50

Murtonen, A., 292n12, 294n24

North, C., 233n87, 271nn50, 51

O'Day, G., 207n8

Overholt, T., 287n51

Pagis, D., 209n17, 211n38

Paul, S., 35, 218n8, 219n10, 220n13, 223n30, 232n85, 234n91, 235n96, 236nn101–3, 276n19, 294n21

Perri, C., 10–11, 19, 208n16, 209nn18, 23–27 passim, 211n36, 214nn56, 57

Petersen, D., 288nn60, 63

Whedbee, J. W., 285n41

Williamson, H., 180, 240n4, 242n14, 250nn40, 45, 252nn59, 63, 253n63, 254nn71, 73, 255n78, 257n89, 259n95, 291n83

Wilson, R., 217n2, 287n52, 288n56, 290n80

Wiseman, D. J., 275n13

Wolf, H., 253nn66, 67

Wolff, H. W., 255n82

Wordsworth, W., 11f, 17

Zach, N., 213nn51, 53, 216n90

Zakovitch, Y., 16–23 *passim*, 30, 203n1, 211nn40, 41, 214nn67–70 *passim*, 215nn76–80 *passim*, 255n75

Zimmerli, W., 297n50

Library of Congress Cataloging-in-Publication Data

Sommer, Benjamin D.

  A prophet reads scripture : allusion in Isaiah 40–66 / Benjamin D. Sommer.

    p.   cm. — (Contraversions: Jews and other differences)

Includes bibliographical references and index.

ISBN 0-8047-3216-7 (cloth)

  1. Bible. O.T. Isaiah XL–LXVI—Criticism, interpretation, etc.   2. Allusions in
the Bible. I. Title. II. Series.

BS1520.S66   1998

224′.1066—dc21   98-20169

                                                              CIP

                                                            Rev.

Original printing 1998

Last figure below indicates year of this printing:

07 06 05 04 03 02 01 00 99 98